The Life of Thomas Burgess

John Scandrett Harford

BIBLIOLIFE

THE

LIFE

OF

THOMAS BURGESS, D.D.

F.R.S. F.A.S. &c. &c. &c.

LATE

LORD BISHOP OF SALISBURY.

BY

JOHN S. HARFORD, ESQ. D.C.L. F.R.S.

" τὸν μακαριώτατον ἐπίσκοπον παρ' ὑμῖν ἐπί τε
ὀρθότητι πίστεως καὶ τῇ λοιπῇ ἀρετῇ διατρέψαντα "

ST BASIL, Ep 70

Second Edition.

LONDON:

PRINTED FOR

LONGMAN, ORME, BROWN, GREEN, & LONGMANS,

PATERNOSTER-ROW.

1841.

TO

THE MOST REVEREND

WILLIAM HOWLEY, D.D.

ARCHBISHOP OF CANTERBURY,

PRIMATE OF ALL ENGLAND, AND METROPOLITAN,

THIS MEMORIAL

OF A PRELATE WHO WAS EDUCATED IN THE SAME SCHOOL AND

IN THE SAME UNIVERSITY WITH HIS GRACE,

AND WHO ADORNED,

WITH CONGENIAL TALENTS, VIRTUES, AND PRINCIPLES,

THE CHURCH OVER WHICH HIS GRACE PRESIDES,

IS MOST RESPECTFULLY INSCRIBED,

BY HIS FAITHFUL AND DEVOTED SERVANT,

JOHN S. HARFORD.

PREFACE

TO

THE SECOND EDITION.

THE rapid sale of the first edition of this work leads the Author to hope that it has proved acceptable to the public. It is now printed in a smaller and cheaper form, with the view of promoting its more extended circulation. Some interesting letters from the Bishop's own pen have been added. For those addressed to the late Dr. Burney the author is indebted to Archdeacon Burney, to whom, as well as to the other individuals who have laid him under similar obligation, he begs to offer his sincere thanks.

Blaise Castle, May 11. 1841.

PREFACE.

If the charm of a biographical work consists in the novelty of its incidents, or in the striking vicissitudes which it records, the life of a learned and pious Bishop, whose time was chiefly spent in labouring for the good of mankind, and in promoting the great objects of the Christian Ministry, would necessarily fail in general interest. But expectations of this description arise, as Dr. Johnson observes, from false measures of excellence and dignity, and " must be eradicated by considering that, in the esteem of uncorrupted reason, what is of most use is of most value." In this point of view, those who teach us by their bright example how to live and how to die, — how to pluck the fruits of imperishable truth and unfading happiness, may well claim our sympathy and fix our attention. Of this number was the excellent Prelate whose life and character it is the object of the following pages to depicture.

To profound and extensive erudition Bishop Burgess united a firm and inflexible adherence to his convictions of Christian duty both in public and private life, accompanied with deep humility, and guileless simplicity of mind and manners.

The particulars of his learned and literary life include much that is curious and interesting.

To trace the formation and developement of his character, and its practical influence in the exalted station which he filled in the Church, has been the Author's endeavour. He writes from personal knowledge and authentic data, having been honoured with the friendship of the departed Prelate, and intrusted by him with the disposition of his papers and correspondence.

His aim being to interest general readers, various particulars, familiar to scholars, are occasionally explained, and when quotations from the learned languages are introduced, upon which the point or meaning of a passage depends, a translation is added.

In the original papers a few inaccuracies of expression, which, however, very rarely occur, have been corrected, and, in some instances, a slight transposition has been made in the order of the sentences, with the view of conveying more clearly the meaning of the writer.

The author cannot conclude without expressing his particular obligation to the Bishop of Nova Scotia, and to Dr. Gilly, for enabling him to present to his readers many interesting particulars respecting the late Bishop Barrington.

To Viscount Sidmouth, to the Bishop of Lincoln, to the Dean of Salisbury, to Archdeacon Berens, to Dr. Wordsworth, to the Rev. Mr. Townsend of Durham, to Dr. Ollivant, to the Rev. Mr. Dansey, and to Mrs. George Marriott, he is also much indebted for the loan of letters, or for useful information.

But above all, he begs to acknowledge his obligations to the Rev. C. B. Pearson, for invaluable co-operation and assistance.

CONTENTS.

APPENDIX.

No. I.

No. II.

No. III.

ERRATA.

In great haste
lest I miss the post
I conclude myself
Your sincere friend
T. Burgess

T. St David's

T. Sarum.

LIFE

OF

BISHOP BURGESS.

CHAPTER I.

BIRTH. — PARENTAGE. — EDUCATION.

1756 to 1775.

DOCTOR THOMAS BURGESS, late Lord Bishop of
Salisbury, was born on the 18th of November, 1756,
at Odiham, near Basingstoke, in Hampshire.

His father was a respectable grocer of that place,
a man of excellent understanding and sincere piety,
who was the object of his son's devoted respect and
affection, and whose memory he so tenderly cherished, that even to the latest period of his life he
could hardly mention his name without emotion.
There was so strong a likeness between them, that
a picture of the father, by Opie, with a wig somewhat of the episcopal cut, which hung in the Bishop's
library at Salisbury, might readily have been mistaken for a portrait of himself. His mother's maiden

B

name was Harding, and her connexions were highly respectable.

Their family consisted of three sons and three daughters. The Bishop was the youngest brother. The eldest, who was a man of great natural talent, inherited a property of several hundreds a year in land from his maternal grandmother. John, the second son, was apprenticed in London, and by his steadiness of conduct and ability established himself in a good business, and acquired a considerable fortune. Of the three daughters, the eldest married Mr. Pinkerton, a gentleman of literary celebrity, whose name is well known as the author of a work on geography, and of other useful publications.

Thomas was sent when a little boy to a dame's school, kept by a Mrs. Fisher, who seems to have been the very counterpart of Shenstone's schoolmistress. In his visits to Odiham, after he had distinguished himself, he never failed to call upon his old mistress, who was exceedingly proud of having had him at her school, and used to call him " *her scholar*."

He was seven years old when he was sent to the grammar school of Odiham. Though living in the same town with his parents, they denied themselves the pleasure of having him home except at the regular holydays, that he might not become unsettled, and inattentive to his studies. As his mother doated on him, this was a great trial to her, especially when she saw him on Sundays, at church, among the train of his schoolfellows, but she repressed her feelings for her child's good. His own feelings, it is scarcely needful to add, were not a little excited on these occasions.

Much pains were taken by this worthy couple to imbue the minds of their children with religious principles. The inscription on the monument to their memory, erected by the Bishop conjointly with his brother John, in Odiham church, expresses in beautiful terms their high estimation of the pains bestowed by them on the education of the family, and of the sacrifices of personal comfort which they had cheerfully made for this purpose.

This wise and faithful discharge of parental duty was peculiarly rewarded in the subject of this memoir. There is every reason to believe that the good seed thus cast into his mind, germinated, by the divine blessing, at a very early period, and that through the restraining influence of the "fear of the Lord," so justly denominated by the sacred penman "the beginning of wisdom," he passed through the dangerous ordeal of a public school, and of college, uncontaminated. He was one of the most dutiful and affectionate of sons, both to his father and mother. The latter was a great invalid, and it was his delight whenever he came home to pass much of his time in her sick-room, and to devise every means in his power to solace and amuse her. Till her death, which occurred about 1798, he made her as large an allowance as he could afford.

He does not appear to have been very fortunate in his first tutor. Dr. Webb, then master of Odiham school, was a scholar of very moderate attainments; an inference which the boys themselves drew from various facts, one of which was, that they frequently observed on his table English translations of the classical authors they were in the habit of construing. It was therefore with no small reason that he said to

his old pupil Burgess, on receiving from him in after
years a present of his youthful publication of a new
edition of Burton's Pentalogia — " You are got far
beyond me."

In the year 1768 he was sent to Winchester
school, and remained there till 1775. Dr. Joseph
Warton, so well known by his Essay on the Genius
and Writings of Pope, was then head-master; and the
Bishop often expressed himself greatly indebted for
the pains which he took in directing the attention
of his pupils to the critical beauties or defects of the
authors they read with him. A poet himself of some
reputation, and passionately attached to literature, it
was his ambition to kindle in their breasts a congenial flame, and under his auspices their ordinary
classical lessons were often converted into an instructive lecture on the principles of good taste in composition. He was also in the habit of lecturing to
the elder boys on Grotius de Veritate during Lent,
out of the regular course of school hours, and contrived to render his comment so interesting that they
listened to him with delight. Warton, however,
though an elegant scholar, was not an able philologist.
He held verbal criticism cheap, and, as a natural consequence, frequently encountered insurmountable difficulties in Greek authors ; while the expedients to
which he resorted in order to conceal the fact were
easy of detection, and excited much amusement
among the elder boys. When, for example, he came
to a passage of peculiar obscurity in the chorus of
a Greek tragedy, he would allow the boy who was
construing to glide through it in the best way he
could, while he raised his own voice to an unusual
pitch, and complained of noises, which to every body

else seemed no more than ordinary in other parts of
the school. It was one of the late Bishop Huntingford's anecdotes, that he so well knew what would
happen on an approach to such passages, that he had
often said to the boy next him, " Now we shall have
a noise." But Warton wanted also other qualities
essential to the head-master of a public school. He
was inconsistent in his plans, and deficient in moral
courage, often conceding with respect to points of
discipline upon which he ought to have been inflexible. These defects paved the way for what was afterwards called *the Row*, when the school was in such a
state of rebellion that the interference of the magistrates was required, and upwards of thirty of the boys
were expelled. Burgess had left the school before this
catastrophe occurred, but used to tell, among other
proofs of the insubordination which prevailed even in
his time, that a riotous boy had the audacity, on one
occasion, to hurl a Latin dictionary at Warton's head.
He himself never participated in any of these tur-
bulent proceedings. Manly and independent in
his disposition, but at the same time mild and in-
offensive, he steadfastly pursued a course of good
conduct. He admired his master's literary enthusiasm, and daily felt in himself the growth of a
congenial taste. Not only did he diligently apply
to the appropriate studies of the place, but found
leisure to peruse in succession some of the best
English classics; and after he had risen high in the
school, it was frequently his habit to sit up for
hours after the other boys had retired to rest, in
order to enjoy undisturbed his favourite authors.

It has been justly remarked, that the future *man*
may usually be traced in the dispositions and habits

of the *boy*. That calm self-possession, that love of
books, that taste for a studious and contemplative life,
which characterised the Bishop to the end of his
career, were not only thus early developed, but had
even stamped a thoughtful expression on his countenance. By way of illustration, some doggerel strains
shall be quoted, which I have more than once heard
him repeat, in which one of his comrades, passing in
review the leading peculiarities of his schoolfellows,
described him and a boy, named Eper Jasper, as
follows : —

> And what's Eper Jasper made of ?
> Of sauntering walk,
> And little talk,
> And that's Eper Jasper made of !

> And what's Tom Burgess made of ?
> Of pensive looks,
> And toys full of books,
> And that's Tom Burgess made of !

I have often wished, he added, on repeating these
lines, that I had preserved a copy of this gallery of
my old schoolfellows.

Fraught with this early passion for literature, he
regarded men of genius, or of extensive learning,
with feelings of admiring reverence, while the
thought would steal through his mind, " Shall *I*
ever participate in similar honours ?" Such thoughts
are natural to every youthful aspirant after fame.
The time came, when, without losing this admiration
for superior talents, his reverence was reserved for
those who consecrate them to the glory of God,
and to the advancement, on Christian principles, of
human improvement and happiness.

Among those who were thus the objects of his

youthful homage, was the highly accomplished brother of his preceptor, still familiarly called Tom Warton. He was a frequent visiter at the Doctor's, and happening one day to want the loan of a volume of Johnson's Shakspeare, inquiry was made in the school whether any of the boys possessed it. Burgess proved to be the happy individual, and in addition to the pride of producing it out of his own stores, he deemed it (he has told me) quite a privilege to render this service, however trivial, to the scholar and the poet. In these early days he delighted in Warton's Sonnet to the River Lodon; and as he was fond of repeating it, or having it read to him to the last, it will not be out of place to introduce it here.

SONNET TO THE RIVER LODON *

Ah! what a weary race my feet have run
Since first I trod thy banks, with alders crown'd,
And thought my way was all thro' fairy ground,
Beneath thy azure sky and golden sun,
Where first my Muse to lisp her notes begun!
While pensive Memory traces back the round
Which fills the varied interval between,
Much pleasure, more of sorrow, marks the scene
Sweet native stream! those skies and suns so pure
No more return to cheer my evening road,
Yet still one joy remains, that not obscure,
Nor useless, all my vacant days have flow'd,
From youth's gay dawn to manhood's prime mature;
Nor with the Muse's laurel unbestow'd.

---

* Near Basingstoke, Warton's native country.

CHAP. II.

1775 to 1778.

IN the year 1775, Mr. Burgess removed to Corpus Christi College, Oxford, upon a Winchester scholarship, which he gained after passing through a severe competition with five or six other candidates. Dr. Lawrence, the future friend of Burke, entered at the same time. They were both good scholars, and their tutor, who soon discovered that their classical proficiency much exceeded his own, intimated to them that he dispensed with their future attendance at lectures. Dr. Randolph was at this time head of Corpus.

The philological deficiencies of Dr. Warton have already been mentioned. His pupil was so sensible of the consequent defects of his own early training, that he now assiduously applied to the study of the best authors on Greek verbal criticism. Hoogeven, Bos, and Vigerus, became his constant companions, and he even submitted to the drudgery of committing to memory the whole of Nugent's Greek Primitives. The solid advantages which he felt that he had thus acquired, often led him to recommend a diligent consultation of similar authors to such of his younger friends as manifested a taste for Greek literature, and he would sometimes expatiate to them upon the great importance of cheerfully submitting, early in life, to the necessary labour of accurately investigating the fundamental principles of those particular parts, whether of learning or science, to which their studies were directed.

His conduct as an under-graduate was, I have every reason to believe, in all respects exemplary. His circle of acquaintance was small, and pretty much confined to such as, like himself, were men of high principle and studious habits.

The four years which he spent at Oxford, previously to taking his degree, were steadily devoted to hard reading and to learned researches. He studied some of the finest works of the Greek philosophers and poets, with critical attention; and being fond of the philosophy of language, applied its principles to the investigation of the origin and formation of that of Greece, with an acuteness which contributed much in its consequences to his future eminence. He delighted also in metaphysical reading and research; and when he relaxed from these severer occupations, it was to cultivate a more intimate acquaintance with the finest productions of elegant literature, both classical and English. From an admirer, he became a votary of the Muses, and, in the year 1777, published, in the spirit of youthful ambition, an English poem, entitled Bagley Wood, which was followed at a short interval by another, the title of which I have been unable to discover. Bagley Wood is situated between Abingdon and Oxford, and was one of his favourite rural retreats. His library has been searched in vain for copies of these youthful productions, which, however useful they might have proved to himself as exercises in composition, were probably of no great poetical merit.

In the year 1778, before taking his degree, he
tried his strength as an author in a way better
adapted to the powers of his mind and to the course
of his learned studies, by editing a new edition of
Burton's Pentalogia. This work, which comprises
five of the finest of the Greek tragedies, illustrated
by Annotations for the use of students, had formerly
been deemed a Cambridge book, but had gradually
fallen into disuse in that University. Mr. Burgess
enriched this edition with an Appendix of additional
and learned notes, with an improved and copious
Greek Index, and with an elegant Preface, in the
course of which he deprecates, in the following
terms, the severity of criticism * : —

" Such as it is, I trust the learned reader will
accept, in a kind spirit, this attempt on the part of a
youth, less skilled, I fear, in Greek criticism, than
becomes one who ventures for the first time to incur
the risk of commenting upon the ancient tragic
authors. Many considerations there are which make
me doubt of the propriety of this publication, and
these doubts would have prevailed, had I not been

---

* Hæc autem, qualiacunque sint, benevolè accipiat, rogo
lector eruditus, quippe quæ a juvene conscripta Græcarum literarum, vereor, rudiori quàm decebat eum, qui primum Critices
periculum, in Tragicis veteribus facere auderet . . .

Multa tamen animo occurrebant, quæ suaderent ne hæc ἀυτοσ-
χεδιάσματα publice proponerem et movebant quidem, in me
firmasset Quintiliani, viri planè gravissimi, judicium Non
differendum *monentis* esse tyrocinium in senectutem : nam quo-
tidie metus crescit, magis fit semper quod ausuri sumus, et dum
deliberamus quando incipiendum sit, incipere jam serum est
Quare fructum viridem, et adhuc dulcem, promi decet, dum
veniæ et spes est, et paratus favor. Et audere non dedecet, et si
quid desit operi supplet ætas, et si quæ dicta sunt juveniliter
pro indole accipiuntur.

encouraged by the authority of Quintilian, a man
of the most profound judgment. 'A youthful
author must not (he says) defer publishing till he
grows old, for fear daily gathers strength; that
which is long meditated appears more and more
awful; and while we deliberate when to begin, the
time itself for beginning passes away. Therefore
the fruit must be gathered while it is yet green and
tender, while there is the hope of pardon, and
favour is at hand. To dare the attempt involves no
dishonour, and age supplies what may be wanting
to the work, and should any thing be advanced
which savours of youth, it is treated accordingly.'"

Such a publication by an under-graduate was so
remarkable an occurrence, that it attracted much attention both at Oxford and elsewhere. Dr. Warton,
on receiving a copy of it from his old pupil, went
into an ecstasy of delight, and holding it up in his
hands before the Winchester boys, addressed himself in particular to one who has since acquired no
small literary distinction, the Rev. W. L. Bowles,
exclaiming, "When will you produce such a work?"
The fact is, that a resident graduate, who had undertaken the office of editor, growing tired of the labour,
had suddenly withdrawn his services. The publisher,
Mr. Fletcher, was one day complaining in the presence of Mr. Buckland a fellow of Corpus, of Burgess, and others, of the embarrassing position in which
he consequently found himself, when Buckland exclaimed, " Burgess, why should not you undertake
it?" The next day Fletcher called, and formally
pressed the office of editor upon him. The youthful critic complied, and had great reason to rejoice
in his decision, for independently of the reputation

which the publication secured him, he derived solid and permanent advantage from the practical application which it involved of his philological studies, from the critical works which it led him to investigate, and from the acquaintance or friendship of various learned men which it procured him.

That Mr. Buckland, who was a man of learning, should have recommended an under-graduate of his college to undertake the difficult task of editing and enlarging a work which required intimate acquaintance with the Greek tragic authors, and much critical acumen, proves the high estimate which he had formed of the extent of his learning, and of the soundness of his judgment.

CHAP. III.

TAKES HIS BACHELOR'S DEGREE. — PUBLISHES DAWES'
MISCELLANEA CRITICA.—OPINION OF SCHOLARS UPON THE
WORK.

1778 to 1780.

In the year 1778 Mr. Burgess took his Bachelor's degree.

His philological ardour now led him to engage in preparing for the press a new edition of Dawes' Miscellanea Critica, a work of great erudition, which had become scarce, and sold at a high price. For the information of general readers, it may be as well to state that it consists of critical disquisitions on, and conjectural emendations of, the text of the Attic poets; of acute remarks on their peculiarities

of construction; of dissertations on various questions
connected with Greek metre; and of elaborate inquiries into the properties of the Æolic Digamma *, a

---

* The acuteness and sagacity of Dr. Bentley were eminently
displayed by the successful application of the properties of the
Digamma, to the removal of many apparent harshnesses and an-
omalies from Homeric versification In what way its disap-
pearance from the Homeric poems is to be accounted for, has
never been satisfactorily explained. Dawes differed from
Bentley, by maintaining that it was not expressed by a letter,
but by a conventional accent. Each theory may possibly be
correct; that is, each mode may have been practised, and the
supposition would aid, we think, in accounting for the final
disuse of the letter. But whenever omitted, its force, if no
longer visibly expressed, must have been understood, and have
been supplied, as a matter of course, in the reading and pronunciation of a polished native, otherwise Homer could not
have been admired in the degree that he was, even in the most
perfect period of Grecian versification, for his metrical harmony.
The form of the letter is settled by the evidence of various
ancient inscriptions, and, to use the words of a distinguished
scholar, Bishop Monk, was similar to that produced by the per-
pendicular union of two gammas, from which it drew its name
Bentley himself affirmed that its sound, as well as that of the
Latin V, answered to our W. Other authorities have asserted
that its power resembled that of our F, or V, or was something
between our V and W; others again have maintained, that it
more nearly approached that of our B The caprices of pronunciation are often inexplicable After all, these various
letters are more or less nearly related B and V, for instance,
were often interchanged in the speech and the writing of the
Dorian Greeks, and also of the ancient Romans; and Scaliger,
quoted by Kidd, observes, Imperiti librarii inter B et digamma
nullum discrimen faciebant. In Spanish, V and B are often,
likewise, interchanged The above contradictory opinions may,
it appears to us, be reconciled by the supposition, that the pronunciation of this letter slightly varied in different states of
Greece Of the existence of the digamma at periods long subsequent to the age of Homer, various ancient inscriptions testify.
Sir William Gell found one of great antiquity in Elis, in which
the digamma occurs no less than seven times Upon this topic
Mr. Kidd has collected much interesting matter in his edition
of Dawes, in addition to the learned researches of Burgess,

letter, for the restoration of which to the Greek alphabet we are indebted to the learning and acuteness of Dr. Bentley. Its exact form and pronunciation have been the subject of much learned discussion, involving questions intimately connected with the prosodial laws of the Homeric poems.

The critical skill and various learning displayed by Dawes in this work have procured for him a distinguished place among those who have aided the progress of Grecian literature in England, nor have foreign scholars been backward in paying a just tribute to his superior learning. It was originally published as a specimen of a projected edition of the Attic poets, a splendid project, which, had it been realised, would have proved an invaluable accession to Classical Literature, and have shed a bright lustre upon the name of its author, and of his country.

The new edition was enriched by Mr. Burgess with a learned Preface, and with an Appendix of nearly two hundred pages, in the course of which he illustrates the critical principles of Dawes, enlarges the sphere of his investigations, or assigns his reasons, in particular instances, for dissenting from his conclusions.

The able manner in which the work was edited, the various and profound learning displayed in the Appendix, and the elegant flow of its Latinity, became the theme of general commendation in the

pp 200 206. 214 ed of 1827. Consult also Bishop Monk's Life of Bentley, vol ii. ch 20. For further remarks on this subject, and upon Homeric versification in general, see a letter from Dr. Vincent to Mr Burgess, at the close of ch. vi. of this volume.

learned world, particularly as proceeding from a
youth who had taken his Bachelor's degree little
more than twelve months. He received accordingly,
from some of the most eminent scholars of the age,
both at home and abroad, very honourable testimonies of their approbation, accompanied by anticipations of the future brilliancy of his career.

The following are extracts from letters addressed
to him at a subsequent period, specially referring to
Dawes, by Everard Scheidius, and by Spalden, Professor of Greek and Hebrew at Berlin, and the
editor of a learned edition of Quintilian : —

VIRO CELEBERRIMO, ERUDITISSIMO
THOMÆ BURGESSIO
S. D.
EVERARDUS SCHEIDIUS.

Nuperrime quum apud Schultensium, amicum inte-
gerrimum, et Ruhnkenium suavissimum meum pre-
ceptorem, in Batavis essem, tanta ac tam honorifica
nominis tui mentio, a duum viris illis, me præsente,
facta est, Burgessi, vir eruditissime, ut te quum antea
ex elegantissimâ tuâ Dawesii Miscellaneorum editione
cognitum habuissem, magnopere jam venerari atq.
amare cœperim, &c. *

EVERARD SCHEIDIUS
TO THE CELEBRATED AND VERY LEARNED
THOMAS BURGESS.

Very lately, when I was with my intimate friend Schultens, and
Ruhnken my most amiable preceptor, in Holland, your name
was mentioned in such honourable terms, most learned Burgess,
in my presence, by both of them, that I found feelings of veneration and love springing up in my heart towards you, whom
I already knew by your most elegant edition of Dawes's Mis-
cellanies.

Spalden writes in English, and says, " A public
disputation at the university of Halle, in Saxony,
which I was lately obliged to engage in, made me
think of publishing the little treatise, which I now
take the liberty of presenting to you. The greater
part of it consisting of conjectural criticism, —
among the teachers of which you hold so particular a rank at Oxford, — I presume that it may,
in some measure, be thought worthy'of your notice.
You will find yourself, and your learned labours
upon the ingenious Dawes, quoted therein. It is
with particular benefit I have studied this book, —
my inclination leading me to aim at the attainment
of a thorough knowledge of Greek antiquity."

The Bibliotheca Critica for 1782, a continental
review of high authority, noticed his editorial labours in the following terms : —

" The critical disquisitions of Burgess extend
through 180 pages ; and display, amidst something
of youthful redundancy, striking indications of intellect, of learning, and of elegance ; so that we
have no doubt that if, with advancing years, discrimination and judgment be added to his various
endowments of learning, he will, hereafter, rank
among the most eminent teachers in this department of literature. Such, indeed, is the copious-
ness and variety of learning in this work, that we
place it among those from which we hereafter propose to extract select passages." *

---

* Ceterum Burgessei Animadversiones paginis constant cir-
citer 180, et habent in juvenili redundantiâ magnam commen-
dationem ingenii, eruditionis, et elegantiæ ; ut minime dubi-
temus, eum, si progressu ætatis, ratio et delectus ad reliqua
doctrinæ bona accesserint, aliquando in præcipuis harum liter-

Dr. Andrew Kippis, to whom he was indebted for various biographical particulars respecting Dawes, writes thus in acknowledgment of a specimen which he had sent him of his Appendix : —

" I return you many thanks for the specimen you have been so good as to present me with, of your very learned and valuable notes. I have read them with particular satisfaction ; and with singular admiration of the profound knowledge of the Greek tongue displayed in them. Critical subjects have always been peculiarly pleasing to me ; and it has been the rule of my life, amidst my various engagements, to read something every day in a Greek and Latin writer."

It would be easy to multiply extracts of this description, and to accumulate the praises bestowed upon the editor of Dawes by his learned contemporaries. But this is needless, since the following pages will fully attest the high opinion entertained of his erudition by such scholars as Wyttenbach and Villoison, Burney and Vincent. Their united commendation forms a decisive answer to the depreciating tone in which his services as a critic and a scholar are sometimes alluded to in the present day, by inconsiderate objectors. The real point to be investigated, in order to form a just estimate of them, is the state of Greek learning at Oxford, at the period of his academic career, and the degree of assistance which he rendered by his writings and influence to the students of his time.

---

arum doctoribus numeratum iri. Et quandoquidem copia et varietas doctrinæ inest huic libro, nos eum in iis reponimus ex quibus specimina alio tempore expromamus

C

The result of such an inquiry would prove every
way honourable to his ability and zeal. Since then,
a great increase of light has been reflected upon
every department of Greek criticism, by a succession
of eminent scholars, and its thorny paths have been
wonderfully smoothed and laid open for students by
their researches. No man was more prompt to recognise, and to hail the progress of this light, than
Bishop Burgess. It was a topic upon which he
delighted to expatiate. Though the results of his
own labours may have been in some degree cast
into the shade by more recent publications, they
have been by no means superseded, as will be evident
to any one who will take the pains to examine into
the use made by Mr. Kidd, in his recent {and able
editions of Dawes, of the learning and researches
of Burgess. He dissents from him, it is true, in
the theory which he adopted respecting the origin
and formation of the Greek language. This, however, is a subtle and recondite question, upon which
eminent scholars have differed, and will continue to
differ; it is a question also, with respect to which
very ingenious, and yet conflicting theories, may be
advanced and defended. After every concession
made in the spirit of the foregoing observations, the
honour will still belong to Mr. Burgess of having
been the most zealous, able, and successful promoter
of Greek learning at Oxford, towards the close of
the eighteenth century.*

* Mr Burgess took his degree of B A. on Dec. 17. 1778,
and of M A. in 1782. He was chosen a fellow of Corpus in
1787, and was soon after appointed logic reader, and then
tutor of the college. He became B D. in 1791, and D D in
1803.

CHAP. IV.

COMMENCEMENT OF FRIENDSHIP WITH MR. TYRWHITT. —
CORRESPONDENCE WITH HIM.

1780.

CONSEQUENCES far beyond the value of any transitory praise accrued to Mr. Burgess from the republication of Dawes, since it procured for him the acquaintance and friendship of Mr. Tyrwhitt, a gentleman who, to a large experience of men and things, united great mental acuteness, elegance, and refinement, enhanced by the polish of the best society. His influence in the literary world was justly extensive; for it was founded not only upon his personal qualities, but also upon works of acknowledged ability and interest.

Mr. Tyrwhitt was educated at Eton and Oxford. In 1761 he became Clerk of the House of Commons; but resigned this office, after occupying it for six or seven years, in consequence of the effects of fatigue and late hours upon his health. Henceforth he devoted himself to learned and literary pursuits, and gave himself up to his beloved books. He was a man of varied and profound erudition. His knowledge of modern languages was very extensive; and he was critically conversant with those of Greece and Rome. Philology was his favourite study; and he applied its principles, with much success, to critical questions connected with the text of our old English poets, particularly Chaucer and

c 2

Shakspeare. He manifested no less acuteness in
dealing with many recondite points of Greek criticism. In private life, he was equally distinguished
by the generosity and kindness of his heart, and by
the mildness and elegance of his manners. His
taste was refined and fastidious, and his mental
sagacity of a high order.

Such a man was justly entitled to the compliment
of a dedication of the new edition of the Miscellanea
Critica. To Mr Burgess's request, that he would
accept this compliment, he not only acceded, but
placed also at his disposal various notes and observations upon Dawes, — the fruit of his own
researches. Many of these were inserted in the new
edition. The intercourse thus commenced led on
to correspondence and acquaintance, and finally terminated in cordial and mutual friendship. Mr.
Tyrwhitt soon proved himself to be a friend of no
ordinary value. He was so struck, on conversing
with Mr. Burgess, with the extent of his learning,
and with the simplicity and integrity of his heart,
with his ardent zeal for mental improvement, and
his candour in the avowal of any mistakes, or errors
of judgment, with the mild suavity of his manners,
and the manly independence of his principles, that
he quickly became affectionately interested in his
success in life. He found, also, great delight in the
interchange of opinion and sentiment with him,
upon many interesting points arising out of their
kindred studies. He, himself, was now advanced in
life, and was capable, from his acknowledged wisdom
and experience, of giving the most important practical counsel to his learned, but, as yet, inexperienced
young friend; and finding that every hint of this

description was gratefully received, he became to him, at length, a sort of Mentor.

He watched over, fostered, and encouraged his learned studies, and became the confidant of his literary schemes and projects. His friendly counsel was always at his command; his animating encouragement stimulated all his laudable undertakings; and, whenever he conceived that he had committed, or was about to commit, an error in judgment, he pointed it out to him with honest sincerity, and with equal delicacy. A remarkable instance of his kindness occurred soon after the commencement of their personal acquaintance, which produced so profound an impression upon the heart of Mr. Burgess, that, even in the latest periods of his life, he was wont to dwell upon it with the freshness of almost youthful gratitude. His pecuniary resources were narrow; and, finding his expenses at Oxford more considerable than his means warranted, he resolved, on principles of honourable independence, to tear himself from this seat of the Muses, rather than contract debts which might prove embarrassing. His plan was, to take orders, and, in the retirement of a curacy, to prosecute his studies in conjunction with the performance of clerical duties. This resolution he communicated to Mr. Tyrwhitt, who replied, " No! you must on no account quit Oxford. You must be my curate there for the next two years."

The assistance thus delicately offered was most gratefully accepted, and, for about that space of time, he received from Mr. Tyrwhitt a pecuniary contribution amounting to the ordinary salary of a curate, for the express purpose of enabling him to retain his situation in the university, and of pursuing, at ease, his learned studies.

A selection of letters and extracts from letters, addressed to Mr. Burgess by this amiable and generous friend, shall now be placed before my readers. Those which refer to subjects of verbal criticism connected with the Miscellanea Critica, are omitted, either wholly or in part, as having special reference to that work, and as unsuited to the taste of general readers. But many are of a more popular nature, and are distinguished by fine sense and critical discrimination, united to a delicate playfulness and humour, which impart to them no common charm. Various letters from other learned correspondents are also interspersed. They have reference to the pursuits and studies of Mr. Burgess, and therefore tend to illustrate his biography. It is justly remarked by Mr. Lockhart, in his Life of Sir Walter Scott, and he quotes Southey's Life of Cowper to the same effect, " that, from the style and tone of such letters, a man's character may often be gathered even more surely than from those written by himself *;" and this is particularly true in the case of a man like Mr. Burgess, of a very retiring and modest disposition. Many of the letters addressed to him at this period have been preserved; but very few of his own have survived, excepting those addressed to Mr. Tyrwhitt, and nearly all of these are elaborately critical. Some of more general interest are introduced.

Two or three letters were exchanged between

* Life of Sir W. Scott, vol. 1. p. 158.

them before they became personally acquainted. They had reference to the forthcoming edition of Dawes, and to notes upon the work, from the pen of Mr. Tyrwhitt, to be inserted in the Appendix.

Previously to the date of the following, Mr. Burgess had called on Mr. Tyrwhitt, and had left on his mind, as will appear, a most pleasing impression

TO MR. BURGESS.

Sir,

Though you seemed willing to allow me as much time as I should desire for drawing up my notes, I thought it best to dispatch them out of hand, lest a longer delay should lead you to expect something more considerable than I have to produce. I will beg the favour of you to read them over with attention, before you send them to the press, and to let me know if you observe any thing which you think wants to be corrected, or more clearly explained. As to style, I have been too little practised in writing Latin to attempt any elegance, but I should be sorry to break Priscian's head, or even to scratch him roughly, if, therefore, I have committed any such enormity, pray tell me of it. I must repeat my best thanks to you for the favour of your visit, and my regret that the shortness of your stay in town prevented me from seeing you again. It is a pleasure which I have very rarely experienced, to converse with one of your age who knows so much, and at the same time shows such an ingenuous and rational desire of learning more.

If at any time you should think that I can be

of the least service to you, I desire you would apply
to me freely, as you may be assured that I shall be
happy to take every opportunity of convincing you
that I am with real regard,

Dear Sir,

Your faithful Servant,

THOS. TYRWHITT.

Welbeck St., Nov. 8. 1779.

TO T. TYRWHITT, ESQ.

DEAR SIR,

I AM really at a loss to express my respect in
terms equal to what my gratitude would dictate.
So much condescension and politeness, with such
sincerity, have convinced me that I had not idly
formed an early attachment to your name It is
my singular happiness to prove, by experience, the
justice of that attachment; though the friendship,
I should rather say the favour of Mr. Tyrwhitt,
was what I had as little reason to expect as merit
to deserve. I am very much obliged for your remarks on Dawes, which I received last Tuesday,
and I join in the thanks which I anticipate from the
reader for the accurate learning which they contain.

[Then follow two long pages, chiefly composed
of critical remarks and questions relative to Dawes.]

I cannot help mentioning a piece of University
news, which I think will interest you. A scheme
is much talked of, and is soon to be introduced into
convocation, by which a fund is to be raised for the
purchasing of books for the Bodleian library, the
defects of which we are now astonished should have
been of so long continuance. The fund is to be

raised principally from an increase of the matricu-
lation fees, and an annual subscription from those
who are entitled to the use of the Bodleian.

I remain, Sir,

with sincerest respect,

T. BURGESS.

C. C. C , Nov. 16. 1779

TO T. TYRWHITT, ESQ.

DEAR SIR,

I KNOW not how to abstain from repeating my
best thanks for the freedom of your censures, and
the unreservedness of your friendly counsel, but
am afraid to venture on a subject in which the
warmth of gratitude might, perhaps, give to my
expressions the colouring of compliment.

I should think myself unworthy of your friendship, and of the favour of your correspondence,
if I did not mention, especially after your polite
and flattering request, what perhaps, when recon-
sidered, you might wish in one instance to alter in
the Latinity of your remarks.

[Then follows a passage in which Mr. Burgess
proposes a slight change in the Latinity of a sentence in Mr. Tyrwhitt's notes; a suggestion, which
as he had not to do with an Archbishop of Grenada,
but a most amiable and candid critic, was received
in the same spirit in which it was offered.]

You see, Sir, (he goes on to say,) how I have
taken advantage of your complaisance to imitate
your sincerity.

When I read your sentiments concerning the

MS. Odyssey, I was quite convinced of the propriety of being silent on it.

> I am happy to subscribe myself, dear Sir,
> Your obliged and grateful Servant,
> T. BURGESS.

C. C. C., Nov 29 1779.

The following letter is a literary curiosity, as
coming from a very eminent scholar. The correspondence does not appear to have proceeded further.

TO MR. BURGESS.

SIR,

I SHOULD have answered your letter before, but
have been much out of order for some time. I
cannot give you any other information or intelligence concerning Mr. Dawes, than that I always
esteemed him as a very ingenious man, and a man
of considerable learning He was quite a stranger
to me. I am much pleased with your intended
publication, and congratulate the University of Oxford on such a worthy young gentleman. There
is one thing in Mr. Dawes's Miscellanea, p. 219.,
which I cannot help taking notice of, where he
has mistaken a passage of Euripid. Troad, for one
of an Ionic poet, which I have given some account
of in my Emendations on Suidas, p. 104. It is well
worth your reading. I shall always be glad to hear
from you, and wishing you success in your studies,
am your

> Most obedient humble Servant,
> J. TOUP.

St. Martin's, Oct. 13 1779.

In the year 1779 the subject for one of the Chancellor's Prizes at Oxford was, "On the affinity between poetry and painting." Mr. Burgess was among the competitors; but the present Lord Sidmouth, then Mr. Addington, bore away the palm. "My failure was a great disappointment to me," said the Bishop, reverting to this event in his latter days, "yet I can truly say I listened to Mr. Addington with the most sincere pleasure, while he publicly recited his successful essay; and I well remember how much I felt the effect which he imparted to it by his admirable voice and manner." His generous nature was, in fact, ever prompt to recognise, and to render homage to rival excellence. Among his manuscripts there is a copy of his own essay on this occasion. It is fraught with learning and research, but the subject was less within the province of his own observation and experience than many which might have been selected.

TO MR. BURGESS.

DEAR SIR,

I HAVE had a very transient glimpse of Valckenaer's Theocritus; but I had time to examine the passage which you pointed out to me, though to very little purpose, as he only observes Dawes rejicit.

I condole with you upon your misfortune that Perizonius lived before you. "Pereant qui ante nos nostra dixerunt*," was an exclamation of some angry critic upon a similar occasion.

* " Perish those who have said our good things before us."

Your etymology of *span new* I should have proposed myself, without much hesitation, if I had not been staggered by another phrase in common use of the same import; viz. *spick* and *span*, which seems to point to something different from *spinning*. The true etymology, whenever it is discovered, will be found, I am persuaded, applicable to both phrases.

I hope to have the pleasure of seeing you here when you come to town, and am in the mean time,

Dear Sir,

Your very faithful humble Servant,

T. T.

Welbeck Street, 25th March, 1780.

TO MR. BURGESS.

Dear Sir,

I am greatly obliged to you for the trouble which you have taken in examining Stobæus, and for your description of the manuscripts, which was new to me.

I am glad I happened to mention Porphyry to you, as it has led you to read the Ζητηματα. He is certainly in the first class of the existing commentators on Homer.

I have received lately four plays of Euripides, from M. Brunck, viz. Hecuba, Medea, Hippolytus, and Bacchæ. I understand that we are to expect nothing more from him till his Sophocles is published. He goes on to take much greater liberties with the text of his author than I can approve of. I have sometimes thought that it would not be an unsalutary law in the republic of criticism, if an editor were absolutely restrained from inserting any conjectures of his own in the text of his author. He might safely, perhaps, be intrusted with a liberty of inserting those of others. We are not apt to exceed on that side.

I shall hope to continue to hear from you at your leisure, and shall be very happy whenever I can find any way of being of the least use to you or your studies. Allow me to mention a little thing which has occurred to me. You intend to spend the vacation in the country, where perhaps you may not be so well provided with books as you are at Oxford. Will you give me leave to make over to you a few useful, not splendid, Greek folios, to be added to your country library? You will, at least, I flatter myself, take this offer as it is meant by

Your sincere Friend,

T. T.

Welbeck Street, 31st May, 1780.

TO T. TYRWHITT, ESQ.

DEAR SIR, C. C. C., 1780.

I WILL take this opportunity of supplying the deficiencies of my last, of the 3d inst., by returning my sincere thanks for the pains you have obligingly taken in reading over the parts of Foster's essay, mentioned in a former letter, and I will certainly take advantage of your observations respecting them.

I lately received some further intelligence of Mr. Dawes and his MSS., communicated to my Cambridge correspondent by Dr. Farmer of Emanuel. He says that the late Dr. Askew purchased his books and

MSS. If you could inform me by what means I may obtain a sight of them I shall be much obliged.

Dr. Farmer has a MS. by Dawes, containing criticisms on Akenside's " Pleasures of Imagination," in which he expresses his sentiments respecting Dr. Bentley very plainly. " Of this celebrated person," says he, " I shall say no more at present, but intend soon to submit to the public censure some animadversions upon his emendations of Aristophanes, Menander, and Philemon ; from which I presume it will appear that his skill in the Greek language has been very much over-rated, both by himself and others, and that there has not been sufficient reason for the mighty expectation long ago raised, by his proposed edition of Homer." Dawes seems on many accounts to have imbibed no small share of the reigning prejudice against the great critic.

I shall return to Oxford through town in the beginning of April, and I am, dear Sir,

Your obliged,

T. BURGESS.

CHAP. V.

OBTAINS THE CHANCELLOR'S PRIZE. — EXTRACTS FROM THE PRIZE ESSAY. — LORD MONBODDO.

1780 to 1781.

IN the year 1780, one of the Chancellor's prizes was adjudged to Mr. Burgess, for an Essay on the Study of Antiquities. It is referred to in the two following letters : —

TO T. TYRWHITT, ESQ.

DEAR SIR, C. C. C., June 25. 1780.
I HAVE just received the MS. belonging to Dr.
Farmer, entitled "Remarks upon a Character in a
late Poem, entitled the ' Pleasures of Imagination,
augmented with critical Notes and Emendations,
particularly some Hints relating to the genuine Pronunciation of the Greek Language, the Imperfection
of the Oxford Edition of Pindar, and the Use of the
Consonant or Aspiration WAW in the Writings of
Homer.'" There were some of Mr. Dawes's neighbours, it seems, who applied the character of Momion
in the 3d book personally to him, which was the
cause of this strange medley of learning and nonsense.
All the critical remarks and emendations are to be
found in the Miscellanea. He sometimes refers, in a
later handwriting, to a supplement of his remarks
on Pindar, Callimachus, and Aristophanes, which I
suppose is among Dr. Askew's papers.
I will just add, that I flatter myself you will not be
displeased to hear that within these few days I have
been so fortunate as to obtain the Chancellor's prize
for an English Essay on the Study of Antiquities, a
copy of which I will take the liberty to send you as
soon as I can get some printed, which I mean for distribution among my friends.
Yours respectfully,
T. BURGESS.

TO MR. BURGESS.

Dear Sir,

I DID not intend to have written to you till I could send you notice of the departure of the books (by the frank acceptance of which you have obliged me very much); but I have been induced to alter my mind by reading in the papers that one of the Chancellor's prizes for this year has been adjudged to you. Though distrustful, in general, of newspaper intelligence, I have a sort of inward persuasion that, in this case, they have told truth, and the warmth of my regard for you will not permit me to delay my congratulations till the fact can be better ascertained.

Having now my pen in hand, I will say a few words on some points in your last. As you will give me no account of the Aristotle, I will tell you, that it is to be published next Saturday, at least so the editor has said, in a letter which I have seen of his own writing, within this week.

You have seen much more of Lord Monboddo than I, who have only dined with him once, at the Archbishop of York's, where he did not open much of his philosophy, perhaps from the fault of his company. Mr. Harris's book I have long heard of. The subject, I should have thought, rather required a volume in folio, than a part only of a loosely printed octavo. However, I shall be glad to see it. I am always,

Dear Sir,

Yours very sincerely,

T. T.

June 26 1780.

TO THE SAME.

DEAR SIR,

I HAVE at length dispatched to you the Greek folios of which I begged your acceptance, — Hesy-chius, Suidas, M. Pollux, Eustathius, Photius, and Athenæus, I wished to have added Stobæus, but I could not find a complete copy. As you are so fresh from the conversation of Lord Monboddo, I shall make no apology for obtruding a set of such rum gentry upon you.

I was happy to hear from yourself that I had not been too credulous in the newspapers, when I congratulated you upon your having obtained the Chancellor's prize. I shall be very glad to read your essay when you do me the favour to send it to me.

By your account of Dawes's MS., I should imagine that you are not likely to make much use of it. I will venture to suggest my private wishes, that nothing may be produced which would be dis-agreeable to Dr. Akenside, if he were now living. I had a considerable degree of intimacy with him for the last ten years of his life, and I consider him as Ἀνέρα, τον ουδ' αινειν εστι κακοισι Θεμις· much less should I like to see published a satire upon him, written by *Dawes in a passion*. But I dare say he is very safe in your hands.

I am to go out of town next Tuesday, for three weeks or a month. I have some thoughts of calling at Oxford in my return, but I am afraid not before you will have left it. Adieu, my dear Sir, and believe me always,

Yours very sincerely,

T. TYRWHITT.

Welbeck Street, 14th July, 1780.

D

TO THE SAME.

DEAR SIR,

I HAVE notice of a parcel from Mr. Brunck , but what it contains I know not, as it must perform quarantine before it can be delivered.

I shall be happy to read your epistle, whenever you think proper to send it. But I hope you do not mean to impose upon future critics any necessity of following your example, and prefacing their lucubrations with verses.* How do you contrive to pursue, together, such different studies, criticism, poetry, etymology, Latin, Greek, and something which people spoke, or may be supposed to have spoken, before Latin and Greek ?

I am obliged to you for your friend's imitations of Chaucer. After the reason which you have assigned for suppressing the tale, it would be impertinent to inquire further about it. As a friend of your friend, I must tell him, that there are some Chattertonianisms in his language which he must avoid in any future work, if he means to pass for Chaucer. A-propos to Chaucer, let me ask you what may seem an odd question, — whether you have got a copy of my edition of the Canterbury Tales? My reason is, that there are very few left ; and if you have not got one already, I would reserve one for you, as the book is not likely to be reprinted, and I should wish to have a copy deposited in your hands.

---

* Alluding to an epistle in Latin verse in the manner of Horace, intended to have been prefixed to the edition of Dawes

I have just put out proposals for publishing, by subscription, two dissertations of the late Dr. Musgrave, one on the Grecian Mythology, and another on the Chronology of the Olympiads. He ordered them to be delivered to me, as I suppose, for this purpose. I am therefore trying to raise what money I can, in this way, for his family, who are in great want of assistance. As I hold myself bound to take off a certain number of subscriptions myself, I shall beg leave to set down your name in my list for a copy L. P., which I shall desire you to accept from me. If you can in any way promote the subscription, it will be an act of humanity.

I am, dear Sir,

Yours very sincerely,

T. TYRWHITT.

A second edition of Mr. Burgess's Prize Essay upon the Study of Antiquities was quickly called for, and published, with additions. His general object in this essay was to give just ideas of the light reflected upon history and chronology, and upon ancient arts and manners, by antiquarian researches; in particular, by the study of architecture and marbles, of coins and inscriptions, of old poetry and records. In the second part, he expatiated at considerable length upon the antiquities and the philosophy of language, and on the utility of etymological researches in the illustration of physics, metaphysics, and other sciences. This being a subject to which he had directed much attention, it is treated of at considerable length.

The Essay on Antiquities is the production of an elegant and ingenious mind, richly stored with classical images, and glowing with sensibility to the sublime and the beautiful in nature and in art. The style, though in some parts incorrect, is in general nervous and elegant. The subject being popular, and different from those which subsequently employed the author's pen, a few extracts are here introduced as a specimen of the mode in which it is treated.

"The mind of man, always active and inquisitive, seems seldom to exert itself with more pleasure than in retracing the memory of those ages which are past, and of those events and characters which are never to return. There is an involuntary attachment to that which is irrecoverably snatched from our presence, and removed beyond the reach of our hopes and wishes, which induces us to behold with a kind of religious awe the obscurest vestiges of antiquity.

"But these sensations of the mind are then most powerful and poignant when they arise from the contemplation of places, once the scene of actions which decided the fate of empires, or rescued an oppressed people from slavery and superstition, or which were frequented by some of the few who have distinguished themselves from the great body of mankind by the invention of arts which contribute to the use and ornament of life, or who stand foremost in the annals of science."

After expatiating upon the inferences which may be drawn as to the customs and manners of nations from their progress in the arts and sciences, from the peculiarities of their language and architecture, and from the nature of their laws and institutions, he beautifully touches, in the following passage, upon the light reflected on classical poetry by the study of ancient sculpture : —

" The same advantage results to poetry from a careful examination of the remains of ancient sculpture. The images of the poets receive new life and spirit from a comparison with the works of kindred artists. Their conceptions seem to acquire beauties which before were unknown, a delicacy and grace which would otherwise have escaped the acutest judgment, and the most refined sensibility. After such a comparison, we see the whole of a poetic attitude or description with more enlightened eyes, purged, like those of Diomed, of the film too gross before to discover the fine texture of celestial forms. It is thus the reader of Virgil's very affecting description feels the powers of his imagination enlarged after studying the Laocoon at Rome. And thus, in the flourishing days of Greece, the astonished spectator turned from the statue of Phidias to the awful and majestic Jupiter of Homer. By studying the works of the best masters, the imagination becomes conversant with images of beauty and grandeur, the combination of which enables the artist to approach nearer to the perfect ideal form than the most exact imitation of ordinary individual beauty. From the invaluable remains of antiquity, Michael Angelo derived the excellence of many of his best performances. Raphael studied their noble simplicity and sedate grandeur of expression with the most diligent attention ; and, as he more correctly imitated the antique than his great contemporary, more successfully expressed its beauties."

The following passages occur in the latter part

of the Essay : — " The investigation of monumental
antiquities contributes much to correct the misrepresentations and supply the deficiencies of history,
as well as to illustrate the state of ancient manners of
which they preserve so many striking images.

" In surveying the proud monuments of feudal
splendour and magnificence exhibited in the remains
of ancient castles, the very genius of chivalry seems
to present himself amidst the venerable ruins with
a sternness and majesty of air and feature, which
show what he once has been, and with a mixture of
disdain for the degenerate posterity that robbed
him of his honours. Amid such a scene, the manly
exercises of knighthood recur to the imagination in
their full pomp and solemnity ; while every patriot
feeling beats at the remembrance of the generous
virtues which were nursed in those schools of fortitude, honour, courtesy, and wit, the mansions of
our ancient nobility.

" The history of monasteries, and other religious
houses, has afforded employment equal to the ardour
of the most industrious antiquary. Nor can we
sufficiently admire the indefatigable diligence and
extensive learning exerted in collecting the im-
mense treasure of records contained in our monastic
antiquities. Though the history of these institutions
exhibits too many instances of licentiousness, indolence, and ignorance, yet we ought with gratitude
to remember that even while the inhabitants of the
cloister were themselves, for the most part, lost to
all good taste, they prevented the surrounding bar-
barism of those dark ages from entirely extinguish-
ing the light of classical learning, and that to them
was owing the preservation of the most valuable

ancient authors, the various discoveries of which constitute so interesting a part in the history of learning.

 * * * * * *

 * * * * * *

 * * * * * *

" The study of antiquities, once so far removed from all the arts of elegance, is now become an attendant on the Muses, an handmaid to History, to Poetry, and Philosophy. From their united influence many are the advantages which have been derived to general knowledge. Much of that obscurity, particularly, which overspreads the first periods in the history of every nation, has been happily removed from our own by the diligence and sagacity of able antiquaries. What, indeed, may we not expect further from an age in which every part of science is advancing to perfection — in which History has attained a degree of excellence unknown to any former period of English literature : and Poetry and Philosophy have gained new honours. and, lastly, in whose character *that* has so conspicuous a place which is essential to the success of this study, an inquisitive curiosity, and love of truth."

Lord Monboddo has been mentioned as one of the correspondents of Mr. Burgess, and many of his letters have been preserved. Some of them are upon recondite metaphysical questions, which he discusses with much subtlety, but they are treatises rather than letters, and quite unsuited to the object of these pages. Others, though tinctured with the peculiar notions and opinions of their ingenious and learned, though often very extravagant writer, are

both curious and interesting, and refer so particularly to the studies of Mr Burgess, that, like those
of Mr. Tyrwhitt, they tend to illustrate this period
of his life. Of these, therefore, a few will be introduced.

TO MR. BURGESS.

DEAR SIR,

BEFORE I left Edinburgh, I received two copies
of the second edition of your Essay on the Study
of Antiquities. One of them I gave — and, I hope,
by your permission — to Mr. Dalzell, Professor of
Greek in the university of Edinburgh, a very ingenious man, and very zealous in the study of
Greek learning. Since I came into the country I
have had time to go through your work, which,
I think, is much improved in the second edition. I
am glad to find that you compose in the true ancient taste, and have not gone into that fashionable
short cut of a style, first introduced by Sallust, and
made worse by his imitator, Tacitus, who have been
the model of French, and of a great deal of English
writing, of late years. It is a style of writing that,
I think, does not deserve the name of composition;
and I would rather call it notes, or memorandums
for composing. But, abrupt and disjointed as it
is, I like it better than such composition as Mr.
Gibbon's, loaded with epithets altogether improper
for prose, and generally concluding his sentences
with two substantives, and each with its attendant
epithet. And I heard an English gentleman observe, what I believe may be true, that there is not
a parenthesis in the whole book Now, I hold that

there is nothing contributes more to diversify a style properly, or to express a thing forcibly, than parentheses, properly used. The finest and best pattern of writing, I mean Homer, has used them very much; and the best poet and greatest writer we have in English, Milton, has both raised and varied his style by the use of them; one beautiful example of which I have given from his Comus, in the third volume of the " Origin and Progress of Language." I am glad to see that you are not averse to the use of them.

I see you have done me the honour frequently to mention me, and with much commendation. You speak of my system of the origin of the Greek language and that of Hemsturhusius being the same; and it is true. But I assure you, that I no more copied from him or Lennep than they did from me When I wrote my dissertation upon the subject, I had only heard, as I have said, that Hemsturhusius had some system of that kind; but the account I got of it was so imperfect, that I could make nothing of it. He never published it himself, as far as I know ; and as to Lennep's work, it did not fall into my hands till about two years ago, nearly six years after that dissertation was printed; and I am not sure (I have not the book by me) but that Lennep's work was printed after mine. Now, that being the case, it is an extraordinary coincidence and agreement of two men in the same system, who knew nothing of one another's opinions; and, in that respect, is a very curious literary anecdote.

There is one thing concerning the Greek language in which you and I seem perfectly to agree,

— that it is the most wonderful piece of art ever
invented by mortal man, as far at least as we
know ; for the Shanscrit language may, according to the account given of it, be as artificial,
or more so, than the Greek. Even a barbarous
language, such as I hold all European languages
to be, compared with the Greek, is a great piece
of art. But, in the first place, the art in them is
not near so great, as they have not the variety
of flexion and termination by which cases and
tenses are formed ; nor even of articulation, which
makes the Greek language the most various, and,
at the same time, the most high-sounding language
in the world. And, secondly, we cannot carry
back the art of any other language so far, nor
deduce it, by a regular and orderly progression,
from a few elementary sounds. But all other languages that I know seem to consist of the cries of
savages, broken, indeed, and distinguished by articulation ; to which, no doubt, an art of language
has been applied, so as to form out of them the
several parts of speech, and connect them by a lame
and inartificial syntax.

There is the language of one author in Greek,
of which you should make a particular study, as it
may be said to be a language by itself, and unique
— such as is written by no other author ; and with
more variety of flexion and termination, and greater
beauty and pomp of sound than any other language
in Greek. By this description you will know that
I mean the language of Homer, in which there is
a variety of beauty that is not to be found in any
other. That this is truly the fact, may be easily
shown by a man so learned in the Greek language

as you are. But it is a matter of curious inquiry,
how it happens that the oldest language we have
in Greek should be the most perfect.

In general, let me advise you to be very sparing
in your censures of the ancients. When I was a
young student, I was as much disposed, or more
than you are, to find fault with the ancients, and I
flattered myself I had detected great errors in
them, but now that I am near the age of seventy
I am come to this firm persuasion, that though
we may know more of facts of natural history than
they did, yet as to arts and sciences, and particularly as to the grammatical, rhetorical, and poetical
arts, and as to logic and metaphysics, and even
as to the philosophy of nature, our knowledge is
quite contemptible compared with theirs. From
this rule I think there is but one exception, and
that is the astronomy of Sir Isaac Newton. But
even the principles of that astronomy have been so
laid down as to lead to downright materialism, and
thus to disgrace one of the noblest discoveries in
science that ever was made by a single man.

I will only further say a word concerning philosophy, and the highest kind of it, to which
Aristotle has given the name of Metaphysics.
About this philosophy I hope you are chiefly employed, and that you will procure to the university
of Oxford the glory of restoring ancient philosophy
to Britain, and, indeed, I may say to all Europe,
where it has now been dead a century, and in place
of it are come materialism and atheism. If you
can contribute to this restoration, or rather the
resurrection of philosophy, you will do great honour
both to yourself and to your university; and I

know some great men in London who will be as
ready to give their countenance and assistance to
you, as they have declared themselves ready to give
it to Dr. Horsley, on account of the help he has
given me to reconcile the principles of Sir Isaac
Newton's astronomy with the genuine principles of
theism.

Wishing you all success, both in your philological
and philosophical inquiries, and hoping to hear
from you soon, I ever am

Your most faithful humble Servant,
JAMES BURNETT.

Give my service to all my acquaintance in Oxford, who think it worth their while to inquire
about me.

CHAP. VI.

LITERARY CORRESPONDENCE WITH LORD MONBODDO, MR. TYRWHITT, AND DR VINCENT

1781.

THE progress of Mr. Burgess's literary life and
occupations at Oxford are so graphically developed
by the letters of Mr. Tyrwhitt, and by those of
some few among his other correspondents, that we
shall subjoin, with brief occasional comments, a
further selection of them.

TO MR. BURGESS.

DEAR SIR,

You have indulged me in such a liberty, or rather
licence, of criticism upon the communications with

which you have occasionally favoured me, that I
should deem myself unworthy of your present confidence if I did not use the same freedom in giving
you my sentiments of your Αναθημα.

A Greek epigram is certainly an ornamentum
ambitiosum ; a sort of hors d'œuvre, which, if not
very exquisite, had better be spared — poterat duci
quia cœna sine isto. I conceive, therefore, the
utmost severity of morose criticism can never be
more properly exerted than in a matter of this
kind. * * * * *
 * * * * * *

[After several critical remarks upon the epigram,
and objections to particular words, Mr. T. adds:—]

I would not have you be offended or mortified
with the number of them, as I scarcely remember
to have read a modern Greek poem, from the time
of Politian to the present, which was not equally
open to censure.

I do not know that Bentley has any where, in any
writing of his own, explained the doctrine of the
digamma in general.

I am glad you continue your researches among
the Bodleian MSS., but (begging your pardon) I
should think you might give us something better
from thence than a metaphrase of Homer. That it
may afford some light to a few passages, is very possible ; but I am sure your time may be better employed than in publishing it at length.

I am always, dear Sir,
Yours very sincerely,
T. T.

Welbeck Street, Jan. —, 1781

TO T. TYRWHITT, ESQ.

DEAR SIR, Odiham, Jan. 16.

I AM greatly and sincerely obliged to you for your remarks on my Epigram, but was not aware that I should have given you so much trouble. To confess the truth, I looked upon it with some degree of complacency, and began to have a more favourable opinion of the practicability of Greek composition, than Mr. Dawes, from his better experience, had. The mortification which so many errors — if pointed out by another person — might have occasioned, was entirely prevented by the real favour of your criticisms.

Your remark on the ill success of Greek composition from the time of Politian to the present is a douceur which I found little difficulty in admitting.

I am, dear Sir,
Your very obliged humble Servant,
T. BURGESS.

LORD MONBODDO TO MR. BURGESS.

DEAR SIR, Monboddo, 27th Sept. 1781.

I THANK you for your letter and your verses; I cannot say with Horace,

——— Carmina possumus
Donare, et pretium dicere muneris;

so I cannot repay you myself in kind; but I send you, enclosed, some verses of a lady in London, an acquaintance of mine, which I think very good. She is the widow of Commodore Walsingham, lately lost; and is by inheritance a wit and a poet, for she is the daughter of Sir Charles Hanbury Williams. And, indeed, she is in every respect a very accomplished woman. The card with which she accompanied the verses is as well turned as any thing of the kind I ever saw; but you are to remember that poets deal in fiction, or, at least, in very extravagant hyperboles.

But lest you should think that, because I cannot write verses, nobody in Scotland can, I send you, likewise, inclosed, a copy of verses that I think truly classical, written by a friend of mine at the bar in Scotland, Mr. M'Laurin.

As to your verses, I must tell you freely that I like the Latin very much better than the English. The Latin are an excellent imitation of Horace's familiar epistolary style; for they are sermoni propiora, affecting nothing of the tumor and pomp of heroic verse which Horace could write too, and could rise even to a higher style of poetry, — I mean the Ode; but he knew how to suit his style to his subject, and could practise his own rule —

Descriptas servare vices, operumque colores.

You have marked your age by a much more memorable event than the consulship of Lollius and Lepidus.

I think it not amiss that you should follow the advice once given to a young student, —

—— det primos versibus annos
Mæoniumque bibat felici pectore fontem.

But attend to what follows, —

Mox et Sociatico plenus grege, &c

I would, therefore, have you use poetry only as the amusement of your youth, and apply your Greek learning to its proper use — the study of the Greek arts and sciences, and particularly the science of sciences, — I mean Philosophy, — in which you will find the principles of all arts and sciences, even of the popular arts, such as Poetry and Rhetoric, as Aristotle has very clearly shown. At the same time, you have no reason to regret the time that you have hitherto bestowed upon Philology, which is the best introduction to Philosophy, and does much better before it than to follow after it; for it was a fall of my friend, poor Mr. Harris, as he observed to me last time I saw him, to descend from Philosophy to Philology.

I have not had time yet to read much of the philological work you have sent me. In the Preface, I observe, you make very honourable mention of me, for which I thank you.

I am much pleased with what you say of the digamma. It is, I think, perfectly clear that the sound, if not the character, of the digamma was used by the Arcadians and Ænotores, who imported the Latin dialect into Latium. And it is clear, from the passage of the Halicarnassian, which you have quoted, and defended against a most audacious criticism of Dawes, that it was noted by the character _V_ among the Latins; the sound of which, as the Halicarnassian tells us, was that of the Greek diphthong ου, which I have no doubt was sounded something like our _W_.* I am further of opinion that it was used, in the days of Homer, both

* On this question, see the note, p. 14.

in the beginning and in the middle of words, in
order to thicken the sound, and to prevent vowels
from gaping upon one another. I have no doubt
but the digamma had the effect of lengthening
the preceding vowel, by thickening, and so retard-
ing the pronunciation of the subsequent vowel,
and in that way a good deal of Homer's metre is to
be explained.

I am, very sincerely,

Your most obedient humble servant,

JAMES BURNETT.

TO MR. BURGESS.

DEAR SIR,

AFTER my shocking rudeness upon a former occasion, I little expected any further employment
from you in the office of censor. But I find I
have to do with a young man of parts and learning,
who is, yet, really desirous of hearing advice.
Where did you acquire this uncommon disposition? Not, surely, from your study of modern
critics. However, as long as you condescend to
consult me in any matter, I shall esteem it ουδε
φιλιον ουδε οσιον * not to give you my opinion with
freedom and sincerity.

I suppose (though you do not expressly say so)
that you have thoughts of printing the Latin verses
at the head of your edition of Dawes? I believe
I threw out, upon a former occasion, my general
notion of the hazard attending hors d'œuvres of
this kind. In the present case, what strikes me

---

* Neither friendly nor equitable.

as particularly liable to misapprehension is, that
you seem to consider the book as entirely your
own. What would Dawes say to that? Exclusive of this point of legal discussion, — how far an
editor acquires a property in the works of his
author, — I have no objection to make to the plan
and sentiments of your address, except, only, to
that part in which you speak of yourself, modestly
enough, indeed : but even that modesty, and the
example of Horace, (whose very words, as I recol-
lect, you have almost transcribed,) will scarcely, I
doubt, completely justify you to that class of
readers who are angry with honest Montaigne for
having told them that he liked white wine better
than red. The manner in which you have marked
your æra is more poetical, I think, than Horace's
naked appeal to the Fasti ; but would you choose,
in a calm philosophical discourse, to adopt the language of political invective ? * Would you wish to
make the war still more general and destructive, by
setting the critics of all the world in arms against
us ;— Brunck, Villoison, &c. &c.? The remainder of
your poem deserves a more serious acknowledgment from me. How far you meant to flatter me,
you know best, but your compliments are certainly
such as I wish to deserve, and such as (from a friend
and a poet) I think I might almost venture to receive
without too much blushing.

I am always, dear Sir,
Yours very sincerely,
T. T.

Welbeck Street, 29th March, 1781

---

* Referring, probably, to some passage of the above description in the Latin poem alluded to.

The following letter from Mr. Tyrwhitt is in reply to one in which his young friend had gratefully adverted to the kind method which he had devised to enable him to continue at Oxford: —

DEAR SIR,

I AM really happy in being able to assist you in the prosecution of a plan which seems as agreeable to your inclination, as I am persuaded it is well calculated for the improvement of your talents. But do not over-rate your obligations (as you call them) to me, by supposing that I am quite disinterested in this transaction. While your chief residence is at Oxford, I shall hope to have the pleasure of seeing you oftener, or, at least, of corresponding with you more frequently, and with more satisfaction, upon the subject of our common studies, than if you were settled in any other place. These, I assure you, I consider as no small advantages, which I am likely to derive from the plan which you have thought fit to adopt at my suggestion. But, where both parties are satisfied, it seems unnecessary to discuss minutely which has most reason for being so.

I am much obliged to you for your information with respect to the translations of Thucydides. It looks as if Sir Isaac's eye had been fascinated by the Latin, so as to prevent him from consulting the Greek.

Do you hear any thing of Mr. Toup's work upon Euripides? I had a letter, not long ago, from Mr. Brunck, in which, without naming Sophocles, he announces an edition of the XI plays and frag-

ments of Aristophanes, of which the text is printed
off. * * * * *
* * * * * *
* * * * * *
* * * * * *
— *A long series of verbal criticism on a passage
in Homer is omitted, which concludes thus :* —

And so, while I only meant to fill two or three
pages with innocent prate, I have stept into the
abyss of antiquarian criticism. Help me out, if you
can ; or, at least, treat me with tenderness as a
young etymologist, and as

Yours very faithfully,

T. Tyrwhitt.

Welbeck Street, Oct. 30 1781.

The edition of Dawes, as appears from the following letter, was published in the summer of
1781 : —

TO MR. BURGESS.

Dear Sir,

I sincerely congratulate you upon the conclusion of your labours, and (by anticipation) thank
you for your intended present to me. It gives me
pleasure to find that you reflect without dissatisfac-
tion upon our first correspondence, and that my
sincerity has, with you, atoned for my freedom.
I am only sorry that you hope, a little doubtingly
(with an if), for the continuance of my esteem. I
have, certainly, more reason to doubt the permanence of your partial attachment. But I trust that
the continuance of our correspondence (which you
will allow me to solicit upon the present friendly
footing) will convince us both that our mutual

regard for each other is more likely to increase than diminish.

> I am always, dear Sir,
> Your very faithful servant,
> T. T.

DR. VINCENT TO MR. BURGESS.

DEAR SIR,

I AM much obliged to you for your kind remembrance of me in your present of the new edition of Dawes. It is a book I have ever valued, and shall have more reason to do so now, from the learning and accuracy of your observations. I hear — but I know not with what truth — that Dr. Bentley's Homer is passed into the hands of Mr. Cumberland; if so, it will be easy for you to obtain a sight of it, and I am well assured it will repay your curiosity. Should you come to London, I hope you will favour me with your company to eat a bit of mutton.

> Believe me to be, with great respect,
> Your most faithful servant,
> W. VINCENT.

Dean's Yard, June 18 1781,

TO T. TYRWHITT, ESQ.

DEAR SIR,   C C C. Nov 15th, 1781

I HAVE examined the MS. Commentary on Aristotle's Rhetoric, and am inclined to think that it differs very much from the printed copy.

[Then follow a long series of extracts in Greek from the MS., accompanied by remarks and criticisms.]

E 3

I am employed in printing a second edition of my Essay on Antiquities, with additions. When it is completed, I shall cry a truce to publication for some time.

As soon as I find myself at leisure, I mean to act upon a hint which you threw out the last time I had the pleasure of being with you, respecting Homer and Plato : I mean to read Homer with Herodotus I shall then give Homer a second reading with the Greek tragedians, to whom I shall unite some of the most comprehensible parts of Plato. But, previously to this, I shall go through one of our own historians, with Barrington on the Statutes, and Blackstone's Commentaries : I shall then take up Montesquieu, as a prelude to a superficial course of the history of modern Europe. I think of choosing Hume, with proper cautions with regard to particular facts : which are, perhaps, sufficiently pointed out by Dr. Towers. I shall be glad if you approve of the preceding plan, and shall be obliged for any further hint on the subject.

I am, dear Sir, &c.,

T. BURGESS.

TO T. TYRWHITT, ESQ.

DEAR SIR,   C. C. C., Nov 26. 1781.

I wish to know about what time Dr. Musgrave's Dissertations will be published, as I am going into Hampshire for the first week in December, and hope to add two or three subscriptions to those which I have collected since my return to Oxford.

I will take this opportunity of answering the critical part of your former letter.

[Then follows a passage on the formation of the Greek word εισοκε.]

Will you be so good as to inform me whether the *god of eating* was worshipped under any peculiar name by the ancients ; and whether Comus was the god of eating, as well as revelling in general ? You will perhaps smile at this inquiry, and may be led to suspect that this unknown god is supplanting the goddess of learning even in our Athens itself. But that you may not think too hardly of us, I will mention the occasion of my inquiry. I lately received from Lord Monboddo some verses written by a Mr. M'Laurin, on the *god of eating,* to which I am threatening an answer. I will transcribe them.*

I am, dear Sir,

respectfully yours,

T. BURGESS.

TO MR. BURGESS.

DEAR SIR,

As you mention a purpose of going into Hampshire for the first week in December, I am a little doubtful whether this will catch you at Oxford ; however, I will risk it.

I am persuaded you will find the plan of reading which you have laid down for yourself answer very well ; — Homer is the great source of prose, as well as verse. When you come down in your course to Euripides, it would be not unpleasant, I should think, or unuseful, to join to him Aristophanes, and the histories of Thucydides and

* The verses are omitted, as we entirely agree in the opinion given of them in Mr. Tyrwhitt's reply.

Xenophon. Those four authors reflect much light one upon another. From them you may proceed to Plato and Demosthenes, and, afterwards, as your inclinations may lead you.

As your plan is for an abridgment of English history, I should think that Hume, with the cautions of which you seem to be aware, would answer your purpose. The books which you propose to read with him are very informing; but I should doubt whether to go through them with proper attention would not require more time than you might, perhaps, find it expedient at present to give up to them.

I do not remember to have read of any altars erected to a god of eating by the ancients. If our northern nations have addicted themselves to that worship, I fear we shall have no more metaphysics. Such poetry as Mr. M——'s, I think, might be composed after a good dinner.

Yours very sincerely,
T. T.

Welbeck Street, Nov. 21 1781.

NOTE TO CHAP VI.

THE following letter from Dr Vincent, upon the style of Homer, and on the nature and uses of the digamma, is introduced in the form of a note, because, though full of interest to scholars, it might, perhaps, be deemed out of place in the text by general readers.

SIR,   Dean's Yard, March 7 1781.

You are so much better informed upon the subject of the digamma, than myself, that it would little become me to offer any opinion upon your general system, which I think very complete, some few particulars you may, perhaps, not think impertinent.

And, first, in regard to Homer's dialects, I entirely agree with you in thinking it the poetic dialect of his age. What words occur that are not *strictly* conformable to this, is impossible for us now to determine; — but I conceive many of this sort to exist — introduced, 1. for their peculiar aptness; 2 their lofty sound; 3 their application; 4. their air of antiquity; — instances of these occur in all our best English poets; and in none more than Shakspeare, Spenser, and Milton.

To imagine that Homer, according to the vulgar error of grammarians (vide tractatum per Plutarchum ap. Maittaire), used all dialects indiscriminately, or any dialect that assisted his measure, is imputing to him a poverty of expression, or want of versification, which every line gives the lie to; for if there ever was a poet whose words flowed into verse, or, if I may say so, jumped into their places of their own accord, such is the versification of Homer : here stands the great difference between him and all his translators; not that we can impute blame to them, — for the nature of translation itself renders the attempt almost impossible, — but the existence of this difference is undeniable. Read the fine simile at the end of the eighth book, in Pope, beautifully paraphrased as it is, you discover a labour, a research, a *curiosity* of numbers and expression derived from consummate art, — while the plain simplicity of beauty flows from Homer with as natural ease as if he had uttered every word with the rapidity of the Italian *improvisatori*.

To impute to such a poet as this the want of licentious dialects, to eke out his versification, is grafting his condemnation upon our own ignorance; — I would as soon believe it, as believe Mr. Wood, when he asserts that letters were not in use when Homer wrote. A language abounding in compound harmony, elegance, and precision of the most exquisite kind, was never formed, or can be formed, by mere oral use; — images sublime and poetical in a great degree, may be the produce of great minds and strong conceptions in the most unlettered age; but to clothe these in harmonious numbers, dignified expression, and precise language, in such a period of arts and manners, is impossible. When people who assert this produce Fingal for an instance, they assert without proof, — but (setting Fingal aside as dubious authority) if we examine the beautiful odes Mr Gray has versified from the Latin translation of Olaus; would Mr Gray, himself, assert the elegance of language in those Runic fragments? Poetical ideas they doubtless contain; and so do the harshest numbers of Chaucer, — translate Chaucer into Latin, and let a Metastasio translate the Latin, would not the images flow in all the elegance of Italian harmony? But this is not the case with Homer: for in the most refined ages of Greece he was still looked upon as a model of language, harmony, and numbers, and with every disadvantage he must now labour under, from our ignorance of pronunciation, &c., no one can read his works over a second time, without feeling this, and acknowledging it in the fullest extent

The conclusion from all this must be, that, as Homer stood in need of no paltry expedients, he certainly made use of none, but used that language which was the language of the age or country he lived in. The fashionable language varied with the age. In Homer's days it was what he wrote; in Herodotus's it was Ionic; and therefore Herodotus, though a Dorian by birth (for Halicarnassus was a Dorian colony, Herod. lib. 2 p. 191. Ed. Wag.), compiled his history in it. In after times, when the writers of Athens were as pre-eminent as the power of her arms, all was Attic.

The dialects of the Greek language are originally only two,— the Doric and Ionic. How the difference of these arose, or what was the original distinction between Dorians and Ionians, does not appear with sufficient precision in history to determine upon; but they were so clearly and radically different, as to cause a degree of difficulty and obscurity respectively (vide Maittaire, page 6. Introd. δυσνοητος). The Attic is, in reality, not a distinct dialect from the Ionic, but a peculiar mode of speaking and writing in that one city, which was the head of the Ionians: but if we choose to call this mode of speaking a dialect, we ought to make a dialect for every separate state of Greece (vide Maittaire, page 3 Introd.) for there were different modes of speaking peculiar to every one, as will appear from consulting the decrees of the cities in Demosthenes's Oration on the Crown, the Ode of Sappho, the Decree of the Lacedemonians against Timotheus; the Cretan marble in Prideaux, and a thousand others (vide Maittaire, page 262. et seq.)

Dr. Bentley has very justly observed, from Dionysius Halicarnassensis, that the old Attic and the Ionic were nearly the same, doubtless they were exactly the same, and continued so in every point, except the contraction and resolution of the vowels: and this is the only characteristic of distinction between them that can be depended on; all the others, upon a nice scrutiny, I conceive would be found promiscuous

If this point was once fairly proved, which I think it easily might, and the Ionic and Attic shown to be one dialect, would not the whole argument about the variety of Homer's dialects drop to the ground of itself? for the Doricisms in Homer are few, perhaps none, but what were common to the poetic language in general; nor are they ever of that kind which cause the obscurity and perplexity of that dialect

The only difficulty, Sir, that you would start here is, that if we make Homer a mere Ionic, we take away from him the use of the digamma, because that is supposed to be merely Æolic, and the Æolic is only a branch of the Doric. That Homer was an Æolian, I think the authority you produce incontrovertible, but, because he was an Æolian, he should therefore write in the Æolic dialect, is no more a consequence than that Herodotus, who was a Dorian, should necessarily write in the Doric

Neither does it follow that Homer used the digamma merely because he was an Æolian, *for it will be found that the digamma was used promiscuously in the early ages of the Greek language.* Dionysius Halicarnassensis, as quoted by Maittaire, page 159., says that the prefixing την ου συλλαβην ενι στοιχειω γραφομενην (F scilicet) συνηθες ην τοις αρχαιοις Ελλησιν. (I have never seen Forster's Treatise, but suppose, when Dawes rejects the authority of Dionysius, he does not sufficiently consider the melting of ου ou — oo, into w in English)

That Homer used the digamma, — that is, that it was in use in his age, and the language he wrote, — I think may be established beyond all contradiction Dr Bentley, by applying it to solve the difficulties of Homeric quantities, and relieve the ear from the ungrateful sound of naked vowels, upon the whole, bids fairest to establish both its use and authority; and though I entirely agree with you, that this may now be impossible to be reinstated with the general consent of all critics on every separate and individual word, yet, to all who are admirers of Homer, every removal of an imperfection is a satisfaction and a triumph

Still there is nothing more difficult than to establish the genuine sound of letters in a dead language. The very vowels themselves are very dubious and confused Our English vowels correspond not with the vowels of any of our neighbours on the Continent, nor do theirs with each other. If I may be allowed the expression, they graduate on a different scale.

		1	2	3	4	5	
French	.	au	a	e	o	oo	== good.
English	. .	a	e	i	o	u	
Italian	. .	ah	a	e	o	oo	

The French have no sound of our long *i* (kind) in their whole language; observe their pronunciation of the word *invincible.* I am not skilled enough in the Italian to assert it, but I think it is the same with them. This, with the variety of pronunciation of each vowel in every language respectively, the distinction into long and short, broad and narrow, grave and acute, produces such an infinity of difficulties in treating even of living languages, that where the same occur in a dead one, it is almost impossible to reconcile them, or lay down any general system that shall find the concurrence of critics and grammarians.

In regard to the digamma, all this is multiplied ad infinitum. The letter itself, the use of it, and disuse of the sound, the manner of its affecting quantities, are all disputable points You will see all this difficulty in its full extent, by referring once more to Priscian, De numero literarum apud veteres, Putchii, page 541., which, in many particulars, militates against Gataker de bivocalibus.

And, from these premises, I do most entirely agree with you in all you assert at the close of your 417th and 418th pages.

And now, Sir, sincerely wishing you all success in your researches and publication, I conclude myself

Your most humble servant,

W. VINCENT.

CHAP. VII.

APPOINTED TUTOR OF CORPUS. — HIS COLLEGE FRIENDS AND ASSOCIATES.

1782 to 1783.

In the summer of 1782, Mr. Burgess was appointed tutor of Corpus, and held the office till the year 1791.

Though his studious habits and retiring disposition prevented his mingling much in general society at Oxford, there was a select set of literary men, including several Wickamites, with whom he lived on terms of intimacy, and to whom he was endeared by the same pleasing and attractive qualities both of head and heart which distinguished him in after life. Of these nearly all have paid the debt of nature; but among the few that survive, those whom the author has had the privilege of consulting, either personally or through friends, bear their united testimony to his superior talents and amiable qualities. Among these may be enumerated the Reverend Dr. Routh, the present learned and venerable President of Magdalen College, Oxford; the late Reverend Gilbert Burringdon; and the Reverend Mr. Putt, of Combe, near Honiton, Devon. The latter thus describes him in a letter to his friend, the late Reverend Francis Huyshe, written in the year 1837: —

" Mr. Burgess was of rather longer standing at College than myself. From my first acquaintance with him, I perceived that he was indefatigable in the pursuit of literature, — more especially in the study of the Greek language. He had a pleasing person, simple, unaffected manners, was truly amiable, and universally beloved. He was as social as a life devoted to study could allow him to be. In short, he was, in every respect, among the most exemplary Academics of his time. I cannot express how gratified I feel at having once again met him at your house and my own."

With Dr. Routh, for whom he felt the highest esteem, he kept up a literary correspondence to the end of his life. In a conversation with which the author was honoured by that eminent individual in the spring of 1837, he described his old friend as wedded from his youth to studious habits and pursuits, but as a most welcome and agreeable companion whenever he allowed himself to indulge

in the pleasures of social intercourse.* He is described by another of his contemporaries as wear-
ing on his fine features, as he paced the streets of
Oxford, " the pale cast of thought ; " and as having,
in youth, been, in person and manner, more like
what he was in advanced life, than is often the case.

About this time, one of his favourite schemes
was the publication of a quarterly Classical Journal,
of which he was to undertake the editorial part.
The nature of the project will be fully illustrated
by the following letter from Mr. Tyrwhitt, — which,
at the same time, forcibly proves what a wise Mentor
he continued to possess in that gentleman.

DEAR SIR,

THOUGH, upon the first reading of your project,
I thought of it as I do now, I did not choose to
make an immediate declaration of my sentiments
to you, for fear you should imagine that I had not
given it all the attention which you had a right to
expect from a friend to whom you had imparted
so confidential a communication. To say the truth
in a few words, I apprehend that your plan is not
likely to answer either in point of reputation or
profit, at the same time that it must necessarily
engross your whole attention, and preclude the
advances which you would otherwise make in more
useful studies. With respect to this last point, I
believe any one, who knows what the life of a
journalist is, will tell you, that it is as laborious as

* Dr. Routh alludes to the Bishop in the following terms,
in his Reliq. Sac. vol i. p 139. " Thomas Burgessius, vir
etiam apud exteras gentes eruditionis laude insignis, nunc epis-
copus Menevensis dignissimus."

that of a galley slave, and as closely confined within a very narrow circle of labour. His trials are literally " never ending, still beginning." While he is copying or extracting one piece of nonsense, he has the satisfaction to see a long succession of new nonsense springing up, and demanding the same kind office.

That no reputation can be derived from such an employment, I think is pretty evident, on the contrary, it is much to be feared that the hurry in which the journalist is obliged to do his business, will often lead him into gross and ridiculous mistakes, not to mention the danger, from the same source, of his acquiring a habit of slovenly, inaccurate composition. I shall say little upon the article of profit, as I cannot suppose that it is a principal object with you. That some of the established literary journals are very profitable to the booksellers, who are proprietors of them, I can easily believe, but whether it be practicable for the author to secure any considerable profit to himself, I much doubt. But, on this head, Daniel Prince can give a better opinion than I can. I do not think that the difference between your proposed publication and the subsisting journals is likely to make it more generally saleable. The taste for Anecdota Græca et Latina is far from universal; and the English part (to which you have assigned a large space) will, I fear, be still less attractive. You will pardon me, I hope, for smiling, when I read in your bill of fare, Poems of Lydgate and Collations of Robert of Gloucester, &c.; but I should be seriously concerned to see you engaged in any undertaking, in which most of your time was to be

thrown away upon such barren objects. I have
found reason to suspect, lately, that the fragment
of Nicetas (supposed to be unpublished) has been
published in the Paris edition of that author among
the Byzantine Historians. When you have an opportunity, I wish you would look into that matter.
                I am, dear Sir,
                        Yours very faithfully,
                                        T. T.
Welbeck Street, Feb 3 1783.

DEAR SIR,

I AM happy to find that we are agreed upon
the subject of your last. I was convinced that the
project was a sudden thought, which might have
been safely left to die away of itself; but, as you
asked my opinion, I thought myself bound to give
it with the sincerity and openness of a friend.
There is something so ingenuous in your manner of
asking and receiving advice, that I have almost persuaded myself that you would be glad at any time
to hear my real opinion, even if it should be different from your own. If I am wrong, give me a
hint, that I may mend my manners.

But how have I deserved, by endeavouring to
keep you out of a scrape, that you should wish to
involve me in a worse? An edition of the Poetics
is no light matter; but leaving that Θεων εν γουνασι,
I must beg you to excuse me for having been a
little dilatory in answering your last.
                Yours very sincerely,
                                        T. T.
Welbeck Street, March 17. 1783.

In the spring of 1783, Mr. Burgess became a fellow of Corpus.

The following letter refers to an unsuccessful canvass which he made for the Greek Professorship.

TO T. TYRWHITT, ESQ.

DEAR SIR,   Oxford, May 7. 1783.

THE business of tuition has so much increased upon my hands this term, by the addition of five new pupils, — three of them scholars, and two gentlemen commoners, — that my time is more than ever occupied.

Since the receipt of your last favour, I have had an opportunity of showing the Dean of Christchurch a specimen of my Logical collection. In a very friendly conversation, he dropped some hints which I shall certainly make use of. He very much approved the design of collecting the fragments of Archytas. I have written a letter to M. Valckenaer, to acquaint him with my intention. He will probably be able to assist the collection a good deal, should he have dropped his intention of publishing the Reliquiæ Pythagoricæ.

Though my late canvass was without success, — and, indeed, from the beginning I was not very sanguine in my expectations, — yet the prospect of an event, which was not impossible, and the consequent lectures, gave a bias to my thoughts and reading, which I have found difficult to interrupt, even in the midst of my present college business, which has no great connection with poetry or criticism. In short, I have been reading the Poetics of Aristotle, with much more pleasure, I am sure, than

F

I ever did before. I shall make no scruple to
trouble you with a few conjectural emendations of
the text, out of a great many, which have occurred
to me

Mr. Randolph's ˉgrace passed last Thursday for
his Doctor's degree, but not without considerable
opposition, which I do not hesitate to call envious
and illiberal.

I expect soon, from Paris, a collation of the four
manuscripts of the Poetics, which I hope to have
the pleasure of bringing with me when I come to
town.

Yesterday was the day of ordination; but I have
not yet the honour of the new title you were so
good as to inquire about. My attention was much
withdrawn from that object by the business of my
late canvass. I shall be better able to prepare for
examination against another time.

I am, dear Sir,
Your very obliged humble servant,
T. BURGESS.

TO MR. BURGESS.

DEAR SIR, Welbeck Street, Sept. 6 1783

I HAD apprehensions, as well as you, that Mr. W.
Jackson, or some other Christchurch man, would
be a candidate for the Greek Professorship; but
the reason why I never mentioned it to you was,
that I did not see the least possibility of being able
to assist you in the pursuit of it. Lord North
will probably dispose of it. If you have any channel of application which you would wish to try, I
could easily rid you of your embarrassment with

respect to delicacy, by inquiring of the Dean, whether his brother is a candidate or not. I rather
believe he is not.

I am (in haste),

Yours sincerely,

T. T.

LORD MONBODDO TO MR. BURGESS.

DEAR SIR,   Edinburgh, Jan. 31 1783.
I THINK myself exceedingly obliged to you for
the trouble you have taken to make so diligent an
inquiry concerning *Peter the Wild Boy.* As there
is nothing I love so much as knowledge, you could
hardly have obliged me more; and I am glad to
find that, at the same time, you have gratified your
own curiosity, — which, I see, rises to higher objects than that of those who call themselves Philosophers in this age. These gentlemen are very
curious about the Natural History of Plants and
Animals, even of the lowest kind; but the Natural
History of their own species has no charms at all
for them: and yet I maintain that, without knowing
the Natural History of Man, — that is, what sort
of animal he is in his natural state, — it is impossible to have any true knowledge of the Philosophy of Man, which, like every other philosophy,
ought to be deduced from facts. I will venture to
affirm that, by your visit to Peter, you have enlarged your ideas of our species, and acquired a
truer knowledge of it than is to be acquired from
all the modern books put together, that have been
written upon the subject. The people that have
not those enlarged views of the species, and cannot
conceive the progress of man from a mere animal

F 2

to an intellectual creature, will not believe but that Peter is an idiot. But this opinion, I think, one half of the facts you have related, are sufficient to confute. And if a man has studied so much of the nature of language, as to know that articulation is the most difficult art among men, he will not be surprised that a savage, who never practised articulation till he was fifteen years of age, should have learned so little of it as Peter has done; though, from what you told me, his vocabulary is much larger than I thought it had been.

The next thing to be inquired concerning him, and which is still of greater importance, is to know the state he was in when he was caught; for this we have nothing, at present, but the information of newspapers, which I have collected, and which all agree in this, — that, in the year 1725, he was caught in a wood in Hanover, called Hamelin, going on all four, and feeding on whatever he could get in the woods; and particularly they mention the leaves and bark of trees; and what you have heard concerning his way of subsisting in his travels, when he ran away, so far confirms this account of his diet in the woods. Sir Joseph Banks, at my desire, has applied to a Hanoverian Baron, whom he names, to collect all the accounts that can be got of him in that country. His going upon all four any more than his feeding upon wild fruits, needs no confirmation with me; as I hold it is impossible he could have walked otherwise, if he was exposed before he had learned to walk erect: and accordingly, all the solitary savages that have been found in different parts of Europe, in the several centuries before this, of whom I have given an account in the first volume of the "Origin of Language," were all quadrupeds. But this, as well as a man's subsisting upon vegetables not prepared by fire, must appear incredible to those whose notions of the human species are so confined, as to believe that man was always in the state we now see him in at present in Europe.

I am sorry that you can hear no more of the gentleman from Africa, who knew something of the orang-outang. He resembles very much what Peter was : only he is in a stage of human nature a little farther advanced, — for he walks upright, uses a stick for a weapon, builds huts, and lives in some kind of society; and, being born of parents that have been wild since the beginning of the world, he is very much stronger and bigger than Peter ever was, who certainly is come of parents such as we are, — but being exposed very early, and leading a savage life till he was fifteen, I do not wonder at what you tell me of his being so much stronger and nimbler than the men of this country.

I am glad to hear that Peter has not employed your thoughts so much, but that both your metaphysics and philology go on. Your Chrestomathia Philosophica will be of admirable use to those who desire to study the ancient philosophy in good earnest. The Isagoge of Porphyry was intended, as the title denotes, for an introduction to philosophy; but you should publish along with it Ammonius Hermeias's Commentary upon it. These two, diligently studied, will be sufficient to give a lad some general idea of logic, which is the foundation of all philosophy; for without logic there is no philosophy.

You have my leave to send to Mr. Gebelen what I have written upon the Pyramids of Egypt; though I doubt he is not so much a Greek scholar as to profit by it. I have dipped but little into his book; but, from what I have seen of it, I would not advise you to bestow much time upon it; for it appears to me to be a perfect dream, — and, I think, the dream of a sick man. You will be much better employed in speculating upon the origin and formation of the Greek language; but I would have you keep to the language, and its grammatical structure, and not seek in it what you certainly will not find, — I mean philosophy. I have not got from Mr. Caddel the packet you mention; but, as he is careful, I suppose it will come.

I shall be glad to hear from you as often as is convenient, in the mean time I am, with great regard and esteem,

Your obliged and faithful humble servant,

JAMES BURNETT.

THE SAME TO THE SAME.

DEAR SIR,

I HAD the favour of your letter, and your packet by Mr. Horner, whom I have not seen, but have desired to inquire after him. I am glad to hear that you have been so busy, though unsuccessfully, in the matter of the Poetical Professorship, in which I learn, with pleasure, that Dr. Jackson stood by you. I beg you would offer my best compliments to him. You need not, I think, doubt of academical preferment, if you continue as zealous as you seem to be in promoting Greek learning and

Greek philosophy. I approve much of your Chrestomathia, which you have begun, very properly,
with Porphyry's Introduction ; — an Introduction,
as I think, not only to Aristotle's Categories, but
to all philosophy. What you have sent me of it
is, I think, very well and very accurately printed.
He is an author whom it is a pleasure to read for
the style, which is both elegant and accurately
philosophical , and it will instruct the young student, more than any thing I know, in the language
of ancient philosophy, which a man may be a very
good Greek scholar, and yet not understand ;
though I think he will be the better Greek scholar
for understanding it, as I have shown in some of
my notes, particularly in one of them, where I
have corrected a very improper translation in a very
important passage in the beginning of St. John's
Gospel, where the doctrine of the Trinity is laid
down, — which, by the leave or without the leave
of Dr. Priestley, I think a fundamental doctrine of
Christianity. In this work of yours, I think you
should collect all the Locrian Remnants, as Milton
calls them ; not only those that are to be collected
from Simplicius, and other commentators upon
Aristotle, and which have never been published by
themselves, but also those which have been already
published by Gale in his Opuscula Mythologica,
— a book that is become rare, and, I believe, almost
out of print ; for be assured you have, in those
fragments, the substance of all the philosophy of
Plato and Aristotle, which certainly came from the
Pythagorean school, as certainly as that school came
from Egypt, — not from Tartary or Siberia, as a
late French dreamer, whose book I have seen,

F 4

would persuade us. You take the true way to restore the ancient philosophy, by publishing such valuable remains of it; for the greatest merit both of Mr. Harris's work and mine, is introducing the young student of philosophy to an acquaintance with such authors. In the publication of them you will find abundance of work for your acumen criticum, as I have shown in some of my notes.

I shall print, with your permission, the account you sent me of the wild boy, by way of Appendix to the volume which I have now in hand; and I shall add something further, in the same Appendix, about the orang-outang, whom I consider as a man of the same kind with Peter, but something more advanced in the arts of civility, — therefore more docile, and more intelligent.

I am ever, with great regard and esteem,
Your most faithful and
obedient humble servant,
JAMES BURNETT.
Edinburgh, Nov. 2. 1783.

CHAP. VIII.

TAKES ORDERS. — CORRESPONDENCE WITH MR. WINDHAM. — MR ROBERTS'S DESCRIPTION OF HIS PURSUITS, ETC AT OXFORD

1784.

THE preceding pages have placed Mr. Burgess before my readers as an eminent scholar, and as standing deservedly high in the esteem and affection of his contemporaries. They are henceforth to view him as discharging the sacred functions of the clerical office. He was ordained both to deacon's and to priest's orders in the year 1784, by Dr. Cornwallis, Bishop of Winchester.

When he was in his seventy-ninth year, circumstances led the author, in the course of an interesting conversation he had with the Bishop on the subject of his ordination, to inquire how far his actuating motives on that occasion corresponded with the high and holy tenor of his ordination vows. This question came home to the feelings of one whose views of the object and end of the Christian ministry were truly elevated; and who, in examining candidates for orders, was in the habit of probing not only their proficiency in learning, but their inspiring motives, and the depth and sincerity of their personal piety. His reply was to the following effect: — " At the time to which you refer, I was full of that ambition for literary distinction natural to a young scholar circumstanced as I was, but, after I had taken orders, and turned my attention to sacred studies, I gradually imbibed deep and serious views of Divine Truth." At, or soon after, this time, he devoted himself with much assiduity to the study of Hebrew.

Among his correspondents in 1784 and 1785 was the Right Honourable William Windham, eminent both as a statesman and a scholar. He delighted in the society and the studies of Oxford, and occasionally spent a few days there. The following letter, referring to his feelings upon the death of Dr. Johnson, will be read with interest:—

Dear Sir,

Having seen in the Almanack, just now, that the
Oxford term ends to-day, I will write you a few
lines in haste, rather than increase my risk of being
too late by the delay of another post. It is difficult for me to begin a letter to you at this moment,
without saying a word on the melancholy event of
Dr. Johnson's death, which casts a darker gloom
over my mind than I was prepared for. I must
despatch, however, what is the immediate occasion
of my writing, and inform you that I have seen
lately, Nicolaides, who is disposed to listen to the
overtures I made to him; and upon receiving, at
any time, a summons from you, will come down by
way of experiment. Some suspicion has got into
my mind, that he is not a pleasant man to deal
with; but, even if that should be true, your intercourse with him may be so managed, as that his
discontents should affect no one but himself.
Should you come to London this vacation, I hope
you will let me have the pleasure of seeing you.
If you can come by Monday next, you may pay
your last tribute to genius and virtue, by attending
the mournful train of Dr. Johnson's friends to
Westminster Abbey. Pray tell this to Crofts.

Yours most sincerely,

W. Windham.

Hill Street, Dec. 17. 1784.

THE SAME TO THE SAME.

Dear Sir,

Your curiosity about Sadler should not have remained so long unsatisfied, so far as it is in my

power to satisfy it, if my absence from town for these last two days had not occasioned a delay in the receipt of your letter. Sadler, after working night and day, got his balloon finished a day or two ago, and is to return from Dover to-morrow, whither he has been to make some necessary arrangements to fetch it. I have procured him permission to share with Blanchard the use of Dover Castle: but I conceive it will be more desirable for him, with the assistance of another letter which I got for him, to provide some private place. After all his exertions, I fear Blanchard will have had too much the start, and the last stroke be added to the disgrace of this country on the subject of balloons, by a foreigner being the first person to cross the Channel. When I have seen him to-morrow, which I expect to do, I will write to you again.

Yours, with great truth,
W. WINDHAM.

Hill Street, Dec 23. 1784.

THE SAME TO THE SAME.

DEAR SIR,   Felbrigg, June 9.

I THOUGHT myself very unlucky on hearing from my servant how nearly I had missed the pleasure of seeing you. The account contained in your letter is a very obliging instance of your attention, and gives me a prospect of executing my friend's wishes in a manner more satisfactory than I could have ventured to promise myself.

I write this from my own house, whither I am come for a fortnight, to enjoy fresh air and leisure; and shall then return to town for about a fortnight

longer, previously to a journey I am to make, this
summer, to Scotland, in company with Mr. Burke.
Should you be passing through London at the time,
I hope I may have the good fortune to meet you:
I must not promise myself any thing so good, as
that Lord Monboddo will prevail upon you to make
this your summer, also, for visiting Scotland. By
the way, the Monthly Review has, as you have
probably seen, fallen upon his last volume with
more rancour than any thing in a work of that
nature can possibly call for, or than the general
respectability of his character can by any means
warrant. It seems to be dictated by the very spirit
that manifests itself sometimes in your common
room, though it has not yet quite gone the length
of wishing that the author might be put to death.
I am sorry that such illiberal things should be said
of a character in many points highly respectable;
and I am more sorry to observe of most of them
(in confidence) non potuisse refelli. One must confess, that of the greater part of this work, the unlucky term chosen by the reviewers — *Anilities* —
is very descriptive.

A day or two ago, before I left town, I found
Mr. Winstanley had done me the favour to call
upon me, let me beg of you to make my compliments to him, and to explain the reason of my not
calling upon him. When I return to town, I will let
you know more upon the American matter, about
which you may possibly receive a letter, in the mean
while, from my friend Mr. Grymes. Believe me
to be, with great truth,

Your obedient and faithful friend and servant,

W. WINDHAM.

During the summer of 1785, Mr. Burgess visited Holland, principally for objects of classical research. The only trace which I have discovered of his proceedings while there is contained in the following extract from one of Mr. Tyrwhitt's letters, dated 26th of November, 1785 : —

" Of literary transactions in other parts of the world, I have not heard any thing for some time. I suppose we shall have Mr. Brunck's Sophocles about Easter. The most promising work of which I have any expectation is the Physica et Ethica of Stobæus, by a scholar of Heyne's, from some MSS. in Spain, probably those of which you saw copies at Leyden. Have you heard from Holland lately? I had an opportunity very lately of sending a copy of Isæus to Ruhnken, Wyttenbach, and Santen, who sent me some poems of his; I forget whether by you, or through Maty."

In the following letter Mr. Tyrwhitt amuses himself with the proofs furnished by a pamphlet of Villoison's, of the diffusion of his friend's fame on the Continent.

DEAR SIR, Welbeck Street, May 11. 1784.

I HAVE, at length, received the Epistolæ Vinarienses, a pamphlet of 120 pages in quarto. Of the first 114 pages I shall say nothing ; but the last six contain the investigation of a point in which you must be interested, as it is declared to have been undertaken in consequence of what *Clarissimus T Burgess* has said, page 501. *Appendicis Doctissimæ.* In pursuance of your suggestion, M. Villoison has examined two MSS. of Arcadias at Paris, and has extracted ea, quæ hanc litem dirimant, ut merito speraverat Clarissimus Burgess.

If your transcript of Trypho is ready, I dare say the Dean of Christchurch, who is expected here at the end of this week, will take charge of it for me.

Yours sincerely,

T. T.

Among his Oxford pupils, he always spoke with particular regard of the late Lord Tenterden. A friendly intercourse and occasional correspondence subsisted between them throughout life. He came to Oxford from Dr. Beavor's school, at Canterbury, a superior scholar; and, while he was yet an undergraduate, obtained a prize for his beautiful Latin poem, entitled Globus Hydrostaticus. He acquired a similar distinction after taking his Bachelor's degree for an Essay on the Use and Abuse of Satire. The Bishop often referred to Lord Tenterden's career at College and in after life, as strikingly illustrative of the intimate connection between studious and moral habits and future professional emience. His own course was another eminent example of it.

The following letter, addressed by him to one of his pupils, a Mr. Patten, who had unexpectedly quitted Oxford, will prove how anxious he felt to promote their welfare and improvement: —

DEAR SIR,

As I have put a gentleman commoner, who is just come, in possession of your rooms, who is disposed to take your furniture, I shall be glad if you will let me know what are the thirds. I wish the rooms may be as well occupied by the present inhabitant, as they were by their last possessor. I am

sure I shall never lose him with more regret than
I did his predecessor. I sincerely wish I could
have been of more use to you in your studies than
I was. I had flattered myself, from what I knew
of your abilities, and from certain symptoms of
diligence and good-will on your part, that you
would have employed the time in a manner which
would have been very useful to yourself, and a
credit to us both. But why should I express these
regrets, since I trust that your own good sense,
unshackled by the restraints of College forms, will
lead you to employ your time still more profitably?
Indeed, I do hope that I shall have the pleasure of
hearing you, one day, spoken of as acting up to all
the public duties which belong to your station and
fortune; as the friend of the poor and the unedu-
cated, the patron of industry, and the promoter of
useful experiment, and as contributing no common
share to the aggregate of the exertions which are
necessary to the happiness of your own neighbourhood, and to the welfare and prosperity of your
country.

I am, dear Sir,
With sincere regard and affection,
Your faithful friend and servant,
T. Burgess.

Mr. Burgess found himself, after holding for a
few months the office of tutor of Corpus, in such
easy circumstances, that he no longer needed the
kind aid which his friend, Mr. Tyrwhitt, had prevailed on him to accept under the denomination
of his Curate. Their correspondence continued to
be frequent; and Mr. Tyrwhitt, while he watched

his proceedings with an interest akin to paternal anxiety, hailed with the sincerest delight his advancing progress in the path of literary and professional distinction. The following letter marks the period at which the grateful Curate relinquished his kind patron's generous assistance : —

DEAR SIR,

I AM ashamed to look at the date of your last favour. A letter which gave me so much pleasure deserved an earlier acknowledgment; but, to say the truth, the late cold weather so benumbed me, that I have [not been capable of attending to any but the mere animal functions. With respect to the resignation of your curacy, I wish you to take your own time. Before you give it up, be sure you have no further occasion for it.

After what I have said of myself, you will expect no news or entertainment from me. I am not yet completely thawed. I hope soon, however, to be alive enough to receive entertainment from you, whenever you have leisure or inclination to give me a line.

Yours very sincerely,
T. T.

Welbeck Street, February 23. 1784.

The following extract of a letter from William Roberts, Esq., author of the Life of Mrs. Hannah More, and who was one of Mr. Burgess's College pupils, gives an expressive sketch of his habits and manners at the time now referred to : —

" My first acquaintance with Dr. Burgess began in 1784, when at the age of fifteen I was elected scholar of Corpus Christi College in Oxford,

of which Dr. Cooke was the President, and Mr.
Thomas Burgess the tutor. I attended his lectures,
which were very able and instructive, for several
years, and was honoured with many special marks
of his kindness and regard. He had then lately
distinguished himself by his edition of Dawes's
Miscellanea Critica, and an Essay on the Study
of Antiquity, which gained the Chancellor's prize,
contended for by the Bachelors of the University.
His great object was the cultivation of Greek
literature ; and during the period in which I received his instructions, he attained the distinction
of being considered the best Greek scholar in the
University. I read through one of Aristotle's
treatises with him in private , and, while I was so
engaged, I had every day fresh reason to be
grateful for his instructions, and for the very kind
interest he took in my progress and improvement.
It was always with real pleasure I ascended the
stairs which led to his apartment over the gateway,
in which I used to admire his well-stored book-
shelves, over which the stained glass in his window
spread a soft and solemn light. His countenance,
voice, and manner were remarkably prepossessing,
from which whatever he taught borrowed additional
efficacy and impression. He was so kind as to employ my humble services in occasionally instruct-
ing some of his pupils, and assisting him in some of
his collations and commentaries, and he rewarded
my industry by implanting in my mind principles
of conduct, and elements of thought and argument,
for which I trust I have had the greatest reason
to be thankful. His own demeanour, sentiments,

G

and habits, were always singularly pure, upright, and exemplary.

" My intercourse with him at that time had relation chiefly, if not altogether, to literary subjects, till I took my Master's degree, when 1 ceased to reside at College; but from that time till the death of the Bishop, a period of near half a century, we kept up an occasional correspondence. The subjects of our epistolary intercourse were generally of a critical or literary cast; and it has been very agreeable to me to receive, through this medium, some of the maturest fruits of the Bishop's reading and meditation, which were always directed to philanthropic ends, and often — very often — to the best interests of the soul. After his eyes began to fail, his letters were necessarily short, but generally comprised some matter of useful information."

CHAP. IX.

APPOINTED CHAPLAIN TO BISHOP BARRINGTON — SKETCH OF THE CHARACTER OF THAT PRELATE. — SUNDAY SCHOOLS. — SALISBURY SPELLING-BOOK.

1785 to 1786.

AT the commencement of the year 1785, Mr. Burgess took an active part in the establishment of an Agricultural Society at Odiham. Lord Rivers was President. The society was supported by annual subscriptions. It invited communications from its members upon subjects of rural economy, offered premiums for useful discoveries and improvements, and rewards to servants for good and faithful service. There was one branch of its operations, — the establishment of Sunday and daily schools, in which Mr. Burgess took a lively interest. Several of his family, his father in particular, were among the active members, and the fundamental rules and resolutions were drawn up by his own pen.

In the course of this year he was appointed chaplain to Dr. Shute Barrington, then Bishop of Salisbury, under circumstances truly honourable to his character. That Prelate had no actual acquaintance with him ; but, being desirous of selecting, as his chaplain, a clergyman of superior worth and learning, he was induced, after due inquiry, to apply to Mr. Burgess. As this event tended much to his subsequent preferment, and as we shall frequently have to allude to the Bishop in the course of the following pages, we shall here pause a little in the direct course of our narrative, in order to make the reader acquainted with the distinguishing traits of his personal history.

The character of Dr. Shute Barrington, as a Bishop, a Christian, and a Gentleman, stood so high, that it is just matter of regret that the literature of our country has not yet been enriched with any authorised memoir of his useful life : the more so, because the fruits of his personal observation of men and things, had they been culled and collected by any of his friends competent to the undertaking, would have been full of interest,— comprising a period extending from the last struggle of the Stuarts, through the Spanish, American, and French wars, down to the year 1826. His memory was richly stored with anecdotes, gathered

in conversation with statesmen who had successively
taken an active part in public affairs during the
whole of the eighteenth century; he was one of
the favourite church dignitaries of George III.;
the associate, and in many instances the patron, of
some of the most distinguished literary characters
of the age.

He was born in the year 1734. His father, the
first Viscount Barrington, was the intimate friend
of Locke and Somers, and was privy to many of the
secret springs which set the revolution of 1688 in
motion, and brought it to a happy termination.
The Bishop himself perfectly remembered many of
the stirring incidents of 1745. And well he might,
for, having been taken as a schoolboy to witness the
trial of one of the rebel lords, who was afterwards
beheaded, his confinement in a close court for
many hours increased the symptoms of a dangerous
malady, the stone, to which he was thus early
subject. He was obliged, in consequence, to
undergo the painful operation of lithotomy in his
twelfth year. Perhaps he was the only instance
of a patient living eighty years after this operation,
and retaining a perfect recollection of all the circumstances and sufferings belonging to it.

He was often known to attribute his health
and longevity to the simple regimen and strict
temperance imposed upon him after this alarming
complaint had discovered itself in his boyhood. It
was also made instrumental, under Divine Grace,
to the production of that mental discipline, and
those religious principles, which distinguished him
in early youth, growing with his growth, and
strengthening with his strength. He was taught,

with his first reflections, to feel that his existence
hung by a thread, and that nothing could avert renewed sufferings and an early and painful dissolution
but the blessing of God upon the means which he
was cautioned to employ to ward off the threatened
evil. Thus early trained to the practice of self-
denial, he obtained an habitual mastery over his
passions, and studiously guarded against excess of
every kind. Looking up to Heaven for protection
against a malady, which might return upon him at
any moment, he learnt to exercise the same principle
of dependence on the Divine Goodness in relation
to the general events and contingencies of life.
These pious dispositions, nourished by the dew of
the Divine blessing, not only rendered him superior
to the temptations most incident to youth, but
elevated his tastes and pursuits above the ordinary
level of those around him, and shed their benignant
influence on his manners and demeanour. At the
time of his taking orders, he was a sincere and
humble learner in the school of Christ. The
assiduous study of the sacred Oracles is known to
have occupied, at this time, as in after life, his particular attention. He justly regarded it as the duty
of a Christian, and especially of a clergyman, to
read the Bible regularly and systematically, and it
was his daily habit to peruse a portion of the Old
Testament in Hebrew, and of the New Testament
in Greek.

He was educated at Eton and at Oxford, and
was an elegant, without being a profound scholar.
After obtaining a fellowship at Merton, he took
orders, and advanced rapidly to the highest honours
of the church. As one of the Royal Chaplains, he

followed George II. to his grave, and was present at the coronation of George III.

Though few Bishops have ever manifested a greater interest in every thing tending to improve and to perfect the parochial economy of our national establishment, it is remarkable that Dr. Barrington never had the charge of a parish himself. His preferment was in cathedrals from the very first. After passing through the preparatory steps of a canonry of Christchurch and a stall in St. Paul's, which he afterwards gave up for a canonry of Windsor, he was consecrated, in the year 1765, Bishop of Llandaff. He owed his elevation to the interest of his brother, the second Viscount Barrington, who was then Chancellor of the Exchequer. It was an extraordinary proof of family merit, combined with good fortune, that all the sons of the first Peer rose to a high grade in their several professions. William, the eldest, held some of the first offices in the state, and served the Crown thirty-four years. John was a General in the army, and commanded the King's forces at the capture of Guadaloupe in 1758. Daines was a Judge, and distinguished himself by his taste for natural philosophy, and by the publication of several learned works. Samuel was an Admiral, and was successful in several engagements with French vessels and squadrons.

The Bishop's first wife was Lady Diana Beauclerk, daughter of the Duke of St. Alban's, and a grand-daughter of the first Duke, who was a son of Charles II. and Nell Gwynn. This lady died in 1766, leaving him no issue. In the year 1770 he was married to his second wife, Jane, only daughter of Sir John Guise, of Rendcombe, Gloucestershire, and heiress of her brother Sir William, by whom he had a son, who died an infant. Her hereditary seat, Mongewell, in Oxfordshire, became a favourite residence with the Bishop during the remainder of his life.

In the year 1783 he was raised to the See of Salisbury by the express nomination of George III., who admired his character. Lord Shelburne, then Prime Minister, intended to have bestowed it on Dr. Hinchcliffe, Bishop of Peterborough.

Dr. Barrington was distinguished in this responsible situation by his episcopal virtues; his liberality was conspicuous in the repair of the palace at a great personal expense, and also in subscribing a large sum for beautifying and repairing the cathedral.

His charities were munificent without being ostentatious. He was a generous and ready contributor to objects of benevolence, or public utility, but these bore only a small proportion to his daily deeds of private beneficence. He delighted in the luxury of doing good, and few have better understood the true value of money, or employed it more judiciously as the instrument of virtue. Such was the individual with whom Mr. Burgess now became associated, officially in the first instance, and ere long by the bonds of intimate and affectionate friendship.

The preliminary movement, on the part of the Bishop, was to address him the following note, which he perused without the slightest anticipation of what was to follow.

Cavendish Square, May 2. 1785.

THE Bishop of Salisbury presents his compliments to Mr. Burgess, and wishes to have the pleasure of seeing him next Thursday morning, May 5th, at the Star Inn, Oxford.

The Bishop hopes to be there by nine o'clock, but, lest he should not be punctual to his time, will apprise Mr. Burgess of his arrival.

My readers shall have, nearly in his own words, the account of what occurred at the interview, just as he related it to the writer in the year 1835, with that genuine simplicity which stamped a peculiar value upon all that fell from his lips.

"I was much surprised," he said, "at the Bishop's note, and could not imagine why he wanted to see me. Upon the day specified I received the promised message, and went to the Star, where I found him with Mrs. Barrington and Mrs. Kennicott. He conducted me into another room, seated himself opposite to me, and at once made me an offer, expressed in the kindest terms, of his chaplaincy. I was really so unprepared for the offer, and so surprised by it, that, to use a homely expression, it struck me all of a heap, and I could make no reply, but sat before him mute as a statue. Many persons would have concluded that I could be no better than an idiot, but he penetrated the real cause of my embarrassment, and after a short pause, rising up, said, he trusted he might construe my silence into consent, he then proposed to introduce me to the two ladies in the adjoining room, whither I followed him."

It has been stated in print, that the appointment

was made in consequence of Mr. Tyrwhitt's recommendation. The real fact is, that the fame of Mr. Burgess, as a man of distinguished learning and character, united to the testimony of his friend, jointly influenced the Bishop's decision. The following letter explains, in this sense, the whole transaction : —

MR. TYRWHITT TO THE REV. MR. BURGESS.

DEAR SIR,

It is very true that your last letter had not the additional pleasure of surprise, as the Bishop had given me reason to expect such an event. I wish I could claim more merit in having brought about a connection, which, I trust, neither side will repent, but, in fact, all my share in the transaction has been the having recommended you, generally, some time ago, to his Lordship's patronage. To this particular situation I should never have ventured to recommend you, notwithstanding all my friendship for you ; nor would he, I am persuaded, have listened to my recommendation, unless he had been assured, by less partial testimony, that you were likely to fill it to his satisfaction. I sincerely congratulate you upon your appointment, as it opens to you a reasonable prospect of advancement in your profession ; and as, in the meantime, your attendance will be as easy and pleasant as good nature and politeness can make it. I am always,

Dear Sir,
Yours most faithfully,
T. T.

Welbeck Street, 7th May, 1785.

Mr. Burgess was quickly called from his beloved retirement in Oxford, to act his part as chaplain in the town residence of his patron. The following kind letter was his summons: —

DEAR SIR,   Cavendish Square, May 27. 1785.

I SHALL want your attendance here at dinner, on Saturday, June 4th ; and as the occasion is formal, a gown and cassock must be a necessary part of the contents of your portmanteau. A bed shall be prepared for you, whenever you are disposed to come. If you are musical, you will probably wish to be in the Abbey on Thursday. Previous information when I may expect you, will enable me to give you the satisfaction of meeting Mr. Tyrwhitt.

> I am, dear Sir,
> With much regard,
> Your sincere friend,
> S. SARUM.

MR. WINDHAM TO THE REV. MR. BURGESS.

DEAR SIR,

I MUCH fear that a letter of mine directed to you at Oxford ετωσιον εκφυγε χειρος, and must reckon as a presumption that you are no longer in college. My concern, however, is not for the letter that is gone, but for that which I am now writing, which will be of no use if not received on the spot, and to which a value is attached ουχ' ὁ τυχων — nothing less, than the pleasure of an introduction to the celebrated Madame de Genlis. Madame de Genlis leaves Mr. Burke

this morning on her way to Oxford, and as she
will want some attendant, capable of answering
questions, not quite within the capacities of our
ordinary Ciceroni, there is no person to whose care
I would so much wish to consign her as to yours.
If you are not in the university my purpose is defeated, and my hopes of serving Madame de Genlis,
and of gratifying you, are at an end; if you are,
more, I know, need not be said, to insure her every
attention in your power. Believe me to be,

Dear Sir,

Very sincerely yours,

W. WINDHAM.

Beaconsfield, July 17. 1785

Mr. Burgess was well acquainted with the celebrated Mr. Porson, and always spoke with admiration of his extraordinary talents and profound
learning. The following note refers to the commencement of their friendly intercourse.

TO THE REV. MR. BURGESS.

DEAR SIR,

UPON my return hither last Wednesday from a
country visit, I was so lucky as to catch Mr.
Porson, who had come from Oxford with the mail
that morning. I am very glad that he has met
with you, and you with him. He brought me the
two books from you, for which I am much obliged.
Mr. P. seems to be very well pleased with his
expedition, and talks of making another visit to his
friends at Oxford, particularly to a Mr. Suidas *

* Alluding to a celebrated manuscript of Suidas in the library
of Corpus

of your college, with whom he was not able to
converse near so much as he wished   *   *
  *   *   *   *   *
  *   *   *   *   *

              I am always, dear Sir,
                      Yours very sincerely,
                                      T. T.
Welbeck Street, Aug. 26 1785.

About the time that Mr. Burgess entered on
the duties of his new office, Bishop Barrington was
much occupied by a benevolent project for extending the system of Sunday schools throughout the
diocese of Salisbury. Sunday schools were at this
time novelties. Hannah More, and Mr. Raikes of
Gloucester, were the first persons who gave a
powerful impulse to them, an impulse which has
since been felt throughout Great Britain, has
extended itself even among the continental nations, and been felt across the Atlantic. The
system furnishes a simple and a most efficacious
instrument for diffusing the blessings of Christian
instruction amongst the rising generation. The
Bishop of Salisbury found in his chaplain a very
able coadjutor in the prosecution of his benevolent
intentions. No better evidence can be adduced of
the good fruit of Mr. Burgess's sacred studies, and
of the growth of the religious principle in his mind,
than the zeal with which he henceforth exerted
himself to promote the Christian education of the
children of the labouring classes, and to train them
up in provident principles and habits. Few objects
were nearer to his heart than these throughout the

remainder of his life. To his first assiduous ex-
eitions, therefore, of this description, for the good
of his fellow-creatures, his biographer may be
allowed to recur with peculiar interest. Suitable
books for Sunday schools were at this time extremely rare, and Mr. Burgess took great pains to
supply the deficiency. Hence originated " *the
Salisbury Spelling-Book,*" the first of a long list
of useful little publications which he compiled from
time to time, at different periods of his life, for the
Christian instruction of the ignorant and simple.
It is a very useful manual, into which, in addition
to the elements of spelling and reading, he introduced many pretty and edifying stories told in the
simplest language ; a series of scriptural lessons ;
and, finally, the church catechism. It quickly obtained a circulation extending far beyond the bounds
of the diocese for which it was specially intended,
as appeared by a letter from Messrs. Rivington,
addressed to the author, and requesting his direc-
tions, when they were about to print a new edition.

This little book was quickly followed by another,
consisting of Exercises adapted to the Spelling-
Book, in which the children were carried further
on in religious knowledge. Then, finding that
something still more elementary than these was
desirable for very young children, he compiled two
more manuals — one entitled " The Child's First
Book ," the other, " The Child's First Lessons in
Religion," with short prayers for children to learn
by heart before they are taught to read.

Unpretending as these little works were, the
detail and the accuracy which they required cost

him no small pains, and subtracted much of his attention from learned studies. But the hope of doing good rendered the employment delightful and attractive.

" Every man," says Dr Johnson in his Life of Watts, " acquainted with the common principles of human action, will look with veneration on the writer, who is at one time combating with Locke and at another making a catechism for children in their fourth year. A voluntary descent from the dignity of science is, perhaps, the hardest lesson that humility can teach." The spirit of this remark may justly be deemed applicable to the case before us, where we find a distinguished scholar and critic, fresh from Aristotle and Sophocles, employing himself with a zeal and energy not less intense than he had manifested in his learned researches, in sedulously framing syllabic forms and scriptural lessons of the simplest nature for early childhood and youth.

The pleasure with which the Bishop contemplated his labours will be evident from the following letters : —

DEAR SIR,　　Palace, Salisbury, Oct. 29 1785.

As I purpose being at Mongewell toward the end of next month, you will reserve the ψυχῆς ἰατρεῖον, which you are preparing for me. till my arrival.

I entirely agree with you, that the addition of our Saviour's Sermon on the Mount would be a valuable improvement to the intended publication ; but I have my fears lest the increase of price may prove an impediment to the sale. These fears arise from the consideration of the villages, inhabited chiefly by rack-renters, where I hope to see the Sunday schools established. Perhaps, should the sale of the first edition be rapid, and the profits not contemptible, Mr. Easton may be inclined to give a little more press-work for the same money. But all these points may be more fully discussed when the time of reprinting arrives.

I am much pleased with the outlines of your sketch, and I think the execution likely to correspond with the design, if carried on while your mind is fresh from your late humble labours, and has not soared into the higher regions of Aristotle's Metaphysics, or Plato's Parmenides. Mrs. Barrington sends her kind compliments, and charges me to inform you that you are much inquired for by the ladies of this place, who express great concern that they are not to see you any more this year.

I am, with true regard,
Your sincere friend,
S. SARUM.

TO THE SAME.

DEAR SIR, Cavendish Square, April 13 1786.
My name is most heartily at your's and Homer's service. May the work to which it is to be prefixed contribute to render the language and the beauties of that Prince of Poets better understood and more admired ! *
I hope to see you next week in perfect health,

* Alluding to Mr B.'s intended publication of the work, entitled Initia-Homerica.

and that you will bring me some tidings of the
Spelling-Book, for which I feel impatient.
I am, dear Sir,
With true regard,
Your sincere friend,
S. SARUM.

By the following letter from Dr. Warton, it will
be seen that about this time he was meditating a
publication of the Opuscula of Gravina, a learned
Italian scholar and essayist : —

DEAR SIR, Wint., Nov. 25 1786
I AM exceedingly pleased with the design of your
publishing some little pieces of Gravina. It is now
just thirty years since, in the Essay on Pope, I endeavoured a little to bring him forward, and make
him more generally known. It is highly useful to
publish small works, which even the lady-readers of
the present time will venture on. I have printed
in London, and it will now soon be published, Sir
Philip Sidney's "Defence of Poesie," and Extracts
from Ben Jonson's Discoveries. In both is excellent stuff. I cannot but be gratified in the compliment you intend me, of inscribing these pieces to me
It is obviously very agreeable laudari à laudato. I
shall always be glad to see you at this place, and am,
dear Sir,
Your faithful friend and servant,
JOSEPH WARTON.

The Bishop's favourite residence, Mongewell, on
the banks of the Thames, about fourteen miles from
Oxford, has already been mentioned. His chaplain

was a frequent guest there. On one of these occasions, somewhere about the period of which we are treating, an incident occurred which showed how much of manly independence was united in his character with modesty and mildness.

Aliquando bonus dormitat Homerus,

His patron one day so far forgot his habitual courtesy, as to reprove his chaplain in somewhat unmeasured terms with respect to a trivial occurrence at which Mrs. Barrington had taken needless umbrage. Mr. Burgess received the reproof in perfect silence, but almost immediately quitted the room, and, ordering out his horse, proceeded to Oxford, leaving the Bishop to interpret, by what had passed, the cause of his departure. His Lordship quickly drew the inference, and feeling that he had been betrayed into an act of injustice towards a most amiable and excellent man, addressed an apologetic letter to the offended party, expressed in such terms of candour and kindness, as at once repaired this momentary breach of a harmony, which appears never after to have been, in the slightest degree, interrupted. The Bishop was in the habit of removing to the palace at Salisbury in the course of the summer months; and Mr. Burgess, freed by the close of the term from his official duties at Oxford, became then an inmate of the family, and daily discharged the functions of domestic chaplain. When ordinations took place during term time, candidates for orders came to him at Corpus for examination. He acquired, at this time, a partiality for Salisbury which made his return to it, towards the close of his life, a recurrence to early and cherished associations.

H

The retired walks of the palace gardens, and the
fine views which they command of the superb
cathedral, were in perfect unison with the contemplative turn of his mind, and the tastes which he
had contracted in the lettered shades of Oxford.

Bishop Barrington was fond of society, and being
himself an elegant scholar, and of a highly intellectual cast, he delighted to gather men of learning
and science around him, and to elicit their various
stores of information and amusement. Without
effort and without artifice, he had recourse to such
topics as interested all, and yet drew forth, in turn,
the peculiar talents of each. To playful humour
and to constant cheerfulness he united a Christian
benignity and a winning politeness, attempered
with the dignity which became his station and character. With such qualities, he made every one
around him feel at perfect ease, and the feelings
which he manifested towards Mr. Burgess were
more than kind, they were almost paternal. Under
such a roof he found himself truly happy; and with
some of the numerous guests who visited the palace
he formed friendships which added much to the
future happiness of his life. Among these he often
recurred, with peculiar pleasure, to the commencement of an intimate acquaintance, in the summer
of 1785, with one of the first female writers of her
age, the celebrated Hannah More.

The following note, addressed to the writer in
the year 1833, refers to its commencement

TO J. S. HARFORD, ESQ.

DEAR SIR,   Palace, Salisbury, Sept 9 1833.

I RETURN you many thanks for giving me such
early information of an event which has terminated

the very protracted sufferings of our dear and excellent friend, Mrs. Hannah More. My acquaintance with her commenced in this house in 1785, when she passed a week here with Mis. Garrick ; Mr Gilpin, of Boldre ; Dr. Henington, of Christchurch ; Mr. Batt, of New Hall, and, I think, Miss Hulse (Lady Bernard) It was a very interesting week, of which our dear friend sometimes reminded me in her latter days. J am much pleased with your sketch of her character for the London papers, which I shall send to the Salisbury Journal.*

Yours, most sincerely,

T. SARUM.

* The following is the tribute referred to in the Bishop's letter to the character and virtues of their mutual and revered friend —

DIED

On the 7th of September, at her residence in Windsor Terrace, Clifton, in the 89th year of her age, after a painful and protracted illness, Mrs Hannah More. Few persons have enjoyed a higher degree of public esteem and veneration than this excellent and distinguished lady. Early in life she attracted general notice by a brilliant display of literary talent, and was honoured with the intimate acquaintance of Johnson and Burke, of Reynolds and Garrick, and of many other eminent men, who equally appreciated her amiable qualities, and her superior intellect. But, under a deep conviction that to live to the glory of God, and to the good of our fellow-creatures, is the great object of human existence, and the only one which can bring peace at the last, she quitted in the prime of her days the bright circles of fashion and literature, and retiring into the neighbourhood of Bristol, devoted herself to a life of active Christian benevolence, and to the composition of various works, having for their object the religious improvement of mankind Her pen could adapt itself with equal success to the instruction of the highest and of the humblest classes, and the numerous editions through which her various publications have passed attest the high sense entertained by the public of their varied utility and excellence. Her practical conduct beautifully exemplified the moral energy of her Christian principles

H 2

My readers will be amused by Hannah More's
own recollections of the above week, which the
writer has often heard her narrate nearly as follows : —

"In the year 1785, during a music meeting
at Salisbury, in what they call St. Cecilia's week,
I formed one of a large party who were staying at the Palace with my old friend, Bishop Barrington. We were all to have gone on one of
the evenings to a concert, but I was prevented from
being of the party by a furious tooth-ache. The

She was the delight of a widely extended sphere of friends,
whom she charmed by her mental powers, edified by her example, and knit closely to her in affection by the warmth and
constancy of her friendship. She lived and walked in an atmosphere of love, and it was her delight to do good ; the poor
for many miles around her felt the influence of her unceasing
benevolence, and her numerous schools attested her zeal for the
improvement and edification of the rising generation. In these
works of faith and charity, she was aided for a long course of
years by the concurring efforts of four sisters, who lived with
her, who regarded her with mingled feelings of admiration and
affection, and towards whom her conduct was ever marked by
the kindest and most endearing consideration. It was truly
a sisterhood animated by all the social and hospitable virtues.
Mrs Hannah More's last illness was accompanied by feverish
delirium, but the elevating influence of Christian principles was
strikingly exemplified even under the decay of extreme old age
and its attendant consequences. Not seldom she broke forth
into earnest prayer, and devout ejaculation, and invariably met
the affectionate attentions of the friends who sedulously watched
over her sick bed, by unceasing and most expressive returns of
grateful love The writer of this tribute to her memory saw
her only the day before her last seizure, when she expressed to
him in a most impressive manner the sentiments of a humble
and penitent believer in Jesus Christ, assuring him that she re-
posed her hopes of salvation on His merits alone, and expressing
at the same time a firm and joyful trust in his unchangeable
promises In her excellent writings she will long live, not
only as one of the brightest ornaments of her sex, but as a bene-
factress of mankind.

Bishop's chaplain, Mr. Burgess, a tall, grave, and sensible young man, rather reserved, and silent, begged to be allowed to bear me company. His reserve, when we were left alone, gradually wore away; our conversation became various and animated; I was struck by his learning and good sense; and out of this interview sprung an intimate friendship, and a correspondence which has been carried on for upwards of forty years."

Some specimens of their correspondence will be found in various parts of this volume, though we regret to say that the greater part of the letters on both sides have perished.

There were many points in common between these excellent persons. Both were devoted to literature, and anxious to consecrate their acquirements to the highest and noblest ends. Both were occupied by objects of practical utility and Christian benevolence. The refinement and vivacity of female society always had peculiar charms for Mr. Burgess; and in the present instance he was delighted by the union of elevated and heartfelt piety, in combination with brilliant wit, extensive knowledge, and admirable good sense.

CHAP. X.

VISITS HOLLAND AND PARIS. — DEATH OF MR. TYRWHITT.— PUBLICATIONS BY MR. BURGESS IN 1787 AND 1788 — CORRESPONDENCE WITH DR. BURNEY, DR. PARR, ETC. — PUBLISHES A TREATISE AGAINST THE SLAVE TRADE.

1786 to 1789.

AT the time of which we are now writing, Mr. Burgess appears to have been the person who did

the honours of Oxford to learned foreigners; and
the following letter from Mr. Spalden, a Prussian
gentleman already referred to in that character
(page 16.), will prove what a pleasing impression
he made upon such occasions : —

TO THE REV. MR. BURGESS.

DEAR SIR,   Amsterdam, October 11. 1786.

I ALMOST despair of being still present to your
memory when this letter reaches you It is not
long since I finally quitted England, a country
which before I had been in it I preferred to all
others, and now having seen it, I still more prefer
to them all. As your friendly reception at Oxford
inspired me with gratitude, and with esteem for
you, and as the analogy between our studies rendered your conversation most agreeable and useful
to me, I hope you will allow me to correspond with
you in English, for I feel myself drawn to you as a
scholar, whose character is as amiable, as his learning and knowledge are extensive.

I am now enjoying the intercourse of gentlemen
in Holland who know very well your name and
your works, especially M. Ruhnkenius in Leyden,
and M. Wyttenbach in Amsterdam.

I am, dear Sir,

Your most obedient servant,

G. L. SPALDEN.

In the summer of 1787, Mr. Burgess, fraught
with schemes of classical research and investigation,
visited Paris and Holland. In the course of this
journey he formed a friendly acquaintance with

many distinguished foreign scholars, among whom
may be enumerated, Wyttenbach, Ruhnken, Heyné,
and Villoison. He kept up with them for several
years an occasional correspondence, and that with
Heyné extended to the year 1800.

Wyttenbach was at this time preparing for the
publication of an elaborate and critical edition of
Plutarch's moral works, and was anxious that it
should be printed at Oxford. Mr. Burgess afterwards conducted a successful negociation on his
account with the delegates of the Clarendon Press
for this purpose. Their subsequent correspondence
chiefly related to this subject. In a Latin life of
his friend Ruhnken, Wyttenbach has depicted, in
the following terms, the pleasant recollection which
that eminent scholar and himself retained of the
visit of Burgess. "Afterwards a most agreeable
guest visited us, Thomas Burgess, an Englishman,
whose superior learning was adorned by a rare integrity of mind and modesty of demeanour. The
friendship we thus formed with him was kept up
afterwards by an interchange of letters and good
offices."*

He received at Paris many kind attentions from
Villoison, whose great erudition, and ardent zeal in
the cause of Greek literature, united to no small
degree of French vivacity, rendered him a very
interesting companion to a traveller, whose objects
were so exclusively of a learned description. Ac-

* Mox gratissimus advenit hospes Thomas Burgessius, Bri-
tannus ; cujus excellentem literarum scientiam, rara quædam
ornabat animi probitas, morumque modestia unde amicitia
cum præsente nobis conciliata, deinde cum absente epistolis
officiisque viguit

cordingly they formed a friendship, which led to
frequent correspondence. On the part of Villoison
it was carried on in French. The other foreign
correspondents of Mr. Burgess addressed him in
Latin. Some few of Villoison's letters will be
found in the ensuing pages, their liveliness and
literary ardour being such as to render them interesting even to general readers.

The following marks the commencement of their
acquaintance at Paris in August, 1787 : —

MONSIEUR,

Je suis bien sensible à l'honneur de vous reçevoir
ce soir, et serai bien flatté de cultiver l'amitié d'un
savant de votre merite. J'en sens vivement le prix.
Si vous vous donnez la peine de relire ma lettre,
vous y verrez, Monsr., que ce n'est point des mes
Epistolæ Vinarienses que je vous avois fait l'offre,
parceque je n'en ai qu'un seul exemplaire, mais
de mon Homère qui s'emprime à Venise, et dont
j'ai donné la notice dans mes Anecdota Græca. Je
vous prierai d'accepter cette faible marque de la
haute estime que je vous ai vouée, et de la reconnoissance que je vous dois du profit que j'ai tiré de la
lecture de vos savans ouvrages. J'espère que vous
voudrez bien me donner votre adresse à Londres,
et que nous entretiendrons un commerce littéraire.

Je suis fâché, Monsr., que vous ne m'ayez pas
fait l'honneur de vous adresser à moi en arrivant
à Paris. Je me serois fait un devoir, un plaisir,
et un honneur de vous rendre tous les services qui
dépendent de moi, et de vous faire avoir chez vous
la communication des MSS. du Roi, ce qui vous
auroit épargné la peine d'aller à la Bibliothéque du

Roi. En un mot disposez de moi librement et sans
façon. J'ai été moimême étranger dans beaucoup
de pays.

Haud ignara mali, miseris succurrere disco.

D'ailleurs j'aime passionement les Anglois, et
surtout les savans, qui, comme vous, Monsr., éten-
dent les bornes de nos connoissances, et dont les
doctes ouvrages ont beaucoup servi à mon instruction. Je cultive les lettres par goût, et pour mon
amusement, et respecte infiniment les personnes
éclairées qui leur rendent les services. Vous trou-
verez ce soir à souper chez moi un jeune homme
nommé M. Lenglés, qui va nous donner la gram-
maire et le dictionnaire de la langue Tartare.

J'ai l'honneur d'être en vous attendant, Monsr.,
Votre très humble et
très obéissant serviteur,
D'Ansse de Villoison.

A letter of nearly the same date, in a similar
strain of esteem and compliment, written to him at
Paris by l'Abbé Desfrançois, " Interprète du Roi,"
proves the kind reception he met with there.

During his stay at Paris the following letter
reached him from Bishop Barrington : —

Dear Sir,   August 24. 1787

I felt no common degree of satisfaction in
learning that your expedition has, hitherto, more
than answered your expectation. May your literary inquiries at the Bibliothéque du Roi be as
fully gratified as your curiosity has been with respect to those objects at Paris with which you have

been as yet conversant. I most cordially wish that I could give you a greater latitude than you ask for, viz. to the 15th of next month. My public confirmations to compensate for the unavoidable omission of last year, are fixed for the 17th and 18th : the examinations of the candidates for the 24th. Notwithstanding these various calls, yet such is my reluctance to bring you from your pursuits a moment sooner than you can relinquish them; that on your immediately notifying your wish to remain, I will supply your place myself as examiner, and provide some other person to assist at the confirmation.

I purpose being at Salisbury, on Wednesday next the 29th inst., and shall be impatient to hear all that you can transmit relative to the state of letters and literary works at Paris. Mrs. Barrington charges me with her best compliments and thanks for your attention to her commission. Allow me to give you a commission as far as 10*l.* or 15*l.* for such books as you conceive will interest me.

Believe me, with the truest regard and esteem,

Your most sincere friend,

S. SARUM.

Soon after the return of Mr. Burgess, an event occurred which deeply affected his feelings. His excellent friend Mr. Tyrwhitt was cut off in his fifty-sixth year, after a short but severe illness. What has already been said of this eminently learned, amiable, and accomplished individual, renders it needless further to dilate on his qualities as an author, and as a man. His name was seldom mentioned by the subject of this memoir, even in his old age without some endearing or grateful epithet.

Mr. Tyrwhitt left materials for a new edition of Aristotle's Poetics, which was printed at the Clarendon Press in the year 1794, under the editorial superintendence of Mr. Burgess, and Mr. Randolph. This edition is extremely elegant, and contains not only Tyrwhitt's commentaries, but also his version of the original.

In the course of the summer of 1788, Mr. Burgess again visited Holland, and the following letter addressed to Dr. Parr from the Hague attests the diligence of his learned researches.

TO THE REV. DR. PARR.

DEAR SIR. Hague, Sept. 26. 1788.

I HAVE been at this place a few days. I had heard much of Mr Meerman's collection of Greek MSS., which were bought by the present baron's father in the year 1764, when the books of the Jesuits' College at Paris were sold; and I was unwilling to leave Holland without examining two of them in which I was most interested, the MS. of Homer, and that of Aristotle's Poetics. The MS. of the Iliad belongs to the 11th or 12th century, and is written on vellum. It contains all the twenty-four books; there are but a few scholia. The MS. of the Poetics is of the 16th century. Though it is of so recent a date, I have met with some variations, which I have not seen noted from any other MS I collated the whole of the first chapter as a sort of estimate of its value, and I also examined various select passages. I did not forget our friend Holmes's undertaking, but looked for MSS. of the

Septuagint. I soon arrived, however, at the end of
my search.   There are but three MSS. and each
of these contains only portions of the Bible.   In the
public library at Leyden there is a very valuable
MS. of parts of the Septuagint, the most ancient, I
think, that I have ever yet seen.   Some persons
have attributed it to the age of Nero.   It is however
summæ et venerandæ antiquitatis.   It was collated
by Mill but very imperfectly.   It contains the books
of Moses, and part of Joshua and Judges.

I have found my summer's excursion amply recompensed at Leyden.   My collection of Anecdota
Græca has been very much enlarged through the
civility of M. Ruhnken and Van Santin.   I have
transcribed a great part of Philemon's Lexicon Phi-
lologicum, and have left a commission to have the
remainder transcribed for me.   Many other particulars you shall hereafter hear.

Ruhnken has printed off some sheets of a new
edition of his Timæi Lexicon Platonicum, and is
thinking of republishing his Elogium Hemsterhusii,
to which will be added an unpublished letter of
Bentley's to that scholar containing some very valuable emendations on the comic fragments of Julius
Pollux.   M. Tollius has just published   a   new
edition of Apollonii Lexicon Homericum in octavo.
Santin has printed a considerable part of a new
edition of T. Maurus, and a specimen of a new
edition of Catullus.   He is also the editor of Bur-
man's Propertius, published a few years ago   You
have perhaps heard that Villoison has at length published his long expected edition of Homer's Iliad.
With my best compliments to yourself and family,

Your faithful friend and servant,

T. BURGESS.

From the six following years, that is to say from 1786 to 1792, the current of Mr. Burgess's life quietly and calmly flowed on in the discharge of his duties as Tutor of Corpus, and Examining Chaplain to the Bishop of Salisbury, and in the publication of various learned works, all of which added to his reputation. The friendship and affection with which he continued to be treated by the Bishop were such as to remove any painful feelings of dependence. Nor did he owe this high consideration solely to his Lordship's genuine benignity and politeness, for as a literary man he was sensibly alive to the credit reflected upon himself by the selection of a Chaplain whose superior learning and character attracted universal esteem. The Bishop was proud of his Chaplain, and took a lively interest in the various productions of his pen, and the chaplain was animated by reciprocal feelings of grateful respect and attachment to his Diocesan.

During the period above referred to, a prebend of some value becoming vacant at Salisbury, it was offered to Mr. Burgess, but he declined it, for a reason which will perhaps produce a smile in the reader, though it was strictly in unison with the shyness and modesty of his character. The reason was, as he himself told a friend, that it would have obliged him to sit in one of the most conspicuous parts of the Cathedral. Another subsequently became vacant, which did not put his nerves to this trial, and he gratefully accepted it.

During the year 1787 Mr. Burgess was much occupied by the study of Hebrew.

In 1788 he published the following works :—

Conspectus Criticarum Observationum in Scriptores Græcos et Latinos. 8vo. 1788.

Initia Homerica, seu Excerpta ex Iliade Homeri,
cum omnium locorum Græca Metaphrasi.   8vo.
1788.   A second Edition in 1820.

Remarks on Josephus's Account of Herod's Rebuilding of the Temple of Jerusalem.   8vo. 1788,
which was followed by Remarks on the Scriptural
Account of the Dimensions of Solomon's Temple.
8vo.*

Sententiæ Philosophorum e Codice Leidensi Vossiano.   12mo. 1788.

These publications were only the precursors of
other learned treatises which followed in rapid succession during the ensuing five years.

Even a cursory inspection of their contents would
impress any intelligent reader with a strong conviction of the mental energy, the various erudition,
and the indefatigable industry of their author.

His correspondents at this time were numerous,
including, in addition to the learned foreigners
above enumerated, Di Pair, Mr afterwards Dr.
Burney, Rev. Mr. Glasse, Dr. Loveday, Mr. T. Fal-
coner, Dr. Heberden, Lord Sandys, &c.

---

* These Treatises are learned and acute   Dr Heberden
and Mr Pierce had contended that the prophecy (Haggai, ii.
6—9) is not applicable to our Saviour, because the Temple
which he glorified by his presence was not the second, built by
Zerubbabel, but the third Temple, rebuilt, according to Josephus, by Herod.   Mr. Hawtry, on the contrary, in order to
remove this objection, contended that Josephus did not mean
to say that Herod took down the temple and rebuilt it, but repaired it only   Mr Burgess differed from both of these views
from the latter, by proving that Josephus does relate that
Herod took down and rebuilt the Temple , from the former,
by maintaining that another rebuilding of the Temple by
Herod is not incompatible with the usual application of the
prophecy of Haggai   But in doing this he disclaims offering
any opinion of his own upon the justice of that application.

Though most of their surviving letters are unsuited to the taste of general readers, from being
chiefly confined to topics of learned criticism, several among them are of a more popular character,
and are introduced here not only as recording the
opinions entertained of the publications of Mr.
Burgess by his learned contemporaries, but also as
interesting specimens of epistolary correspondence.

MR. BURNEY TO THE REV. MR. BURGESS.

Sir,   Hammersmith, Sept 8 1788.
I BEG leave to return you my sincere thanks for
the present of the Initia Homerica, which you did
me the honour of sending to me, and, at the same
time, permit me to congratulate teachers and pupils,
on the appearance of a publication from which they
cannot but derive mutual advantage. In a country where the aspirers after knowledge are so
numerous, it is very strange that elementary books
should always have been so few in number, and
generally so useless, from the injudicious manner in
which they have been compiled or written. In the
present age, however, it is surely an occasion for
triumph, that while Mrs. Barbauld and Mrs. Trim-
mer have successfully employed their talents to
smooth the road to the English student, Mr. Huntingford and Mr Burgess have laboured to render
the avenues which lead to an acquaintance with
the writers of Greece, more easy of access than
they were ever found by our ancestors.
            I have the honour to be, Sir,
                  Your obliged
                        CHARLES BURNEY.

TO THE REV. MR. BURGESS.

REVEREND SIR,   Greenford, Feb 27. 1787.

I HOPE you will forgive the liberty I take in thus introducing myself to you with a request of so much consequence to me, that I am obliged to wave the circumstance of my not having the honour of your acquaintance.

It is now about three years since I began the task of putting Milton's Samson Agonistes into a Grecian dress. After a variety of interruptions, occasioned by the laborious employments in which I am engaged, I am now bringing it very near its conclusion. It has been, as yet, submitted to no eye, save that of one highly honoured friend, who had the goodness to revise it in a very imperfect state, and to suggest several alterations of great consequence.

Before it makes its appearance in the world, I am very anxious that it should have the advantage of your critical knowledge: if I can be so happy as to obtain your permission to transmit you the MS., it is a favour I shall never be able to repay, but I shall always consider myself as most essentially obliged to you.

I hope, Sir, my presuming to address you personally, instead of transmitting you this request through the medium of any of our common friends, will be attributed only to the impatience I feel to be gratified in this object so very near my wishes.

I have the honour to be, with the utmost respect, reverend Sir,

Your most obedient humble servant,
GEORGE HENRY GLASSE.

The above request was acceded to, as appears by a subsequent letter of grateful acknowledgement from Mr. Glasse.

TO THE REV. MR. BURGESS.

Fair Lawn House,
SIR,   Hammersmith, Nov. 6. 1788.

I SEIZE eagerly the first leisure moment, since the arrival of your letter, to answer it. Some years ago, Terentianus Maurus * employed my thoughts almost wholly, and engaged my hours almost continually. The delight which he then afforded me, and the knowledge which I derived from him, make me still reflect on him with respect, and hear him mentioned with pleasure. My views with regard to an edition of his works are, perhaps, entirely defeated; but I resemble the coachman, who, when he could no longer, from infirmities, sit on the box, was charmed with the *smack of the whip.* I had, indeed, a firm intention of publishing him, and had made considerable collections for the purpose; but more serious avocations soon demanded my time and care, and as I became better acquainted with books, and the serious duties of an Editor, the difficulties, at which I had once been scarcely startled, appeared terrific, and my mind was by degrees weaned from its favourite purpose.

I am truly happy to hear that there is a chance of a new edition, by Santenius; but should this hope be frustrated, or should the edition of Santenius not answer the wishes of the public, I believe that

* An elegant Latin poet and grammarian.

I

I should almost be tempted to renew the charge; to forget my former dangers and difficulties, and to brush up my rusty arms : —

> Saucius ejurat pugnam Gladiator — at idem
> Immemor antiqui vulneris arma capit.

For though I have not opened Terentianus for several years, except accidentally, your account of Santennus has awakened my former enthusiasm, and I exclaim with Propertius,

> Nam me ab amore tuo deducet nulla Senectus,
> Sive ego Tithonus, sive ego Nestor ero.

I lost no time, dear Sir, in sending for your Conspectus, which I perused with avidity, and am bound to thank you for it. I am really delighted to find that you have so much good treasure in store, and that these jewels have not fallen into the hands of those who are insensible of their value.

Many of the articles have roused my curiosity in an uncommon degree, and most impatiently shall I expect their publication. Those to which I principally allude are the notes to, and various lections of the Tragedies, all that relates to Demetrius Phalerus, Bentley's letters, Sanctamand's notes on the Anabasis of Xenophon, the Libellus de Metris, Excerpta Herodiani, and Philemonis Lexicon.

Let our countrymen remember that the foundation of the Miscellaneæ Observationes was laid in England, and let us hope, that such another valuable structure may be raised in our days, and become the envy as well as the admiration of the learned in Holland and Germany.

Your intention was mentioned to me some time

ago by Parr, who, as he spoke warmly in praise of it, will, I hope, become a contributor.

Will you pardon the liberty I take in earnestly recommending to your notice, the valuable Lexicon of Photius. The original exemplar, from which the various copies that are scattered through Europe have been made, is in Trinity College Library at Cambridge. But you have a transcript at Oxford. Do then, by your love of learning I conjure you, and by your endeavours for the promotion of Greek Literature I beseech you, let this inedited treasure make a part of your publication. It might be merely reprinted, without a single note; and Alberti's Index in his Glossaria Græca might be completed, for some omissions have been remarked by subsequent critics. Were it once in print, some scholar might be induced to give a proper edition of it.

If you come to town, I shall think myself much honoured and feel myself much pleased, if you could venture so far as the three mile stone. The Oxford coach, indeed, passes my door. I have several books with marginal notes, and some curious papers of a critical nature, some of which, if you approve of them, I should not be unwilling to see in your work.

May I beg you to pardon this rambling letter, and to command my services whenever you are in need of them.

I am, Sir,
Your very faithful humble servant,
CHARLES BURNEY.

P. S.   My friend Porson had copied nearly half of Photius, when the College lent the MS. to the

intended editor in Denmark. The book however
is returned, and was on Porson's table, when I
heard from him lately. He will not be tempted
to complete his manuscript, nor to publish the
work.*

Mr. Twining of Colchester has almost printed
his translation of Aristotle's Poetics. This will be
one of the most valuable books that has appeared
for many years, on account of its learning, taste,
and sagacity.

TO THE REV. DR. PARR.

Nov. 19 1788.

I am very glad that the object of my Initia
Homerica has met with your approbation. It was
to consult such opinions as yours with respect to the
object, that I published the book. I hope to make
it, in another edition, more useful to beginners, and
more deserving of your approbation.

I have inclosed a copy of my Conspectus, which
I have printed in Latin, and have endeavoured to
put into a rather more readable form than it was
in the English Advertisement, which you did me
the favour to accept. I have lately had a very
friendly letter from Mr. Burney on the subject of
it, and I hope to profit, towards the completion of
my undertaking, from his kindness and learning.
Our common friend Mr. Routh has promised some

---

* Mr. Porson did, however, complete his transcript, in that
exquisite style of Greek penmanship for which he was celebrated, when it was unfortunately consumed by fire. He had
the patience to go through the labour a second time, and the
work has since been published from his manuscript by Trinity
College, Cambridge.

remarks on Epiphanius, and I flatter myself that
Dr. Parr will not be ασυμβολος. I have not the
art of making fine speeches, and therefore I must
omit the opportunity of telling you why I should
be proud to have your assistance and contribution
to my intended publication.

The question which you ask me about the eligibility of any particular College is not easy to answer.
However, upon the whole, I am inclined to think
that Oriel is most likely to answer the views of
your young friend. The fellowships are exceedingly good, and are open to the University. The
present Provost is a very learned and excellent man,
and your young friend will certainly have it in his
power to recommend himself to him by his diligence and regularity. In our College we have no
Warwickshire Scholarship.

M. Wyttenbach has finished the Miscellaneous
Works of Plutarch ; they are ready for the press ;
and I think it is not unlikely that we shall have the
honour of printing the book at Oxford. But of
this, more in another letter. He has printed off
half a new number of the Bibliotheca Critica, *i. e.*
of the second number of the third volume. Brunck's
Sophocles is one of the articles. The latest intelligence that I can give you of Heyné's Pindar, is
the following extract of a letter which I received
from him the 12th of last April : —

"Nihilne apud vos adhuc constitutum est de
Pindaro recundendo, de quo ante annos aliquot me-
cum egit vir doctus Oxoniensis. Non alienus eram
ab eo concilio, ut mitterem interpretationis copias,
quas in Pindarum paratas habeo. Nunc eas hac

urbe evulgandas typis curabo.   Gottingæ, d. xii
Apr. 1788."

M. Santenius has printed off a considerable part
of a new edition of Terentianus Maurus, some of
the sheets of which I saw when I was at Leyden
at the latter end of September.   I told him of the
expected edition in England.   He was very anxious
that I should send him all the particulars about it,
which I could collect.   You will oblige me very
much by any information respecting it which you
can give me.

I am, dear Sir,

Yours, most respectfully,

T. BURGESS.

P.S.   White has mentioned to me your generous
exertions for a certain distressed family.

TO THE REV. MR. BURGESS.

DEAR SIR,   Hatton, Nov. 29. 1788

I APPROVED, and meant to express my approbation
of the object, and of the execution of your Initia
Homerica.   After the noble specimens you have
given us of your deep erudition and correct taste, I
was naturally led to wish for some of your own observations upon Homer.   Clarke, whom I reverence,
is sometimes wrong.   Ernestus, whose knowledge in
Latin Literature seems to me unequalled, and who
upon various subjects is a scholar and a philosopher
of the first class, has not been very useful in his
notes on Homer.   I am sorry to add, that he is now
and then unnecessarily captious; and I know that
you sincerely dislike this temper in philological
writers.

I rejoice exceedingly to find that you have so
many precious remains of that great and good man
Mr. Tyrwhitt. I am glad to see your prospectus in
Latin, for you have the rare and happy talent of
writing upon philological subjects, without the ridiculous and offensive quaintness which has long been
so fashionable among philologists. Burney told
me of his letter to you. He wishes, as I do, that
you would give us Photius, before it comes out in
London. I have seen fac similes of your three Oxford copies. When I inquired at Cambridge about
our famous manuscript, which belonged you know
to Gataker, and is deposited in Trinity Library, it
was gone, I think, to Stockholm. Porson, four
years ago, had transcribed down to iota. It is now
returned, and I have repeatedly urged him to publish it ψιλῶς, if he should find himself too idle to
write emendations or notes. At all events, dear Sir,
pray let us have it. I have very little leisure myself, and, strange as it is, I feel an almost invincible
aversion to inspect my very numerous papers. Yet
I am not without hopes of affording you a little
contribution some time or other. The Review upon
Glasse is to come out in January. I have seen the
greater part of the intended strictures, and I assent
to many of them. I need not tell you who the two
critics in the Monthly are. I dissent a little from
some of their principles, and think they impose unnecessary fetters upon a modern Greek writer ; for,
as respects the Musæ severiores, we may say with
Martial —

Nobis non licet esse tam disertis.

True it is, that I am an advocate for great precision,
and so far I must commend the general exactness of

I 4

Mr. Glasse's critics. But in writing, as in manners, it is easier to lay down rules than to observe them. I confess of myself, what I think of almost all other scholars, that, whatever faults they may find in the translation, neither they nor I could, upon the whole, have translated the Agonistes so well. I am very sorry that the negotiation between Heyné and your university is broken off. I wait eagerly for his notes upon Pindar.

The Cambridge delegates are naturally enough out of humour with the delay of Tunstall in the T. Maurus, and of Porson in the Æschylus.

I am, like yourself, very little in the habit of saying fine things. But I say only what is true, when I assure you of my great respect for your diligence, judgment, learning, and candour, all of which give me an interest in your projects and your fame. Under the impression of that respect, I feel myself inclined to acknowledge that I have some doubts about two or three passages in your Conspectus. But I will not presume to point them out, unless you give me leave. They are of no great consequence, yet I wish to be satisfied how far they are right, and I would be understood not to condemn, but only to doubt. I thank you for your very kind account of your College, and for your advice about Oriel. As I am not acquainted with the Provost, I wish you would be so good as to ask him a few questions, and then I will write to him myself. My efforts for Dr. Brown's family have been very successful, which you will be glad to hear.

I have taken the liberty of sending this letter to the Bishop of Chester, and must desire you to apologise for it: an apology is the more requisite as

the Bishop probably knows how much I am displeased and even shocked at his treatment of a poor
curate in his diocese. The curate is much to blame
from imprudence and rashness in two or three
measures, which he has taken *without my knowledge*,
and in consequence of which he is now smarting
under a most heavy scourge of persecution. I have
seen all the letters, and it is a deplorable case.
Very good bishops are often grossly misled by prag-
matical secretaries; and in the church, as well as
in common life, the poor and friendless too often
meet with little candour.

I am, dear Sir,

Yours very respectfully and truly,

S. PARR.

TO THE REV. MR. BURGESS.

DEAR SIR, December 1. 1788.

I HAVE recommended your Conspectus to the
attention of my friend Mr. Griffiths, who has promised to insert any account of it, which I may draw
up, in the Appendix. This I shall do with much
pleasure, though I have long since ceased reviewing
any thing but my boys' exercises. But I feel very
desirous that so useful a plan should be generally
known; and how can it be better circulated than in
the Monthly Review?

Of Mr. Glasse's Samson I have much to say.
The mistakes are numerous, and many of them sur-
prisingly gross. On the whole, however, it is the
most astonishing performance which any modern
writer of Greek verse ever produced. Did I tell
you that I have a Collation of Juvenal, and part of

a Collation of Lucan, which I shall be happy to
present to you for your Observationes Criticæ?
My hopes about Wyttenbach's Plutarch are revived
by the renewal of the Bibliotheca Critica, whence,
among other good things, we learn that a Polybius
is to be expected from Schweighauser. *De hoc
viderint Oxonienses.* I shall always be happy to be
favoured with hearing from you, and remain,

Dear Sir,

Your very faithful servant,

C. BURNEY.

TO CHARLES BURNEY, ESQ.

DEAR SIR,   C. C. C , Dec. 14. 1788.
I SHALL be very much obliged to you for the collations of Juvenal and Lucan, which you are so
good as to offer me, as indeed I shall be for any
contributions that you may do me the favour to communicate. I am much gratified by the opinion you
express of my Conspectus, and of the collection
which I am forming. I have great pleasure in
finding that you take so much interest in both, and
shall think that the pains I have already taken, and
my advertisement of what I have done and mean to
do, will be fully answered, and most satisfactorily
recompensed, by the advantageous manner in which
you kindly offer to make them more known. You
will be glad to hear that M. Wyttenbach means to
contribute largely I shall give his promise to me
in his own words, from a letter which I very lately
received from him. You will pardon my vanity
in adding the few words which introduce what he

says of the Conspectus. "Imprimis mihi placuit
cum delectus et elegantia animadversionis in Ho-
mericis Initiis, tum acumen et doctrina in dispu-
tatione de Josepho. Nunc de criticarum observationum Conspectu quid dicam? Ita me libellus
cepit et allicuit ad studium tuum jucundum, ut
si quid habeam ineditæ scriptionis vel meæ vel
alienæ, vel antiquæ, vel novæ, illud lubens tecum
communicaturus sim; siquidem post editas amplius
tres particulas, atque adeo absolutis tribus volu-
minibus, mihi finem Bibliothecæ criticæ impositurus
videor." * I think I mentioned to you before that
M. Wyttenbach has promised me his observations
and emendations on the Poetics of Aristotle to add
to Mr. Tyrwhitt's. Dr. Parr does not absolutely
promise, but gives me reason to hope that he will
not be quite ασυμϐολος. As to Photius, there is one
circumstance which would determine me to publish
the whole. You must be aware of the difficulty of
getting good copyists for works of any length. I
have been solicited on many hands, from the Continent as well as at home, to bring out the whole of
Damascius, which it is my intention to do. But
the only amanuensis I can get in Oxford, is at
this moment employed upon Damascius, and my
college engagements will not allow me to think of

* "The judgment and elegance displayed in your critical
remarks upon Homer, as well as the acumen and learning of
your Treatise on Josephus, particularly pleased me. And, now,
what shall I say with respect to your collection of critical observations? So much did this little work attract and allure
me to your agreeable occupation, that if I find I possess any
suitable inedited materials, written by myself or by others, be
they ancient or modern, I will readily communicate them to
you; the more so, as after the three next parts of the Bibliotheca
Critica are published, I propose to bring that work to a close."

transcribing from Photius more than excerpta. But
if Porson would do me the favour to contribute
what he has transcribed, Photius's Lexicon should
be the first philological matter that I would print,
and it should not be long before I would put it
to the press. You must use your interest with
him I have desired Dr. Parr to do the same. I
would write to him myself, if you could let me
know where a letter would be likely to meet him.
Wyttenbach's Plutarch, I have the pleasure of informing you, will be printed at Oxford. The negotiation between him and the delegates of our
press, which my summer's excursion in Holland
gave me an opportunity of setting on foot, is
settled to the satisfaction of M. Wyttenbach. I
agree with you perfectly in your opinion as to the
conclusion of Mr. Glasse's preface. I read through
the Samson Agonistes with pleasure, and with as
much diligence as my many engagements would
allow me. But I would never be answerable for
the errors of the best modern composition in Greek.
Those who are best able to discover the faults of
the translation, will, I think, agree with you, that it
is the most astonishing performance which any modern writer in Greek verse ever produced.

I am, dear Sir, your faithful humble servant,

T. BURGESS.

The following will be read with interest, both on
account of the writer and his expected guests.

Oxford, Saturday, 1788.

Mr. ROUTH presents his compliments to Mr.
Burgess, and requests him to accept his thanks
for his elegant, and, if he may be allowed the ex-

pression, well-reasoned treatise on the dimensions of the Temple. Mr. Routh expects the pleasure of Mr. Porson's and Mr. Banks's company at dinner on Monday, and should be extremely glad if Mr. Burgess would meet them.

MR. VILLOISON TO MR. BURGESS.

MONSIEUR, ET SAVANT AMI,

J'AI reçu avec bien de la reconnoissance la lettre que vous m'avez fait l'honneur de m'écrire par M^r. Barrois. Je suis bien sensible, M^r., aux preuves de souvenir et d'amitié que vous voulez bien me donner.

Mon Homère paroîtra enfin à Venise dans environ trois mois. Vous y verrez M^r., dans la preface, l'usage que j'ai fait de vos savantes remarques, et la justice que je vous rends. Aussitôt que j'aurai reçu des exemplaires, je m'empresserai de vous en envoyer ainsi qu'à Milord Stormont.

J'ai lu avec beaucoup d'intérêt et de profit votre excellente dissertation sur Joseph (Josephus) : elle est pleine de critique, de logique et d'érudition, et répond d'une manière victorieuse à un des argumens les plus forts qu'on ait faits contre la Religion Chrétienne.

Vous m'obligerez infiniment, si vous aurez la bonté de me donner de vos nouvelles dans le plus grand detail, et de me marquer en même temps les nouvelles littéraires. Comment va votre traité de l'Analogie de la Langue Grecque ? quand paroîtra votre édition du troisième livre de l'Iliade, votre nouvelle édition en 8vo. des Marbres d'Arundel ?

*　　　*　　　*　　　*　　　*

*　　　*　　　*　　　*　　　*

Then follow notices of works in progress by savans at Paris, Florence, Rome, Parma, Naples, &c.

A succeeding letter gives a list of nineteen different works in progress on the Continent.

Mr Villoison seems to have been the general reporter of all literary gossip. Wyttenbach, writing to Mr. Burgess in the ensuing year, amuses himself with transcribing Villoison's list of savans and their works, and then archly adds, — Quis credidisset tot esse tamque egregios μουσαγετας de quibus vix unquam fando audiveramus.*

TO THE REV. DR. PARR.

DEAR SIR,   C C C., January 5. 1789

THOUGH the receipt of your last kind letter, which has laid me under many obligations for the amusement and instruction which it afforded me, and for your very liberal offer of communications on Terentianus Maurus, made me very desirous of hearing from you again, not only on the subject of Terentianus, but on the Latinity of my Conspectus; yet a variety of engagements prevented my sitting down to write to you. Not a day, however, has passed without my thinking of the debt I owe you. One of these engagements has been the preparing a pamphlet for the press on a temporary topic, which has lately occupied all the attention

* Who could have imagined that there are so many and such illustrious companions of the Muses, of whom we had scarcely ever even heard mention ?

which I could spare from other engagements, of this you shall hear in my next.

As to your pupil, the chance which he has of becoming a fellow of any College will depend entirely on his own behaviour, the connections he may make, and accidents which it is impossible to foresee, but which he may, in some degree, be able to prepare himself for, when he has resided a little at the University. If he enter a commoner at any College where there are open fellowships, there is certainly a greater probability of his succeeding to a fellowship of that society, than of any other. The best Colleges for him to enter with this view are, Oriel, Brazennose, University, Balliol, and Queen's. Though it is not easy to decide which is preferable, yet I have made my inquiries ; and, upon the whole, I should recommend Oriel. His situation in Oriel will give him a prior chance in his own society, and will not intercept his views upon any other.

I congratulate you most sincerely on the success of your efforts for Dr. Browne's family. I have desired Dr. White to consider me as responsible for a small sum. But to return to the literary part of your letter. You will oblige me very much by pointing out any exceptionable words or expressions in my Conspectus. I did not send it you out of mere compliment, nor did I wish to have your good opinion only, but I hoped to profit from your judgment.

I am very much satisfied by your approbation of my specimen of Initia Homerica. The whole of this work will consist of two parts: to the first I shall prefix a collection of grammatical principles from the writers on dialects, as an introduction to

the grammatical knowledge of Homer; to the
second part I shall prefix a collection of critical
principles, as preparatory to a critical knowledge of
Homer.

Mr. Burney has been at Oxford lately, and I am
very happy to have made his acquaintance.

I remain, dear Sir,

Your most obedient friend and servant,

T. BURGESS.

Dr. Warton, his old preceptor, continued occasionally to correspond with Mr. Burgess; but his
letters, though expressive of sincere regard and
esteem, are in general brief and hurried. In the
course of one of them, written in 1788, he expresses regret that it will not be in his power to
make any contributions to his " Conspectus," because, to quote his own words, " In all intervals of
leisure, I never lose sight, for a moment, of my
own great work, the ' History of Grecian Poetry.' "
It is humiliating to human pride to compare the
projects of superior minds with their actual achieve-
ments. This work, it is scarcely needful to add,
was never finished.

About this time the public mind was much engrossed by discussions upon the proposed abolition
of West Indian slavery. The powerful eloquence
and philanthropic energies of Mr. Wilberforce were
exerted in its behalf, in the British senate, for the
first time, in the spring of 1789. He was nobly
supported by the united influence and the splendid
talents of Pitt, Burke, and Fox; but though the
advocates of abolition proved invincible in the field
of argument, Prejudice and Interest prevailed for a

time against Justice and Humanity. The immediate object of Mr. Wilberforce's motion was defeated; but a lodgment was made in the public mind in its favour, which proved the harbinger of final success. The attention of the nation was roused to a full investigation of the question ; and, in every part, committees and associations were formed, whose fixed resolution it was, that they would wage interminable war against a system which they justly deemed disgraceful to their country, and an outrage upon Christianity. Happily, this great question, after a long and arduous struggle, has been terminated (as far as Great Britain is concerned) in a manner equally consonant with Justice and Humanity. But those who ventured, at the time to which we now refer, to declare themselves the determined supporters of Abolition, had to incur no small degree of obloquy. Among these early champions Mr. Burgess may justly be numbered. While the question was yet fresh, and the prejudices stirred up in opposition to its calm discussion were hot and powerful, he published, in the year 1789, a treatise entitled "Considerations on the Abolition of Slavery and the Slave Trade, upon grounds of natural, religious, and political Duty." It is a powerful and eloquent exposure of the futility of the arguments advanced in support, not merely of West Indian slavery, but of slavery itself. It explains, in a clear and satisfactory manner, its inconsistency with the principles of Christianity; it proves in what a mitigated form it existed among the Romans; it touches in forcible terms upon the fatal consequences of the slave trade to the progress of civilisation in Africa, and among her swarthy sons in the West

K

Indies ; it describes in glowing language the genius
of the British constitution, and the claims which the
negroes have to a share in its paternal influence,
and it anticipates, with certain and assured hope,
the final triumph of the cause of emancipation, in
spite of every opposing effort and influence.

It is remarkable that his proposition, in the year
1789, was exactly accordant with the measure finally
adopted by the British Parliament. He argues in
his treatise, not for immediate emancipation, but for
an Act of the Legislature which should prohibit all
further importation of slaves into the British islands
from the coast of Africa ; and which should abolish
slavery itself after a limited period : and he proposes to prepare, in the mean time, for this final
measure, by the Christian instruction of the Black
population.

One passage, and one only, shall be adduced as
a specimen of the style in which the work was
written.

" There are those who think it is in vain to oppose the established practice of slavery and of the
slave trade, by reasons derived from morality and
religion , that all complaints of cruelty and oppression will avail nothing against the pleas of commercial and national interest.

" And can any thing be really and ultimately
useful to England, which is inconsistent with her
political constitution ? to Christians, which offends
against the very genius and spirit of their religion ?
or to men, which violates the first duties of human
nature ? It is impossible to believe (however industriously the doctrine has been circulated) that
such sentiments can be general, and we ought to

have much better hopes of the deliberate judgment of a whole people. If, indeed, the event of the question were left to a body of slave merchants, some apprehension might reasonably be formed about the issue. But the cause of slavery and the slave trade is no longer a subject of mere private speculation. This cause of human nature is brought before the tribunal of that nation, which has always been celebrated for its mercy; the cause of liberty is submitted to the arbitration of that country, whose freedom and happiness are founded on the general rights of mankind. And we cannot doubt that the great principles of political justice, which form the basis of our constitution, and which ought to come home to the breast of every British subject, will have their full weight in the deliberations of those august assemblies, which are to decide on a cause that involves the purity of our holy religion, and the credit and consistency of our national character."

Coming from an individual of such learning and character as Mr. Burgess, this publication proved both seasonable and influential; and a vote of thanks for it, as such, was soon after passed by the London Abolition Committee, and transmitted to him by the late Bennet Langton, Esq.

TO C. BURNEY, ESQ.

Dear Sir,

I have at last sent you the long talked of Photius. I shall be obliged to you if you will be so good as to take as early an opportunity as you conveniently can to lodge it safe in Porson's hands.

I have lately received a letter from Villoison with

K 2

an offer of Observations on Hippocrates, by Mr. Corai, a native of Smyrna, with an assurance on the part of Villoison, that they will be *l'ornement du recueil*, &c.

You will do me the favour to accept the inclosed copy of my pamphlet on Slavery. If Elmsley has already sent you a copy, you will oblige me by sending this with my compliments to Dr. Burney.

I am, dear Sir, &c. &c.

T. BURGESS.

C. C. C., May 10 1789.

TO THE REV. MR. BURGESS.

DEAR SIR,

THE Photius arrived safely, and I directly wrote you ten words to say so. What can have become of the letter? Do the Oxford postmen play these tricks, or the Hammersmith? I hoped you would have let me see you when you were in town, as I had much to say on many subjects.

What thought you of the review of your Prospectus and Initia Hom.? Pray publish a number soon, and let not curiosity be deadened by long delay.

You will see the opening of my critique on Glasse in the next review. I know not how he will like it — or Parr — or yourself; but I trust myself to the candour of you all. If I am wrong, correct me, and I will publish the corrections in the next article: if I am rude or pert, scout the whole as unworthy of notice: if I am right — why, you will know how to act, without my venturing to say a word.

My *troops* are just dispersing, so that I am just now more than usually hurried. One of my young

men, who is a tolerably decent scholar, is intended
for Oxford, and I am extremely solicitous to have
him placed at *Corpus,* in order that he may benefit
by your lectures, and watchful eye. Can you give
an idea of what chance he would have of getting
a scholarship, and what likelihood there would
ultimately be of his arriving at a fellowship? The
young man has talents and industry, but requires
rather a tight rein.

Many thanks for your treatise on the slave trade;
which I consider to be a strong proof of the mental
powers and diligence of its author. Did I not, in
my last, send you my father's best thanks for *his*
copy? How does Plutarch go on?

Your faithful and obliged friend,

C. BURNEY.

June 15 1789.

TO C. BURNEY, ESQ.

DEAR SIR,   C. C. C., June 19 1789

YOUR partiality to Corpus I consider very flattering, and I beg you to accept my particular acknow-
ledgements. I should be very happy to see any
friend of yours a member of Corpus, and wish
that there may be an early opportunity for his
offering himself as candidate for a scholarship.
Every scholarship is filled up from particular counties, and always from the county of the person who
was last made fellow, whose succession to a fellowship makes the vacancy among the scholars. I do
not foresee any probable vacancy for the next year
and a half: the senior scholar, however, is a Kentish
man, and of course the vacancy will be filled up
from Kent. From these particulars you will judge

K 3

of the first circumstance of eligibility in your young friend. The number of *independent* members is limited by statute to six : and that number is at present full.

I am glad to hear that the opening of your critique on Glasse is to be in the next Review. I anticipate from the review of Monostrophica much amusement and instruction ; from the review of Glasse I cannot anticipate any possible room for displeasure. Were I the author of the work, I think, at least I hope, that I should not be offended by the correction of errors *committed ,* much less do I expect to be displeased with the enumeration of errors *overlooked.** And I have no doubt, from the fairness of your review of the Monostrophica, that Glasse will see enough to compensate for the exactness of your criticism.

If I did not tell you before, I certainly have had the impression on my mind of having told you, that nothing could be more satisfactory to me than the review of my Conspectus in the Monthly Appendix , both from the private satisfaction of having your opinion of my undertaking, and the additional pleasure of seeing the objects of that undertaking so advantageously reported to the public. I was not less pleased with the notice which was taken of those circumstances in the contents of the *Initia Homerica†* on which it was always my wish the reader should lay most stress. When I read the review, I confess I did not think of you. I am persuaded

* Alluding to the friendly part he had himself acted, at Mr. Glasse's request, of critically examining his translation.

† A new edition of this valuable work was published at Glasgow in 1820.

you will not think I mean to flatter you, when I add that your experience in education, and knowledge of the Greek language, render the opinion of the Initia Homerica expressed in the review very valuable to me.

I am sorry that you have not had a copy of my pamphlet on the slave trade. It was my wish that Elmsley should send you one immmediately after its publication. If you will take the trouble to send for a copy in my name, you will do me a favour in accepting it. I am proud that it has met with Dr. Burney's and your approbation. I hope to send you the first number of the Critical Observations in the course of Michaelmas term. All arrangements about Plutarch are settled much to Wyttenbach's satisfaction : but his papers will not be in the hands of our delegates these twelve months.

I am, dear Sir,
Your faithful and obliged friend,
T. BURGESS.

My compliments to Porson when you see him. *

TO THE REV. T. BURGESS.

DEAR SIR, Dec 20. 1789.

I BEG leave to thank you for the letter with which I have been this day honoured, and to assure you that I shall receive with pleasure, and read with the

---

* In a letter from Bennet Langton, Esq. to Mr Burney, Dec. 1789, he says, —

" I had the good fortune, when I arrived here (which I did yesterday se'nnight), to find that Mr. Porson was upon a visit to Oxford, and have been favoured on two days with some of his conversation. On the last occasion, Mr. Burgess was of our party "

K 4

greatest attention, the conjectures of your learned
friend Corai. True it is that I am tolerably well
versed in Hippocrates. Bentley is said to have
possessed an ample store of verbal corrections of
this author, and to have been ambitious in conversation of displaying his fondness for Hippocrates.
But I know not where they are deposited. I have
often been surprised in the course of my philological
inquiries at the little notice which is taken of this
writer. But I dare say that you will agree with me
in commending and even admiring the emendations
which are scattered in Heringa's Observationes
Criticæ.

Towards the end of Hare's strictures upon Bentley
there are some observations which Dawes had probably read, and which explain the Ictus Rhythmicus
in its principles, so as to illustrate Dawes's hypothesis. But of this you will judge. I never read
the close of the letter to Bland without laughing at
the solemnity and the virulence of the whole
metrical tribe. I rejoice at the intelligence you
send me about the publication of Valckenaer, and I
am very much obliged to you for being permitted
to peruse the precious MS.

How does Santin go on with his T. Maurus? I
rallied Burney about his *former* intention of publishing T. M., and gave him a long catalogue of
reasons for my incredulity. He replied, that his
intentions were so vague and so loose that he never
thought it worth while to mention them to me. But I
goaded him to think seriously, and to resolve firmly
about the business, *in future*. I tell you in confidence, and in great, very great confidence, that
something will be done, and I beg of you never to
open your lips upon the subject till I have a right

to speak more plainly ; and, alas ! I have now spoken enigmatically enough.

I have lately been much pleased with Verheyk's notes upon Antons. What does Porson say to you about his Æschylus ? He is busy in chastising the advocates of a disputed text in St. John. I have urged him to publish a just pamphlet, and put an end to the controversy. In your book upon the slave trade I saw good sense, good writing, and good intention. But I remain unconvinced. What signifies writing, when Mr. Pitt can speak on one side and act on the other ? So it was in the reform of Parliament ; and when the test subject comes on, he will speak for the church, but propitiate the dissenters by losing the question in the House of Commons. I hate these virtuous, honourable men. Will the bishops do nothing except voting ?

Have you seen my friend Wakefield's Sylva Critica ? He is a greater heretic in metre than in theology. But I admire his book much, and I love it yet more, for it is the exact picture of his mind.

I am, dear Sir,

Yours very respectfully and truly,

S. PARR.

TO THE REV. DR. PARR.

DEAR SIR, January, 1790

MANY thanks for your obliging letter. The additions to Fletcher's Miscellanea Metrica which you were so good as to suggest, I have mentioned to him, and he is glad to find that his intended publication does not meet with your disapprobation. Heath's introductory pages, and Dawes's metrical canons, shall certainly be added. I could wish to add Brunck's metrical observations, as well as

Dorville's, Markland's, &c., if I did not think that
I shall be able to execute that part of the publication more advantageously another time, should
a second edition be called for. I shall make it a
lecture book, which will afford me opportunities of
reading it frequently and diligently.

The intelligence which you sent me respecting
Emmanuel College and Fair Lawn House gave me
great pleasure. I rejoice that Burney has renewed
his connection with Cambridge, and that he is engaged to publish Terentianus Maurus.

The conclusion of your letter reminds me of
some conversation we had at Oxford on the subject
of the Test Act. You say, " Will the Bishops do
any thing besides vote ? " Perhaps they will : perhaps they are now doing something : though I do
not know that they are, nor have I any authority
to support it. I remember you thought that the
avowed countenance of the Bishops was necessary
on this occasion. But why should you wait for the
countenance of any men of any rank ? Your talents
require no exterior assistance to give efficacy to
your language or argumentation. You have the
means of rendering incalculable service, not merely
to the Church, but to your country, on this occasion, if you do not leave those means unexerted,
because they are not solicited. Excuse my freedom. I speak as I feel : and my feelings are excited by sincere respect for you, and by the interest
which every friend to the present form of government, as well as every Churchman, must take in
the present question. Compliments to Mr. Smelt.

I am, dear Sir, yours, respectfully,

T. BURGESS.

CHAP. XI.

FROM the moment that Mr. Burgess took orders, his attention was directed in a serious and compre- hensive manner to theological pursuits. That he might be able to consult the Old Testament in the original, he was assiduous in the study of Hebrew, while his intimate acquaintance with the Greek language gave him every advantage that learning can impart for the critical investigation of the New. He also commenced, about this time, a perusal of some of the principal Greek and Latin fathers; and he soon after applied his studies in this line to a useful purpose, by addressing an able letter to the Monthly Review, in refutation of a charge which they had made against the orthodoxy of the Anti- nicene Fathers with respect to the doctrine of the Trinity. In the year 1790, the first sermon which he published, issued from the Clarendon Press. It was preached before the University, and, as the subject was highly interesting, and the mode of treating it original, we shall be excused for dwell- ing upon it a little in detail. It was entitled "The Divinity of Christ, proved from his own Declarations, attested and interpreted by his living Witnesses the Jews." Respecting the great doc- trine of which it treated, it may truly be said, in the language of his preface, "that there is the best evidence for asserting that it has always been be- lieved in all ages of the church, and the best

grounds for maintaining that it will so continue to be
believed by infinitely the greater part of those who
study the Scriptures seriously and without prejudice." The evidence of its truth is cumulative ;
that is, it consists of a series of direct, and of
many collateral proofs. The sermon of Mr. Burgess
was confined to a particular class of those proofs,
which, though occasionally glanced at by preceding
writers, had not been hitherto placed in a light
so striking, or in a form so original. The following statement will illustrate his ground of argument : — On various occasions our Saviour uses
language respecting his own nature and attributes,
which, interpreted according to the acknowledged
and established rules of criticism, amounts to nothing less than the assertion of his Divinity, and of
his equality with the Father. If any doubt could be
entertained whether his words are to be interpreted
in this their plain and obvious sense, that doubt is
removed by the testimony of his Jewish hearers,
who, being familiar with the same customs as himself, intimately conversant with their own native
phraseology and idiom, in which he addressed them,
and fully alive to all the circumstances of time,
place, and occasion, were much better judges of the
sense which his words conveyed, than even the
most learned and critical scholars of modern times.
Now their words and their conduct furnish, on the
occasions alluded to, convincing proof that they
understood him in this high and peculiar sense ;
for they are not only represented as stirred up to
the greatest pitch of indignation, at the supposed
blasphemy of the claim, but as attempting to inflict
upon him, in consequence, the summary punishment

directed by the law of Moses against offenders guilty
of this crime. (Vid. Lev. xxiv. 14. 16.)

On one of the occasions referred to (John viii
57—59., compared with Exodus iii. 14.), He declares his pre-existence in language which implied
an assumption of the name and prerogative of
Jehovah, which so incensed his hearers, that they
instantly took up stones to cast at him.

On another occasion, it is declared that the Jews
sought to kill him, because he claimed to be the Son
of God in a sense *, which, to use the words of the
Evangelist, was "making himself equal with God."
John v. 18. 23.

On a third, when he remonstrates with them
for being about to stone him, they justify their
rage by replying, " For a good work we stone thee
not, but for blasphemy: and because that thou,
being a man, makest thyself God." (John x. 33.)
And in this latter instance, although in the ex-
ordium of his reply, He parried for a moment
their anger by a certain degree of ambiguity in the
comment he gave upon his own previous words
(John x. 36.), yet that anger revives in all its force
when he closes by re-asserting his claim to be the
Son of God in such a sense, as that the Father was
"in Him, and He in the Father." (ver. 38.)

On none of these occasions does Jesus contradict
their inferences, which, in his zeal for the honour
due only to God, he certainly would have done,
had they mistaken his meaning.

But the most remarkable of these examples is

---

* The force of the original is lost in our English version, by
the omission of the word ἰδιον, that is, *own* or *peculiar* (his own
Father).

connected with the closing scenes of our Saviour's
life; for it appears, on a calm consideration of the
facts as recorded by the Evangelists, that the immediate cause of his condemnation was a solemn
attestation of his own Divinity. His enemies, it is
true, were bent upon his destruction; but, until he
himself furnished them with a pretext for com-
passing it, by a clear and express claim to that
effect, they were baffled in their attempts to adduce any plausible reason for such a sentence.

"And the chief priests and all the council (says
St. Mark) sought for witness against Jesus to put
him to death; and found none. For many bare
false witness against him, but their witness agreed
not together." (Mark xiv. 55, 56.)

Finally, after other vain attempts, it is added:
"And the high priest stood up in the midst, and
asked Jesus, saying, Answerest thou nothing?
what is it which these witness against thee? But
he held his peace, and answered nothing. Again
the high priest asked him, and said unto him, Art
thou the Christ, the Son of the Blessed? And
Jesus said, I am: and ye shall see the Son of man
sitting on the right hand of power, and coming in
the clouds of heaven. Then the high priest rent
his clothes, and saith. What need we any further
witnesses? Ye have heard the blasphemy: what
think ye? And they all condemned him to be
guilty of death." (Mark xiv. 60—64.)

St. John, in like manner, testifies to the real
ground of his condemnation in the following words
addressed to Pilate by his Jewish accusers: "We
have a Law, and by our LAW he ought to die,
because he made himself the Son of God." (John
xix. 7.)

That Christ applied to himself the terms " Son of the Blessed," and " Son of God," in that high and peculiar sense which involved the claim of Divinity, is therefore equally clear from their language, and from his own undisguised admission.

This sermon contained a series of admirable remarks upon the intimate connection between sound and scriptural views of doctrine and the virtues of a Christian life.

In the year 1797, the Rev W. Wilson, Fellow of St. John's College, Cambridge, published a learned and able work, intitled " An Illustration of the Method of explaining the New Testament by the early Opinions of Jews and Christians concerning Christ." In its most important parts it pursued a line of argument and illustration closely accordant with that which we have just particularised ; but as Mr. Wilson had neither read nor heard of the sermon of Burgess, he took credit to himself for being the first person who had placed the argument derived from the Jewish testimonies concerning Christ in a prominent light. Meeting subsequently with that sermon, he at once saw that to it, and not to his own work, belonged the claim of originality ; and therefore, in a spirit of candour and equity, he addressed the following letter to its author, which, though it is here introduced out of date, belongs to this branch of my subject.

St. John's College,
Cambridge, July 17 1798

Sir,

I HAVE directed to you by the mail coach, a copy of a very imperfect book, which I ventured to publish about a year since under the title of " An

Illustration of the Method of explaining the New Testament by the early Opinions of Jews and Christians concerning Christ." My only reason for taking such a liberty, and for troubling you with this letter, is, to apologise for a sentence at the bottom of the 122d page, which I am convinced, after reading your sermon on the same subject, is a very improper one

Though I was by no means unacquainted with some parts of your writings, I had not seen the title of your sermon till after the middle of the last month, and I have not had an opportunity of seeing and reading the sermon itself before yesterday. Not being aware that any of our Saviour's doctrines had been regularly and fully ascertained, or confirmed by his words *as interpreted by his Jewish hearers*, I had rather pleased myself with thinking that both the design and execution of my work had novelty as well as truth to recommend them I find, however, much of the reasoning of my first six chapters in your sermon; and, though not mortified at discovering my want of originality, I am exceedingly concerned at having published a passage, in which I may appear to think slightly of your work, to which, had I known of it, I should most certainly have appealed with pleasure and pride, in support of some of the principal opinions which I have advanced

I am, Sir, with great respect,
Your obedient servant,
W. WILSON.

The reply of Mr. Burgess was as follows: —

Sir,

The obliging present of your book reached Durham a few days after your letter. I should have written earlier to thank you for both, if I had not been prevented from reading your very learned work till lately. Single sermons engage so small a share of the public attention, that no apology was necessary for overlooking that of which you speak so kindly. I should certainly have been much pleased to have seen my endeavours to interpret our Saviour's testimony of Himself by the opinions of the Jews, who lived at the same time with him, noticed in your book. But I am much gratified by finding this first, and, as I conceive, most important but neglected branch of the historical evidence of Christ's Divinity so largely and decisively confirmed by you.

I am, Sir, very respectfully,

Your obedient servant,

T. Burgess.

What the impressions of the public and of learned contemporaries were of this Sermon, will appear from the following letters: —

Dear Burgess,   Mongewell, June 29 1790

Your argument, on a second attentive perusal of your sermon, strikes me with its original force. On considering it in every point of view I can discover no weak part. You are armed at all points, and invulnerable; though you must not suppose that an attempt will not soon be made by Dr. Priestley to convince the world to the contrary.

L

If Dr. Price has any real candour belonging to his nature, he will be inclined to re-examine the foundation of his own opinions relative to the appellation of " Son of God," and about the strength of your reasoning.

I am, with true regard,

Your sincere friend and brother,

S. SARUM.

The succeeding letter is from the Reverend G. Huntingford, then Warden of Winchester College, and afterwards, successively, Bishop of Gloucester and Hereford. He was about eight years the senior of Mr. Burgess. Their acquaintance ripened from this time, under the influence of mutual esteem, into warm and affectionate friendship.

Dr. Huntingford united superior learning to eminence in Christian piety. His amiable and cheerful countenance was the index to a guileless heart. He diffused comfort and happiness around him by his social and domestic virtues; and the sphere which felt the influence of his truly Christian benevolence was not less illumined by the instruction, vivacity, and anecdote which marked his conversation. He died at Winchester College in 1832.

TO THE REV. MR. BURGESS.

MY DEAR SIR,

A DISCOURSE on subjects at all times most important, and in the present age most universally examined, must be acceptable to every reader who knows only your name. To me it is doubly va-

luable, as I am well acquainted with that simplicity
and sincerity of heart from whence the thoughts
proceeded. I have, indeed, thought long, seriously,
conscientiously, anxiously, on the great doctrines
of our religion. I have explored, too, the dark
and boundless abyss of infidelity. I have stood on
the slippery and unbalanced ground of scepticism.
I have perilously faced all dangers of the most
free inquiry, insomuch that I believe few have
searched more diligently for truth, and I trust none
will hold it more tenaciously now it is found, than
myself. What I mean by truth, is the Gospel religion. In the government of the universe, and
more particularly in the scheme of man's redemption, I discover One Divine Power, Μιαν Θεοτητα,
participated from Eternity by Three Eternally Divine Minds, inseparably united in one consciousness. This proposition appears to me perfectly
intelligible, and seems to comprise the whole of
what need be laid down as the first and grand article of Christianity. Were I called upon for my
second proposition, I would distinguish it by Αυτο-
Θεος, Θεος εκ Θεου, Πνευμα εκπορευομενον.*

These would be followed by Θεος εκ Θεου εφανε-
ρωθη εν σαρκι, εδικαιωθη εν πνευματι, ωφθη αγγε-
λοις, εκηρυχθη εν εθνεσιν, επιστευθη εν κοσμω, ανε-
ληφθη εν δοξη. †

According to these leading and indispensable
principles of my religion, I could never join in communion with a Socinian nor with any Arian who

* God, God of God, the Proceeding Spirit.
† God of God was manifested in the flesh, justified in the
spirit, seen of angels, preached unto the Gentiles, believed on
in the world, received up into glory. — Vid 1 Tim. iii. 16.

denied the Eternal Pre-existence of Christ. With you, therefore, I see the absolute necessity of excluding Socinians from our Establishment; to effect which our Establishment must be guarded in its chief points ; and a considerable defence is provided for its security by the Test Laws. Still, however, I think our Articles may be more simplified; and some parts of our Liturgy, intelligible enough to thinking men, but dark to the generality, might be so framed as to admit more into the congregations of our Church, though not into the ministry. Yet, should you ask me how and when this work might commence, and whether unanimity would probably be found in the very persons who should begin it, I am afraid I should be forced to say, Αλλοι μεν αλλο τι εκραζον· ην γαρ η εκκλησια συγκεχυμενη * in the last century, and perhaps the same would happen in this.

You have rested the Divinity of our Saviour on most sure grounds, the testimony of the Jews themselves, by an interpretation of words explicit and unequivocal The merit of your Discourse and weight of your argument are not the less, whether the same testimony has or has not been adduced on the same account by preceding writers. Perhaps in so prominent a manner, it has not stood foremost. In a general way, all writers notice it. You will do infinite service at Oxford, by bringing the argument forward in so strong and striking a light ; and your Strictures on Priestley and Price will put young men on their guard against such pestiferous empirics in theology

* Some cried one thing, and some another for the assembly was divided.

I have to lament that my situation has hitherto left me no leisure for reading or writing, except when with Mr. Vivian, my pupil. The secular employments of my office call for much attention; and I feel it my duty to discharge every function to the best of my abilities. Still, however, I have the mind of one " multa et præclara minantis." Stobæus is always before my eyes, and often in my thoughts, and I wish you to inform me whether you think labours might usefully be employed on his Fragments? and whether that ground be still unoccupied? This I ask in confidence and secresy; for I should not choose to stand pledged for any publication, nor to have mentioned, for many years, what, after all, might never be accomplished. In the intercourse of public life, " pendent opera interrupta." If you should be of opinion that a new edition might be acceptable, I should take pleasure in a work of such variety of matter and diversity of style, and should expatiate on subjects which pleased my fancy.

When you can find leisure, favour me with a letter, and add the time when you think to be at Salisbury.   I am,

Your ever affectionate friend,

G. I. HUNTINGFORD.

Winton College, June 11. 1790.

The concluding passage of the following letter from Dr. Parr is curious, as an anticipation of what Porson afterwards effected in his letters to Travis, though with little idea of the prominent part which Burgess was in after days to take in the question alluded to : —

DEAR SIR,

YESTERDAY I was favoured with your letter, which reached me about the time that the post sets off from Warwick; of course, I could send no answer before to-day.

I desired Mr. Paradise to thank you for the honour you did me in sending me your sermon, which, from my respect for the writer, and my serious attention to his subject, I had before purchased. The composition is masterly, and many of the observations are highly interesting.

What tidings have you of Lennep? I wish we could prevail upon Porson to collect and fairly state the evidence pro and con relating to the two disputed texts, and in his luminous way to subjoin his own opinions. Perhaps I wish for that which, in your very orthodox University, would be thought indecorous, when I say, that the learned world would be obliged to any scholar for republishing what has been written on them by Emlyn, Martin, Newton, Mills, Bengelius, Wetstein, Benson, and Griesbach. I have the honour to be, dear Sir,

Your very respectful and obedient

SAMUEL PARR.

TO THE REV. G. HUNTINGFORD.

DEAR SIR,

MANY thanks for your obliging letter. The approbation you are so good as to bestow on my sermon has given me much real pleasure. The ground of argument which I chose in proof of our Lord's Divinity, I am glad you think with me is sure ground. In the midst of difficulties and embarrassments on the subject of our religion, I have always found it sufficient to fix me. If I had any satisfaction in the composition of the sermon, on the mere score of writing, it was in bringing forward an argument, which, though not unnoticed, seemed not to have been made enough of, that is, not to have been exhibited as a leading and fundamental proof of our Lord's Divinity.

I rejoice to hear that you have been thinking seriously of Stobæus The ground is not, indeed, unoccupied. Mr. Heeren, a German, is employed in the Ecloga Physica, and Mr. Schow, a Dane, on the Ecloga Ethica. But so little has been done to Stobæus, that there is room for employment in every species of criticism and illustration. My information respecting Mr. Heeren and Mr. Schow, I owe to the following paragraph in a letter which I received last January from Mr. Heyné; "a nostro Heeren, (cujus Menandrum Rhetorum sub- tili criticâ expolitum, meministi,) futuro anno excu- detur nova recensio Eclogarum Physicarum multis modis plenior, e codd Italicis et Escurialensi. Ec- logæ autem Ethicæ, ab alio meæ disciplinæ alumno, qui nunc Romæ degit Schow, Dano, curantur simili modo."

If you are in Winchester in about a fortnight's time, I shall have the pleasure of calling on you, and shall be happy to meet you in good health.

I am, dear Sir,

Your sincere friend,

T. BURGESS.

C. C. C , July 25. 1790.

TO THE REV. G. HUNTINGFORD.

My dear Friend,

I have many thanks to return you for your last letter, and for what I have since seen on the subject of my Reflections. As I greatly value your good opinion, I have a sincere satisfaction in knowing to whom I owe so favourable a representation of them. I can make every allowance, for the different points of view in which believers and unbelievers see the same article of faith; but such allowance gives neither truth nor probability to opinions which every page in the Gospels convinces me are untrue. I can make every allowance, without being able to alter my persuasion that they who deny the truths of the Gospel, and reject the faith which Christ has enjoined, are not Christians. An unbeliever may sincerely hold the opinion which he avows, but his sincerity can never make that true which is false, nor relax the meaning of our Saviour's denunciation against unbelief.

I have well weighed in my own mind the difficulties which you start; and the more I think on the subject, the more and more I am convinced of the necessity of marking, as fully and plainly as possible, the limits which separate what we believe to be true, because revealed, from what we believe to be untrue; and what we believe to be Christianity, from what we believe is not Christianity. Without a full and decided perception of such limits, I think we cannot contend earnestly for the faith. If belief in the Divinity of Christ be necessary to our salvation, as Christians; which, as a believer in

Revelation, I cannot doubt; to deny that faith, must (I have as little doubt) exclude unbelievers from the benefits of Christianity. Therefore, what even the Racovian Catechism pronounces of those who do not worship Christ, I think myself bound to apply also, though the Socinian Catechists do not, to those who deny the Divinity of Christ.

I have read, with much pleasure, your letter to the students of Hackney. I wish they may have minds well enough disposed to profit by it. I am printing a new edition of my sermon, which I hope to send you soon.

I am, dear Sir,

Your affectionate friend,

T. Burgess.

C. C. C., 1790.

In the course of the same year he followed up the subject of his first sermon by another, the object of which he thus describes in a letter to Dr. Parr : —

" I am at present employed in preparing an Ordination Sermon for next Sunday, which occupies all my leisure. My subject is ' the distribution of the gifts of the Holy Ghost at the first establishment of the Christian Church,' and by way of introduction to the main subject, ' Scriptural proofs of the Personality of the Holy Ghost distinct from the Father.' "

CHAP. XII.

CHARACTER OF MR. CORAI. — MR. BURKE'S WORK ON THE
FRENCH REVOLUTION. — PROPOSAL OF CONFERRING THE
DEGREE OF LL.D. ON HIM BY THE UNIVERSITY OF OXFORD
FRUSTRATED. — LETTERS ON THE SUBJECT.

1788 to 1790.

AMONG the foreign correspondents of Mr. Burgess
in 1788, and for several successive years, was a
young Greek, a native of Smyrna, of the name of
Corai. He was introduced to his notice by Villoison, to whose generous exertions he had already
been much indebted, and who hoped that some
appointment, suited to a man of learning, might be
procured for him in England. He had been educated as a physician, and was passionately fond of
Greek literature. The works of Hippocrates had
engaged his particular attention, and he had prepared a mass of critical materials with a view to a
new edition of his works; on which, however, his
want of pecuniary means forbade him to venture.
The literary ardour of this young man comes into
touching contrast with his poverty in the course of
his correspondence with Mr. Burgess, who did his
best to bring him into notice, by publishing, in the
second Fasciculus of the Museum Oxoniense (a work
of which we shall hereafter have to speak), a specimen of his learned lucubrations. There is a passage in one of Villoison's letters, by which it seems
that the University of Oxford had manifested a
disposition to print the whole of them; but if so,

the intention was abandoned. This letter is so amusing a specimen of the levity with which this sprightly French scholar treats the formidable dif ficulties of emendatory criticism, that we cannot forbear inserting it : —

`A Paris, 13 Mars, 1791

Monsieur et cher Ami,

Je profite avec bien d'empressement du premier moment que j'ai de libre pour vous témoigner ma vive et éternelle reconnoissance du service important que vous avez rendu à la littérature Grecque, à l'Antiquité, à la Médecine, à moi, Monsieur, et à M. Corai, en déterminant l'Université d'Oxford à se charger de l'impression de son ouvrage immortel. Vous en serez étonné quand vous le verrez, et vous conviendrez qu'il n'y a point de livre de critique qui renferme tant de découvertes. Il a restitué Hippocrate d'un bout à l'autre, et chemin faisant, il corrige une foule de passages d'Hérodote, d'Athénée, Platon, Sophocle, Aristophane, Hésychius, &c. Il me montre son travail à mesure qu'il avance, et mon admiration va toujours en croissant. Son premier volume sera prêt et livré à l'impression dans dix mois. Dieu veuille seulement conserver des jours si précieux aux lettres ! Sa santé est très-foible, et la position précaire où il se trouve, la pauvreté où il est réduit, ses inquiétudes sur l'avenir, aggravent ses infirmités. De revers ont fait perdre à cet homme vertueux une fortune considérable, dont jouissoient ses parens qui étoient les plus forts négocians de Smyrne. Je vous prie en grâce d'insérer dans vos deux premiers cahiers de vos "Observationes Miscellaneæ Criticæ" toutes les

observations qu'il vous a envoyées, afin d'annoncer
son ouvrage à l'Europe savante.

Marquez-moi donc, mon ami, quand paroîtra la
nouvelle édition, en 8vo, des Marbres d'Arundel.
Le Strabon d'Oxford avance-t-il ?   Y a-t-il d'autres
nouvelles littéraires ?

Aimez toujours votre meilleur Ami,

D'ANNSE DE VILLOISON.

Meetings frequently took place between Mr.
Porson and Mr. Burgess, both at his own lodgings
in London, and at the house of Dr. Burney.   He
always spoke with admiration of the singular acuteness of Porson's mind, as well as of his great learning.   He described his conversation as turning
much upon points of Greek criticism, and abounding in curious anecdotes.   Being one day questioned
respecting Dr. Parr, after he had been dilating
in this manner upon Porson, he gave the following
sketch of him. — " Parr's forte was a wonderful
memory.   His conversational dexterity far exceeded
his powers as a writer.   His composition was
pompous and verbose ; but his table-talk at the
house of such men as Dr. Routh, where I used to
meet him, was very agreeable.   As for his Latinity,
it is a mosaic, composed of sentences from the Latin
classics, curiously but incongruously assorted.   He
had little or nothing of Porson's surprising skill in
conjectural criticism, the result of profound learning and a sort of wonderful intuition, by means of
which he corrected or restored so many corrupt
readings in Greek authors." *

* The skirmishes of these literary Goliaths are naturally
matter of curiosity and amusement to ordinary scholars. Parr

In the year 1790, when the public mind in England was agitated by fierce and conflicting opinions upon the moral and political tendencies of the new order of things in France, Mr Burke, no less a philosopher than a statesman of the highest order, published his celebrated work, entitled, " Reflections on the French Revolution," &c. in which he not only exposed, with masterly skill, the

---

was always submissive in the presence of Porson, and did homage to his immeasurable superiority, but he lorded it in his turn over others with the mixture of good-natured vanity and insolence which were natural to him. I have found among the Bishop's papers a curious instance of his style of dealing with an antagonist, in the following particulars of a rencontre between him and a very eminent critic, the late Bishop Marsh, then Margaret Professor at Cambridge. It took place in the Combination Room of Trinity College, where Parr, Marsh, Mr. Jones, one of the college tutors, and others, were seated at the head of a table. Dr Parr, who had been talking of Sir William Jones, mentioned the epitaph on his monument in University College, Oxford, and, addressing himself to one of the company, inquired what he thought of the word " florruisset," which, he said, was in the inscription. Dr Marsh now broke forth. " I do not like it. Had it been floret, he does flourish, or floruit, he has flourished; or florebit, he will flourish, it might have done very well, but floruisset never can be right." By a wink from Mr Jones some of the party were now apprised that Parr himself was the author of the epitaph. He could bear no more, but, with a sort of good-humoured indignation, exclaimed, — " I'll tell you what, Marsh, you have thought proper, in the most rampant, audacious, and obtrusive manner to give your opinion. I will bet you a rump and dozen that it should not be floret, and another rump and dozen that it should not be floruit, and another that it should not be florebit, and another that it should be floruisset, and these gentlemen shall decide." Marsh was evidently discomposed, for many persons had gathered round them.

———— Now dreadful deeds
Might have ensued ;

but one of the party, by an ingenious turn in the conversation, contrived to avert the gathering storm.

levelling and destructive character of Jacobinism, but did noble justice to the principles of rational liberty as exemplified in the British constitution.

The benefits resulting to his country from this timely interposition were eminently great, and an earnest wish was excited, in consequence, among the resident Graduates of Oxford to give appropriate expression to their gratitude by conferring on Mr. Burke academical honours. Mr. Burgess was among the foremost in furthering this proposition, and the course which the affair took is fully explained in the following letter, addressed by him to the Bishop of Salisbury : —

MY LORD.   C. C. C, December 7. 1790.

My pamphlet I reserve till you arrive at Mongewell. Your account at Fletcher's I will take care of. I have inclosed the title-page of a publication, which I have suggested to Nichols, and which he has very readily undertaken to print. I think it will be an useful introduction to St. Paul's Epistles.

Mr. Burke's book, as you may imagine, has been much the subject of admiration in this place. It is become, indeed, a very general wish of the resident Members of Convocation, that a diploma degree might be conferred on him, in return for the services which his book is likely to render, by the admirable representation which it contains of the true principles of our constitution, ecclesiastical and civil. I cannot represent this wish as universal, and, indeed, I am sorry to add, that it is not the wish of some respectable persons in high stations of the University. It was suggested to the Vice Chancellor, about three weeks ago, under the sanction of one of the

Heads of Houses. Ten days elapsed without any progress in the business, and as the term was hastening towards a conclusion, the Vice Chancellor was consulted whether it would be considered by him and the other Heads as disrespectful, if the Masters were to express their wishes by requesting him to propose it to the board ; which would enable him, at the same time, to judge how far it was the general sense of the resident members. The Vice Chancellor said he saw no impropriety in the proposal. Accordingly, an address to him, to the above effect, has been signed by forty-nine Members of Convocation. The address will be presented to-morrow. Forty-nine are, I believe, full half of the resident members, who answer for themselves and their friends. We count upon full eighty Members of Convocation who are decidedly for the degree. There are, however, some doubts whether the meeting in Golgotha will defer to the general sense of the Masters. It certainly will not be the first time they have obstructed the wishes of the University.

As to absolute unanimity, Mr Burke, as a public character, cannot reasonably expect it ; but if this could be deemed a sufficient objection to the intended compliment, a few disaffected or self-willed persons might at any time obstruct the best measures of the place. I have troubled you with these particulars, because, as I had my share in promoting the application for the proper degree, I thought it due to your Lordship.

I am, my Lord,

Your Lordship's dutiful and

obedient servant,

T. BURGESS.

P S. — I have delayed my letter for the sake of stating the result of to-day's meeting. The Heads have met, and decided against the degree.*

* The following was the address alluded to in the preceding letter, and presented to the Vice Chancellor : —

We, the undersigned, beg leave respectfully to suggest to the Vice-Chancellor, that we believe it to be a very general wish of the Members of Convocation, that the degree of LL. D. by diploma might be conferred on the Right Honourable Edmund Burke, in consideration of his very able representation of the true principles of our constitution, ecclesiastical and civil, in his late publication, entitled, " Reflections on the Revolution in France, and on the Proceedings in certain Societies in London relative to that Event."

James Adams, M A. New C.

Henry Beeke, B D. Oriel C.

John Buckland, B D C C C

Thos Barnard, B D. C C C.

R. Baxter, M. A Jesus C.

Thos Burgess, M A. C. C C

Thos Boys, M. A. New C.

W Bryant, B D Linc. C.

W Clarke, B D Trin C.

R. Churton, M. A. Brazennose C.

Sept. Collinson, M A. Queen's C.

J Crouch, M A. St Edmund's Hall

John Davies, M. A Jesus C.

Henry Davies, M A Wadham C.

J Denison

W. Flamant, D.D Trinity C.

W Fothergill, M A Queen's C.

W Green, M A Magd. Hall.

G Griffiths, M. A Hertford C.

J. Gutch, M. A. All Souls C.

G. Harper, M A. Brazennose C.

W Holywell, B. D Exeter C.

W. Hooper, M A. Univ. C.

R Heslop, M A Univ C.

D. Hughes, D D. Jesus C.

J L Jacob, M. A. Worcester C

II. Kett, M A. Trinity C.

S Kilderbee, M A Univ C.

W. Landon, M A. Oriel C.

W Lee, M. A. New C.

J Parsons, M A Brazennose C.

R Pritchard, M A. Jesus C.

J Roberts, M A Jesus C.

W Rhodes, M A Worcester C.

Edward Stretch, M A. C C C.

J Skelton, B D C C C

C. Smith, M A New C

J Smith, M A Pembroke C

M Surtees, M A University C.

J. Tesh, B D. C. C. C

T D. Trollope, M A Wadham, C.

W Towney, M A Wadham C.

J Thompson, M A. Queen's C.

D Veysie, M. A. Oriel C.

T. Winstanley, M A Hertford C

W. Williams, M A Wadham C.

R. Wright, M. A. Brazennose C.

J. White, D. D Wadham C.

J Yeomans, M. A. Wadham C.

The decision of the Heads was not allowed to frustrate the main object of the resident Graduates.

They effected their purpose of doing honour to Mr. Burke, in the following address, from the pen, we believe, of Mr. Burgess, and transmitted by him, at their request, to Mr. Windham, to be presented by him to that gentleman : —

"WE, whose names are subscribed, resident Graduates in the University of Oxford, request you to accept this respectful declaration of our sentiments, as a tribute which we are desirous of paying to splendid talents employed in the advancement of the public good. We think it fit and becoming the friends of our Church and State to avow, openly, their obligations to those who distinguish themselves in the support of our approved establishments; and we judge it to be our especial duty to do this in times like the present, peculiarly marked by a spirit of rash and dangerous innovation.

" As members of a University whose institutions embrace every useful and ornamental part of learning, we should esteem ourselves justified in making this address, if we had only to offer you our thanks for the valuable addition which the stock of our national literature has received by the publication of your important reflections. But we have higher objects of consideration, and nobler motives to gratitude. We think that we consult the real and permanent interests of this place, when we acknowledge the eminent service rendered to our religious and civil constitution by your able and disinterested vindication of their true principles. And we obey that

M

more sacred obligation upon us, to promote the
cause of religion and morality, when we give this
proof to the world that we honour the advocate by
whom they are so effectually defended."

TO THE REV. MR. BURGESS.

DEAR SIR,

I AM sorry to have delayed, a day longer than was
necessary, the transmitting to you the inclosed letter to me, from Mr. Burke, expressive of his sense
of the approbation signified of his work, and of
the honour done him by the resident Graduates of
Oxford. By some accident, it did not come into
my hands till Saturday, after the post was gone
out.

Mr. Burke is a man to feel, on all occasions, more
what is of service to the general interests of mankind than what is personally flattering to himself;
and, in that view, thinks less, I dare say, of the
compliment you have paid him, however honourable,
than of the effect of that compliment in counteract-
ing what I must think a great reproach to the
governing power in the University. It certainly
reflects no great honour on the sincerity and purity
of their zeal, to whom the more valuable of our
establishments are, in a peculiar manner, intrusted,
that they should be slow in thanking a person who
had stepped so zealously and so ably forward in
their defence as Mr. Burke.

It gives me infinite pleasure, both as a zealous
promoter of the same general principles as Mr.
Burke, and as a member of the University of Oxford, that you have, in so great a degree, rescued its

character from this reproach, and confined the blame within its proper limits.

Let me, in conclusion, repeat my satisfaction, in having been made the medium of a communication so creditable to both parties, and, with my best compliments to all friends who may be at Oxford, I beg you to believe me,

Dear Sir,
Most truly and faithfully yours,
W. WINDHAM.

Hill Street, Dec. 29. 1790.

TO THE RIGHT HON. WILLIAM WINDHAM.

My DEAR SIR,

THE valuable tribute of approbation which I have received from so many distinguished Graduates in the University of Oxford, becomes doubly valuable by passing through your hands. Gentlemen so eminent for their erudition and virtue, and who possess the uncommon art of doing kind things in the kindest manner, would naturally select a person, qualified like themselves, to convey honours and distinctions to those whom they are inclined to favour.

Be pleased to assure those learned gentlemen that I am, beyond measure, happy in finding my well-meant endeavours favourably received by them ; and I think my satisfaction does not arise from motives merely selfish, because their declared approbation must be of the greatest assistance in giving an effect (which, without that sanction, might well be deemed wanting) to an humble attempt in favour of the cause of freedom, virtue, and order united. This

cause it is our common wish and our common interest to maintain, and it can hardly be maintained
without securing in a stable perpetuity, and pre-
serving in an uncorrupted purity, those invaluable
establishments which the wisdom of our ancestors
devised, and thus of giving permanency to those
blessings which they have bequeathed to us as our
best inheritance. We have, each of us, a common
interest in maintaining them all; but if all, excepting those who are more particularly engaged in the
conduct of those establishments, and who have a
peculiar trust in maintaining them, were wholly to
decline all marks of concurrence of opinion, it might
give occasion to malicious people to suggest doubts
whether the representation I had given was really
expressive of the sentiments of the people on those
subjects. I am obliged to those gentlemen for
having removed the ground of those doubts, and

I have the honour to be,
      My dear Sir,
  Your most faithful and obliged humble servant,
             EDMUND BURKE.
Duke Street, St. James's, Dec. 22 1790.

CHAP. XIII.

TRANSLATION OF DR SHUTE BARRINGTON TO THE SEE OF
DURHAM. — MR. BURGESS RESIGNS THE TUTORSHIP OF
CORPUS. — A PREBENDAL STALL GIVEN HIM AT DURHAM
— AND SUBSEQUENTLY THE LIVING OF WINSTON — HIS
STYLE OF LIFE THERE.

1791 to 1795.

UPON the death of Dr. Thurlow, Bishop of Durham,
in 1791, Dr. Shute Barrington was translated to

the vacant see. This event naturally produced a great change in the plans and professional avocations of Mr. Burgess. The duties attached to the office of Bishop's chaplain in a diocese so remote and important, being incompatible with those of Tutor of Corpus, he prepared to bid adieu to Oxford. In quitting the scene of his early literary triumphs, endeared to him also by so many ties of friendship, and by such varied and interesting associations, a heart even less susceptible than his would naturally have been agitated by conflicting emotions. Not only a separation from friends, but from the libraries, and other learned advantages of the University, were painfully felt by one so wedded to study and contemplation. But the bright star of his patron's favour and friendship summoned him away, and above all, the guidance and disposition of that gracious Providence which had opened to him, step by step, and by means unlooked for and unexpected, the path of usefulness and honour, and which was preparing him for extended services and further advancement.

In his intervals of leisure Mr. Burgess still kept up a correspondence both with English and foreign literati. In the years 1791 and 1792, he was much occupied with preparing for the press the edition of Aristotle's Poetics, with Mr. Tyrwhitt's commentaries, referred to in chapter x. The following letters will illustrate these particulars.

TO MR. BURNEY.

Dear Sir,   Auckland Castle, Aug. 25 1791

THE day before yesterday I received a letter from Santenius, with one inclosed for you, which I take

M 3

the earliest opportunity of sending you. I have just
received the third sheet of the Poetics.

Adieu! yours sincerely,

T. BURGESS.

P.S. Santenius is much pleased with Porson's collation of the Parma Catullus. These are his words,
which I wish you to send Porson: " Suo tempore
accepi, quem ad me dedisti, libellorum fasciculum;
quæ qui continebat, quin omnia mihi fuerint non
modo gratissima, sed vel maxime jucunda, me quoque
tacente, divinare potuisti: inprimis vero cum de
Rhythmis dissertatio tum optatissimus ille Catullus
Parmensis. Et pro hoc quidem, quo nihil accu-
ratius nec intelligentius fieri potuit, meis verbis
humanissimo et doctissimo Porsono gratias velim
agas cum maximas tum sincerissimas, nec me tanti
officii aut æstimatorem imperitum, aut hominem
accepti immemorem, ab illo censeri patiare." *

---

* " I received, in due course, your present of a collection of
tracts; and you may easily imagine, without my saying so, that
all which they contained was not only most agreeable, but even
delightful to me, particularly the dissertation on metres, and
that most desiderated, Parma Catullus. With respect to this,
which could not possibly be executed more accurately or more
judiciously, I beg you to offer my warmest and sincerest thanks
to the accomplished and most learned Porson; nor let me, on
any account, be regarded by him either as an incompetent es-
timator of such an undertaking, or, as not duly sensible of the
obligation."

TO DR. CHARLES BURNEY.

DEAR BURNEY,   Edinburgh, Oct 29 1792

I HOPE that you received safely my last letter with the inclosed.

I left Durham on Wednesday last, and arrived here yesterday morning. I have hitherto had very favourable weather for my excursion. What I have seen of Scotland, and of this place especially, very much exceeds all my expectations. I have no literary news to give you. I have just seen Dalzel, and am to sup with him this evening, and go to-morrow with him to Munro's introductory lecture. I shall stay here till after the 12th of November for the sake of meeting the old Greek veteran*, who is not expected till the Court of Session opens. Remember me to Porson when you see him; and if the news of his appointment to the Greek Professorship be true, do give him my hearty congratulations.

> I am, dear Burney,
> Very sincerely yours,
> T. BURGESS.

TO THE REV. MR. BURGESS.

SIR,   Cambridge, Dec 4. 1793

THE desire you are pleased to express of conveying to the public your intended remarks on Aristotle's Treatise, in a letter addressed to me, certainly does me too much honour to allow me to hesitate in complying with your request; and I shall be happy to receive from you any further communication on that subject.

* Lord Monboddo.

M 4

I am very glad to learn from you that Mr. Tyrwhitt's edition is likely to appear soon. I have so high an opinion of his critical judgment and sagacity, that the difficulties in Aristotle's text which *he* has not been able to remove, I shall almost despair of ever seeing removed at all.

I am here on a visit to Dr. Hey, and shall return to Colchester in a few days.

Your obedient servant,

T. TWINING.

A conscientious desire to promote men of learning and piety formed one of the distinguishing features in the character of Bishop Barrington; and it was his happiness, in the great majority of instances in which he disposed of his extensive patronage, to find that he had not been deceived in his estimate of character. Never had he more reason to indulge this pleasant reflection than in one of the earliest of his acts of this description after his translation. In the course of the year 1794, he gave the first stall which became at his disposal to his excellent Chaplain, and before the close of the same year changed it for another more valuable. In addition to learned and professional eminence, attained by a path every step in which had been honourable to his character, Mr. Burgess now found himself in possession of a lucrative piece of preferment, and in a post of honour and usefulness in the church. The mutual feelings of the Bishop and Chaplain are most pleasingly developed in the following letter : —

Mongewell, Dec. 5. 1794.

It may be matter of doubt, my dear Burgess, whether you derive more pleasure from your pre-

ferment, or I from having bestowed it. The thanks
of both are due to a gracious Providence : from me,
that it has given me the power of rewarding distinguished and unassuming merit : from you, that
you have been the object of my choice. You have
obtained the comforts which flow from ease and independence : I, those which result from the consciousness of having acted right ; from the credit of
my appointment, and from the friendship which
this connection has produced between us, and which
I value among the happy circumstances of my life.
Be that life long or short, may I, during the remainder of it, never forget, that patronage is a trust
to be rendered subservient to the great interests of
religion and learning.

As this will probably find you within forty-six
miles of this place, I wish you to be informed that I
do not mean to stir from hence till after Christmas-
day, when the meeting of Parliament will compel
me to remove.

  Believe me, with the truest regard,
    Your affectionate friend,
      S. D.

For three years Mr. Burgess assiduously discharged the various duties which devolved upon him
as Bishop's Chaplain and Prebendary ; and, according to ordinary estimate, few situations in the Church
could have been more enviable. He was surrounded
with the luxuries attendant on high station, without
its cares and responsibility. He had continual access to agreeable and literary society, and such was
his patron's Christian benignity and politeness, that
he was free from all painful feelings of dependence.

So simple and primitive, however, were his tastes,
and such was his love of learned leisure, that he
often sighed in secret for a state of life more congenial to these predilections. He was actuated,
also, by motives still more elevated. The religious principle had been silently deepening in his
mind, and he felt anxious to employ his talents for
the promotion of the glory of God and the salvation
of souls, in the active discharge of pastoral and parochial duties. In prosecution of this, the favourite
bent of his wishes, and the highest point of his
ambition, he requested his kind friend the Bishop
to bestow upon him the living of Haughton, then
vacant, and to permit him to relinquish his stall
and the chaplaincy. " You shall have it," replied his
Lordship, in his courteous manner ; " but you must
now, in your turn, do me a favour. You must give
it me back again ; you shall have a living, but it
must be one which will not dissolve our connection,
nor sever you from Durham." " He accordingly
gave me," added my venerable friend, (whose very
words I nearly quote,) " in 1795, the sweet and
delightful living of Winston ; so delightful, that the
Editor of the Beauties of England and Wales expresses his surprise that an incumbent once in possession should ever quit it for any situation under
the sun. Arthur Young says it is worth going a
thousand miles to see , and Mr. Frederic Vane,
Lord Darlington's brother, used to call it the
Northern Tivoli. The landscapes which it commands are absolutely enchanting. You have Raby
Castle ; you have richly wooded acclivities, a fine
bridge over the Tees, the hills of Cleveland ! Such
a combination of beauty is rarely found centred in

any one place." Nearly in these words did Bishop
Burgess, in his 80th year, recur, with almost
youthful enthusiasm, to these scenes, in which he
had spent many of the happiest hours of his life.
He there found a retreat from the round of company, and the frequent calls of public duty, which
had hitherto absorbed the greatest portion of his
time. But the Bishop added still further to his
happiness by releasing him from his more onerous
duties, those incident to the station of domestic
chaplain, and restricting them, in a great degree,
to the office of examining candidates for orders.
For this service he was peculiarly fitted by his
learning and piety, and he could not but feel
that he who, in addition to active parochial labours,
faithfully discharges the important functions of such
an office, occupies a very useful and honourable
situation in the church of Christ. Winston was
only ten miles from Auckland Castle, where Mr
Burgess was a frequent and cherished inmate. The
feelings of the Bishop towards him have been already described as next to paternal, and what had
recently occurred tended to augment their mutual
friendship and esteem. He divided his time of residence pretty equally between Durham and Winston, though the peaceful and pastoral delights of
the latter increasingly riveted his affections. The
income of the living was moderate, from 200*l.* to
300*l.* per annum, and the population did not exceed
a few hundreds. They very soon became animated
by feelings of cordial respect and affection for their
new Rector, in whom they found a kind and liberal
friend, a Christian teacher and benefactor, and a
bright example of personal piety. He set himself

to do good among them, in conjunction with his
curate, not only by a zealous discharge of his public
duties, but also by visiting his people in their respective homes and cottages, and there conversing
with them in the true spirit of a Christian pastor.
Among many other modes of administering to their
temporal comfort, he constantly kept a large assortment of blankets and other useful articles in his
house, to lend out among the sick or necessitous.

Throughout life, his heart melted upon an appeal
to his benevolence; and he felt not only for the
trials of the more indigent poor, but for those, also,
to which industrious men in respectable situations
are occasionally liable, from peculiar vicissitudes.
For example, one of his parishioners, a tenant of
the Bridgewater estate, was in arrear for rent, for a
considerable sum ; a distress was about to be levied
on his effects, when he generosly interfered, and
advanced the whole amount, consenting to receive
it back by degrees, in hay, cheese, and such articles.

His pastoral care was specially extended to those
of his flock who were precluded, by distance or bodily
infirmity, from attending the services of the parish
church. Two cottages, situated in suitable quarters of the parish, were fixed upon, where such persons assembled at a specified hour, every Sunday,
and Mr. Burgess and his curate divided the duty of
meeting them, and of ministering to their spiritual
edification. Sir Thomas Bernard, a name pro-
verbial in the annals of benevolence, was so much
pleased with "The Poor Man's Club," as this
plan of instruction was called at Winston, that
he gave an account of it in one of his publications, and it thus became the germ of those extra-

official ministrations, which, under the name of cot-
tage lectures, and, in most instances, with episcopal
sanction, are doing extensive good in many of our
populous parishes, destitute of due church accommodation. Disinterested efforts like these, on the
part of the clergy, are now of ordinary occurrence,
and, while they essentially promote the important
ends of the Christian Ministry, they win the affections of the people, and cement the bonds of their
attachment to the Established Church, its ministers,
and offices.

The instruction of the children and of the youth
of his parish was another branch of pastoral duty to
which Mr. Burgess assiduously devoted much of his
time and thoughts; and many were the little cheap
publications on religious subjects which he printed
at Durham for their benefit.

The Titles of some of these were as follows : —

A Catechism on the Ten Commandments, for
the Use of Parents and Visiters of Sunday Schools.
Price Twopence.

Selections from the Old and New Testament, and
the Book of Common Prayer.

Moral Annals of the Poor, in two Parts.

Sacramental Questions and Answers, extracted
from the Book of Common Prayer, to which is
added, Paraclesis, or a Compendium of Christian
Consolation. Price One Penny.

An Easter Catechism, in two Parts.

A Christmas Gift.

A large assortment of his sermons, preached at
Winston and at Durham, are in the possession of
the writer. They bear the impress of a heart truly
devout, and of a judgment which clearly appre-

hended the great scope and aim of the Gospel of Christ. The fallen condition of man, his redemption by the atoning sacrifice of Jesus Christ, the session of the Saviour at the right hand of the Majesty on high as Mediator and Intercessor, the renewing and sanctifying influences of the Holy Spirit, these were the great truths upon which he supremely dwelt, and which he applied to the consciences of his hearers, with affectionate seriousness and energy.

And, in order that his people might profit by the Liturgical part of the services of the Church, and "pray with the understanding," he was careful to instruct them in the object and end of its various offices. " The Church keeps up," as Isaac Walton observes, in his life of George Herbert, " an historical and circular commemoration of times, as they pass by us ; of such times as ought to incline us to occasional praises, for the particular blessings which we do, or might, receive by those holy commemorations. To these, whether involving calls to special humiliation, or to devout thanksgiving, he directed the attention of his hearers, and he was no less assiduous in explaining to them the nature, obligations, and privileges of the Sacramental ordinances.

Deeply attached to the Church of England, convinced that its doctrines are scriptural, its mode of government apostolic, and its formularies impregnated with the elevated yet chastened devotion of the purest ages of Christianity, he was among the most devoted of her sons. But, although, in this sense, a high churchman, there was no bitterness in his orthodoxy. However uncompromising in his opinions, charity and kindness influenced his whole mode of communicating them to others ; nor could a Dissenter, after personal conference with him, fail to bear away the impression that he was one in whom the love of God and of his neighbour was predominant, and who had a smile for real goodness, wherever it was to be found.*

CHAP. XIV.

SACRA PRIVATA OF MR. BURGESS.

The life of Mr. Burgess at Winston was divided between the faithful discharge of pastoral and parochial duties, the prosecution of his learned studies, and the assiduous cultivation of personal religion. The piety and integrity of his heart, and his conscientious desire to consecrate his various talents to the glory of God, have already been described ; but his portraiture as a private Christian has not been attempted. We shall now place him before the reader in this character ; and in doing so, shall not be reduced to indulge in imaginary traits, since he has himself furnished the requisite particulars in

---

* Although it is anticipating the order of events, the following extract from a letter of Hannah More to the Rev. C. Wilks, written in 1809, is so much in unison with the above statements, that we venture to insert it here — "The good Bishop of St. David's has paid us a second visit. He drove over from Bath to breakfast, and, as it was Easter Monday, he desired, after breakfast, to read the whole church service to us. It was so primitive, and so like all he does, it pleased me. With guests and workfolks, we mustered a decent congregation."

a variety of private reflections and soliloquies, written at different intervals, though chiefly about the time to which we now refer, and which prove him to have been, early in life, a bright example of faith and holiness. To subdue his own will, and to bring his senses, passions, and affections into subjection to the law of Christ, had so become his predominant object, that, without any hyperbole, it might have been said of him, —

> Thy care is fix'd, and zealously attends
> To fill thy odorous lamp with deeds of light,
> And hope that reaps not shame.   MILTON.

At the same time it will appear how sensible he was that his best services were marred with imperfection, and that "he gloried only in the cross of Christ, by which he was crucified to the world, and the world to him."

The reflections alluded to were chiefly written in the blank leaves and in the margins of some of his favourite devotional writers, among whom may be enumerated Bishop Wilson's Sacra Privata, Doddridge's Rise and Progress of Religion, Payne's Thomas à Kempis, Robinson's Scripture Characters, Nelson's Practice of True Devotion, Law's Serious Call, and Baxter's Saint's Rest. (Only eighteen months before his death, he took down from a book-shelf a copy of Payne's Kempis, and pointed out with much feeling to the present writer its numerous marginal annotations, as indexes of the state of his mind while residing at Winston, and as no less expressive of his latest convictions. He added, that he had written many notes and reflections in the margin of another devotional book, which, how-

ever, has unfortunately been lost. His Nelson on
True Devotion is also replete with similar annotations. These, and a few sheets of manuscript, are
the principal sources to which we are indebted for
the means of graphically developing his inmost
thoughts. To such spiritual exercises he could have
been no stranger before he came to Winston, but
the opportunities he there enjoyed for calm and uninterrupted reflection tended, as he himself avowed,
to deepen and confirm in his soul every holy principle.

By some memoranda referable to this period, it
appears that he so apportioned his time as to assign
particular hours to study, to devotional exercises,
and to his active duties; and in order to compass
these objects without injury to his health, he practised the strictest temperance. We shall now, without further preface, place before our readers the
following specimens of his " Sacra Privata : " —

A HEATHEN Emperor used to say of a day in
which he had performed no good action, " *I have
lost a day.*" Go and do thou likewise. Look out
for objects, and seek for opportunities of doing
good ; and when thou hast neglected any such, then,
at least, say, " I have lost a day." Record omissions.
Keep a moral register, with a column for omissions.

If we expect no return for any good we do but
from God, he will repay us with infinite interest.

Those occasions in life are truly valuable which
give exercise to the best Christian virtues, such as
long-suffering, gentleness, meekness, forgiveness,
and all other gifts of the Spirit, and the graces of

N

charity — that charity " which suffereth long and is kind."

Thou hast been all mercy to me, O God! May I be so to others!

Labour after and pray for simplicity of intention.

In every act of good which you do, endeavour to perform it from love to God, and obedience to his will.

All is vanity, but the love of God and a life devoted to his will. O my soul! consider those words — " Son, remember that thou in thy lifetime receivedst thy good things."

" Lord, increase my faith; " increase my love of Thee, and my hatred of sin.

Bring thyself every day to such particulars of

SELF-EXAMINATION

as will be satisfactory to recur to at the hour of death.

1. Dost thou believe that Almighty God hath by his power made heaven and earth, and all things therein, and that he doth by his Divine Providence govern the same?

2. Dost thou confess that thou hast transgressed and broken the holy commandments of Almighty God in thought, word, and deed? Art thou sorry in thy heart that thou hast so broken his laws, and neglected his service, and so much followed the world and thine own vain pleasure? And wouldst thou not lead a holier life if thou wast to begin life again?

3. Dost thou from thy heart desire to be reconciled unto God, through Jesus Christ, his blessed

Son, thy Mediator, who is at the right hand of God in heaven, now appearing for thee in the sight of God, and interceding for thy soul?

4. Dost thou renounce all confidence in all other mediators, saints or angels, believing that Jesus Christ, the only Mediator of the New Testament, is able to save " them to the uttermost that come unto God by Him, seeing He ever liveth to make intercession for them ? " And wilt thou, with David, say unto Christ, " Whom have I in heaven but thee, and there is none upon earth that I desire besides thee ? " — Psalm lxxiii. 25.

5. Dost thou hope to be saved by the only merits of the precious death and passion which thy Saviour Jesus Christ suffered for thee, not putting any hope of salvation in thy own merits, nor in any other means or creatures, being assuredly persuaded that " there is no salvation in any other ; " and that " there is none other name under heaven whereby thou must be saved ? "

6. Dost thou heartily forgive all wrongs and offences offered unto thee, and dost thou cast out of thy heart all malice and hatred, that thou mayest appear before the face of Christ, the Prince of Peace, in perfect love and charity?

7. Dost thou firmly believe that thy body shall be raised up out of the grave at the sound of the last trumpet; and that thy body and soul shall be united together again in the resurrection day, to appear before the Lord Jesus Christ, and thence to go with Him into the kingdom of heaven, to live in everlasting bliss and glory ? Thank God, I do. — Lord, teach me.

STUDYING THE CROSS.

Blessed are the evils which lead us from the world to Christ.

Blessed are the wrongs which bring us to a willing conformity to Christ.

Blessed are the injuries which wean our affections from things on earth, and fix them on God.

Have your crosses done you any good ? Cast all your care upon God.

" Blessed Lord, who hast caused all holy Scriptures to be written for our learning," &c. &c.

I pray God to fix in my mind what I have read, to convert my reading into holy resolutions, and my resolutions into practice, in every part of my duty to God and man.

ON EARLY RISING.

Consult Wesley and Law on early rising. Wesley rose at four.

RESIGNATION.

Whatever evils and losses you suffer, regard them as ordered by God for your good.

It is the Lord's doing.

" Whom he loveth he chasteneth." " Every branch that beareth fruit, he purgeth it, that it may bring forth more fruit." — John xv. 2.

Blessed are the injuries which render you dependent upon God, and independent of creature comforts. " In patience possess ye your souls." " Come unto me, all ye that labour and are heavy laden ; and I will give you rest."

A serious view of Death, proper to be taken as we lie down in our beds.

O my soul! look forward with seriousness and attention, and learn wisdom by the consideration of thy latter end. Another of thy mortal days is now numbered and finished; and as I have put off my clothes, and laid myself upon my bed for the repose of the night, so will the day of life quickly come to its period; so must the body itself be put off, and laid to its repose in a bed of dust.

There let it rest, for it will be no more regarded by me than the clothes which I have now laid aside. I have another far more important concern to attend to. Think, O my soul! when death comes, thou art to enter upon the eternal world, and to be fixed either in heaven or hell.

All the schemes and cares, the hopes and fears, the pleasures and sorrows of life will come to their period, and the world of spirits will open upon thee. And, oh! how soon it may open! perhaps before the returning sun brings the light of another day. To-morrow's sun may not enlighten my eyes, but only shine round a senseless corpse, which may lie in the place of this animated body: at least, the death of many in the flower of their age, and of many who were superior to me in capacity, piety, and the prospects of usefulness, may loudly warn me not to depend on a long life, and induce me rather to wonder that I am continued for so many years, than to be surprised if I am suddenly removed.

And, now, O my soul! answer, as in the sight of God, art thou ready? Art thou ready? Is there no sin unforsaken, and so unrepented of, to fill me with anguish in my departing moments, and to make me tremble on the brink of eternity? Dread to remain under the guilt of it; and this moment renew thy most earnest application to the mercy of God and to the blood of a Redeemer, for deliverance from it.

But if the great account be already adjusted; if thou hast cordially repented of thy numerous offences; if thou hast sincerely committed thyself into the hands of the blessed Jesus, and not renounced thy covenant by returning to the allowed practice of sin, then start not at the thought of a separation. It is not in the power of death to hurt a soul devoted to God, and united to the Great Redeemer. It may take me from my worldly comforts, it may disconcert and break my schemes for service on earth; but, O my soul! diviner entertainments and nobler services await thee beyond the grave. For ever blessed be the name of God, and the love of Jesus, for these quieting, encouraging, joyful views! I will now lay me down in peace, and sleep free from the fears of what shall be the issue of this night, whether life or death be appointed for me. O Lord, thou God of truth and mercy, I can cheerfully refer it to thy choice, whether I shall wake in this life or another. *

All religious consolation is founded on faith in God, and that on a knowledge of the Scriptures. (Romans x. 17.) There can be no religious consolation without repentance, the first motion towards

---

* The last Reflections are taken from Dr. Doddridge's "Rise and Progress," but were found carefully written out by Mr. Burgess, in connection with his own heads for daily self-examination — thus appropriating them to his own use.

which is the grace of God producing in the heart effectual conviction of sin. The next is, a perception and acknowledgment of the mercy of God in producing this conviction ; confession of sin, renunciation of self-righteousness, and full dependence on the merits of Christ's atonement, bring the mind first to the hope, and then to the assurance of pardon, for the sake of Christ. Thus the heart is " renewed," and " created in Christ Jesus to good works," which, springing from faith and a deliberate principle of obedience and love, now become acceptable to God.

A devout participation of the sacrament of the Lord's Supper, as it is a high exercise of repentance, contrition, and grateful adoration, so is it also an efficacious means of consolation.

" Injuriarum remedium est oblivio," says the heathen moralist. " Injuriarum remedium est ignoscere *," says the Christian : and both upon rational principles; but the Christian remedy is the surest, because without forgiving an injury it is not easy to forget it : in practice, also, it is infinitely the best, because it is in obedience to the express command of God.

To forgive injuries on a religious principle is an act of grace, not of nature ; and the surest means of attaining it is to exercise the mind in that entire resignation to Providence, which sees the hand of God in all events which happen to us.

* " To forget injuries is the best remedy for them," says the heathen moralist.

" To pardon injuries is the best remedy for them," says the Christian

N 4

Memento mori — perhaps to-morrow, perhaps to-night.

O Death, how bitter is the remembrance of thee to the man who is at ease in his possessions, &c.

O Lord, into thy hands I commend my spirit, that whether I live I may live unto Thee, or whether I die I may die unto Thee; for, whether I live or die, I am thy creature, thy property. Lord Jesus, mercifully receive me.

Now, while the time of gathering heavenly riches is, in much mercy, continued, lay up for thyself the substantial treasures of eternity — treasures of prayer, forgiveness, meekness, patience, humility, beneficence, contentment, temperance, purity. Study the one thing needful. Suffer not the censures of men to deter thee from treading the path of duty. Their scoffs cannot do thee the slightest injury, if thou have the courage to despise them.

Love and wish well to every soul that lives. Dwell in love, and then you dwell in God. Hate nothing but evil. Give me grace, O Lord, to love Thee more and more, to love thy name, to love thy will.

Suffer not your peace to depend upon any created good. Study the one thing needful.

Assist me, O Lord, in my endeavours to withdraw my mind from the actions of others, and to turn my eye inwardly on myself. Be thou, O Lord, the pure object of all my intentions and desires, so that I may seek myself in nothing that I do. Keep me always mindful, that many actions assume the appearance of charity that are only selfish and carnal;

preserve me from that self-deceit which seeks itself
in all things, without perceiving it : deliver me from
all self-will and inordinate affection. grant me that
true and perfect charity " which envieth not, which
seeketh not its own," but desires that God may be
glorified in all things, through Jesus Christ.

STUDYING THE CROSS.

They who would bear crosses only of their own
choosing would sacrifice to God only that which
cost them nothing.

Christ has said, " How hardly shall the rich man
enter into the kingdom of heaven ! " And shall we
labour through life to acquire wealth, and be miserable from the want or loss of such an obstacle to
our everlasting happiness ?

Christ has said, " Woe be to you that are rich,
for ye have received your consolation." And may
we not therefore aspire to great spiritual consolation,
even in the absence of human comforts?

Christ has said, " How can they believe who receive honour one of another, and seek not that
honour which cometh from God only ? " And shall
we all our life long be grasping after honours and
distinctions, and be miserable at the smallest dimi-
nution of them? Is wealth " the one thing needful ? " No. Is it not a great hinderance to our
salvation ? On many accounts it is. Is the privation of it, therefore, any real loss ? It may be
converted into a gain. Is the grandeur, wealth, or
happiness of this world " the one thing needful ? "
No : they may be a great hinderance to our salvation, by withdrawing the soul from God, and fixing
it on the objects of this life.

Are the troubles, the losses, the crosses which interrupt our happiness in this life to be lamented, or to be thankfully accepted? They are to be thankfully accepted as mementos that this world is not our home; as motives to repentance for past sins, and to the redemption of lost time, as lessons and trials of meekness, patience, humility, and fellowship with Christ.

Why should we hope to escape those trials from which no human being has been exempt? Who among the servants of God accomplished his earthly pilgrimage without experiencing adversity and distress? Christ and his apostles, the martyrs and pilgrims of old, all suffered persecution. Do not they deserve the name of hirelings, who are for ever seeking after comfort? Repine not, therefore, at the want of riches and honours, which, by gratifying and nourishing our self-love, self-esteem, and self-seeking, are very dangerous impediments to our salvation. He that is overwhelmed by what are called the evils of life, forgets that he is a Christian; forgets that Christ has said, without taking up our cross daily we cannot be his disciples; forgets that tribulation is the direct path to God, the path to heaven.

Remember thou art here in a state of probation; that thy trial may perhaps be thy conduct under evils, as another's may be his conduct under prosperity.

Whatever trials befall thee, regard them as permitted by God for thy good. Make it thy daily object to have a conscience void of offence towards God, and towards man, and then commit thy cause, joyfully and confidently, to Him who careth for thee.

Convert all injuries into occasions of spiritual profit, by seeing the hand of God in them, by making them the means of dying to thyself, and of attaining to more intimate communion with a neglected and long-suffering Saviour.

We enter into the fellowship of the sufferings of Jesus Christ when we endure injuries with a composed mind, patiently, and, if possible, cheerfully, in obedience to his commands, in imitation of his example, and therefore for his sake.

Simple obedience is to be more highly prized than refined subtilty, and a pure conscience than learned philosophy, that is to say, a conscience purified by the blood of Christ, and freed by it from the condemning sense of sin; a mind and heart spiritualised, sanctified, and bent on a course of renewed obedience to God.

In these thoughts and aspirations, so simple, and yet so elevated, the reader has before him a picture of the interior mind of the subject of this memoir. It was thus that he acted on the principle of the Psalmist, "Thy word have I hid in my heart, that I might not sin against Thee;" and in reliance on that animating promise, "If a man love me, he will keep my word, and my Father will love him, and we will come unto him, and make our abode with him." — John xiv. 23.

The communion of the devout soul with its Creator, Redeemer, and Sanctifier, is the employment of its spiritual and immortal faculties in the highest, purest, and noblest manner of which they are capable. It is an approach, by the way of his own special appointment, and in compliance with his own gracious invitation, to the mysterious presence of the " First Perfect" and the "First Fair," of the Central Source of Light and Life, of Holiness and Happiness. It is to look up to Him, through faith in the Great Mediator of the New Covenant, with humble, yet filial confidence, as to a reconciled Father; and to claim the fulfilment of his infallible promises, of renewing the soul that seeks Him, and of stamping upon it, in some degree, the image of his own moral perfections. So far, then, as this devout temper of soul is habitually cultivated, it will be found to include the germ and principle of every excellency of which created nature is capable. This is to cull, while still mortal, immortal fruit, the pledge and foretaste of an eternal and unfading inheritance. The production of this state of mind is, in fact, the object and aim of all religious ordinances, the ultimate scope, as far as man is concerned, of that glorious Revelation, "which has God for its author, salvation for its end, and truth without mixture of error for its matter."

From an early stage in his clerical career, Mr. Burgess was animated by this devout spirit. To its purifying influence is to be ascribed that superiority to the temptations of the world and of high station; that indifference to wealth; that patience, self-denial, and charity, which were such distinguishing features in his character. At this particular period, there is reason to believe that he carried some of the habits and tastes of an ascetic life further than his better judgment afterwards approved; but, even if it were so, what was it but the excess of a noble principle, " terrena calcantis, cœlestia sitientis ? "

Nor let any sneering objector presume to say, " Pretty language, indeed, this depreciation of wealth and honours from a man who was in the high road to the possession of both ! " Wealth, in the degree that he enjoyed it, had sought him ; he was disposed to make the best use of it in every way ; and had it by any accident been wrested from him, he would have practised, himself, the magnanimity which he inculcated ; he would even have said that he might have learnt this lesson in a much lower school than that of Christ, the school of his favourite Epictetus. And as for honours, it will be seen by the sequel, that he was never found among those who coveted them. Such objectors have yet to learn that Christianity, when it truly animates the heart with its superhuman philosophy, can impart poverty of spirit in the midst of affluence, and unaffected humility beneath the shade of a mitre.

CHAP. XV.

HIS MARRIAGE. — DOMESTIC LIFE AT WINSTON, ETC. — IS APPOINTED TO THE BISHOPRIC OF ST. DAVID'S.

1799 to 1803.

THE following letter to Dr. Parr illustrates the interest with which Mr. Burgess continued to recur to classical and learned topics : —

TO THE REV. DR. PARR.

DEAR SIR, Durham, Dec. 9. 1797

I EXPECTED long since to have had an opportunity
of returning your H. de Noris, as I intended to have
been in London the summer after I saw you last,
but as I shall still defer my visit to the south for
another year at least, it may perhaps be some time
before I meet with a good opportunity of sending
your valuable little book : unless you think I may
trust it in a parcel addressed to Payne.

The Art of Poetry of Horace I have hardly looked
at since I left London. I have been a good deal
occupied with his great master. You will oblige
me by letting me know if you have received a copy
of my *Fasciculus secundus.* I am very desirous that
you should have one; as I shall be happy to hear
your opinion of some matters, which I have touched
upon in the last pages of the Preface, and in the
Postscript.

I have seen and read Wakefield's Diatribe. With
so much real learning and acuteness as he has, how
could he venture *so hasty* an attack upon such learning as Porson's? I have not seen his Lucretius,
but I heartily wish it success, and will certainly
procure a copy.

With your feeling, and knowledge, and opportunities of information, and your vicinity to the
great theatre of politics, I do not wonder at the
lively interest you take in the present state of public
affairs I have long since endeavoured to resist solicitude — not from indifference, but my principle
is hope. The kind wishes which you express are

not lost upon me : I most cordially return them, and
should be happy to see you in any situation that
would give a full exercise to your talents.

I am, dear Sir,

Yours sincerely,

T. BURGESS.

Five years of the life of Mr. Burgess glided happily
away in the peaceful and faithful discharge of pastoral duties at Winston, varied by official residence
at Durham, by occasional visits to Bishop-Auck-
land, and by the discharge of his important functions as examining chaplain. His retirement had
occasionally been pleasantly interrupted by visits
from Oxford friends, and from others of more recent standing ; but in the year 1799 he effectually
relieved the solitude of his situation, by entering
into the married state.

The object of his choice was Miss Bright, daughter of John Bright, Esq. Mr. Bright was of an
ancient Yorkshire family, whose ancestors suffered
greatly in their property during the usurpation of
Cromwell. In addition to his landed estate he
possessed a house in Durham, in which his widow
continued to reside after his death. The present
representative of the family is the Rev. John Bright,
of Skeffington Hall, Leicestershire.

Mrs. Burgess survives her husband, and che-
rishes his memory with unceasing and affectionate
veneration During the long course of forty years,
through which this union extended, their harmony
and happiness were uninterrupted. Those who have
had the privilege of sharing their social board will
fully enter into the spirit of this description, and

can never forget the respect and tenderness which he unceasingly manifested towards his amiable consort.

My readers will not be surprised to hear, that his thoughts had hitherto been so exclusively bestowed upon his learned studies and his religious duties, that he had little attended to the cares of housekeeping. In allusion to his inexperience in all such matters, the Bishop of Durham smilingly said to the lady, a short time before their marriage, " Miss Bright, you are about to be united to one of the very best of men, but a perfect child in the concerns of this world; so you must manage the house, and govern not only your maids, but the men-servants also." A piece of friendly advice for which Mrs. Burgess, however unwilling to outstep her proper province, soon found reason to perceive the necessity.

On the day of their marriage, the Bishop drove into Durham from Auckland Castle, to unite their hands, and it was arranged that they should go to Winston Parsonage immediately after the ceremony. Conjecturing that his chaplain might probably have forgotten to furnish his larder suitably to the occasion, the kind and thoughtful Prelate had sent over an ample supply of delicacies to await their arrival. Just as they were about to drive off, he amused himself by probing the fact. " You have, no doubt, taken good care to provide every thing in the best manner for Mrs. Burgess's reception at Winston ? " The chaplain started at the question, and was obliged to own that really it had never occurred to him. He was at once relieved from his embarrassment, and had reason, as on many former occasions, to recognise in his diocesan his good genius.

But while he thus occasionally lost sight of what referred to personal comfort or gratification, Mrs. Burgess was most pleasingly impressed, on settling at Winston, by the minute attention which she found that her husband had been in the habit of paying to the comfort and relief of the poorer classes of his parishioners.

In after life, they both delighted to recur to the happy days they spent in this peaceful parsonage. The situation was so retired, that, excepting in the summer months, they saw little company; but their evenings were rendered delightful by the constant fund of interesting reading which the library, seconded by its owner's intimate acquaintance with its stores of knowledge and entertainment, supplied.

Their time was divided between Durham and Winston, though the habits of the two places were necessarily very different. Mr. Burgess retained all his love of studious and devout retirement; but his marriage naturally led him more than formerly into mixed society, where he was always a great favourite. He was never inclined to take the lead in conversation, or in any way to obtrude his opinions, but was always willing to be drawn out by others, when, from the strength of his memory, his excellent understanding, and his acquaintance with general literature, he poured forth a bright stream of instruction and amusing information. But he was most happy himself, and most of all attractive to others, when engaged in a tête-à-tête with some kindred spirit upon any subject of mutual interest.

His person, as described to me, at this time, cor-

o

responded with my own impressions at a much later
period.   It was tall, erect, and dignified, and there
was a cast of pleasing, not repulsive gravity over
the calm expression of his intellectual features. His
smile was peculiarly winning. The Reverend Mr.
Smelt, a very accomplished man, and sub-tutor to
George IV., who often met him at Durham, used
to say, " Of all the sweet things I can think of,
there is nothing quite equal to Burgess's smile."

He had always been a cherished guest at Auckland Castle, occasionally spending many weeks
there.   During one of these visits, after his marriage, Mrs. Burgess was walking in the park with
the Bishop and a lady, when they saw him approaching.   " There," exclaimed the lady, " comes
' an Israelite indeed, in whom is no guile.' " " Yes ; "
replied the Bishop, " or, as Pope has elegantly
expressed it, —

>   " ' In wit a man, simplicity a child.' "

Dr Paley, to whom the Bishop had given the
valuable living of Wearmouth, occasionally visited
at Auckland Castle, and Mr. Burgess often amused
himself with contrasting the open-heartedness and
honest simplicity of his manners and conversation
with the obsequious complaisance of some of the
guests.   Mrs. Barrington was one day very eloquent
about the happiness of a certain married couple,
whose days, she said, passed in perpetual harmony,
so entirely did they think alike on all subjects.
" How delightful ! how enviable !" one and another
exclaimed ; but Paley was silent.   At length Mrs.
Barrington addressed him thus : " But, Dr. Paley,
what do you say to it ? "   " Mighty flat, Madam,"

was his short but expressive comment on this description of connubial bliss.

As the love of literature was ardent in Mr. Burgess, the love of books was its natural attendant. When he went from Winston to Durham for a few days, the carriage was often so loaded with them, that Bishop Barrington, in his pleasant way, told Mrs. Burgess she really ought to stipulate as to the number and weight to be admitted at any one time.

His various duties, and the increasing demands upon his time, now left him, it is true, little leisure to pursue those critical and philological pursuits, which had hitherto continued pleasantly to employ some of his hours of relaxation, the fruits of which still exist in a series of small manuscripts, written in a neat style of penmanship, and entitled " Otia Dunelmiana." They consist of critical notes, various readings, and conjectural emendations, having reference to the text of some of his favourite classical authors.

The two following letters, the latter of which is from Bishop Porteus, will prove that any leisure he could command was principally occupied by theological studies, and in preparing cheap and useful publications, for the religious edification of the humble and industrious classes. —

TO THE REV. MR. BURGESS.

My dear Friend,

I HAD not otherwise intended to thank you for the very *elegant compliment* of your Dedication, till I could have read the work, " Paulina Initia : " but Mr. Sharp's Tract, and your additions to it, have

o 2

reached me this day ; and I should be very culpable
to delay a week in returning you my sincere acknowledgments for your very kind attention, and
in expressing my astonishment at your unwearied
powers and incessant exertion in behalf of the most
interesting of all causes. I think that Mr. Sharp's
remarks are not only ingenious, but in many instances true. Beza, as I see in Poole, has been before him : indeed Mr. Sharp's letter mentions this
circumstance.

Your affectionate friend,

G. J. HUNTINGFORD.

W. C. April 4. 1802.

TO THE REV. MR. BURGESS.

REVEREND SIR,   Fulham House, June 4. 1802

I AM very glad you continue your pious and
judicious labours for the instruction of the lower
classes and middle orders of the people. Mr. Sharp's
Tract * is a very valuable one, and I cannot have
any objection to my little book on the Evidences
being bound up with it.

You would oblige me by sending me a copy of
your " Selections " when finished, and also copies
of the three parts of the Easter Catechism, and of
the Christmas Gift. They might be sent by different posts under different covers.

I am, with much regard,

Your faithful and obedient servant,

B. LONDON.

* Mr. Granville Sharp's Tract on the Greek Definitive Article. It was first published in a number of the Museum
Oxoniense, by Mr. Burgess, who was a zealous advocate in
support of Mr. Sharp's theory. Some account of it, and of the
important questions connected with it, will be found in the Appendix.

After Mr. Burgess had taken his degree of B.D., Dr. Cooper, one of his brother prebendaries, and his next door neighbour at Durham, used frequently to urge him to proceed to take that of D.D. Most of the prebendaries at this time had done so. "Burgess," he would say, "you ought to take your Doctor's degree. It is a compliment you owe your college." In the summer of 1803, business calling him to London, he stopped at Oxford in his way, and did take it. During his stay in town, the Bishop of Durham told him that Mr. Addington, then Premier, had a few days before said to him, in the course of conversation, "I wonder Burgess does not call on me: I was with him both at Winchester and Oxford." The Bishop added, that, after hearing this, he really ought to call. His shrinking, modest nature recoiled, however, on the present, as on many former occasions, from obtruding himself into notice, or in any way courting patronage, and he returned to Durham without profiting by this friendly hint. Even Mrs. Burgess heard nothing of it till several days after his return home, when he casually mentioned what had occurred, and she very naturally exclaimed, " Then, of course, you called in Downing Street ? " to which he replied in the negative. She tacitly acquiesced in his decision.

About a fortnight afterwards, as they were sitting together, the post came in, and among various letters which it brought, Mrs. Burgess called his attention to one franked by Mr. Addington. " Some friend," he replied, " must have asked him to frank a letter to me," and he put it aside for the moment, not having the slightest suspicion of its contents. Mrs. Burgess, who soon after left the room, observed on her return, that he looked grave and thoughtful, and inquired the cause, when he showed her the following letter from Mr. Addington : —

Sir,　　　　　　　Downing Street, June 5. 1803.

THOUGH we have been separated almost thirty years, I have not, let me assure you, been a stranger to the excellence of your private character, nor to your exertions for the interests of learning and of religion ; and I have been anxious that your services should be still further noticed and distinguished, and your sphere of being useful enlarged. These considerations, alone, have led me to mention you to his Majesty as the successor of the late Lord George Murray, in the diocese of St. David's, and I am happy to say that his Majesty has entirely approved of the recommendation. It will not be expected that you should relinquish your prebend in the cathedral church of Durham.

I have the honour to be, with true esteem,

Sir,

Your most obedient and faithful servant,

HENRY ADDINGTON.

To the Rev. Dr. Burgess

The feelings of Dr. Burgess on the perusal of this letter were mingled and conflicting. The tribute of respect and esteem which it conveyed, from a distinguished and upright statesman, writing from an accurate knowledge of the nature and circumstances of his career, both public and private, could not but highly gratify him. His conscience,

also, testified that he had in no way courted this
flattering offer. It came to him unsought and unexpected. But his reflecting mind could not be
dazzled into a forgetfulness of the great responsibility attendant upon the episcopal office, nor of the
onerous public duties which its acceptance would
impose upon *him*, whose cherished wish had been the
quiet life of a country clergyman. His first impression, therefore, was, to decline the offer; and, in
allusion to this fact, he said to a friend, a short
time only before his death, " I had not lost the
feelings which prompted me, some years before, to
request permission to retire from Durham into a
less public station." Further reflection, however,
outweighed his scruples; he felt convinced that
should he return a negative reply, the friends whose
judgment he most valued would unite in condemning his decision; and this conviction, together with
the spontaneous nature of the minister's offer, and
the anticipations which his letter threw out of his
increased usefulness, finally induced him to return
an affirmative, and, of course, a grateful answer.
Some idea existed that Mr. Addington would have
given the vacant bishopric to a learned divine in
the North, long since dead, an old friend of Burgess, and a worthy man, but pompous and pushing.
One who knew them both observed, in allusion to
this report, " It was well he did not give it to
Dr. —— ; he would have died of inflation It is
best bestowed on that humble, apostolical man."

The see of Exeter became vacant about ten days
after the appointment of Dr. Burgess to that of
St. David's, and Mr. Addington told him that it
would have been offered to him had it first been at

his disposal. The Bishop replied, that he much
preferred St. David's, as he delighted in the charm
of a country residence. Exeter was given to the
late Dr. Fisher. They were consecrated on the same
day, and were in consequence called, at the time,
the Twin Bishops.*

When he attended the levee to do homage,
George the Third surprised him by one of those
instances of accurate recollection of old incidents
in the lives of his subjects, for which he was so
remarkable; and it was not less an instance of his
kindness, and his power of paying a just and elegant
compliment. " You were chaplain, I believe, to
the Bishop of Durham, twenty years ago, when he
was Bishop of Salisbury?" " Yes, please your
Majesty." " I thought so," the King replied; " I
remember his saying he went to Oxford to select
the person best qualified to serve him in that capacity, and that he fixed on you. It was equally
honourable to you both."

Among the many heartfelt congratulations which
poured in upon him on this occasion, none could
have awakened such emotions as those which he
received from his old and revered friend the Bishop
of Durham. They were equally affectionate and
cordial, though mingled with many regrets at the
prospect of losing his valued chaplain's efficient
services.

The friend of his youth, Dr. Huntingford, who

* The consecration sermon, on this occasion, was preached
by his old and highly valued friend the late Archdeacon Churton, with whom he kept up an intimate friendship and frequent
correspondence, until it was terminated by the death of the
latter, after his own translation to Salisbury.

had become Bishop of Gloucester, and was also Warden of Winchester College, addressed him as follows : —

MY DEAR FRIEND,

I HAVE again and again contemplated your promotion with unspeakable joy. On your own account, and for the sake of the church and religion, I seriously think it a most interesting event.

It is not impossible that you may see me either in London, where I must preach the Fast Sermon, or at Gloucester, through which you will pass in your way to Abergwilly. The greater leisure we should probably have at Gloucester, would make that place the more eligible for our meeting.

I am, my dear friend,

Your sincere and affectionate

G. J. GLOUCESTER.

The boys of Winchester School proffered their congratulations in a Latin letter, in which, while they plumed themselves on the honour of claiming him as a Wykehamist, they further urged it as a plea for his applying to the Warden to grant them an additional week at the ensuing holydays. His reply, in the same language, conceived in terms of terse elegance, signified his ready assent to their wishes, his zeal for the college, and his kindest wishes for all its youthful occupants; while the Bishop of Gloucester testified both his private regard for his friend, and his public sense of the merits of the Wykehamist Bishop, by granting more than was requested; a decision which he communicated in the accompanying letter.

My dear Friend,

The young men were much gratified by your epistle. I deem it of consequence that they should be deeply impressed with a sense of the effects which arise from laudable exertions. I have therefore given them a fortnight; one week to you as a Wykehamist, and one to my friend. The inclosed is my formal and official answer.

Your ever affectionate friend,

W. C., July 7. 1803. G. J. Gloucester.

My Lord,

I am honoured with your Lordship's application. The interest I take in the prosperity of every deserving Wykehamist will induce me to give one week; and the personal respect I feel for your Lordship will prompt me to add a second.

I trust the scholars of this college will retain a due sense of your kindness, and look up to your example as an object for their imitation.

I am, my Lord,

Your Lordship's affectionate friend and servant,

G. J. Gloucester.

Winton College, July 7. 1803.

CHAP. XVI.

SETTLEMENT OF THE BISHOP IN THE DIOCESE OF ST DAVID'S. — HIS PRIMARY CHARGE.

1803 and 1804.

In the autumn of 1803 the Bishop of St. David's took possession of Abergwilly Palace. Situated two miles from Carmarthen, in the vale of Towy, on the edge of the river of that name, amidst meadows of exquisite verdure, skirted by lofty wooded acclivities, this peaceful residence was in perfect accordance with the taste of its new occupant. Its rural beauties and secluded character delighted him, and his love of the picturesque found ample scope in the scenery of the neighbourhood. His predecessor in the see, Lord George Murray, had much improved and beautified the principal apartments of the palace, but it was substantially in great want of repair; and in many respects its defects proved incurable. The passing traveller must not judge of what it was during the occupancy of Bishop Burgess, by the elegant and spacious mansion which now forms the palace. This was exclusively the work of Dr. Jenkinson, the succeeding bishop, who also added much to the beauty of the pleasure grounds by judicious improvements. At the time to which we refer, it was a large, straggling house, cheerful in its appearance, but without any pretension to architectural character and effect.

The year 1803 closed before the Bishop found himself comfortably settled in his new residence. His primary visitation of the diocese took place in the year 1804. During the preceding months he had made himself fully acquainted with its condition, and had anxiously reflected upon the best means of exerting himself for its improvement.

The charge which he delivered on that occasion was equally beautiful and impressive. He touched upon the high responsibility attached to the cure of souls, with the earnestness of one who deeply felt its weight; but he more especially dwelt upon the happiness arising out of the mixture of studious, peaceful habits, and active duties naturally connected with the clerical profession. In dilating on this subject, he had the advantage of speaking from intimate experience. At Winston he had himself acted the conscientious part which he now recommended to others, and had largely tasted of the pure and elevated happiness which he depictured. So faithfully, indeed, does this charge reflect the image of his own feelings, tastes, and predilections, that we shall further the object of this memoir, as a portraiture of his character, by introducing a brief analysis of some of its most interesting and impressive passages.

He makes, at the outset, some striking reflections upon the testimony borne by the experience of all ages to the vanity of every scheme of human happiness which is not based upon religion. He then refers to the witness of the Royal Psalmist to the same truth, and cites various sublime passages in which David declares that in the love, the service, and the favour of God, he found the alone adequate object of his soul's noblest powers and affections. " Whom have I in heaven but Thee ? and there is none upon earth that I desire in comparison of Thee. My flesh and my heart faileth : but God is the strength of my heart, and my portion for ever."

For the attainment of happiness thus deeply founded, the Christian minister, he proceeds to prove, enjoys singular advantages. His profession naturally keeps him aloof from the violence of civil discords and contentions, and the law fortunately disables him from those competitions of interest,

those hazards of commercial speculation, which tend
to fill the mind with uncharitable selfishness and
irreligious anxiety. The opportunities for mental
advancement and for self-inspection which he possesses, may be improved to the most valuable ends ;
and if, as is often the case, the scene of his clerical
labours happens to be a retired situation in the
country, he may convert this allotment of Providence into an additional means of happiness. In
retirement, all nature assumes new beauties. In this
garden of Eden the voice of God is more distinctly
heard than in the din of crowds and cities. The
mind here disengages itself from the contagion of
earthly cares, and fits itself for the finest exercise of
all its powers.

To be employed in the acquisition of knowledge,
or in the contemplation of important truths, is
not only one of the purest pleasures of which the
human intellect is capable, it is also the most permanent, the least dependent upon accidents, and
the most worthy of a rational and intelligent nature.

The love of knowledge is an original innate principle. For what is mind but the faculty of perceiving knowledge ? The pleasure arising from
what we did not know before, is, too, as universal
as it is innate ; is seen in the infant and the savage,
in the scholar and the philosopher. It is also as
active as it is universal. One man it sends to the
utmost bounds of the habitable globe, through the
severest extremities of heat and cold, of danger and
disaster ; another it impels with the same ardent
spirit of inquiry, to exhaust, in his laboratory or his
study, the vigour of his healthiest days, the flower

of his animal spirits, perhaps the very power of his reason.

Happily for him who devotes himself to the Christian ministry, no other professional study combines so many of the most valuable parts of learning.

Whatever can in any degree recommend the cultivation of general knowledge, or give value to books, those inestimable repositories of its treasures, may be eminently said to the praise of sacred learning. The antiquary, the philologist, the historian, the moralist, the poet, and the artist, will all find, in the study of the Bible, ample stores to interest their respective tastes, and exercise their talents.

But in the vast concerns of eternity, how much greater is its value? They that fear God and know the depth of their own sinfulness, and look with awe and terror to the demands of divine justice, will there meet with the most consolatory grounds of hope and confidence in the mercy of God, and motives to gratitude for the means ordained for their salvation.

They who, under the impressions of the merciful goodness of God, hunger and thirst after righteousness, will there find food that will satisfy their longing after divine knowledge, their desire of growth in grace and moral improvement, food that will never fail, but endure unto everlasting life.

The Christian minister derives from the study of the Bible all the interest and pleasure which might be expected from the only authentic history of the first origin of the human race, of the progress of society, the destruction and renovation of mankind, the institution of religion and law, and the revolutions of a people separated from all other nations, and under the immediate government of God.

In the second part of this wonderful book he finds the highest affections of the mind excited by an account of the birth, life, sufferings, death, and resurrection of an extraordinary person, professing himself to be the SON OF GOD — the only-begotten SON OF GOD; and dying, not for himself, but (through the ignorance and malice of his enemies providentially permitted) for the sins of mankind. By a connected view of the two parts of this inestimable book, he sees God's great plan of the redemption of the world gradually unfold itself, from its opening in his gracious promise at the Fall, through a series of literal and typical prophecies, to its final accomplishment in the advent of the Messiah. With awe, and admiration, and gratitude, he contemplates the deep unfathomable mystery of incarnate Deity : a mystery which for ages lay hid in the designs of Providence, and was at length manifested to the world, attested by men and angels, declared by miracles and signs, by the glorious ascension of Jesus Christ, and by the effusion of the Holy Spirit on the day of Pentecost. This series of events, combining all the dignity of truth, with more than the wonders of fiction, deeply interests even an indifferent reader : but a religious man and a Christian, and above all a minister of the Gospel, is touched with a more affecting sympathy, when he finds himself a party concerned ; when he sees that he himself is one of the transgressors for whom the great sacrifice was offered, when he beholds his own cause pleading, and nothing less than everlasting happiness or misery at issue. How greatly, then, must

the effect on his own mind be increased, when, by
" rightly dividing the Word of Truth," and by
combining with the grandeur of the subject his own
personal interest, he sees at one view, by the light
of Scripture, the relative points which connect this
great plan together.

To the interesting pursuits of a studious life,
the habits proper to the clerical office add the comforts of a peaceful life, infinitely enhanced in its
value by the ends and sanctions which regulate it.
To have the " affections set on things above, and
not on things on the earth," and so to "overcome
the world;" to find the yoke of Christ easy; to
" come with boldness to the throne of grace;" to
be assured of acceptance with God in the name of
Christ; — these are the privileges of a sincere
disciple of Christ, and sources of happiness eminently resulting from the conscientious exercise of
the pastoral duties.

Having thus dilated on the blessings of a life
devoted to the Christian ministry, he next touches
upon its inestimable utility. He then briefly refers
to the chain of evidence which establishes the authenticity of the Holy Scriptures, and the truth of
Christianity, after which he enters upon a consideration of what may be called the difficulties and
discouragements of the clergy. To these he op-
poses many wise, consolatory, and animating observations, and winds up this part of the subject by
the following passage : —

" Justice can never be done to any profession
which is pursued with aversion or indifference.
Without loving his profession no one can become
an able and faithful minister of the Gospel of

Jesus Christ. But to such, the love which David had for the priesthood, for its occupations and duties, will become a living principle of conduct. ' Oh! how amiable are thy dwellings, thou Lord of hosts! My soul hath a desire and longing to enter into the courts of the Lord. My heart and my flesh rejoice in the living God!' "

The charge concludes with a description of the ends and objects proposed by a society to be called the Church Union Society, the establishment of which is described in an ensuing chapter. In an appendix the Bishop ably defends the principle of Mr. Granville Sharpe's Treatise on the Greek Definitive Article, in reply to the objections of the Rev. C. Winstanley.

CHAP. XVII.

PLANS PURSUED BY THE BISHOP FOR THE IMPROVEMENT OF HIS DIOCESE.

WE shall now place before our readers a general sketch of the plans pursued by Bishop Burgess to promote the diffusion of Christian light and knowledge throughout his extensive diocese. These plans were adopted within the first twelvemonth of his occupation of the see, and were carried on with little deviation, and with his characteristic steadfastness of purpose, throughout the long period of twenty-two years, during which he presided over it. His own personal habits and proceedings were scarcely less uniform than his plans. His life was divided

P

between the active discharge of his episcopal duties
and the laborious pursuits of an author and a scholar. Early and late he was employed with his books
and his pen: the dawn of day beheld him at his
labours, whether in grappling with difficult theological questions, or composing catechisms for children, or instructions for his clergy ; and the midnight oil was not spared in the prosecution of these
important objects.

The general sketch, therefore, which we contemplate, will be equally that of the Bishop's life in
1803 and in 1820, varied only by official residences
at Durham and attendance on parliamentary duties
in London. The same may be said of his private
history during the same long period. Nothing
could be less diversified. His habits at the age of
forty-seven and at seventy were perfectly similar,—
studious, self-denying, temperate, assiduous. The
same simple tastes and pleasures also accompanied
him from youth to age : the love of picturesque
nature, of a meditative or social walk, or an agreeable drive, poetry, music, especially sacred music.
Such also was the tenor of his mental qualities
and feelings; he was habitually amiable, gentle,
humble, affectionate; but firm and inflexible in
the maintenance of principle and the discharge of
duty : equally immovable in these respects, whether
pressed to relax from his purposes by the first
nobleman, or the humblest curate of his diocese.
As a life of this description admits of no variety,
the particulars will be included in a brief compass ;
and this will the more especially be the case between the years 1804 and 1823, because little of
his correspondence during this period is in pos-

session of the editor. The greater part of it was destroyed at the time the Bishop quitted Abergwilly for Salisbury.

By way of introduction, the following particulars respecting the see of St. David's will not be found irrelevant.

The see of St. David's is of very great extent, comprehending at the time now referred to the counties of Pembroke, Carmarthen, Cardigan, Brecknock, Radnor, a fourth part of Glamorganshire, eight parishes in Herefordshire, and a small portion of Montgomery and Monmouth shires.

It was constituted a metropolitan see of the British Church as far back as the sixth century. Twenty-five Archbishops succeeded each other in its administration. Sampson, the last of them, lived A. D. 915. His successors, though they lost the title, exercised archiepiscopal functions over the suffragan Bishops of Worcester, Hereford, St. Asaph, Bangor, and Llandaff, until the reign of Henry the First, when Bernard, a Norman, was violently planted in the see by that monarch, and surrendered his metropolitan powers to the Archbishop of Canterbury.

Carleon was the original seat of the Archbishopric. It was probably abandoned in consequence of the outrages to which it was exposed by invasions from the adjoining counties of England. This translation took place somewhere between A. D. 550 and 609, when St. David occupied the see. The reverence inspired by his Christian virtues, and the zeal and ability with which he opposed the pernicious doctrines of Pelagius, had called him from the seclusion of monastic life to the possession of the first honours of his native Church. It is in Wales, and within this period, that the original British Apostolic Church maybe distinctly traced. Stillingfleet proves, in his Origines Britannicæ, that the see of St. David's was not subject to the Pope before the Conquest; consequently that for many centuries it existed in an independent form. Giraldus Cambrensis maintains that this state of independence continued until the reign of Henry I.

The history of the see may be divided into three periods : —

1st. From its foundation, in the sixth century, to the abdication of the metropolitan authority of its bishops in the twelfth.

2d. From the commencement of its suffragan state to the beginning of the Reformation in the sixteenth century.

3rd. From that time to the present.

The first portion of this history is designated by Bishop Burgess as a period of holy austerity and venerable poverty ; the second, as the period of establishment and endowment; and the third, as respects the external condition of the see, as one of declension and dilapidation. The noble architectural buildings, the ruins of which attract so many travellers to St. David's, were erected subsequently to the extinction of its metropolitan state. They were the works of individual wealth and liberality. The palace of St. David's, which must originally have been a splendid residence, was built about the middle of the fourteenth century. It was out of repair early in the sixteenth, and, before its close, was no longer habitable. There were two other episcopal mansions at this time, Lamphey and the Lawhaden ;

and no less than four collegiate establishments within the diocese, for the promotion of learning and clerical education.

The present Cathedral was commenced in the year 1180, by Bishop Peter de Lien, and was completed by his successor, who dedicated it to St. Andrew and St. David. Though built at different periods, and exhibiting consequent incongruities of style, and mingled vestiges of solidity and decay, it is an edifice which, in conjunction with the ruins of the Bishop's palace, is fraught with interest to the antiquarian, so beautiful are some of its chapels, and so interesting many of its architectural features and accompaniments. The following particulars are curious : —

In the year 1287, Bishop Becke made a statute, by which he binds himself and future bishops to leave to their successors 32 ploughs and 256 oxen, that is, eight oxen to each plough, for the cultivation of the episcopal estates. These ploughs and oxen appear to have been attached to the several manors according to the relative magnitude of the estates.

In the year 1379, by a statute of Bishop Haughton, the number of episcopal mansions and manor-houses was reduced to eight, — " sustinenda et reparanda ex necessitate et statuto ecclesiæ Menevensis;" and for the use of the episcopal estates, only 10 ploughs and 79 oxen were to be left by every bishop for his successor. The difference in the number of ploughs and oxen appears to have arisen from the reduction of the manor-houses, and the leasing out of many of the estates, not from any alienation of property; for in Henry VIII.'s survey, more than

thirty manors are enumerated as belonging to the
Bishop of St. David's.

The charge from which the above facts are taken
was printed at Carmarthen, 1811.

The revenues of the see had, in the course of
time, become so much straitened by alienations, en-
croachments, and spoliation, more especially at the
period of the Reformation, that their average produce in 1804 amounted only to 1200*l.* per annum.
Without the retention, therefore, of his stall at
Durham, Bishop Burgess could neither have met the
needful expenses of such an extensive diocese, nor
have exercised that enlarged charity, and that kind
hospitality, for which he was so much distinguished.

He found the see, in all important particulars, in
a neglected condition. Too generally, indeed, it
had been regarded as a stepping-stone to preferment, a prospect fatal to the conception, and still
more to the prosecution, of any continuous and well-
organized system of improvement. "If I had
looked for translation," said the Bishop, "after I
was appointed to St. David's, I should have done
nothing." So far was any such wish from his
thoughts, that he was known, again and again, to
say, in the course of the twenty-two years during
which he held the bishopric, that he should be content and happy to live and die there. These casual
statements gave rise to a report that he had publicly
expressed a firm resolution never to accept an offer
of translation. I can venture to say on his own authority there was no truth in this report. But he
entered on his episcopal functions firmly bent on
making a faithful discharge of his various and com-
plicated duties the business and the happiness of his

existence, and anticipating no other reward than the
testimony of his own conscience, and the approving
smile of the " Chief Shepherd." Secular considerations could weigh but little with one whose motives
of conduct were thus elevated.

The condition of the diocese, as respected the
education of the clergy, and the due enforcement of
discipline, was lamentable. The ancient collegiate
seminaries had long been stripped of their revenues,
and fallen into utter decay. There were no suitable establishments for clerical training, while the
general poverty of the benefices was such as wholly
to preclude the great majority of candidates for
orders from the possibility of aspiring to a University
education. As a necessary consequence, there was
scarcely one among those who presented themselves
at the Bishop's first ordination, who had enjoyed
this privilege. He afterwards ascertained that a
youth, who proved peculiarly ignorant and incompetent, had occupied, only a short time before, the
situation of a livery servant. The general custom
was for young men to continue at the plough till
the year before they attained the age of twenty-three,
when, after spending a single twelvemonth at the
Seminary of Ystrd Merug, they were deemed competent for ordination.

As a first step towards a better system of clerical
education, the Bishop licensed four schools, to
which he exclusively assigned the preparation of
candidates for orders within the diocese. Seven
years of previous study were required, and competition for the scholarships or exhibitions instituted under the Bishop's direction by the Church
Union Society was confined to these schools. In

order to promote the study of Hebrew, various
prizes were offered to the best proficients in that
language. Though the efficiency of these seminaries necessarily depended in a great degree upon
the ability and character of the master, whose incompetency occasionally frustrated the hopes of
the Bishop, a great and beneficial change resulted,
on the whole, from his regulations ; students of real
merit were sure to be brought under his special
notice, and an efficient master became the object of
his encouragement and patronage. Among such,
it may be permitted us to pay a passing tribute to
the memory of the Rev. Eliezer Williams, who for
many years presided over the school of Lampeter,
of which place he was Vicar. His learning, abilities,
and Christian character were of a superior order ;
and while he sedulously laboured to render the
young men under his care good scholars and sound
theologians, he was no less anxious to instil into
their minds principles of vital piety, and to train
them for active duties. His temper was benevolent,
his dispositions were amiable, and his manners engaging. His deportment in his dying hours was in
unison with his living example; for he was enabled
to testify to his pupils, on the approach of the last
enemy, that through faith in his Redeemer he par-
took of that divine, that inestimable support, which
wrests the sting from Death, the victory from the
Grave. So embalmed was his memory in their
love and veneration, that they united in subscribing
a sufficient sum to raise a simple but elegant monument to his memory, with an appropriate Latin
inscription, in the parish church of Lampeter.

The foundation of the most important reforms
effected by the Bishop was laid in the institution

of a Society, in the year 1804, intitled, " A Society
for Promoting Christian Knowledge and Church
Union in the Diocese of St. David's." The meeting for its establishment took place at Abergwilly
Palace on October 10th, 1804; a day memorable
in the annals of South Wales, as the College of
St. David's at Lampeter, which now imparts, on
very moderate terms, an excellent education to
students for orders, may justly be said to have emanated from its proceedings.

The general object was to form a society, or
religious and literary association, for the purpose of
promoting charity and union among all classes of
Christians in the diocese, and of diffusing useful
knowledge among the poor. To effect these ends,
it undertook, —

1. To distribute Bibles, Common Prayer Books,
and religious tracts in Welsh and English, at reduced prices, or gratis, among the poor ; especially
such tracts as are recommended by the Society for
Promoting Christian Knowledge.

2. To establish libraries for the use of the clergy
of the diocese.

3. To facilitate the means of education to young
men intended for the ministry of the Church of
England in the diocese.

4. To encourage the establishing of English
schools for the benefit of the poor.

5. To promote the institution of Sunday schools.

6. To form a fund for the relief of superannuated
curates.

The Bishop, on first placing these objects in detail before the assembled clergy, concluded his remarks as follows : —

" With our united endeavours for these several
purposes, let us daily and earnestly pray God to
bestow his choicest blessings on the Established
Church of this country, and to grant that all dissen-
sion and schism may yield to the due influence of
the Gospel, to juster notions of our Christian calling, and to that spirit of obedience and charity
which may bring all believers in Christ into one
fold under one Shepherd, striving together for the
faith of the Gospel, with one mind and one mouth
glorifying God."

With reference to the third object he thus expressed himself : —

" It would be very beneficial to the Church, if
young men intended for the ministry, who are precluded the advantages of a University education,
were enabled to employ their time in strictly professional studies during the four years preceding
their ordination. An establishment of appropriate
education for the ministry of the Church in this
diocese is very desirable. But, for the support of
such an establishment, much ampler funds are requisite than are necessary to our present undertaking. For the present we may, with very good
effect, assist young students in divinity with books
and some pecuniary aid. For the accomplishment
of this object, I earnestly recommend that every
incumbent may contribute the tenth part of one
year's income of his benefice ; and in the case of
new incumbents, that the benefaction be payable at
the end of the second year of his incumbency.
And I trust that such a contribution from the patrimony of the Church towards the better support of
the 'household of Faith,' will not be thought bur-

densome to any sincere friend of the Church. To this object I am willing to contribute a proportionate part of what I am told is the average income of this See."

On a subsequent occasion it was resolved to collect separate contributions for the projected College. The Bishop proposed that the society should also form a fund for the support of superannuated curates, so that when disabled by incurable infirmity, or by extreme old age, they might retire from duties to which they were become incompetent, and close their lives in peaceful and humble independence. Every minister, a candidate for this benefaction, must have been a subscriber of at least five shillings per annum to this fund, for two years previously to his application.

The clergy of the diocese, though in the great majority of cases possessed of very slender preferment, cheerfully responded to this appeal of their Diocesan. Each year the sums of money accruing from collections made for the intended College, for superannuated curates, and for exhibitions for students were funded. The interest annually accruing was employed in payments for exhibitions to students, and in stipends to the curates; and the sum total in the year 1820, including benefactions from liberal and Christian friends beyond the bounds of the diocese, amounted to nearly 11,000*l*.

In the same year it will be found that fifteen exhibitions of 10*l*. each were paid to the said number of students in divinity who had acquitted themselves in a superior manner at the public examinations; that eight superannuated curates received a stipend of 25*l*. each; that two sums, one of 20*l*., a second of 25*l.*, were paid as prizes for the best Essays on two subjects in Divinity; and that 75*l.* were distributed in smaller prizes to students for their proficiency in various branches of study.

The greater proportion of the fund which has been specified accrued from the contributions of a clergy of very straitened incomes, many of them with large families, and forced to struggle against severe difficulties. The result forms a most honourable proof of their Christian zeal and charity, while the magnitude of the amount gradually created by this annual accumulation of small donations forms a striking comment on the important consequences of steady perseverance in the prosecution of a noble and well-conceived scheme of utility and benevolence.

In the year 1807, the Bishop, on delivering his second Charge to the Clergy of St. David's, adverted in the following terms to the successful progress and beneficial influence of his plans of improvement : —

" I cannot dismiss the subject of our society, without cordially congratulating the clergy of the diocese upon the progress of its several plans, and on the liberal encouragement which it has received. At the same time I must be permitted to renew my former recommendation, that all who partake of the patrimony of the Church would contribute the tenth of one year's income of their benefices to the fund, which is devoted to the education of young persons intended for orders, but who cannot partake of a University education.

" The patrimony of the Church is an awful subject to those who consider for what purposes it was endowed with the temporalities which it possesses. The labourer is certainly worthy of his hire : they that serve at the altar have a right, no doubt, to live by the altar, but it would be well for every incumbent to balance carefully the emoluments he has received with the good he has done; and to remember that Church benefices were intended for the support of religion, and for the honour of the Church, not to confer worldly superfluities and luxuries on individuals, nor for the enrichment of their families. In that portion of the Lord's vineyard which is situated in this diocese, our benefices, in general, are not much in danger of the charge of superfluities and luxuries; and the liberality of the resident clergy is greatly to the credit of their profession. I only wish to suggest to all whom it may concern, that spiritual incomes, which are in a great measure diverted to mere worldly and selfish advantages, will be sources of spiritual uneasiness in the hour of serious reflection, and at that trying season which is to separate us for ever from all our earthly concerns."

The operations of this society not only effected much direct good, but were also eminently useful to the diocese, by the frequent intercourse to which they led between the Bishop and his clergy. They found in him a faithful monitor, anxious to impress upon them the importance of a zealous and conscientious discharge of their various duties, a wise adviser in their doubts and difficulties, and a kind sympathising friend in the hour of trial and affliction. Those who sincerely did their duty were sure to be singled out by him for encouragement and promotion. His approving smile ani-

mated their pious exertions, his liberal hand was
prompt to minister to their necessities, his hospitable mansion was always open to them, and he
invariably met them with cordiality and kindness.
Whatever were his studious pursuits, they were
never allowed to interfere with his giving audience,
whether to the incumbent of an important living,
or to the poorest curate of his diocese The inter-
ruption to his studies was occasionally not a little
trying ; but this was never visible in his looks or
manner, though, when a very wet day occurred,
he not unfrequently expressed pleasure in the anticipation of having a long morning wholly to himself.

A room was expressly set apart for the reception
of his clergy, and they always found it hospitably
provided with substantial refreshments. He was,
in fact, a sort of Elder Brother among them, uniting
a singularly mild, winning, and gentle demeanour,
with a constant endeavour to encourage and ani-
mate their exertions, and to acquire as well as to
impart instruction and information. Nor, when the
occasion called for it, did any one know better how
to assume that dignity of manner which effectually
represses undue familiarity.

CHAP. XVIII.

THE BISHOP'S MODE OF PREPARING FOR, AND OF CONDUCTING, HIS ORDINATIONS

In preparing for, and conducting his ordinations,
the Bishop acted in the spirit of the Apostolic in-

junction, "Lay hands suddenly on no man;" and in order fully to ascertain the competency of candidates, he himself performed the functions of examining chaplain. The onerous duties which this office imposed upon him so entirely engaged his thoughts and attention for the week preceding an ordination, that all other engagements were superseded; and he passed his time in the examining room, sedulously superintending the proceedings of the candidates, and satisfying himself as to their qualifications and attainments.

Whenever, after due examination, he met with cases of incompetency, he was inflexible in withholding orders, but it was his study and delight to encourage and to draw forth modest merit.

Accurate Biblical knowledge, a competent acquaintance with the Greek Testament, and facility in English composition, were among the leading qualifications which he required. But he also held out particular encouragement to the study of Hebrew; and in order to facilitate the acquisition of the language, he published various useful elementary works, which were introduced into the schools of the diocese, and have gone through many editions. The principal are entitled as follows: — Hebrew Elements; or an Introduction to the Reading of the Hebrew Scriptures, 8vo. A Hebrew Primer, 12mo. Motives to the Study of Hebrew, in two parts, 12mo.*

He had also turned his attention to the Arabic as

* " These little works," says the Reverend Hartwell Horne, " form the simplest and clearest introduction to the reading of Hebrew *without* points that have ever been published."

A new edition of the two first, neatly printed in one volume 12mo., issued from the University Press, Glasgow, in 1823.

a cognate language, and published, in 1809, a little work, entitled "The Arabic Alphabet, or an Introduction to the Reading of Arabic."

That candidates should have attentively studied and should well understand the Articles of the Church of England, was another qualification which he justly deemed essential. But, idependently of the learned preparation which he thus required, he did his utmost to impress upon them the absolute necessity of personal piety in order to a faithful and effectual discharge of the clerical functions. He would, in a kind but scrutinising manner, inquire into the motives of those who applied to him for orders ; and unless they proved to be such as would stand the test of reason and of conscience, he gave them no encouragement.

Besides touching forcibly upon this subject in private, he published several small Treatises, with the view of deterring men from inconsiderately selecting the clerical profession, and of stirring up those who were ordained to a faithful and exemplary discharge of their pastoral duties. Among these the following may be enumerated : —

" The Importance and Difficulty of the Pastoral Office, and the Danger of rashly undertaking it." 8vo. 1811.

" A Collection of such Scriptures as ought to be seriously and frequently considered by all who are preparing for Orders, or are already ordained." 12mo. 1816.

" A conscientious Minister's Compunctions on the Recollection of his Want of Preparation for the Ministry of the Church, before his first entering into

Holy Orders, extracted from the Rev. T. Scott's Force of Truth." 12mo.

Though we cannot pretend to give a particular account of his episcopal admonitions, as contained in these publications, and in his various charges, their leading principles may be epitomised as follows : —

That the foundation of clerical usefulness must be laid in just and serious views of the sacredness and importance of the Christian ministry, and of the solemn responsibility which the " cure of souls " involves.

That the pastoral office, when undertaken and discharged in this spirit, will open to the mind sources of the most interesting employment and the purest happiness.

That the Christian Church and Ministry were instituted by Christ himself, to promulgate from age to age the terms of his Gospel, to promote its vital efficacy, and to administer the sacred rites and ordinances which he enjoined in connection with it.

That the Gospel is a message of grace and reconciliation from an offended but merciful God to a sinful world, that its benefits are inestimable; but that those only who are brought to a penitential conviction that they are sinners will duly comprehend its object, or estimate its value

That it unfolds the wonderful means conceived in the counsels of Infinite Wisdom and Love, for the expiation and pardon of sin, and for the restoration of an apostate race to the favour and image of their Maker. That its principles, therefore, comprehend the sole philosophy adapted to the peculiar

Q

condition, the nature, and the exigencies of man,
providing for the pacification of his conscience, the
moral renovation of his nature, his present happiness, and the discipline of his soul for a glorious
Immortality.

That a cheering and celestial light is thus cast
upon human existence, the way of access to a
reconciled God, through faith in the Great Mediator, laid open; "Heaven is added to Earth,
Eternity to Time," and the devout soul placed in a
condition of ineffable alliance and amity with the
Father of Spirits.

That the grandeur of the facts connected with
this dispensation is no less stupendous than its
object is merciful. That the life and death, the
resurrection and ascension of the Son of God, are
events of such transcendant and touching interest,
as will not only be celebrated by the latest accents
of the Church on earth, but will perpetually furnish
matter of wonder and admiration to the hierarchies
of heaven.

That the " Ambassadors of Christ," the delegates
of his mission of Redeeming Love, appointed to
gather his sheep, from amidst an unbelieving world,
within the precincts of his heavenly fold, should be
men participating in that supreme love to God, that
zeal for his glory, and for the eternal welfare of
souls, which characterized Him whose ministers
they are, and whose message of mercy they proclaim.
That they should preach to the world and to their
flocks by their practical example, no less than by
their addresses from the pulpit, and labour both in
public and in private for the spiritual edification of
the souls committed to their charge, as those who

will hereafter have to render an account of this sacred trust to the " Chief Shepherd."

That those only who really love their profession will thus efficiently discharge its duties, and that none but such as are anxious about their own salvation will duly sound the alarm, to awaken to a life of righteousness a world " dead in trespasses and sins."

That personal religion is therefore no less essential to a clergyman, than professional learning. That they should never be disunited : that prayer and the devout perusal of the Holy Scriptures should daily sanctify study, and that study and prayer should lend their combined influence to the public ministrations and the private labours of the Devout Pastor.

What was the impression produced by the mode in which the Bishop conducted his examinations, will be best conceived by my quoting the words of an excellent living clergyman ordained by him, who, in reply to some queries on this subject, thus expresses himself : —

" He did not entrust to others the examination of candidates for Holy Orders. He took upon himself that important task ; and no man was better qualified ; for, having once satisfied himself of the competency of the person examined, he blended his queries with such admonitions as were likely to produce the most beneficial effects. For my part, I trust, the benignity of his countenance, and the kind, the solemn, the emphatic manner in which he spoke to me, once in particular, during my examination, concerning my duties as a Christian Minister, will never, ° while memory holds her

seat,' be erased from my mind. During the ordination week he frequently exhorted us to be constant and regular in the practice of family devotion,
of which he every morning gave us a beautiful example."

It was solely for the purpose of impressing the
Clergy of his Diocese with just views of the importance and responsibility of the Pastoral Office,
that he proposed some remarkable subjects for prize
essays in the year 1810. In the List of Essays
to which premiums were assigned by the Church
Union Society in the Diocese of St. David's, are
the two following. — In 1811, a premium of 10*l.*
was adjudged to the Rev. Johnson Grant, for the
best Essay on " Conversion," and on the three following questions — " Whether a Minister of the
Church can be an unconverted professor of Christianity? What are the marks of unconversion in a
Minister of the Church? What are the means most
likely to excite in the mind of such a Minister (if
such can be) a sense of his unconverted state?"

In 1812, a premium of 10*l.* was adjudged to Mr.
(now the Rev. C.) Wilks, of Edmund Hall, Oxford,
for the best Essay on the Signs of Conversion and
Unconversion in Ministers of the Church.

These are startling questions; and yet a moment's
reflection upon the secular motives which frequently
induce men to intrude themselves into the sacred
profession, furnishes the best comment on their
aptitude and propriety. The Essay of Mr. Wilks
treated this delicate subject with so much practical
discrimination, and touched in so impressive a manner on the responsibility, dignity, and importance
of the Clerical Office, that the Bishop to the close

of his life was in the habit of keeping a large number of copies of it in his house, and of presenting
them to Clergymen after ordination. An abridgment
of this Essay was also one of the exercises frequently
required from candidates for Orders.

The following letter, addressed in the year 1815
by the Bishop to G. Marriott, Esq., will be read
with interest in reference to this subject.

DEAR SIR,

I have unsealed my letter for the sake of giving
you an anecdote respecting the usefulness of a book,
which you, I remember, approved on its first publication, — the Essay on the Signs of Conversion and
Unconversion in Ministers of the Church. The
Bishop of Gloucester *, previously to his late ordination, required of his candidates, who were six, that
they should read and give him an account of the
Essay. On the day of examination, only *five* candidates presented themselves. A letter was delivered to the Bishop from the absentee, declaring
himself no longer a candidate. My correspondent
adds, " You will be able to judge of, and to participate in, the feelings of the Bishop when he read the
young man's letter, in which he expresses the deepest sense of gratitude to the Bishop for his kindness
in putting the book into his hands, which had been
happily the means of saving him from plunging into
the sacred office inconsiderately, and without any
adequate impression of its importance, and of the
responsibility attached to it, and declining being
considered as a candidate." My correspondent

* Bishop Huntingford.

Q 3

adds, " If no other advantage had arisen fiom the St. David's Society than that little Tract, the Society would have ample cause of satisfaction and congratulation."

I am, dear Sir,
Yours very faithfully,
T. St. David's.

The Bishop attached the greatest importance to the sedulous preparation of young people for the Apostolic rite of Confirmation, and his exhortations to his Clergy on this subject were earnest and impressive. He entreated them to devote part of each Sunday to this duty ; or, in cases where that was not practicable, to give up some day in the week to it. On account of the great extent of the Diocese and the badness of the roads, he found it impossible satisfactorily to discharge his Episcopal functions in respect to Confirmation by a triennial Visitation. He therefore made a division of his Diocese into three districts, one of which he annually visited ; and though the consequent sacrifice of time and of personal labour was considerable, he cheerfully made it, in order to accomplish the end in a manner satisfactory to his Clergy, and beneficial to the youthful objects of their care.

He was in the habit of concluding the administration of this rite with an affectionate and impressive address, after which he presented a Religious Tract or Treatise, suited to the occasion, to each of the children.

The Welsh gentry were truly hospitable in their reception of the Bishop in the course of his journeys.; but it often happened that he was obliged to stop at small inns and put up with sorry accommodations, when his coachman, who was very proud of his black horses, was frequently put not a little out of humour by the badness of the stabling. After he had been long enough in his place to identify himself in a certain degree with his master's duties and dignities, he would sometimes say, with an air of importance, "*We* are always confirming or ordaining."

With respect to the most solemn and impressive of the Christian ordinances, the Bishop thus expresses himself. " Next to the duties of catechising the children, and preparing them by *precious* and *gradual* discipline for Confirmation, is the other great duty of preparing the people for the Sacrament of the Lord's Supper by appropriate instructions. This cannot be better done than by appointing one evening in the week preceding the Sacrament Sunday for this purpose. The influence," he adds, " which this attention to your people will have on their minds and conduct, is greater than any one can imagine, who does not know it by experience. The effect produced is the joint result of your instructions and of the impression made on them by your solicitude for their spiritual welfare."

Justly conceiving that a Clergyman must be a very incompetent instructor of the ignorant, or comforter of the sick, who is not familiar with the vernacular language of his parish, he introduced into his Diocese a regulation, requiring that all persons presented to Welsh livings, or nominated to Welsh curacies, should give satisfactory proofs of their proficiency in Welsh to Commissioners specially appointed by himself to examine them; and further, that candidates for Orders, having Welsh titles, should furnish similar evidence of their sufficiency in this respect, before they were admitted to further examination.

In order to correct another very prevalent evil, the hasty or inarticulate reading of the service of the Church, he not only in his Charges called the special attention of his Clergy to the subject, but induced the Church Union Society to offer an annual premium to the best reader of a Sermon, and of the Common Prayer Book of the Church of England, in each of the four Archdeaconries of the Diocese His great object was to introduce an impressive but natural mode of reading the service.

On this subject he thus expresses himself · " The advantages of a just and appropriate elocution in the duties of preaching and praying cannot be too highly valued, or too diligently cultivated, if we consider the unspeakable importance of those duties; and the difference between a cold and monotonous, or hasty utterance, and the enunciation which marks the affection of a heart 'that ' believeth unto salvation,' and is 'strongly impressed with the greatness of the duty in which it is engaged."

With a view to elevate the social intercourse and habits of his Clergy, he recommended monthly meetings in the different Archdeaconries for conference on subjects of professional and learned interest.

" Habits of duty in our profession," he says, " are, in themselves, habits of holiness. But as a further aid to the success of his ministry, and to his own growth in grace, I know nothing so desirable to the Minister of a parish, especially to our younger brethren, as a monthly or quarterly meeting of serious and devout Ministers, anxious to learn and ready to communicate. Such meetings were strongly recommended by Lord Bacon, Bishop Burnet, and Archbishop Tenison.

" The monthly meetings I recommend to be for prayer, for reading the Scriptures, and for religious and literary conversation ; the quarterly meetings to be accompanied with the public service of the Church, and a sermon."

He also established a week-day evening lecture for the special benefit of the labouring and industrious classes, to be delivered for sixteen successive weeks at churches in two principal places in each of the Archdeaconries.*

---

* The following Rules of the Ultra-Ayron Clerical Society are introduced as a specimen of the mode in which the Bishop's advice was acted on

At a Meeting of the Clergy of the Upper and Lower Deaneries of Ultra-Ayron, October 6. 1807,

RESOLVED,

1. That our Meeting be called a Clerical Society.

2. That we meet on the first Wednesday in every Month during the Summer ; and Quarterly from Michaelmas to Lady-Day

3. That the object of our Society, or the purpose for which we meet, be to edify one another, and to promote the success of our Ministry, by friendly and professional communications.

4 That a book be provided for entering the Minutes of our Meeting, and a Secretary chosen : that the names of the Members be called over by the Secretary at every Meeting, and then the business of the day to begin with reading the Word of God and prayer.

5 That every Member of our Society, whether he be a housekeeper or a lodger, has, or will endeavour to have, family prayer at home

6 That every Member of our Society has, or will endeavour to have, a Sunday School in his parish, or in the parishes of which he has the care.

7 That every Member of our Society does and must faithfully observe the 75th Canon of our Church.

8. That every Member of our Society be able to give account at every Meeting of some book that he has read during the preceding month, and that we be ready to lend one another books.

9 That brotherly admonition be administered and received in the spirit of love, without giving or taking offence.

10. That whatever passes at our Meetings be confidential, and not to be reported elsewhere

11. That if any Member violate any one of the solemn resolutions or rules of our Society, notice thereof may be sent to the Secretary, for him to lay the matter before the Society at a subsequent Meeting

12. That the Reverend *R. Evans,* Vicar of Lanbadarn-fawr, be appointed Secretary to our Clerical Society.

13. That any future Meeting, when no fewer than three fourths of the Members are present, be competent to revise or add to the preceding resolutions.

14. That at every Meeting, a subject, a text of Scripture, or some useful question in Theology, be proposed, to be considered and discussed at our next Meeting; and that every Member of our Society be expected to bring an essay, or at least come prepared to speak, on the subject to be discussed

---

CHAP. XIX.

THE BISHOP'S MODE OF LIFE IN LONDON AND AT DURHAM — GROUNDS OF HIS OPPOSITION TO THE ROMAN CATHOLIC CLAIMS. — HIS CONTROVERSIAL WRITINGS AGAINST POPERY. — HIS TRACTS ON THE INDEPENDENCE OF THE ANCIENT BRITISH CHURCH.

THE dispositions and tastes of the Bishop, the bent of his talents, and his studious habits, rendered frequent attendance in Parliament irksome to him; but while in Town, during the Session, he made a point of being present in the House of Lords whenever questions came on affecting the interests of Religion and Morality, or those of the Established

Church. From speaking in public he shrank at all times ; and although he did on some few occasions deliver his sentiments upon momentous subjects, and in strong language, in his place in Parliament, yet such were his diffidence and modesty, that the effort never failed to cost him much previous conflict. In his absence, his proxy was usually entrusted to some Peer whose principles and opinions accorded with his own.

The time, however, which he thus passed in London, was actively employed in the support or promotion of objects of a charitable or professional character, or in literary studies and researches. The transfer of his person to the gay and busy Metropolis made but little change in the prevailing bent of his thoughts and pursuits, which were usually revolving around some question of theological interest, or of public or private duty ; and his habits of temperance were so strict, that he was at his studies early and late without suffering from the effects of severe application.

In one respect, however, he did painfully feel its consequences ; and that was in his eyesight, which gradually became so much impaired, that during the last twenty years of his life he was constantly obliged to wear a green shade. The weakness of his eyes rendered preaching a painful effort to him. Neither had nature endowed him with oratorical gifts. His voice, though remarkably sweet, was low, he had not much of fancy or imagination, and the calm equanimity of his mind unfitted him for acting with power on large assemblies. He took his turn as a Prebendary at Durham, and he occasionally composed and delivered sermons on public occasions.

Thus, in the year 1804, he preached before the
Royal Humane Society; in 1807, before the Lords
Spiritual and Temporal in Westminster Abbey; and
in 1808, before the Society for the Propagation of
the Gospel in Foreign Parts. The time which he
spent at Durham, to keep residence, was employed
much in the same studious manner as in London;
varied, however, by the calls of hospitality, and by
his public duties within the precincts of the Cathedral. The house which he finally occupied in virtue
of his Stall, commanded from the drawing-room
window the finest among the many fine points of
view which crown the course of the river Were, as
its silver waters lave the rich groves, and the base
of the stately and venerable piles which enchant the
eye by their picturesque combinations, in the very
centre of the city of Durham.

The two following letters, addressed at intervals
of several years to Dr. Burney, attest the interest
with which he continued to revert to topics of critical and literary interest.

DEAR BURNEY,   Durham, Feb. 21. 1805

I wish it were in my power to supply you with a
copy of Ruhnkenius's De Gallâ Placidiâ.* I do not
think I ever saw it.

I am very glad to hear that Lunn is going to publish the smaller pieces of Ruhnkenius, and that Mr.
Kidd is to have the superintendence of the work. I
should rejoice to hear that it was to be followed by
Leopardus. Will you desire Lunn to send me his
catalogue of foreign books?

* Galla Placidia was wife of the Gothic monarch Adol-
phus Theodosius the Great.

The Dean of Christ Church informed me not long since that a young man of his college was employed on Hephæstia. I am glad to hear that Mr. Gaisford is to have the advantage of your valuable communications.

I have at present in the press here, a συγγραμμα-τιον of Tzetzes, Περι Διαφορας Ποιητων, περι Κωμῳδιας και περι Τραγῳδιας, of which you shall have a specimen soon.

I am glad you think my Initia Paulina may be useful in a school. I am very uncertain whether I shall be in town before I return to Wales, but I think not.

Though I am sorry that Porson quits Euripides, I am glad to hear that Aristophanes is likely to be the better for him.

Yours very sincerely,

T. St. David's.

TO DR. BURNEY.

Dear Sir,   Abergwilly Palace, August 5. 1812.

I have inclosed a few pages which I am preparing for a preface to a sermon, which I preached lately at Camarthen, before our St. David's Society. In these pages I have occasion to controvert a date or two of Bishop Pearson in his Annales Paulini. We have both of us a common interest in respecting the authority of the incomparable author of the Exposition of the Creed. You will therefore not impute my difference of opinion to any want of deference for his judgment.

There is a passage in p. 21. of the Annales, " Jo sephus post annum — to per triennium," which ap-

pears to me to be very defective both in the assertion
" incunte anno lx." and in the conclusion respecting
Josephus, " familiares dici non poterent." I reserve
what I have to say on it for a little further enquiry.

Tell me if any doubts or difficulties occur to you
in the perusal of the inclosed.

I am, dear Sir,

Yours very faithfully,

T. St David's.

I sincerely congratulate you on all your late
honours.

Among the few public questions in which he did
take an active part was that of Roman Catholic
Emancipation. From the commencement to the
close of the struggle which terminated in its enact-
ment, he gave, on grounds both Political and Religious, his inflexible opposition to that measure,
and in various publications, as well as occasionally
in his Charges, he stated his objections to it with
much energy and ability. He contended that the
admission of Roman Catholics to legislative power
would be not only inconsistent with the principles
of our Protestant Constitution in Church and State,
but would be fraught with danger to both. The
fundamental principle of the British Constitution,
he maintained, was to support with the utmost te-
nacity the Protestant Established Church, as the
fructifying source of that Religious influence and of
that well-balanced Civil Freedom upon which the
security of the State depends. Now the consequence
of granting Emancipation would be the admission
of a body of seventy or eighty men into Parliament
who, if true to their Faith, would spare no efforts

to degrade or subvert the Protestant Established
Church, and to augment the influence of their own.

In addition to these objections, he urged his
strong conviction that the proposed concessions, instead of allaying, if granted, the existing differences
between Protestants and Roman Catholics, would
have a directly contrary effect, by stirring up in the
latter ulterior objects of ambition, and by producing
an increase of demand and rivalry, forming new and
perpetual sources of future contention.

No calculations of expediency, he contended,
ought to create any wavering in the minds of men
who shared with him in these opinions, as to the
course to be pursued. Every religious consideration which made the Reformation necessary should
still endear to them their Protestant constitution ;
and, trusting in the equity and the sanctity of their ı
cause, they ought inflexibly to maintain their principles and to commit the issue to Providence.

The pervading spirit of all that he spoke or published on this subject was that of uncompromising
objection, upon religious grounds, to the proposed
concessions. He deemed it inconsistent with his
office and clerical character to take up the question
in any other way.

But he was also the author of several publications*,

* The following is a list of the principal : —
Bishop Bull's Letter to Mr. Nelson on the Corruptions of
the Church of Rome in relation to Ecclesiastical Government,
the Rule of Faith, &c. 18mo. 1813.

Two Letters to the Clergy of the Diocese of St David's on
the Independence of the ancient British Church on any Foreign
Jurisdiction. 8vo 1813.

A volume of Tracts on the Independence of the ancient
British Church, on the Supremacy of the Pope, and on the

in which, without reference to the Roman Catholic question, his learning and researches were success-fully applied to expose the errors and corruptions of the Church of Rome; to vindicate the nationality and independence of that of England, and to assert its claims as a branch of the Church Catholic. He had read and reflected much upon the principal points of difference between the two Churches, and he ably defended and illustrated the grounds upon which our own proceeded in her solemn and deli-berate separation from that of Rome.

The Protestant zeal of the Bishop, as displayed in these publications, proved both seasonable and useful in directing the inquiries of the Clergy to subjects connected with the Antiquities of the Pri-mitive Church, within that period of its history in which it was uncontaminated by Romish cor-ruptions.

They also did much to elucidate a principle the importance of which is daily becoming more un-derstood, and which ought never to be lost sight of by the Church of England in controversial dis-cussions with that of Rome ; and that is, the broad, the vital distinction which exists between *Catho-licism* and *Romanism*.

Differences between the Churches of England and Rome 8vo 1815

The Protestants' Catechism. 8vo 1818

English Reformation and Papal Schism 8vo 1819

Remarks on the Western Travels of St Paul, as an Argu-ment of Proscription against the Supremacy of the Pope and Church of Rome 1820

Popery incapable of Union with a Protestant Church 1820

A Speech delivered in the House of Lords on the Roman Catholic Question 1821

By the term Catholicism, the Bishop meant the fundamental doctrines of the Christian Faith, derivable from, or provable by, Holy Scripture, and maintained by the Primitive Catholic Church in her Creeds, Sacraments, and Ordinances.

By the term Romanism, he meant the corruptions of Faith and Worship gradually introduced into the Western branch of the Christian Church, first by the contagion of superstition, and subsequently by the subtle arts and usurpations of Popery As the Church of Rome is Episcopal in her form of government, and receives the Apostles' and the Nicene creeds, she may be said to hold the fundamental principles of Catholicism; but she has engrafted upon them such a mass of novel and erroneous doctrines, and superstitious observances, that it is impossible to defend the opinions and the worship of that Church by the authority either of Scripture or Primitive Antiquity.

There is no warrant, for instance, in the inspired writings of the Evangelists and Apostles, for the Supremacy of the Bishop of Rome as Head by Divine Right of the Catholic Church of Christ, nor yet for the Infallibility, however modified and explained, which is claimed for their Pontiff by Romish writers. We look in vain in the Holy Scriptures for any passage which gives countenance to the worship of the Virgin Mary, or which assigns to her the office of a Mediatrix between God and Man, or invests her with the Divine Attributes of Omniscience and Omnipresence. The Romish Doctrine concerning Purgatory, Pardons, Worshipping and Adoration as well of Images as of Reliques, and also Invocation of Saints, is (as our

R

twenty-second Article expresses it) "a fond thing vainly invented and grounded upon no warranty of Scripture, but rather repugnant to the Word of God." The same judgment is pronounced by our Church upon ministering "in a tongue not understood of the people," upon Transubstantiation, and the denial of the Cup of the Lord to lay-people. The system of auricular confession, as practised by the Roman Church, is another abuse deriving its origin from the lust of power, which was "the Mystery of Iniquity," working in the minds of the Clergy, from the third century downwards; and the monstrous invention of Indulgences, which roused the indignation of Luther at a time when he would have shrunk as yet with horror from the idea of calling in question the divinely appointed Supremacy of the Bishop of Rome, is a convincing proof how far that Church, in her ambitious and covetous grasping after worldly advancement, and in her arrogant assumption of spiritual prerogatives, had departed from the simplicity of the faith which was once delivered to the Saints. The Infidelity and Irreligion which these corruptions have engendered, are prominent in every country subject to the Papal sway.

But Romanism is not only not discoverable in the Bible; it is equally undiscoverable in the writings of the immediate successors of the Apostles,— St. Clement, St. Polycarp, St. Ignatius. The Epistles of these holy men are written with primitive simplicity, with a firm adhesion to the fundamental principles of the Gospel as developed in the New Testament, and with an utter absence of any approach to the peculiarities of Romanism. Equally catholic is the spirit of Justin Martyr, a

venerable writer, and a scion of the Church of Pa-
lestine; and of Irenæus, who, though, born in Asia,
was transplanted early in life to a distinguished
station, and finally, to a Bishopric in the Western
Church, and is therefore an unimpeachable witness
of what her faith was in the days of her primitive
purity. Irenæus was a learned and a devout author,
and his principal work is a refutation of the heresies
which had even then widely diffused their baneful
influence. His subject necessarily led to precise
statements, and to definite distinctions between truth
and error. A member of the Church of England,
a Church purified from Romanism, but essentially
and vitally possessed of Catholicism, will find the
scriptural faith and spirit of his Church embodied
in the creeds and in the doctrinal statements of Irenæus. but the Papist will in vain search his writings
for the peculiar dogmas and pretensions of Romanism. He will find, on the contrary, that the
first lordly aspirings of the Church of Rome recorded in history, were signally checked by Irenæus
himself. He it was, who, when Victor, Bishop of
Rome, imperiously attempted to exercise spiritual
domination over the churches of Asia by imposing
upon them the Roman mode of celebrating the
festival of Easter, not only aided in defeating his
object by convening a synod of the churches of
France in opposition to him, but reproved with dignified mildness his rashness and inconsideration.
This fact is the more interesting, because the advocates of Papal supremacy pretend to urge in
defence of this tenet the authority of Irenæus. They
do so, by misinterpreting a passage, in which he
simply states, what has never been disputed, that

R 2

deferential honour and respect were always paid to
the Bishop of Rome as presiding over the See
planted in the capital of the Empire. This species
of honour ceased, however, to be peculiar to the See
of Rome when the Imperial Dynasty quitted what
has been so proudly denominated the Eternal City.
Constantinople, as new Rome, then claimed for her
Bishop equal dignity (τα ισα πρεσβεια) with the
Roman Prelate, and this claim, allowed and recognised by the third canon of the first council held in
that city, was ratified by the canons of the council
of Chalcedon. Authorities still more antient and
venerable may, however, be quoted in proof of the
fact that Papal supremacy was altogether the offspring of Papal arts and usurpation during ages of
growing superstition and ignorance. Among these
none are more conclusive than the Canons of the
earliest General Council, that of Nice, which decree a
simple patriarchate to the Bishop of Rome, and place
the Bishop of Alexandria on an equality with him.[*]
It was the distinguishing glory of the Church of
England at the Reformation, under the guidance of
our Cranmers, Ridleys, and Jewels, that while she
renounced and repudiated the errors and corruptions
of Romanism, she steadfastly adhered to genuine
Catholicism. Exercising her unquestionable rights
as a national and independent Church, she cast away
the foul garments of Superstition and Idolatry with
which Popery had invested her, and shone resplendent
in the bright robe of Scriptural and Primitive Truth,

* Council of Nice, Canon VI., A D. 315. Ruffinus (Hist. i.
6.) explains this Canon as giving the Bishop of Rome authority over the " *suburbicariæ ecclesiæ*." First Council of Constantinople, Canon III., A.D 381. Irenæus, adv om Hær
l iii 3.

steadfastly adhering to her Apostolic form of Church Government, and inserting into her formularies, from amidst the Romish breviaries and ancient liturgies, the scattered pearls of Catholic verity.

But though her appeal is to the Scriptures as a complete rule of faith upon all fundamental doctrines, she makes a wise use of the light afforded by Primitive Antiquity upon various important particulars, which, in the nature of things, admit not of being proved by a reference to this standard. It is thus that she proceeds in defining the authority upon which the Canon of Scripture itself, which she makes the rule of Faith, is founded. Thus, also, she has manifested her deliberate conviction of, and reverence for the Scriptural Faith of the early Church by the retention in her formularies of the Nicene and Athanasian Creeds. And thus, by a series of authentic and unquestionable historical facts, the conclusion is established that Episcopacy was the form of government universally prevalent in every branch of the Church Catholic from the Apostolical age to the era of the Reformation.

Such, in a general way, was the strain of sentiment by which Bishop Burgess illustrated the distinctive differences between Catholicism and Romanism.

The Apostolical origin of the British Church, its priority, by several centuries, to its Saxon sister, founded by Austin, and its consequent independence of the Church of Rome, was another topic intimately connected with that which we are quitting, upon which he published several Treatises, and as the historical facts which they involve are highly interesting, we will here introduce a brief analysis

R 3

of them *, subjoining only a few necessary links and authorities.

In the history of the British Church he traced several epochs, the first of which embraced the question,—by whom Christianity was first introduced into this country. His general argument on this point may be stated as follows. Eusebius and Theodoret assert that some of the Apostles visited the British Isles †, and that the Britons were among the nations converted by them. The testimony of Eusebius on such a point is of great weight, because his undoubted learning, judgment, and experience were expressly and laboriously applied to the investigation of the origin and history of the Church of Christ. His intimate acquaintance also with Constantine the Great, whose father Constantius governed and died in Britain, and who was himself proclaimed Emperor there by the army, must have given him the means of superior information on this particular question.

But who among the Apostles are alluded to by Eusebius, is a question less easy of solution. Nicephorus, speaking of the provinces chosen by those holy men, says that one went to Egypt and Libya, and another to the extreme countries of the ocean, and to the British Isles. From the plural term used by Eusebius it might be argued that this was true of more than one of them. But there is a remarkable coincidence of circumstances which renders it not

---

* Some of the principal learned authorities only generally alluded to by the Bishop are specially referred to in this chapter, and a slight addition has been made of some interesting facts.

† Euseb. Demonstr. Evang. l. iii. c 5. Theod tom iv. serm. 9.

improbable that the first missionary to Britain was St. Paul.

St. Paul was sent to Rome, according to Eusebius, in the second year of Nero, that is, A.D. 56, and he stayed there, according to St. Luke, two years.

Caractacus, the British chief, upon his defeat by the Romans, was sent, as Tacitus has recorded, prisoner to Rome, where his magnanimous behaviour procured him better treatment than was usually bestowed upon captive princes. A very ancient document, the British Triads, published in the Myvyrian Archæology, states that the father of Caractacus went to Rome, as a hostage for his son, with others of his family, and that on his return he brought the knowledge of Christianity to his countrymen from Rome. That the family of Caractacus were sent with him to Rome, about the year 51, to grace the triumph of Ostorius, and remained there several years, we know from Tacitus, consequently, it is probable they were there during the period of St. Paul's residence in that city, and some of them might therefore have been among his auditors.

There were two distinguished ladies at Rome at this period, both natives of Britain, who had embraced Christianity : the one was Pomponia Græcina, the wife of Aulus Plautius, the first Governor of the Roman province in Britain, of whom Tacitus* says, that she was accused of having imbibed a " foreign superstition," and that her trial for this crime was committed to her husband. She was

* Tacit. Ann. xiii 32

pronounced innocent, he adds, of any thing immoral,
and lived many years afterwards, " but always a
gloomy, melancholy kind of life." Such is the description which a Pagan writer would very naturally
give of the manners of a Christian convert. It is
therefore highly probable that Christianity was the
foreign superstition alluded to, and that Pomponia
had become acquainted with it in Rome before the
arrival of St. Paul, or during his first residence there.

The other lady was Claudia, mentioned with
Pudens (2 Tim. iv. 21.), and supposed to have
been Claudia Rufina, the wife of Pudens, a lady of
whom Martial has spoken in terms which convey
the strongest impressions of her beauty and accom-
plishments, and to whom he alludes as a native of
Britain.*

Claudia cæruleis cum sit Rufina Britannis
  Edita, quam Latiæ pectora plebis habet !
Quale decus formæ ! Romanam credere matres
  Italides possunt, Atthides esse suam.   Lib. ii. Epig 54

Claudia, Rufe, meo nubit Peregrina Pudenti :
Macte esto tædis, O Hymenæe, tuis !   Lib. iv. Epig 13

Those who know how diffusive a principle Christian zeal is, will not doubt that these distinguished
converts would be anxious to communicate by every
means in their power, to their native country, the
blessings of which they had been made the happy
partakers.

Britain was, at this time, an important Roman
province, and London and Verulam were become
large, rich, and flourishing towns, crowded with

* The Reverend W. L. Bowles, in a very interesting little
Treatise, entitled " Pudens and Claudia of St. Paul," has placed
in strong relief the argument glanced at above.

Roman citizens. The communication between the colony and the capital of the mother-country must have been constant. It is, therefore, by no means improbable, that the attention of St. Paul should have directed itself to Britain, as an interesting and extensive field of labour, nor that the British converts in Rome should have pleaded in its behalf with the Apostle.

The detention of the British captives who accompanied Caractacus, was not only coincident with St. Paul's residence at Rome as a prisoner, but there is evidence to render it probable that they were released from confinement in the self-same year in which he himself was liberated, and no opportunity can be imagined more convenient for a visit from the Apostle to Britain, if it ever took place.

From the time that St. Paul was set at liberty, A.D. 58, to that when, according to Eusebius, he suffered martyrdom at Rome, A.D. 67, in the last year of Nero, an interval of nine years elapsed. What were the occupations of the great Apostle of the Gentiles during this long period? St. Chrysostom, among the Fathers, and some eminent modern authorities, favour the idea that he returned to Greece and the East, but this is an opinion unsupported by any authentic data. The Asiatic Churches, as he himself said in his exquisitely touching address to the Elders of the Church of Ephesus, were to " see his face no more." * Yet his ardent mind must have been actively employed in the service of his great Master in some quarter; and we know, on his own testimony, it was his delight to preach the Gospel

* Acts, xx. 25.

in countries where its sound had never been heard, " that he might not build on another man's foundation."

The desire which he expresses to visit Spain, naturally directs our attention to the West, and the tradition that he visited both that country and Britain, is supported by ancient and venerable authorities, whereas the traditions of a similar description respecting St. James the Less, St. Peter, and Joseph of Arimathea, are in the highest degree fabulous and absurd. Stillingfleet, in his Origines Britannicæ, has collected many early testimonies in favour of this hypothesis.

Theodoret, who, in common with Eusebius, has been cited as stating that Christianity was introduced into Britain in the days of the Apostles, insinuates that the Apostle Paul preached the Gospel in this island, as well as in Spain, and other countries of the West

Clemens Romanus and Jerome relate, that after' his imprisonment in Rome he carried the Gospel to Spain, " *and to the utmost bounds of the West, and to the islands that lie in the ocean.*"

That he did visit Spain, is supported by the authority of Athanasius and Chrysostom, as well as of Theodoret; and the latter affirms, that he also brought salvation (ωφελειαν) ταις εν τῳ πελαγει διακειμεναις νησοις * — which is in perfect accordance with the assertion of Jerome, that after his Spanish mission, he went from sea to sea, and preached the Gospel in the West. The language of St. Clement, in describing his final travels to the confines of the West, is επι το τερμα της δυσεως.

* To the islands lying in the ocean

Catullus calls Britain the utmost island of the West, and similar epithets are used respecting it by Theodoret and Nicephorus.

The above ancient testimonies furnish, therefore no small probability that St. Paul preached Christianity in Britain; but thus much is historically certain, that it was planted in our island in the course of the first century, either by one of the Apostles, or by some apostolic man.

The second epoch in the ancient British Church was the public profession and protection of Christianity by Lucius, a Prince who flourished in the second century; but the acts ascribed to him are so involved in fable, that little more can be extracted from them than the general inference, that a chieftain, favoured by the Romans, did probably, at the time specified, himself embrace the profession, and foster, by his influence, the diffusion of Christianity in this country.

That the British Church was existing in the third century, we know, not only on the authority of Tertullian and Origen, but also on that of our native historians, Gildas and Bede. It gradually advanced, under peaceful auspices, till the time of the Diocletian persecution, A. D. 303, when, for two years, the faith of its members was exposed to severe trials, and many of both sexes suffered martyrdom in the spirit of primitive devotion. *

The historical fact of the presence of three British Bishops at the Council of Arles, which was convened by the Emperor Constantine, shows the consideration attached to that Church in the fourth

* Gildas and Bede both testify to this fact

century. Athanasius speaks of British Bishops as present at the celebrated Council of Nice, and that of Sardica, and among various Churches which he enumerates, he makes mention of that of Britain. *

Jerome also particularly alludes to the British Church in this century.

In the fifth century one of the most learned and acute men of his age issued from her bosom, and gave birth to an animated controversy upon a question which is still distinguished by the impress of his name. This was the celebrated heresiarch Pelagius. He is said to have been Abbot of the Monastery of Bangor, and after having diffused the poison of his opinions both in the East and West, to have returned to England, whither St. Germain of Auxerre was sent by the Bishop of Gaul to oppose and refute him, One auspicious result of this conflict was the establishment of religious seminaries in Britain for the renovation of Christian learning.†

The sixth century formed a new era in the British Church, by the removal of the Metropolitan See from Carleon to Llandaff, and thence to Menevia, afterwards St. David's, so called from the holy and venerable Bishop who first presided over it. He established many monasteries and schools for the cultivation of religion and learning, and was an able and successful opponent of Pelagianism. The Synod of Llanddewi Brefi affords an efficacious example of the influence and orthodoxy of the British Church at this epoch.

---

* Athanasius, Ep. ad Jov.; Apol. ad Monachos; et Apol. cont. Arianos.

† Stillingfleet's Orig. Britan pp. 74. 89. 135.

We now come to the period of the Saxon invasion, the final success of which was fatal to the British Church in most parts of the island. Heathenism, under the sway of these barbarous conquerors, became again triumphant, and the British Church was no longer visible, excepting in Wales, Cornwall, and Cumberland, for in those places the Britons still maintained their independence

After the Saxons had been partially converted by St. Austin and his companions, under the auspices of Gregory the Great, the existence of the Original British Church became to them, as was natural, a subject of curiosity and interest, and they took great pains to induce its Bishops to conform to the customs, and to acknowledge the jurisdiction, of the See of Rome. Two conferences between the Bishops of the respective Churches are especially noted by Bede with reference to this object; the first of which, according to the same historian, occurred at a place called afterwards Augustine's Oak, upon the frontiers of the West Saxons, probably in Worcestershire. And here Bede observes that the British Christians were singular in their manner of keeping Easter and administering Baptism, and that their customs, in many other respects, differed from the Romish ritual.* The two parties could by no means agree upon terms of union. The British Bishops asserted and maintained their independence, and when subsequently further pressed by Laurentius, the successor of Austin in the See of Canterbury, to Catholic unity, as Bede † terms it, all his endeavours were in vain. Hence

* Bede, lib ii cap. 2   † Id. cap. 4

it is plain that the British Christians formed an independent Church, were under no foreign super-intendence, and yielded no homage to the See of Rome.

There is a curious passage to the same effect in an old Chronicle, which is preserved in a letter from Bishop Davies to Archbishop Parker : — " After that, by the meanes of Austin, the Saxons became Christians in such sort as Austin had taught them, the Bryttaynes wold not after that either eate or drinke with them, because they cor-rupted with superstition, ymages, and ydolatrie, the true religion of Christ."

The Metropolitan authority of the British Church subsisted till the reign of Henry I., when the See of St. David's was forcibly subjected to that of Canterbury.

From the preceding facts it may be inferred that the British is an Original National Church , that it raised its mitred head, both in England and Wales, for some centuries before the mission of St. Austin , that during the almost total extinction of Christian light in England beneath the sway of Saxon Paganism, it still flourished in Wales and Cornwall; that it protested against many of the usages introduced by the missionaries of the Romish Church among their Saxon converts, and that it maintained its own peculiar hierarchy until the reign of Henry I., when it was finally merged, by regal compulsion, in the Saxon division of the Anglican Church.

CHAP. XX.

RELIGIOUS SOCIETIES

1804.

THE year 1804 was marked by the establishment of the British and Foreign Bible Society. Among the earliest of its friends and supporters, in addition to its learned and philanthropic president, Lord Teignmouth, and many eminent persons belonging to the peerage and gentry of Great Britain, were those venerated prelates, Bishops Porteus, Barrington, and Burgess. Its fundamental principle, the dissemination of the authorised version of the Holy Scriptures without note or comment, united in its support Protestants of all denominations. Strong objections, however, were urged by many men of high character and influence in the Church to the union of her members in such an association, not only with Dissenters, but possibly, even with heretics and unbelievers; and earnest protests were published in opposition to it. These quickly produced an animated controversy. The opponents of the Society denounced the union as tending to give countenance to schism, and to level important distinctions. They also stated that one of the objects of the Society for Promoting Christian Knowledge being the dissemination of the Bible, the new association, as far as churchmen were concerned, was altogether needless and uncalled for.

To this it was replied, that the union so much censured involved no sacrifice of principle, opinion, or consistency on the part of its supporters, or that

if a relaxation of principle could fairly be imputed
to any among them, it must be charged upon Dissenters for aiding in giving away the particular version of the Scriptures authorised by the Church.
"If the Bible Society," said Bishop Burgess, who
at once set himself to grapple with the most formidable among the objections urged against it,
"were an association of preachers, or for theological inquiry, there would be some justice in the
charge. But as the distribution of the Bible is not
an act of heresy or schism, a clergyman cannot be
accused of either, for giving it away in concurrence with heretics or schismatics. Must we decline any opportunity of doing good to the souls
and bodies of men, because unbelievers are willing
to co-operate with us, and to increase our means of
doing good? Must we refuse to give our aid to
infirmaries or other charities, because unbelievers
are our associates; or withdraw our arm from a
drowning fellow-creature, because a heretic is giving
him the same assistance? Yet churchmen, it seems,
subject themselves to the charge of heresy and
schism, by being members of the Bible Society together with heretics and schismatics. If churchmen may, by such association, be liable to heresy
and schism, are not heretics and schismatics equally
liable to truth and orthodoxy? What can be
more likely to bring them into one fold, under one
Shepherd, than concurring with members of an
orthodox church in disseminating the Gospel of
Christ, in that translation which belongs peculiarly
to that Church? Such a union is, to say the least
of it, a temporary suspension of unbelief, of heresy,
and of schism, in favour of Christianity and ortho-

doxy. How happily a connection with the Society, even in its subordinate agencies, may operate in the furtherance of the Gospel, is evident from the instance of a Roman Catholic, who was lately converted from popery by correcting the press of one of the Society's Bibles." *

To the argument that the new Society was needless for Churchmen, as being already possessed of a Bible Society, it was replied : —

That although the Christian Knowledge Society had rendered eminent service to the cause of religion, by printing the Scriptures in a cheap form, and selling them to the members at reduced prices, yet the result of a diligent inquiry, which had been instituted throughout the kingdom, proved that the means of that Society were wholly inadequate to supply the national want of and demand for the Scriptures, even were those means exclusively directed to it, whereas only a portion of them could be so employed.

But that even had those means been more adequate to such an end, the supply of our own population formed only a part of the work of benevolence contemplated by the Bible Society. That it embraced also the supply of our colonies, and extending its views even beyond these, that it aspired to be, in

* The Bishop of St David's Letter to Lord Kenyon, pp. 34. 36, 37.

Though the author is convinced that the Bishop's sentiments, as described above, were, in the main, steadfastly maintained by him, he ought perhaps in candour to add, upon the authority of two most respectable clergymen connected with his lordship, that after the year 1830, when so lamentable a spirit of hostility to the Church began to be manifested by many of the dissenting sects, he did not *invariably* express himself in favour of clergymen joining the Bible Society.

connection with its foreign auxiliaries, the Bible Society of the world.

The lapse of thirty-five years has put to the test the validity of the arguments urged on both sides, and the general result might perhaps not unfairly be stated as follows : —

The Christian Knowledge Society, which it was predicted would suffer seriously in its resources from the liberal support given to the Bible Society, has incalculably profited by its establishment. Roused from a state akin to torpor, by the supposed rivalry of the new institution, it made an appeal throughout the country to the friends of the Church, to enrol themselves among its members, which was instantly responded to, and the result was a vast augmentation in its income, in its energies, and in the extent and efficiency of its exertions — a result which gladdens the hearts of all sincere Churchmen.

The Bible Society itself has steadily pursued its course of usefulness, hailed in its progress by the grateful plaudits and benedictions of Protestants on both sides of the Atlantic. The fulminations of the Vatican against it, and the scornful expressions of infidels, may justly be regarded as striking testimonies in its favour. By its own vast resources, and through the medium of foreign auxiliaries, it has extended its gigantic roots into all lands, and will not deem the benevolent object of its establishment attained until the Bible shall be translated into every language and diffused through every portion of the habitable globe. The Established Church, in the mean time, has been incalculably augmented in the number of its members, and has no less advanced to energy and usefulness. Those among her clergy

who have supported the Bible Society have maintained an undiminished attachment and preference
for their own communion, while a large influx of
Dissenters into the Church has taken place ; one
of the causes of which may fairly be referred to
their becoming better acquainted with the principles
of her members, from occasional intercourse with
clergy at meetings of this Society.

The cordial interest taken in the circulation of the
Scriptures at home and abroad by so large a body
of Churchmen, through the instrumentality of these
two Societies, has averted from the Church what
would otherwise have been urged upon her as a signal
reproach. It has rendered it impossible for her
enemies to say that she has regarded with indifference the duty of promoting that great and beneficent
object for which in her beautiful formularies she
unceasingly prays, " that God's way may be known
upon earth, his saving health among all nations."

To another religious association, the Church Missionary Society, which, by its zealous and useful
labours, has done much to remove from the Church
of England the reproach that she is deficient in
missionary zeal, Bishop Burgess also gave his early
support and countenance. The venerable Societies
for promoting Christian Knowledge, and for the
Propagation of the Gospel in Foreign Parts, had already received signal proofs of his attachment. The
Church Union Association in his own diocese had,
in fact, become, under his auspices, an active and
efficient auxiliary to the former, and he felt deeply
interested in the support and extension of the latter,
as a Society almost identified with the Established
Church, and capable, if duly supported, of diffusing

her pure forms and apostolical influence throughout our vast foreign dependencies. He justly regarded it and the Church Missionary Society as occupying distinct fields of labour; the one being specially devoted to the diffusion of Christian knowledge throughout our colonial possessions, without altogether overlooking the claims of the heathen ; the other labouring principally for the evangelization of the heathen, without excluding the benefit of our colonies. Between societies thus constituted on the principles of the Church, employed in works of such disinterested benevolence and such arduous difficulty, and with a World to operate upon, " bursting," to use Johnson's expressive words, " with sin and sorrow," he was not disposed to admit that any other rivalry ought to exist than a generous emulation which should most extend the kingdom of the Redeemer, and most effectually minister to the good of mankind.

Upon the same general principles he cordially supported the London Society for the Conversion of the Jews; and as it is the only association in connection with the Church of England which embraces this object, he regarded it with particular interest. He thought that Christians, instead of treating Jews with contempt and prejudice, should act towards them with a charity inspired by the recollection that their own choicest blessings and privileges have descended to them through the channel of Judaism, and with the hope of being instrumental in hastening the advent of that day, the pledge of increased glory to the Christian Church, when the veil shall be removed from the hearts of God's ancient people, and they shall acknowledge and adore in Jesus Christ the true Messiah. His love of Hebrew learning added to the force of these and similar considerations ; and so strongly did they act upon his feelings, that a box for the receipt of subscriptions and donations, in aid of the Jews' Society, usually lay upon his library-table.*

The part taken by the Bishop in the exercise of his independent judgment, with respect to these Societies, was closely accordant with the course pursued by his friend Bishop Barrington. Like him, also, he was a zealous promoter of the Madras system of education, and like him (as far as his much narrower means permitted), the liberal patron of a great variety of other public institutions and charities, having for their object the temporal and spiritual welfare of his destitute fellow-creatures.

CHAP. XXI.

GENERAL REMARKS ON THE BISHOP'S TRACTS IN REFUTA-
TION OF UNITARIANISM.

1814 to 1820.

BETWEEN the years 1814 and 1820 the Bishop published various tracts in refutation of Unitarianism,

* The above-mentioned Society has recently established a mission at Jerusalem, and a chapel is at this moment in course of erection under its auspices, in which the service of our National Church is to be daily performed in the Hebrew language. Within the last twenty years, the Jews at Jerusalem have very considerably increased in number, and there is a constant influx thither from various parts of Europe. Hitherto, Jewish inquirers after Truth, in the Holy City, have only known Christianity through the Greek, or Romish, or Armenian Churches, in connection, therefore, with revolting superstition and gross errors. They will now have access to it through the medium of our own scriptural services and beautiful formularies.

s 3

and re-published the whole in one volume in the
year 1820. They are marked by extensive scriptural and theological learning. The critical skill with
which they develope the force and meaning of various
important texts connected with the main subject,
the ability with which they condense proofs derived
from the writings of the Fathers, in attestation of
the Trinitarian faith of the primitive churches ; the
skill with which they accumulate authorities from
the works of the most eminent modern critics and
divines, in support of this fundamental doctrine of
the Church Catholic, and their tone of earnest piety,
illustrate the various learning, the mental acuteness,
and the devout feelings of their author, while they
no less forcibly expose the futility of the evasions
and sophistries beneath which Unitarians are forced
to take shelter in their vain endeavours to sustain a
hopeless cause.

Among these tracts, that addressed to a Lay
Seceder combines in a superior degree these qualities, though it is to be regretted that the Bishop
in this, as well as in some of his other publications,
has occasionally pressed a doubtful text into the
service of orthodoxy, which needs no other support
than that which it derives from the plain tenor of
the Bible, from the particular evidence of incontrovertible texts and passages of Scripture, and from
the general consent of Christian antiquity.

It should always be borne in mind that the
question of truth or error in reference to the doctrine of the Trinity is one in which not a single
secure step can be taken excepting under the light
and guidance of Divine Revelation. Having reference to so mysterious and awful a subject as

the mode of the Divine existence, no arguments
drawn from the common resources of reason, no
analogies derived from visible objects, can be safely
trusted to in such a discussion. "Canst thou by
searching find out God? Canst thou find out the
Almighty unto perfection? It is high as heaven;
what canst thou do? deeper than hell; what canst
thou know? The measure thereof is longer than
the earth, and broader than the sea," Job xi. 7, 8, 9.
Every thing around and within us tends to illustrate
the ignorance of man and the narrowness of the
sphere to which his researches are necessarily
limited. His proudest discoveries amount, in fact,
to little more than a scratching on the superficies
of knowledge. With effects and with the mutual
relations and properties of material objects he is
familiar; and the study of these unfolds to him
many of the mysteries of nature, and arms him, by
means of them, with new and extraordinary powers.
But the ultimate causes of the commonest of these
effects are hidden from his scrutiny, and lie en-
shrined in the abyss of Deity. And even every
advance which he accomplishes in science, every
secret which he penetrates, every fresh discovery
which he makes, serves, by opening to him new
and unexplored fields of investigation, to suggest to
him extended ideas of what is still unknown, and
thus to convince him more forcibly of his ignorance.
If the most ordinary works of the great Creator are
thus pregnant with mysteries which baffle human
intelligence, how presumptuous any attempt to
penetrate the secrets of the Divine Essence itself,
or to pretend to determine, by any analogies derived

from present experience, what is possible or impossible as to the mode of the Divine existence!

We have a full right, nay, it is an obvious duty, closely to investigate the authenticity of an alleged Revelation of the nature and will of God ; but when it is once admitted, the most implicit and reverential submission of reason to its discoveries is a consequence equally consonant with sound philosophy and good sense.

In the transcendant and spiritual nature of the Deity, and in the Unity of his Essence, there may, for aught we know, be that mysterious distinction of Persons implied in the doctrine of the Trinity. It will be quite sufficient for the conviction of any candid and reasonable inquirer, if he finds that the plain, unvarnished language of Scripture declares that so it is. The Divine testimony will be with him an all-sufficient warrant for the reception of the doctrine, and when he meets with individuals who, though unable by any shifts or evasions to refute the scriptural proofs of its truth, yet take refuge in the weak, though plausible objection, " we cannot on any evidence receive a doctrine contrary to common sense," he will no less pity, on the preceding premises, their obvious want of this quality, than he will condemn the presumption of their scepticism.

Such are the general principles upon which alone the doctrine admits of being investigated, and it is from not keeping them steadfastly in view, that individuals are often hurried into opinions respecting it, which the Church has ever deemed heretical. Men of speculative and excursive minds are apt to reason and conclude under very erroneous notions of the extent and powers of the human intellect, and especially of their own. One of the greatest triumphs of reason is to be duly sensible how many things there are which transcend its comprehension.

The doctrine of the Trinity is thus reduced to the test of the simple question, what is the testimony of Holy Scripture concerning it? — a question, the reply to which, if there be any force in the general consent of the Church, and in the authority of the greatest critics, divines, and scholars in the interpretation of Scripture, must be, that it is the fundamental article of the Christian faith.

Throughout the volume of Tracts above referred to, the main object of the Bishop was to expose the errors and sophistries of Socinian writers, and in particular, to bring forward incontestable evidences of the Divinity of Christ. He has clearly proved, that the infinite and incommunicable attributes of Deity are ascribed equally to the Son as to the Father, and that texts apparently of an opposite description refer exclusively either to his human nature, or to his voluntary assumption of the subordinate office of Mediator and Intercessor. He has shown that by keeping this distinction in view any difficulty arising out of the language of Scripture with respect to this doctrine is done away, and that the very texts which to a careless or superficial reader may seem contradictory, beautifully harmonise in the testimony which they render to the Divine and to the human nature which meet in the person of the adorable Saviour. Thus, while in one sense He is the " Lord of glory " and " God over all blessed for ever," He is in another and a no less important sense, " the Son of Man," and " the Man Christ Jesus," the Root, at once, and the offspring of David — David's God, and David's Son.

Such are the leading points which the arguments
of the Bishop embrace throughout these Tracts. Independently of their main scope, he has introduced
in the course of them, much of interesting disquisition and of curious learning on various collateral
topics. He has also vindicated the orthodoxy of
some eminent critics and scholars to whom Unitarian
writers have been used to defer, and whom they
would gladly claim as their own. Among these are
Schleusner and Griesbach ; the former the author
of a learned Lexicon of high authority upon the New
Testament, the latter, the editor of one of the most
critical editions of its text.

Unitarians flattered themselves, upon the eve of
its publication, that the rigid collation of numerous
manuscripts undertaken by Griesbach as the foundation of this edition would have been fatal to the
cause of orthodoxy, by disproving the authenticity
of many of the texts most relied upon for its support.
The result was quite the contrary ; for this extended
enquiry with very few exceptions of any importance
tended to establish the truth and correctness of the
received readings.

But independently of direct and positive proofs
that the Trinitarian faith is matter of Divine Revelation, the indirect and inferential proofs are so
numerous and decisive, that it would be about as
easy to dispense with the principle of gravity, in accounting for the phenomena of the universe, as it
would be to give a rational and connected elucidation
of the doctrines of Christianity without admitting
that of the Trinity.

What the final conclusions of Griesbach were
upon the termination of his rigid and extensive col-

lation, the following passage will clearly testify. In his preface to the Apostolical Epistles, published in 1775, he thus expresses himself : —

" In order that I may, as far as in me lies, remove all unjust suspicions, and wrest from malevolent men the handle of calumny, I publicly profess, in the first place, and call God to witness, that I have no doubt whatever as to the truth of that doctrine (the Deity of Christ); for there are so many and such lucid arguments and places of Scripture by which the true Deity of Christ may be proved, that I can scarcely understand how, if the Divine authority of Holy Scripture and the just rules of interpretation be admitted, this doctrine can be questioned by any one. Above all, that passage, John, c. i. v. 1, 2, 3, is so clear, and so above all exceptions, that never can it be perverted and wrested from the champions of the Truth by the audacious efforts of interpreters and critics." *

That the convictions of Schleusner upon this point were no less strong than those of Griesbach may be seen by referring to a passage in his Lexicon very similar in its spirit to the above, under the word Πνευμα.

* Ut iniquas suspiciones omnes, quantum in me est, amoliar, et hominibus malevolis calumniandi ansam praeripiam, primum publice profiteor atque Deum testor, neutiquam de veritate istius dogmatis (Christi Deitatis) dubitare ; atque sunt profecto tam multa et luculenta argumenta et Scripturae loca, quibus vera Deitas Christo vindicetur, ut ego quidem intelligere vix possim, quomodo concessâ Scripturae sacrae divinâ auctoritate, et admissis justis interpretandi regulis, dogma hoc in dubium a quoquam vocari possit. In primis locus ille, Jo. i. 1, 2, 3, tam perspicuus est, et omnibus exceptionibus major, ut neque interpretum neque criticorum audacibus conatibus unquam everti atque veritatis defensoribus eripi possit.

Porson is acknowledged to have been the most
acute and able Greek critic of the last century, and
his testimony upon a point connected with the interpretation of that language is the more impartial,
because he never manifested any zeal in the cause
of orthodoxy. A friend once said to him, " Is the
doctrine of the Trinity that of the New Testament?"
His answer was to this effect: " If the New Testament is to decide, and language has any meaning,
there can be no doubt that it is." *

To the treatise addressed to a Lay Seceder, its
author prefixed a dedicatory address to his old and
beloved friend Bishop Huntingford, who had been
recently visited by a severe domestic affliction. The
strain of piety and feeling in which he alludes to
this visitation, and the intimate connection which
he traces between the orthodox faith and the only
effectual springs of Christian consolation, form a
passage in itself highly interesting, while it forcibly
illustrates his views of the practical evils of Unitarianism and its deadening influence on the Christian
character. We shall therefore introduce some passages from it as a suitable termination to the present
chapter.

TO THE RIGHT REVEREND THE LORD BISHOP
OF GLOUCESTER.

Abergwilly Palace, October, 1814

MY DEAR FRIEND,

A MIND exercised by affliction is tenderly alive to
the impressions of religious truth. In such seasons,

* Communicated to me by the Bishop of Lincoln. The
same anecdote is told in the Quarterly Review, vol xxxiii.
p. 99

the emptiness of earthly comforts, and the want of some consolation which the world cannot give, prepare it effectually for the reception of those promises of light and aid, which the Scriptures abundantly supply. How sweetly then are those passages of David and Isaiah in unison with the feelings of a resigned and believing spirit, — " Tarry thou the Lord's leisure ; be strong and he shall comfort thine heart, and put thou thy trust in the Lord." " Who is he that feareth the Lord, that obeyeth the voice of his servant, that walketh in darkness, and hath no light ? Let him trust in the name of the Lord, and stay upon his God ?" — Isaiah, l. 10.

Our beneficent Creator, who, for the wisest purposes, has implanted in us affections and sensibilities, which attach us closely to those whom we respect and love, but which by the loss of such connections, give occasion to the most acute and painful trials, has also blessed us with a religion which, above all other means, can mitigate the visitation, which deprives us of [them. I need not remind you of His promises, who said, " My grace is sufficient for thee ," nor bring to your recollection that those consolatory words were an answer to St. Paul's request, addressed in prayer to our Saviour. Such trust in his assistance Christ had encouraged by his promise, — " Whatsoever ye shall ask in my name, I will do it, and, Lo, I am with you always, even unto the end of the world." And therefore St. John said, " This is the confidence we have in him, that if we ask any thing according to his will, he heareth us." The same confidence in Christ's divine power to hear and to save induced St. Stephen to say, in his last moments, " Lord Jesus,

receive my spirit." St. Thomas, who in the public
service of the Synagogue had been accustomed
to hear him whom they expected as the Messiah
called the mighty God and the Lord of righteousness, when he saw his Lord after his resurrection
from the dead, exclaimed in a transport of conviction and joy, " My Lord and my God."

Nothing but belief in Christ's Divinity, his omnipresent influence and omnipotent power, could
have induced his disciples and apostles to honour
him with divine worship, and to endure the pri-
vations, indignities, and sufferings which they un-
derwent for his sake. The Divinity of Christ was
not with them a speculative notion, a disputable
dogma, as the Unitarians represent it, but a great
practical principle, which influenced their whole
conduct, and infused into their minds a fortitude
and constancy, which made them rejoice when they
were counted worthy to suffer shame and death for
his name. To die and to be with Christ, they
counted better than life. What things were gain in
a worldly sense, they counted " loss for Christ;"
" yea, they counted all things loss, for the excellency of the knowledge of Christ Jesus."

Their belief in Christ's Divinity, their confidence in him as God, ever present to sustain them
in all difficulties, was the governing principle of
their minds through this life; and their trust in
his Atonement was the ground of their hope of
happiness in the next. They knew that the blood
of bulls and of goats could not put away sin ; and
the Psalmist had long before declared that man
was utterly unable to redeem his brother. But in
Christ, who was with God and was God, who was

" over all God blessed for ever," their " great God
and Saviour" — " God manifest in the flesh,"
who was made flesh and came in the flesh, that he
might by his death be a propitiation for the sins of
mankind — in him they trusted, as a Saviour able
to save to the uttermost all who should come to
God by him.

In the following letter the Bishop of Gloucester
replies to this Christian address.

MY DEAR FRIEND,

YOUR last merely intimated you should take
London in your way to Durham; but mentioned
neither time of continuance nor place of lodging at
the metropolis To that spot therefore I could
direct with less propriety than I can to Durham. I
calculate you are now keeping prebendal residence;
and I hope, after a journey favourable in all respects
to Mrs Burgess and yourself.

For the consolation which your Letter Dedicatory imparts, and for the delicacy with which
you touch on my afflicting loss, I return you equally
my thanks and praise. You have poured balm into
the wound, and not increased the pain by unskilful
handling. In truth, with much dexterity you pass
on to the main subject, a subject more than all
others interesting to a reflecting mind. For if
there be no Divinity in the nature of Christ, there
is no Atonement for transgressing man; if no
Atonement for man, we are yet in our sins; and
where in natural religion can we find any other
dictate or principle than that sin is obnoxious to
punishment?

You have in passages innumerable exposed the

ignorance (I might have said, the impudence and
disingenuity) of Belsham and his adherents. I am
particularly pleased that you have refuted the claim
they have made as to Grotius, Newton, Locke, &c.

With repeated thanks for the well-chosen topic of
your consolatory Dedication, for the abundant illustration and apposite erudition displayed throughout
the whole of your book,

I am your much obliged

and ever affectionate Friend,

G. J. GLOUCESTER.

Wint. Coll. May 8. 1815.

CHAP. XXII.

BENEFICIAL RESULTS OF THE BISHOP'S PLANS — PROGRESS
OF HIS COLLEGIATE SCHEME — EISTEDDFOD — CONTRO-
VERSY WITH PROFESSOR MARSH AND R. P. KNIGHT, ESQ.

1810 to 1820.

OCCUPIED in these various studies, and energetically exerting himself for the improvement of his
diocese, the life of the Bishop of St. David's
glided on in a peaceful flow of serene happiness.
An improved race of clergy was trained up in his
seminaries, from among whom he selected individuals of superior merit for preferment; such of
the beneficed clergy as were most distinguished
by their professional acquirements and active piety
frequently received gratifying proofs of his esteem,
and the name of Dr. Burgess was associated
throughout South Wales with epithets of respect
and veneration.

The fame of his useful exertions extended far beyond the boundaries of his diocese; an assertion which the Quarterly Review for November, 1810, forcibly illustrates in the following passage, which associates in a just eulogy the two names which we have so often ourselves linked together in the preceding pages. After touching on some existing defects in clerical education, it adds, — "Let it not be supposed that, in thus saying, we are depreciating the Church of England at a time when it boasts the learning and piety of so many of its members — when Barrington, at Durham, vies in the munificence of his charitable foundations with the most splendid of his predecessors : and Burgess, at St. David's, performs all the duties of his apostolic function with a zeal worthy of the best ages of Christianity." Surprise was justly felt that, amidst such active employments, he could secure time for numerous publications, many of them bearing the stamp of great research and erudition. Among his various plans of diocesan improvement, none excited so much public interest as the projected Collegiate Seminary for Clerical Education. The slightest acquaintance with the circumstances and condition of the Welsh Church was sufficient to vindicate its necessity, and it therefore daily attracted increased attention, commendation, and support. Letters were addressed to him to this effect by Dr. Manners Sutton, Archbishop of Canterbury, by Bishops Barrington and Huntingford, by the Rev. Charles Daubeny, and by some of the leading nobility and clergy connected with South Wales. Pecuniary subscriptions in aid of the plan flowed in from various parts of England, and liberal

T

contributions, or legacies of books, anticipated the
period when it should have a local habitation and a
name. Among the English friends who thus gave
it their liberal support, the name of Bishop Barrington appears as a donor of 500*l*., and within
the precincts of the diocese a clergyman was found
who contributed no less than 750*l*. in one donation.
The late Rev. T. Beynon, Archdeacon of Cardigan,
was the munificent contributor.

In the year 1809 the Bishop thought he might
venture to commence this great undertaking. A
plan for the intended structure was accordingly
procured, and a quarry was opened near Llandewy
Brefy, then its intended site; but upon a comparison between the probable expense and the
amount of the subscriptions, the necessity of further
delay became apparent. In the mean time the
Bishop's hopes had been so highly excited, that
he had not only sketched on paper, but even circulated in a printed form, a scheme for the government of the College, and for the course of studies
to be pursued in it.

The Eisteddfod, a triennial festive meeting held
by rotation at Carmarthen, Brecon, and some
other leading towns of the Principality, for the
cultivation and encouragement of the ancient language and literature of Wales, was more than once
honoured by the presence of the Bishop and Mrs.
Burgess. The literary spirit which glowed in his
own breast led him to sympathise warmly with the
national predilections, which imparted peculiar enthusiasm to these celebrations. The interest which
he thus felt and displayed was very grateful to the
natives of the Principality, and augmented the hold

which he had obtained on their affections by higher
and more sacred obligations. Though his studious
habits, and numerous professional engagements,
prevented his being a frequent visiter at the houses
of the gentry, he was often indebted to their hospitality in the course of his long Confirmation
tours; and I have heard him speak with great
pleasure of visits which he had thus paid to the
late Mr. Johnes of Hafod, to Colonel Lewis of
Llanayforion, to the late Mrs. Lloyd of Bronwydd,
and to the hospitable mansions of others of the Welsh
gentry. Mrs. Lloyd, whose enlarged Christian benevolence and many amiable qualities endeared
her to a large circle of friends and acquaintance,
regarded the Bishop with friendship and veneration.
She delighted in welcoming him beneath her roof;
and sacred music being her favourite relaxation,
she was able, with the assistance of some of the
members of her family, to gratify his own taste for
it by the united powers of the organ and the voice
The general impression produced by the Bishop on
the minds and hearts of his various hosts was that
of affectionate esteem and regard. Often has the
writer of these pages heard him spoken of in such
terms by various gentlemen of manly sense and
great discrimination within the precincts of the
Principality. They looked upon him, in fact, as the
Bishop Bedell of South Wales.

In the year 1814 he engaged in controversy with
Professor, since Bishop Marsh, upon the following
occasion. The latter, in a treatise entitled Horæ
Pelasgicæ, had questioned the correctness of some
of his opinions as expressed in his notes to Dawes'
Miscell. Crit. upon certain properties of the Æolic

T 2

Digamma. The learned Professor, while he recognised the existence of such a letter in the Greek
alphabet, and its influence on Homeric versification,
differed both with Dawes and the Bishop as to its
shape, properties, and pronunciation, and insisted
that Pelasgic, not Æolic, was its proper designation.

The question was one of a subtle and recondite
nature, and which furnished ample occasion for the
display of learning and ingenuity in the demolition
or construction of a theory. Though Dr. Marsh
could not possibly write on such a subject without
his characteristic acuteness and ability, his mode of
treating it was deemed arrogant and hasty by one
of the first Greek authorities of the day, in an
article in the Quarterly Review. The Professor
came to the subject fresh from studies and pursuits
congenial to it, and with the advantage of living in
an advanced period of Greek criticism. The Bishop
had long since laid aside the polished weapons
suited to such an encounter; but at the sound of
this trumpet of defiance, he broke away for a
moment from his professional occupations, and
seizing

Arma diu, senior, desueta,

descended into the arena; where he quickly proved
that he was still capable of all his youthful prowess.
The pamphlet which he published, in defence of
himself and of Dawes, was entitled " A Letter to
the Honourable and Right Reverend the Lord
Bishop of Durham, on the Origin of the Pelasgi,
and on the original Name and Pronunciation of the
Æolic Digamma, in answer to Professor Marsh's
Horæ Pelasgicæ ," and it treated the points at issue
with so much learning, and vigour of intellect, that

in the opinion of those most competent to decide
upon such erudite questions, his adversary, if not
absolutely unhorsed in this intellectual tournament,
was rudely shaken in his seat. *

* Our learned readers will not be displeased, we think, by
our extracting the brief summing up of the Bishop's arguments
in page 36 of his treatise, it being admirably calculated to give
a just view of the critical offences charged by him on that of the
Professor

" I said, in a former part of this letter, that the positions of
Dr. Marsh cannot be supported without many great hallucinations and offences against first principles   I have shown this
from the Professor's *anachronism* in denominating the Digamma from the *Pelasgi* , from his choice of the Latin F, as
his *sole* criterion of the power of the Digamma ; from his
adopting the *modern* pronunciation of the Latin F as the sound
of the Digamma, and the barbarous term *Faf*, as the name of
the Digamma , and from many strange inconsequences in his
reasoning, such as the following   Oϒ is not a right representation of the Digamma, because B is at least as good, the
Latin V is not *generally* represented by the Greek Oϒ, therefore
Dionys Halicarn, Plutarch, Procopius, &c , who have so expressed it, have not *correctly* represented it, the *vowel* V is
sometimes expressed by ε, ο, υ, ω, ευ, therefore the *consonant*
V is *not generally* represented by Oϒ , the Digamma is *not so
often* expressed by V as F, therefore it is *not rightly* expressed
by V, the Digamma is *not generally* represented by the Latin
V, therefore it is *not rightly* represented by it; V cannot be
pronounced like W, because it is exchangeable with B , the
Digamma could not have been pronounced like W, because the
latter has a broad coarse sound, intolerable to Greek ears, and
which they could not have pronounced

" All these hallucinations are the consequences of the Professor's attempting to supplant the common doctrine of the Digamma by his F and *Faf*   Dawes, then, had good reason for
saying — Ex locis jam descriptis illud in transcursu observare
est, quam frustra sint ii, qui Æoheum F *eidem apud Latinos
figuræ* potestate itidem respondisse contendunt

" That the theories of the Horæ Pelasgicæ, respecting the
language of the Pelasgi, and the *pronunciation* of the Æolic Digamma, are erroneous, might, indeed, be inferred from their
opposition to the testimonies of Herodotus, Thucydides, Dionys' Halicarnas', Varro, and Priscian "

T 3

The following passage, with which his treatise closes, is so characteristic of the amiable feelings of the writer, that it seems to belong to his biography. " I cannot dismiss these pages, without thanking the Professor for bringing to my recollection some of the studies of my first seven academical years, and with it the grateful remembrance of the valuable society in which I passed them, and of the inestimable advantages which it possesses for the cultivation and encouragement of learning. These impressions bring with them some of Gray's exquisite feelings on a distant prospect of Eton College :—

> " I feel the gales, that from you blow,
> A momentary bliss bestow."

Mr. Payne Knight subsequently became the object of his critical censure with respect to two positions in his Analytical Essay on the Greek Alphabet; the first was his calling the Digamma Pelasgic, and the Capuan figure its Pelasgic form, the second, his new, and, as he deemed it, his improved reading, of the Lacedemonian decree against Timotheus.* Upon both of these points the Bishop assailed his opinions, and defended those of Bishop Cleaver, whom Mr. Knight had censured as an unskilful and blundering editor of the Decree.

The title of the Bishop's treatise was, " A Vindication of Bishop Cleaver's Edition of the De-

---

* Timotheus incurred the censure of the Spartan senate for corrupting, as they maintained, the ancient gravity and simplicity of their national melodies, by adding four additional strings to the lyre, which had hitherto contained only seven He was also censured for the immoral tendency of a poem which he composed for the Eleusinian festival

cretum Lacedemomorum contra Timotheum, from the Strictures of R. P. Knight, Esq. 8vo. 1821."

It is written in a vigorous and caustic style of criticism, is fraught with deep and various learning; and, though the subject is one of scholastic nicety, it contains a great deal that is both amusing and interesting.

Though we have very few letters of any interest to produce belonging to this period of the Bishop's life, the following note places him in a very amiable light, and the succeeding letters are specimens of the correspondence which we have already mentioned was frequent between him and Mrs. Hannah More : —

TO GEORGE MARRIOT, ESQ.

DEAR SIR, 188 Piccadilly, Jan 15. 1813.

I CALLED at your rooms in the Temple yesterday, and Tuesday, to consult you about shaping a case, which is to come to you through Taylor for your opinion. I wished also to thank you for your two kind notes; and to say how sorry I was that my momentary inaptitude for a joke should have given you the trouble of writing your very friendly note. The words of my oldest and best friend could not possibly give me any real offence; and still less the repetition of them by a person whom I most sincerely respect and value, like yourself. But, as I said before, the spirits and the reply are often, in some mechanical constitutions, very different before dinner and after.

If you have changed your hours of attendance

T 1

at the Temple, I will trouble you to inform me, as
I wish to have your advice about shaping the case
before noticed

> Yours very faithfully,
> T. St. David's.

My dear Lord,   Dawlish, Sept 23 1810

I am indebted to you for so many attentions, and
so many interesting papers, that I can only thank
you for them in the lump, which I very cordially
do. I received your present of several copies of a
valuable sermon, as also of the able and well-written
Essay on Elocution, which I hope will stir up a spirit
of exertion among your young candidates, and teach
them the necessity not only of delivering good things
but of delivering them in a good manner. Your
little Hebrew stories are delightful — they would be
encouraging too, if I were a little younger and a
little healthier. So far I had written before I left
home, from which I was driven by so great an influx
of company, that I was obliged to fly away for retirement. This seems to be the quietest place on
the coast, and very interesting, and I find some
pleasant society. We hope ere long to visit the
beautiful scenery with which, I am told, the neighbourhood abounds.

I do not wonder, my dear Lord, that the regulations for your truly magnificent collegiate scheme
cost you so much time and thought. I sympathise
with Mrs. Burgess on this damp weather.

> Yours, my Lord, very faithfully,
> H. More.

TO THE BISHOP OF ST. DAVID'S.

My dear Lord,

My conscience would be twitching me night and day, and I could not sleep in my bed, if I any longer delayed stripping off the laurels with which you have bound my brows. It is high time to consign them to the right owner.

My friend the Rev. Mr. Cunningham, vicar of Harrow, is the author of the " Velvet Cushion." I was in his confidence, and kept his secret, while it remained such. I think it a very pleasant little work. Your Lordship was not singular in ascribing it to me; an ascription, however, not very flattering to the real author. My friends in London said they suspected me the *first* half of the book. Why they changed their opinion I know not. While the mystery lasted, however, I got a very lively epigram, which would have been flattering had I earned it.

You have strengthened your cause as far as human authority *can* strengthen that which was so strong without it. With such a confederated band of Trinitarians as your Lordship has mustered in your last treatise, I think Mr. Socinian Attorney-General would not much care to fight single-handed.

I shall be happy to see the whole of this able defence and complete exposure, when finished. Your printer has fallen into the common error in spelling Lord Lyttelton's name

I am ever
Your Lordship's very faithful
H. MORE.

Bailey Wood, 5th November, 1814.

CHAP. XXIII.

THE AUTHOR'S FIRST ACQUAINTANCE WITH THE BISHOP
OF ST. DAVID'S. — DESCRIPTIVE CHARACTER OF BISHOP
RYDER

1820

HITHERTO the writer of these Memoirs has spoken
of the Bishop from authentic documents, or from
the report of others; but in the spring of 1820
he became personally known to him, and their acquaintance, from a concurrence of various circumstances, quickly ripened into an intimacy, the memory of which will ever be grateful to his feelings.

We met, for the first time, in the spring of 1820,
at the Palace, Gloucester, as guests of the late Dr.
Ryder, then Bishop of that See, who was there quite
alone, having come from the Deanery of Wells,
during his residence, to entertain the Judges at
dinner, according to ancient custom, in the Assize
week.

I was struck, at first sight, by the fine countenance
and the dignified person of the Bishop of St. David's.
He was then about sixty-three years of age, tall and
upright, well proportioned in his limbs, and active
in his movements. His features were fine, and cast
in a regular mould. Over them was diffused a
pensive, contemplative air, blended with the expression of deep thought and mild composure.
When he smiled the effect was truly pleasing, like
a ray of sunshine lighting up the serene beauty of
an autumnal landscape. Though his manner was
somewhat grave, his disposition was evidently social;

and the moment that any literary topic or subject of religious interest was started, he became animated, and spoke from the stores of an acute, a learned, and pious mind, and a tenacious memory.

The two Bishops, though not altogether belonging to the same school of doctrinal theology, were substantially agreed upon the most important points, were both spiritually-minded, and were reciprocally animated by sentiments of affectionate regard and esteem. A full flow on both sides of affectionate kindness, of serene and cheerful hilarity, united to a pleasant playfulness of thought and illustration in touching on the various topics upon which conversation turned, banished every approach to the starch or the severe in this spiritual symposium.

Both of these excellent men are now gone to their rest, the subject of this Memoir full of years and honour; his brother and friend in Christ cut off by an unexpected stroke in the maturity of manhood and usefulness. The characters of eminently good men in high stations are the public property of the Church. Their bright example excites to virtuous imitation. What others have been, we ourselves may be, if not in talent and acquirement, at least in the higher range of moral excellence. For the sake of the living, therefore, we will indulge in a brief pause from the immediate object of these pages, in order to introduce a few particulars drawn from long and intimate friendship, respecting Bishop Ryder.

Born of a noble family, familiar from his youth with the best society, naturally kind and affectionate, he united to gentlemanly ease and polish a peculiar suavity of demeanour and manners. He

left the University of Cambridge, where he completed his education, an elegant scholar; and literature, both classical and general, never ceased to
form, in subservience to higher and professional
pursuits, one of the pleasures of his existence. The
'rectory of Lutterworth, in Leicestershire was his
first preferment; he afterwards became Dean of
Wells, but the former place was his home, except
when officially resident at Wells, until he was raised
to the Episcopal bench. At an early period of his
clerical career, he attained to such "ripeness and
perfectness of age in Christ," that he gave himself
wholly to the duties of his office, and proved himself worthy of filling the pulpit of Wicliffe, by
faithfully preaching the great doctrines of the
Gospel, and by earnestly labouring for the salvation
of souls.

His piety was both elevated and practical. It
was accompanied by a humility and gentleness,
which shed their benignant influence over his whole
deportment and conduct, blended with a cheerfulness which rendered the intercourse of friendship
with him peculiarly attractive. Happy himself,
it was his delight to see others happy also, and
his presence in the friendly circle, among his clergy,
or in general society, operated as a sunbeam, so
diffusive was his kindness, so winning his cordiality.
His style of conversation was lively, interesting, and
instructive. It abounded in anecdote and incident,
and the desire to do good was always predominant.
It was pleasant to behold him in the prime of his
days, sustaining, in the midst of a blooming and
delightful family, all the charities of domestic life,
with the purity and tenderness of a human angel,

and discharging the duties of his high station with the zeal of an apostle. Prompt at every call of duty, his professional engagements, his extensive correspondence, and a frequent attendance at religious and charitable meetings, left him little time for personal recreation of any kind ; but when he was able to relax, he was the life of every party of innocent pleasure, and a visit to the Rocks of Cheddar, or the ruins of Glastonbury, under his auspices, never failed to leave behind it the most delightful impressions.

Few Bishops have been more zealous or successful in promoting the building of new churches in populous or neglected districts of their dioceses, and none according to his means contributed more liberally to their erection and endowment. His labours as a preacher, even after he became a Bishop, were incessant, and exceeded those usually undertaken by active parochial clergymen. It was sometimes suggested to him that he preached too often, and made himself too common. In allusion to this charge, he one day said to a friend, " Does not the consecration service for Bishops exhort us ' diligently to preach God's Word ? ' and is not the clerical body solemnly warned by St. Chrysostom to take heed, lest indolence and secularity should exclude more of their order from heaven, in proportion to their number, than from any other profession ?"

During his residence at Wells, he usually preached twice on the Sunday, — once at the Cathedral, and again in the large parish church, which was then destitute of any evening service, except when he thus voluntarily officiated. The crowded auditories on these occasions attested his powers as a preacher. His sermons were truly impressive, and composed in a strain of simple, persuasive, and affectionate eloquence. Their great object was to arouse the slumbering souls of men to a lively concern for their eternal interests, and to attract them in the spirit of deep humility and penitential faith to the Cross of Christ. It is often difficult to select particular incidents out of the daily tenor of a life spent in doing good, but the following will illustrate some of these general statements.

Observing, on various occasions, that on Tuesday mornings, when at Wells, the Bishop disappeared at a very early hour, and did not join the party again till dinner time, I was induced to inquire into the cause; and learned that the two large parishes of Mark and Wedmore, forming part of his Peculiar as Dean, the former distant from Wells twelve miles, the latter eight, were in a state of much spiritual destitution, from the distance of a great part of the population from their respective churches, as well as from the want of church-room.

The state of these parishes had so deeply affected his feelings, that he could not be easy to bestow upon them only a barren sympathy; and finding that the prompt and effectual remedy would be to act the part of Curate to them himself, he undertook and discharged this office with equal zeal and cheerfulness, every other week for many successive years, during his official residence in Wells. Early in the morning of the day mentioned, he mounted his horse or drove over thither, in order to give the full service of the Church in each; and so much was his heart interested in this labour of love, that no weather, however unfavourable, no guests, however distinguished, were allowed to interfere with it. His Christian kindness was quickly rewarded by the attendance of large congregations. The people belonged almost exclusively to the labouring class ; and such kind condescension in a Bishop, such disinterested zeal for their spiritual good, naturally excited their gratitude and attachment ; an impression which was greatly heightened by his amiable, affectionate manners, and by the earnestness of his preaching. Before he quitted the Deanery of Wells, he perfected this work of charity by raising a sum of money to establish a second full service every Sunday in the parish of Mark, where also he built a National School. In the parish of Wedmore, aided by the contributions of the public and the landholders, he was the means of building and endowing two chapels in the hamlets of Blackford and Theale, and also of founding a school. In his Tuesday pastoral visits the instruction of the children was not overlooked. His benevolent care was repaid by the affectionate gratitude of those who were its objects ; and so long as any among the inhabitants survive, who personally attended his ministry, the name of Bishop Ryder will not cease to be pronounced with a heartfelt blessing. Only a short time before his lamented death, I reminded him of his constant rides to Wedmore and Mark, when he told me that he looked back to the hours which he had thus spent as among the happiest of his life. Such was Bishop Ryder — such were the lessons he had learnt in the school of Christ. The same spirit of charity, the same zeal for the salvation of souls, which prompted him, overlooking ordinary considerations of personal dignity, to go to these two neglected parishes, and to labour assiduously and in the most disinterested manner for their good, influenced the daily course of his life and feelings. His memory is fragrant in the affections of his family and friends, and it is embalmed in the veneration of the Church of Christ.

CHAP. XXIV.

PROGRESS OF THE COLLEGE-SCHEME. —C R COCKERELL, ESQ APPLIED TO FOR PLANS.

1820 and 1821.

AMONG the topics to which the Bishop of St. David's adverted with much interest in the course of our meeting at Gloucester, was his projected college for clerical education in South Wales ; but at this time he did not appear to be sanguine in the hope of speedily realising the plan. The subject was brought home much more closely to myself before the expiration of the year, by the following incident. Happening to be on a visit to my estate at Lampeter, in Cardiganshire, I was informed that the Bishop was inclined to erect the college at this place, in preference to Llandewybrefy, the site hitherto proposed, because, though these places are only a few miles distant from each other, Lampeter is much more accessible and convenient.

The pressing want of such an institution in South Wales, its literary and theological objects, and the probability that, independently of its direct and obvious influence, it would tend to civilise and improve the vicinity, naturally interested me, as they would any reflecting landholder, in its favour. A piece of land suitable for the projected building quickly suggested itself. The Castle of Lampeter once stood on a gentle eminence, in extent about three acres, called in modern times Castle Field. The only trace of the ancient edifice is a small acclivity, once the castle-keep. The situation is healthy, and the view which it commands beautiful, extending over the vale of Lampeter and the windings of the Tivy, and surrounded by a fine range of lofty hills. As it appeared, from its healthy and commanding position, peculiarly adapted for the intended purpose, I made (in conjunction with two of my brothers, who were also interested in the property) an offer of it to the Bishop, in the course of a visit which I paid him at Abergwilly, in the autumn of the same year. This offer he very gladly accepted. The subject of the college naturally became during my visit a leading topic of our conver sations ; and from this time I felt a cordial interest in the promotion and success of the project. Henceforth our intercourse, both personally and by letters, became frequent. A fresh impulse was gradually imparted to the whole plan, and strenuous and successful efforts were made to augment the list of subscriptions. The Bishop, in adverting to these measures, often expressed great satisfaction that they had been resorted to at this particular period. " Had I left the diocese," he would say, " before the college was actually in course of erection, it would probably have never been built, and there would have been a scramble for the money subscribed."

U

At this time the sum actually available for the undertaking was under 10,000*l.* : it was afterwards augmented by the transfer to the Building Fund of another sum which had hitherto been appropriated to exhibitions.

The whole amounted to somewhat more than 13,000*l.* , part of which had been contributed by liberal English benefactors, and by the Welsh nobility and gentry; but by far the greater proportion was the produce of the annual accumulation of small contributions from the clergy of the diocese, who, throughout the long space of sixteen years, had cheerfully complied in this manner with the wise and provident suggestion of their revered Diocesan. It was a remarkable proof of their confidence in him, and of his great personal influence, that he was able to induce them cheerfully to continue throughout so long a space of time these annual donations in aid of a distant, and, as it appeared to many, an uncertain object. Most of them, in conformity with his earnest request, had contributed, either by one payment, or by small annual instalments, one tenth of the annual produce of their respective benefices , and when the poverty of those benefices, with few exceptions, is considered, the result is highly honourable to the principles and feelings of that reverend body.

The more intimate opportunity I now enjoyed of studying his character, confirmed the pleasing impressions produced on me at Gloucester by the mild benignity of his manners and the simplicity of his mind and character.

I found the Bishop and his lady living at Abergwilly, in an easy hospitable manner, surrounded by a train of old and attached domestics. After the morning had been devoted to his professional duties and learned pursuits, he usually took a long walk ; and I look back with pleasure to some very pleasant rambles with him in the neighbourhood of Aber gwilly, in the course of which I was much interested by the unconstrained and agreeable flow of his instructive conversation, as well as charmed by the scenery of the vicinage.

One of the first steps taken by the Bishop, in immediate furtherance of the resolution he had now formed with respect to the College, was to apply, at my suggestion, to C. R. Cockerell, Esq., an architect whose name is associated with the purest classical taste, and with assiduous attention to the interests of his employers, requesting him to visit Abergwilly, and to receive his instructions for a suitable plan for the contemplated structure.

None of those who were present when the Bishop and his architect met for this purpose, will readily forget how interesting an occasion it proved. The Bishop's feelings were pleasurably excited by the prospect of actually realizing a scheme which he had projected no less than sixteen years before, and for which he had long been accumulating funds, but which hitherto had eluded his hopes and endeavours.

> Jam tandem Italiæ fugientis prendimus oras.

Mr. Cockerell, an artist no less than an architect, after being made acquainted with the Bishop's general object, and with the limited extent of the sum collected for it, assiduously applied himself to the conception of a plan which should at once be

picturesque and economical ; and, before the close
of his visit, had the pleasure of producing a drawing of this description. It so entirely met the
Bishop's views, and so fired his fancy, that after
surveying it for some time, he exclaimed with enthusiasm, "Should I ever be so happy as to witness
the erection of such a building, I shall be ready to
exclaim, with good old Simeon, 'Lord, now lettest
thou thy servant depart in peace.' "

CHAP. XXV.

THE BISHOP PUBLISHES A VINDICATION OF THE DISPUTED
VERSE IN ST JOHN'S FIRST EPISTLE. — THE KING'S LET-
TER TO THE BISHOP, ANNOUNCING HIS SUBSCRIPTION
OF ONE THOUSAND POUNDS TO THE COLLEGE. — THE
BISHOP'S REPLY. — THE UNIVERSITIES OF OXFORD AND
CAMBRIDGE ALSO SUBSCRIBE

1821 to 1822.

IN the winter and spring of 1821 much of the
Bishop's attention was occupied by the subject of
the college; yet he found time for publishing several
treatises, among which were the following : —

A Vindication of 1 John v. 7., from the Objections of M. Griesbach. 8vo. 1821.

Dr. Owen's Tract on the Nature of the Protestant
Religion. 12mo.

Adnotationes Millii, Bengelii, Wetsteinii, &c., in
1 Joann. v. 7.

Marci Celedensis Explanatio Fidei.

The Bishop, by the publication of the first of the
treatises enumerated in the above list, committed

himself as a Defender of the authenticity of the controverted text, 1 John v. 7. In a subsequent and enlarged edition of this work, as also by various supplementary publications, he entered still more earnestly and resolutely into the controversy. As the prosecution of it formed the principal subject of his literary and theological writings in the latter stages of his life, we shall place before our readers, in a subsequent chapter, and within as small a compass as possible, some account of its distinctive and historical features.

The first edition of this publication was dedicated to the Bishop of Durham, in the following expressive and grateful language : —

To the Honourable and Right Rev. SHUTE BARRINGTON, LL.D., Lord Bishop of Durham.

MY DEAR LORD,

THE long interval which has elapsed since your acceptance of my first endeavour * to assist the acquisition of religious knowledge among the poor, presents to me so many recollections of your Lordship's kindness and friendship, that, if I could forget them, I should be most ungrateful to that directing Providence which first brought me within your Lordship's notice, and which enables me, at this late hour of an advanced life, to offer you this humble tribute of my affection and gratitude.

That the same gracious Providence may long pre-

---

* The Salisbury Spelling Book for the use of Sunday Schools, 1786.

serve you in the enjoyment of perfect health, the
reward of a temperate life, is the ardent wish of,

My dear Lord,

Your Lordship's

Ever obliged and affectionate friend,

T. St. David's.

The Bishop's reply, upon the receipt of this feeling address, was as follows : —

My DEAR LORD,   Mongewell, June 11 1821

My earliest and best thanks are due for the
very gratifying terms in which you make the world
acquainted with the cordial friendship which has
subsisted between us for thirty-five years. In looking back to that long interval, those parts of it
afford me most peculiar pleasure, when, from the
nature of our connection, I was a daily witness to
your virtues, your talents, and the extent of your
various and deep erudition.

May that gracious Providence which has prolonged my life prolong yours also, accompanied by
similar blessings, — freedom from those painful infirmities which usually attend age advanced as
mine !

Believe me, my dear Lord,

With true regard and esteem,

Your faithful and affectionate friend,

S. DUNELM.

P. S. Why should you not take your dinner and
bed here on Friday? Your speech, which you have
done well in printing, contains the soundest arguments in the smallest compass.

The speech alluded to in the preceding letter was delivered in the House of Lords in the Session of this year, in opposition to Roman Catholic Emancipation. I saw him frequently about this time, and witnessed the effort which it cost him to steel his nerves with sufficient resolution for the task of addressing that illustrious assembly So great was his natural modesty, that nothing but a high and paramount sense of duty could have in·duced him thus to come forward. But so great were the evils, both religious and political, which he anticipated as the infallible consequence of admitting Roman Catholics to legislative power, that, after the effort was made, he felt thankful and happy at having raised a warning voice, and delivered a solemn protest, against any such measure.

In the autumn of 1821, in compliance with the Bishop's wishes, I met Mr. Cockerell at Abergwilly for a reconsideration of his plan of the College. The success which had attended the appeal for additional subscriptions during the preceding spring and summer, and the expectation of obtaining a grant from Government, had encouraged the Bishop to authorise an enlargement in some important particulars of its projected accommodations, as well as the introduction of a little more embellishment into the general design. Quarries were now opened at Lampeter, and various other preparatory measures taken. A further impetus was given to the subscription when the same parties met in London in the spring of 1822.

About this time an opportunity presented itself, through the medium of Mr. Hart Davis, an intimate friend of the late Sir William Knighton, the

Keeper of the Privy Purse, of placing before his Majesty George IV. the nature and necessity of the Collegiate undertaking. It being clearly ascertained, through this channel, that the King was favourably disposed to the scheme, the Bishop was induced to address a letter to his Majesty, humbly soliciting his Royal patronage The King was so much interested by the facts of the case that he not only subscribed the sum of 1000*l* in aid of it, but most graciously accompanied the announcement of his intentions with the following letter, addressed to the Bishop and penned by his own hand : —

THE King acknowledges with great pleasure the Bishop of St. David's letter, relative to his pious and useful scheme for the benefit of those who are in future to constitute the great body of the Welsh clergy. The King cannot express in terms of sufficient commendation this most laudable effort of the Bishop of St. David's Whenever the money is wanted, the King has ordered his Privy Purse to transmit 1000*l*. in aid of the Bishop's benevolent intentions.

G. R.

Carlton House, May 17th, 1822.

The receipt of this gracious communication was acknowledged by the Bishop in the following letter, addressed to his Majesty : —

SIRE,

THE very gratifying intelligence which Mr. Hart Davis has communicated to me of your Majesty's paternal attention to the religious and literary interests of the Principality in general, and of my diocese in particular, by your Majesty's munificent contribution of 1000*l.* towards the building of our long-projected College for the education of young men intended for Holy Orders who cannot afford the expense of an University education, claims my most grateful and humble acknowledgments of your Majesty's goodness.

My most ardent prayer is, that your Majesty may very soon see the good fruits of your bountiful protection of Religion and Literature. It will always be to me a source of the most heartfelt pleasure that I have been honoured with your Majesty's confidence, as a very humble agent of your Majesty's bounty.

> I am, Sire,
> With every sentiment of the profoundest
> Respect and devotion,
> Your Majesty's
> Most loyal and grateful subject,
> T. St. David's.

London, August 13. 1822

The public press quickly made the country acquainted with this act of Royal generosity; and the impression which it produced was not only highly honourable to his Majesty, but attracted general attention to the object of his bounty. Throughout South Wales in particular, where, strange to say, prejudices had been stirred up against the college in various quarters, the effect of the King's munificence was electrical, heightening every feeling of affectionate loyalty among the members of the

Church of England, and converting many lukewarm approvers, and even decided opponents of the plan, into professed friends and admirers.

The time was now arrived when it appeared expedient to submit the particulars of the collegiate scheme to the two Universities, accompanied by an application for their sanction and support, which were justly deemed of no trifling importance to its final success. Dr. Kaye, then Bishop of Bristol, and Master of Christ's College, Cambridge, undertook to bring the subject before the Heads of that University; and the same kind office was performed at Oxford by Dr. Copleston, then Provost of Oriel, and now Bishop of Llandaff. The cordial support given by each of these learned and eminent persons to the application in question, and the kind interest which they manifested in its favour, tended in a great degree to insure the favourable result which followed. A donation of 200l. was voted by each of the Universities towards the erection of the College; the additional sum of 100l. was subscribed by Oriel College; and liberal donations of books were made by most of the colleges, in aid of the future library of the projected institution. The Rev. Mr. Tyler, then Tutor of Oriel, and now Rector of St. Giles's, displayed a most friendly zeal in promoting these latter contributions.

CHAP. XXVI.

THE BISHOP'S NOBLE SACRIFICE OF FINES FOR THE
AUGMENTATION OF THE INCOME OF THE SEE OF ST.
DAVID'S.

1823.

CHRISTIANITY is the fruitful parent of the noblest
and purest principles of conduct. In place of those
selfish and contracted motives which so commonly
sway the conduct of men of the world in pecuniary
matters, it prompts to deeds of generosity, and to
habits of self-denial. While it exhibits to the eye
of Faith glorious objects of pursuit, and a standard
of action no less elevated, and stamps comparative
littleness on earthly concerns and interests, it en-
forces by the highest sanctions the faithful and
conscientious discharge of every relative, social, and
civil duty — inseparably conjoining charity to man
with love to God.

Such was the tendency of religion in the mind
and heart of the good Bishop of St. David's. He
was moreover reflective and persevering. He
framed his plans wisely, and he pursued them
steadily ; and qualities like these are an overmatch
for all ordinary difficulties. After eighteen years
of previous patient preparation, the College was on
the eve of foundation. Only a short time before
this work was accomplished, he completed another
plan for the benefit of his diocese, which had long
been maturing; a plan at that time little known,

even within its precincts, but which so eminently illustrates his disinterestedness and liberality, that generous minds will delight to dwell upon its details.

Upon his occupation of the See of St. David's, its annual produce was only about 1200*l*. The palace, which was ill built and ancient, needed frequent repairs, and there were various other local drawbacks on his income.

This See had therefore been usually regarded as a stepping stone to better preferment, a circumstance which naturally operated very detrimentally with respect to any permanent plans for its improvement. The prebendal stall at Durham, held by Dr. Burgess, produced, together with his bishporic, an income which, though not large, considering his station in the Church, his necessary expenditure, and his munificent disposition. was adequate to his wants; and he had devoted himself, with an entire singleness of heart and intention, to the great work of ameliorating the condition of his diocese.

As there was then no reason to expect any of the public enactments which have since been made for augmenting the annual value of the poorer bishoprics, the reflection often occurred to him, when anxiously occupied in promoting his own measures of improvement, " Unless the exertions I am making, the plans I am pursuing, are followed up by my successors, the good I may be enabled to effect may very possibly prove only temporary, and my best endeavours be finally frustrated. Can I devise any means of improving the annual value of the See to such a degree as will place future bishops in a state of comfortable independence, and induce

them to regard it as their permanent field of
labour and usefulness?" After these questions
had been much and often revolved, the following
mode of effecting his object occurred to him. It
is well known that before the passing of the Act
of 6 & 7 William IV. cap. 77. the revenues of our
bishoprics mainly arose from fines accruing upon
the renewal of lives on leases of the Episcopal
estates, occasionally amounting to very large sums.
These fines he determined to relinquish on certain
estates best adapted to the purpose he had in
view, and to run his own life, which he had reason
to believe was a good one, against the remaining
life or lives on them, till they should all fall in.
when he proposed to annex the estates by act
of parliament, in perpetuity, to the See. He calculated that in all human probability he should
finally secure to his successors, by this sacrifice,
a liberal income, and as he had no wish for translation, he saw his way clearly to the entire completion of the plan. As far back as the year 1807
he requested the late Lord Eldon to give him
his legal opinion upon the project. It received the
cordial concurrence of that eminent and upright
lawyer, and thenceforwards the Bishop steadfastly
kept it in view. In the year 1822, several of the
leases having expired, and others being likely to fall
in, he gave the finishing stroke to his design by
bringing a Bill into Parliament, restraining himself
and all future Bishops of St. David's from ever again
letting out on lives the estates enumerated in the
Act, which were thus permanently annexed to the
See, and have doubled its income. The value of
the fines which the Bishop sacrificed in order to

effect this important object was upwards of 30,000*l.*, to every shilling of which he was fully entitled, and which was therefore his free gift, prompted by Christian principle, to Religion and to the Church. It was reserved for his successors to enjoy the benefits of his liberality, for he himself was translated to Salisbury soon after the Bill came into operation.

Let those in the ranks of Nonconformity, who have been used to think of Bishops as secular, selfish persons, bent chiefly on personal or family aggrandisement, follow this Prelate through his whole career; let them especially contemplate this bright display of every opposite quality, and hence learn to discard those blind and systematic prejudices in which they are too prone to indulge against the Heads of our Ecclesiastical Establishment. This sacrifice was scarcely ever mentioned by the Bishop. Few are the persons who have heard him even allude to it. His object was to be generous and charitable on Christian principles, to the exclusion of all display or ostentation. A sentence now and then fell from his lips, which proved how superior he was to every thing little and sordid. I well remember, on a particular occasion, that, on my strongly commending one of his many generous acts, his reply was, " As to money, I regard it no more than as dirt, when an important object calls for support."

His private charities were dispensed in the spirit of this noble sentiment. His applications were numerous, and were seldom unheeded. Sometimes it turned out that his goodness had been abused.

" Well, and if I have been deceived," he would say, when remonstrated with on such occasions, "does not God make his sun to shine on the evil and on the good ? " He often said that avarice was the vice of old age, and that he was anxious to guard against its first approaches

The late Mr. Wilberforce, whose principles and feelings were in complete unison with those which prompted the generous sacrifice above described, expressed, on hearing the particulars, his determination to take the first opportunity of mentioning it in Parliament, to the honour of the Bishop and of that Church of which he formed so bright an ornament.

CHAP. XXVII.

THE FOUNDATION STONE OF ST DAVID'S COLLEGE LAID BY THE BISHOP.

ALTHOUGH the amount of contributions for the building of the College fell considerably short of the estimated expense of its erection, it was resolved immediately to commence the most essential parts of the fabric: sanguine hopes being entertained that a grant from Government and additional subscriptions would ere long provide for the completion of the remainder. This resolution being taken, the Bishop, with his accustomed loyalty,

fixed on the 12th of August, the birth-day of the
Royal Patron of the undertaking, for laying the
foundation-stone.

A few days before the ceremonial took place, the
Bishop and his family proceeded to Dery Ormond,
near Lampeter, the seat of the late John Jones,
Esq.*, who had kindly insisted on their making his
house their home upon this joyful occasion. The
party assembled there was a most happy one.
The Bishop was in delightful spirits, and often recurred in after years to this visit as one of peculiar
interest.

The little town of Lampeter, which seldom knows,
except on market days, what a crowd is, beheld the
assemblage of a great concourse of strangers on the
morning of the 12th of August.† The proceedings
commenced by the performance of Divine Service
in the parish church, which, even before the Bishop
arrived, was crowded to excess, and after his entry
was so thronged that many who longed for admit-
tance came away disappointed. An able and appropriate sermon was delivered on the occasion by
the Rev. John Williams, vicar of Lampeter, and

* The name of Mr Jones deserves to be specially comme-
morated for the services which he rendered to the College
scheme. His liberal mind at once scanned the importance of
the object; and he not only contributed the sum of 500l in
aid of it, but accepted the office of treasurer of the subscription
fund, in which capacity his good sense and knowledge of business rendered him a very useful coadjutor. The county of
Cardigan lost in him an amiable enlightened friend and
benefactor

† My own recollection of the above facts has been assisted
by a manuscript account of them, from the pen of the late Rev
Professor Rees, of St David's College, Lampeter, whose recent
death has deprived that society of an invaluable member

now archdeacon of Cardigan, from Mal. ii. 7., " The
Priest's lips should keep knowledge."

From the Church the congregation proceeded to
the site of the College in the following order : —
First, the Royal Cardigan Military Band ; next, the
scholars of Lampeter Grammar School, two and
two ; then the Rural Deans, and a numerous body
of the Clergy in their canonical habits. Several of
the magistrates and principal gentry of Cardiganshire, and from the adjoining counties followed,
succeeded by the carriage of the Bishop, who was
seated in it in his episcopal robes, with his Chaplain,
the Rev. C. Phillipps. The procession was closed
by several private carriages, and was accompanied
and surrounded by a great concourse of people,
who took a lively interest in the passing scene ; the
band playing a piece of music in slow time, suited
to the occasion. A platform for the accommodation
of ladies and of gentry, who did not take part in
the procession, had been erected above the area on
which the ceremony was conducted, and was immediately filled The writer of these pages and one of
his brothers, as lords of the manor, now presented
to the Bishop the conveyance of the site of the
College, accompanied by a brief address, to which
he replied as follows : —

" Gentlemen, if you are gratified with the thought
of being instrumental in promoting my plan for the
advancement of religion and learning in my diocese,
how deeply must I feel on this occasion, especially
witnessing as I do the general enthusiasm with
which its commencement is attended. It would
have been in vain for me to have planned, had I not
received such efficient support from the clergy and

x

gentry of my diocese ; but I feel that to none is the
institution more indebted than to the lords of the
manor of Lampeter. Sanctioned as the undertaking
is by our gracious King, and favoured with the
support of the Universities; with the blessing of
Providence it must and it will prosper. I am
thankful to God that I have been in His hands the
humble instrument of providing a remedy for the
serious obstacles in the way of education in this
country. May His blessing rest upon the work,
and may it, under the guidance of His spirit, con-
duce to the unity of the Church, to the refutation
of error, to the propagation of sound knowledge,
and above all to the salvation of souls ! "

As the Bishop approached the conclusion of this
address, his voice faltered, and the tear of sensibility
moistened his venerable cheek His emotion was
evident, and excited responsive feelings in the
hearts of those by whom he was surrounded.

The band then played a sacred overture, after
which the Hundredth Psalm (old version) was sung
by the boys and girls of the Lampeter Sunday
School, in which the clergy and gentry cordially
joined. A glorious summer sun shone on the occasion, and the effect of the whole was highly impressive.

The foundation stone, a block of black marble,
was now let down into its place, the Bishop having
previously spread some mortar over it with a silver
trowel. He then struck it with a hammer, repeating a passage from the 90th Psalm, " Prosper
Thou the work of our hands, prosper Thou our
handy work." A set of coins of George IV., presented by John Jones, Esq., were next inserted into

a cavity of the stone, and over it was fixed a brass plate with the following inscription : —

ON THE 12TH DAY OF AUGUST, 1822,
BEING THE BIRTH-DAY OF HIS EXCELLENT MAJESTY
KING GEORGE THE FOURTH,
THE FIRST STONE
OF
ST DAVID'S COLLEGE, NEAR LAMPETER,
TO WHICH HIS MAJESTY WAS A MUNIFICENT BENEFACTOR,
WAS LAID BY
THE RIGHT REV THE LORD BISHOP OF ST. DAVID'S,
ASSISTED BY THE RURAL DEANS OF THE DIOCESE
AND OTHER
BENEFACTORS AND SUBSCRIBERS TO THE
BUILDING OF THIS COLLEGE

The prayer for the King's Majesty from the Liturgy, and three appropriate Collects selected for the occasion, were read with much solemnity, and in an audible voice, by the Bishop's Chaplain, the Rev Mr. Phillipps, preceded by a prayer, the principal passages of which were as as follows ;—

" O Lord ! who hast appointed an order of men to serve in the sacred ministry of thy Church, as stewards of thy Gospel, as teachers of thy Holy Will, and as watchmen to warn men of their sins, ' and to call them to repentance, prosper Thou, we beseech Thee, the work which we have undertaken for the instruction of those who shall hereafter be set apart for thy service. Give thy blessing to their studies, that they may become apt and meet for their future duties. Give them grace to discern diligently and faithfully the signs of the times, that they may all labour in their several stations to turn the hearts of the people from the vanities of tho

X 2

world to the things which belong unto their eternal peace, before they are hid from their eyes.

" Awaken and touch all their hearts most powerfully with thy grace, that they may never forget their ordination vows, and that they may become good and faithful guides to others. Enable them, we pray Thee, so to conduct themselves, that by good example they may lead the people committed to their care in the way of eternal life ; and that they may not by any irregularity of life or conversation render their instructions ineffectual, or cause the ways of religion to be evil spoken of. Teach them to be every day more mindful of their charge, more qualified to perform it, and more solicitous to do their duty, as they that must hereafter give account.

" Grant them, O Lord! a sincere love of thy Scriptures. Enable them by thy Holy Spirit rightly to understand and truly to teach the Gospel of thy Son Jesus Christ, and give them grace so devoutly to pray, and so faithfully to preach thy Word, that all who hear them may be made sensible of the reality of religion, and know that Christ is indeed their Saviour and their Redeemer.

" Direct and bless all their labours, give them a discerning spirit, a sound judgment, and a religious heart, that, in all their studies, their aim may be to set forth thy glory by setting forward the salvation of men.

" Magnify the power of thy merciful goodness by disengaging their hearts from the love of worldly goods, and from the fear of worldly evils. And while Thou raisest their minds above the dread of earthly wants and difficulties, make them rich in the abundance of thy grace, rich in good works,

rich in treasuie laid up 'where neither moth nor
rust doth corrupt, and where thieves do not break
through nor steal.'

" To Thee, O Lord! and to the guidance of thy
Holy Spirit, we commend them, and our labours
for their good, in the name and through the mediation of thy Son Jesus Christ our Lord. Amen!"

At the conclusion of the prayers the Bishop
pronounced the blessing. After a suitable pause,
the National Anthem was sung by the whole assembly, accompanied by the band, and three hearty
cheers were given at the termination of the ceremony.

In the afternoon a large and respectable party
dined at the Town Hall in honour of the occasion,
the Bishop presiding at one table, and John Lewis,
Esq. of Llaniron, at the other. It may be imagined
with what enthusiasm the health of the King,
the generous patron of the College, was drunk
on this occasion. When that of the Bishop was
given, it was responded to with warm hearts and
glistening eyes, but his feelings were too much
affected to allow of his addressing the meeting;
at his earnest desire, therefore, a friend who was
seated by him returned thanks for him, in a few
words, the sentiments of which he himself suggested.

The company separated at an early hour, and
before the evening closed, Lampeter resumed its
wonted tranquillity.

In the course of the day, a petition was signed
by the Clergy and benefactors to the College, so-

x 3

liciting such Parliamentary aid as might enable them to complete the erection of the edifice.

The two following letters have reference to the above events.

TO J. S. HARFORD, ESQ.

Abergwilly Palace, August, 1822.

DEAR SIR,

I WAS glad to see in the Morning Post your account of our Ceremonials at Lampeter. I was particularly pleased with the notice of the King's benignity, as also of our having used on the occasion the prayer for his Majesty, &c. from the Liturgy.

I returned on Wednesday, the 28th, from my fortnight's tour of confirmation, and have hardly had time to read and sort the numerous letters which have accumulated during my absence. One of the earliest I have written since my return has been to acknowledge the receipt of my friend Seyer's letter, and list of Bristol benefactions. His situation, as examining Chaplain to the Bishop of Bristol, gives him an opportunity of knowing a little what a Bishop's correspondence is, and what an occupation also is a long tour of confirmation. He will not, therefore, I hope, have felt much disappointment at not hearing from me before.

You will be glad to hear of the increased number of catechumens in one parish in Cardiganshire, Llanbadarfawr, the mother church to Aberystwyth : —

In the year 1809, I confirmed there 225
            1812   -   -   252
            1815   -   -   354
            1818   -   -   482
            1822   -   -   702

I hope that St. David's College will increase this growing attachment to the Church.

I regret as much as yourself our distance from each other; so much more is done in an hour's conversation than in a week's correspondence.

I rejoice to hear from all quarters such good accounts of the health of our excellent friend at Barley Wood.

Yours very truly,
T. St. David's.

TO THE SAME.

Dear Sir,

I ARRIVED at Llanidloes this morning, and have employed part of the two hours which I have to stay here, in my way to Kerry, in writing to Mr. Cockerell about the Corridor of the College, and to invite him to meet you at Abergwilly on the 28th of August, the day on which I hope (Deo volente) to return home.

I am delighted with your account of our excellent friend Mrs. H. More. It is most consolatory to think that a life which has been so beneficial to the world may yet be continued much longer than there was any hope of last year. I regret extremely that Wales is separated from Barley Wood by " a world

of waters," which makes it impracticable for me to
visit it, and your own romantic residence.

The horses are getting ready. Adieu. Remember me kindly to Mrs. Harford, and believe me,

Yours very truly,

T. St. David's.

CHAP. XXVIII.

THE BISHOP'S CATHOLIC SPIRIT. — BY COMMAND OF THE
KING HE FRAMES A PLAN FOR A ROYAL SOCIETY OF
LITERATURE. — SOME ACCOUNT OF IT, AND OF HIS AN-
NIVERSARY DISCOURSES. — HE QUESTIONS THE AUTHEN-
TICITY OF THE POSTHUMOUS WORKS ASCRIBED TO
MILTON.

1823.

In the Spring of 1823, the Bishop and his co-
adjutors were actively engaged in bringing the
case of the Welsh College before influential members of both Houses of Parliament, in the hope
of procuring, by their exertions, a public grant
in aid of it. He himself applied to the Archbishop of Canterbury and the Bishop of London,
for permission to refer Lord Liverpool to them, in
testimony of the merits of the scheme, a request
which was readily granted. The Premier, in the
course of various interviews with the Bishop, expressed himself favourably disposed to a public
grant, provided it could be so made as not to
establish an inconvenient precedent; but he objected
on this ground to the proposed application to Parliament.

Our frequent meetings upon the business of the
College afforded me, during this spring, continual
opportunities of studying his character and habits.
He was employed early and late with his books and
his pen, and led the life of a laborious student.
After breakfast he gave his attention for some
hours to professional business, and to the claims of
correspondence, and later in the day he often drove
to the British Museum to consult manuscripts and
learned works, or went to some literary, charitable,
or religious meetings. Occasionally he attended
the House of Lords.

His daily dinner was two mutton chops, with
little or no wine. He usually devoted his evenings
to study and writing, and often sat up late at these
employments. Such, at this time, was the daily tenor
of his life ; and his habitual temperance, as we have
already remarked, enabled him to pursue this sedentary course without injury to his health. " Spare
fare, which oft with gods doth diet," was a topic
upon which he loved to expatiate. It had been
the habit of his own life, and, in order to point out
its advantages to others, he published in a small tract
some useful and amusing particulars of the life and
maxims of Cornaro, the Italian philosopher, whom
Addison has celebrated in the Spectator, as having
lived by means of resolute temperance to a very
great age, in spite of a delicate and frail constitution. The more I became acquainted with him, the
more I was struck by the purity of his feelings : his
guileless confidence in the intentions of others , the
unvarying peace and cheerfulness of his mind ; and
his habitual kindness of manner and address. His
recreations were equally simple and innocent. Re-

ligious or literary conversation; the perusal with
a friend of fine passages of poetry; a pleasant
walk; listening to the tunes of his musical boxes,
of which he had several of exquisite quality; such
were some of his favourite relaxations, and he
enjoyed them with a keen relish. When his
nights proved, as they sometimes did, wakeful,
he would solace the time by a tune from one of
those boxes, which usually stood by his bedside,
or by repeating favourite pieces of poetry. Nor
were his "Songs in the night" exclusively "*the*
songs of Sion.*"* I have heard him expatiate on
the pleasure with which he often, on such occasions, went through the whole of Gray's Bard, with
a lively admiration of its lofty numbers and sublime
imagery. In an age and period when so much of
party spirit prevailed in the Church his mind soared
above its influence. He had his own firm and
decided opinions upon those controverted topics,
respecting which good men of the same communion
may be allowed to differ; but he was too well
acquainted with the facts of Ecclesiastical History,
and with the nature of the human mind, to imagine
that all can be made to think alike with respect to
points upon which the statements of Scripture are
not so direct and positive as to preclude reasonable
diversity of opinion. He never allowed names of
contumely to prejudice his mind, à priori, against
any individual. He well knew with how much
levity such names are often applied, by those who
have no religion themselves, in order to depreciate
the character and labours of men eminently pious.
Any clergyman who faithfully devoted himself to
the discharge of his duties, and led a useful and

religious life, was sure of his favour and protection, whether he was called " high church " or " evangelical." Such were the principles upon which he acted, not only in the daily intercourse of life, but also in his disposal of church patronage, and the consequence was, that he was occasionally censured as preferring men, who according to the objectors, did not faithfully preach the Gospel , while he was perhaps still oftener cavilled at by those of opposite opinions, as an exclusive patron of evangelical clergymen. His real object was to prefer men of enlightened zeal, and unquestionable piety ; and his great wish was, that they should so feed the flocks committed to their charge, and in such a manner be examples to them, as that when the " chief Shepherd " should appear, they themselves might receive " a crown of glory." He discouraged all detraction both by precept and practice , he never gave encouragement to gossip or scandal ; and was equally unwilling, except on the clearest evidence, to hear or to believe ill of others.

The following letters belong to the period of which we are now treating. The second was addressed by the Bishop in answer to objections made by a friend whom he highly valued, to some expressions in a prayer in " Law's Serious Call." It is taken from a MS. copy in his own hand-writing.

TO THE LORD BISHOP OF ST. DAVID'S.

MY DEAR LORD,

I MUST be more brief than I could wish in reply to your very interesting letter. Mr. ―― objects to the " two-fold change " spoken of in Jerram's treatise. I asked, whether, *substantially*, there is any thing more in it than the most high church writers (such as Jackson, Jones of Nayland, Skelton, &c.) have maintained, and begged to know to *what* the " new man created in righteousness and true holiness," and the " old man corrupt according to the flesh," &c. refer. He answered, " merely to baptism." I replied that I could not think so, as the context (Ephes. c. 4. v. 22.) shows. At this moment we were interrupted, but I shall hear from him again. In his 3rd vol. (p. 284.) Jones says, " The same baptism which is sufficient to save an infant is sufficient only to *condemn* those who *might*, but never do, get any further. As the Christian advances in life, there must be *other* evidences of his spiritual union with Christ; for as by baptism he is born into a *new state*, so by faith, by a partaking of the other sacrament, by prayer, and by a godly life, it must appear that he *liveth* in Him unto whom he was born again." Jones has another passage equally strong, beginning (p. 391.): "If any man have not the spirit of Christ he is none of his ," — " he is without Christ's spirit if without its fruit." And in Scott's Christian Life (part 2nd, cap. 7.) there is a very striking passage on the same subject. It is singular that on both sides we should still be contending for first principles; but so it is.

*   *   *   *   *

Believe me, my dear Lord,
Devotedly yours,
G. W. MARRIOTT.

DEAR ——, London, Dec 24. 1823

I AM grieved to think that two sincere Christians (as I trust you and I are) should differ so widely as we do in our opinion of a prayer for faith and holiness, such as Law's is. You think *that* prayer very objectionable; and I think you are mistaken in all your objections.

You say it ought to be addressed to Jesus as God. It is certainly addressed to Him as God; He is God as well as man, and a prayer addressed to Him is addressed to God. The term, "Lamb of God," does not at all detract from His divinity. Divine honour is paid to Him as the Lamb of God in the 5th and 7th chapters of the Revelation. And in the 21st and 22d chapters, " the throne of the Lamb " is " the throne of God , " and God and the Lamb are the Temple of the New Jerusalem (Rev. xxi. v. 22.). But under whatever name our Saviour is addressed, prayer can be addressed to Him only as God.

The term *regeneration* is undoubtedly confined by Scripture and by our church to baptism , that is, to the being " born of *water* and the Spirit." But it does not therefore follow that we cannot be " born of God" and of Christ, any otherwise than by *water* and the Spirit The term " born again " is altogether *metaphorical ;* it is used in distinction from our *natural* birth, and to express a change from one state to another, from unbelief to belief, from sin to holiness, &c To be " born of God " is to be " born again;" but " born of God " is not synonymous with baptism. For " whosoever is born of God sinneth not" (1 John, c. 5. v. 18.), whereas we cannot say whoever is baptized sinneth not. It is also said, whoever believeth that Jesus is the Christ, is " born of God " (1 John, c. 5. v. 1.). " God is love,' and whoever loveth is " born of God " (1 John, iv. 7.).

" We are passed from death unto life because we love the brethren " (1 John, iii. 14.). We may have been baptized, and yet be living in habits of sin, and while in this state we cannot be said to bear upon us the impress of the children of God. St. John says, " we are then not of God but of the Devil " (1 John, iii. 8, 9.). But we may be converted from this state of sin, and then we are " born of God " and of Christ.

We may after baptism fall into doubt and unbelief, as St. Thomas did ; and we may, like him, be *begotten again* to a good hope, by the resurrection of Christ. This expression is not actually applied, 1 allow, to St. Thomas, but appears to be a fair inference from the facts of his case.

The expressions, " born of Christ and of God," cannot be restricted to baptism, for we pray thus (in the Ash Wednesday Collect), " Create and make in us *new* and contrite hearts." We may therefore be " born of God " after baptism.

You object to the expression, " O fill me with Christ's holy nature," as impossible in itself and blasphemous.

We might say, in the language of the Apostle, " O make us partakers of the *Divine* nature " (2 Pet. c. 1. v. 4.). which is a stronger term than *holy* nature. But perhaps you will say it is impossible to be holy as Christ is holy. True ; yet Christ himself bids us to be perfect even as our Father in heaven is perfect (Mat. v. 18.) And St. John says, that believing Christians purify themselves "even as Christ is pure" (1 John, c. 3. v. 3.). Now this, in any literal sense, is impossible, but there is no blasphemy in praying that we may be thus perfected. Nay, St. Paul prays for his Ephesian converts, that they may be "filled with all the fulness of God" (Eph. iii. 19.); and says that Christ appointed the different orders of the Christain ministry in His church, that we might come "to a *perfect* man, to the measure of the stature of the fulness of Christ" (Eph. iv. 13.).

Again, St. Paul says,' "Let this mind be in you which was also in Christ Jesus," that is, the spirit of meekness, lowliness, charity, the same spirit, tempers, and dispositions, which Christ bids us learn of him.

We are "born of Christ" when we live in the spirit of Christ. St. John says (1 Eph. ii. 29.), "every one that doeth righteousness is *born of Him.*" Why? because we then follow the example of Christ, who is emphatically called the Righteous;" for " he that doeth righteousness is righteous, even as Christ is righteous (1 John, iii 7.), and he that doeth righteousness is born of Christ."

You object also to the expression, "a new creature," yet St. Paul says, "if any man be in Christ, he is *a new creature*" (2 Cor. v. 17.). To be in Christ is to be a faithful disciple of Christ; or, as the sacramental prayer expresses it, "that we may evermore dwell in Him and He in us."

We are born again when Christ, that is, the spirit of Christ, is formed in us. This appears from the language of St. Paul (Gal. iv. 19.), "My little children, of whom I travail in birth again until Christ be formed in you." These words were ad-

dressed to his Galatian converts who had been
baptized but had departed from the purity and simplicity of the Gospel. The expression is remarkable. Of whom I labour again in birth until Christ,
that is, the spirit of Christ, be formed in you, or
revived in you.

The prayer, therefore, of William Law, which
you think is objectionable, appears to me to be
conceived in the purest spirit of Christianity For
what is true religion but (as Scougal says) "a union
of the soul with God," a real participation of the
Divine nature, the very image of God drawn upon
the soul.

I am, &c. &c.

T. St. David's.

At the time now referred to the Bishop was
often a good deal engaged by the concerns of the
Royal Society of Literature, of which he was
President. It was founded in the year 1820, under
the special patronage of his Majesty George IV.,
who, being himself an accomplished man of letters,
and desirous of giving a stimulus to the promotion
of general literature, and especially to that of his
own country, had summoned the Bishop of St.
David's to his presence, soon after his accession to
the throne, and committed, in a most flattering
manner, to his judgment the task of framing the
plan of a society for the advancement of these objects. The Bishop, aided by a provisional council,
submitted to the King, in November 1820, the
general outline of the Royal Society of Literature,
which received his Majesty's approbation. The
same parties proceeded to ingraft upon it such
regulations as they deemed best calculated to give

full effect to the proposed institution, and to accomplish his Majesty's patriotic intentions. On
the 29th of May, 1823, the Provisional Council
laid before the King the proposed Constitution
and Regulations of the Society, when they received
his final sanction, and were embodied in a Royal
Charter. The principal means of advancing literature proposed by the Society are described in
the charter to be, " by the publication of inedited
remains of ancient literature ; by endeavours to fix,
as far as is practicable, the standard of the English
language, and to preserve its purity by the critical
improvement of English Lexicography; by the
reading at public meetings of interesting papers
on history, philosophy, poetry, philology, and the
arts , by the publication of such of these papers as
should be approved by the Council of the Society ,
and by the assigning of honorary rewards to works
of great literary merit, and to important discoveries
in literature."

The Society, it was enacted, should consist of
Fellows and Associates, and be governed by a
President, eight Vice-Presidents, and sixteen Fel-
lows, constituting a Council.

The annual subscription of Fellows was to be at
least 2*l*. 2*s*. per annum ; or in lieu of annual payments, a composition was allowed at the rate of
ten years' purchase, for that or any higher subscription.

Through the munificence of his Majesty, the
Society was enabled at its outset to assign to ten
Associates the annual sum of 100 guineas each,
payable out of the privy purse ; and they were to be
termed Royal Associates.

Y

An equal number of Associates with similar allowances was engrafted on the funds of the Society.

These Associates were to be men of distinguished learning, and authors of some creditable work; and were bound to communicate to the Council, once a year at least, a disquisition or essay on some literary subject.

A further annual sum of 100 guineas was also contributed by his Majesty out of the privy purse for two gold medals, to be adjudged as honorary rewards to literary works of eminent merit, and to important discoveries in literature.

The ordinary meetings of the Society were to take place in the first and third week in every month from November to June; the anniversary on the last Thursday in April.

We have been thus particular as to the constitution and objects of this Society, because its successful establishment, in the face of many difficulties, was chiefly to be ascribed to the Bishop's anxious care and sedulous exertions; as also because he continued to the latest period of his life to rank among its most zealous supporters. In the seventh year of its institution, he states in the Discourse which he delivered as President, at its anniversary meeting, that its actual and honorary members amounted nearly to three hundred, — a number greatly beyond the expectation of its most sanguine friends.

It is a curious fact, which his Majesty George the Fourth himself mentioned with a smile to the present Dean of Salisbury, that the Bishop, from a misconception of his meaning at their first interview, committed the King as an *annual* subscriber of 1000*l.*, a sum which he had intended only as a donation to the Society at its outset, while his annual subscription was to have been limited to 100*l.* As, however, his Lordship in his zeal had immediately proclaimed the King's munificence, and Fame, through the medium of the press, had almost as quickly trumpeted it with her hundred tongues throughout the country, there was no retreat; and his Majesty not only cheerfully acquiesced, but amused himself with the incident.

The Bishop delivered an annual Discourse for eight years successively at the anniversary meetings of the Society. They are written with learning, elegance, and spirit; but were perhaps a little too much pervaded by his own favourite topics and objects of research, for such occasions

Thus the Discourses of 1826, 1827, and 1828, are chiefly occupied by a detail of the evidence which he regarded as conclusive against the authenticity of the posthumous work De Doctrinâ Christianâ, ascribed to Milton. This work was published by his Majesty's command in 1825, in the Latin original, as discovered by Mr. Lemon in the State Paper Office, and also in the form of an English translation from the pen of Dr. Sumner, then Librarian to the King, and now Bishop of Winchester. In addition to the arguments adduced in these three Discourses, the Bishop entered into a further and more extended discussion of the question, in a Treatise entitled " Milton contrasted with Milton and the Scriptures," which was published together with the Discourses in an octavo form in the year 1829.

It may appear strange to some of my readers

Y 2

that he should have devoted so much valuable time
to a critical question, apparently foreign to his
professional duties and avocations. His actuating
motive, however, was not literary ambition, but
that same zeal for the Trinitarian faith which
had been one of his distinguishing characteristics
throughout life. An intimate study of the writings
of Milton had led him to the conclusion that the
Treatise in question was, as far as his name was
concerned, a forgery; and fearing that the heretical
opinions by which it is pervaded would circulate
more freely under so imposing an authority, he
deemed it a positive duty to vindicate the claim of
the illustrious poet to the praise of orthodoxy.

It is needless to enter into any minute detail of
the circumstantial evidence in favour of the authenticity of the Treatise thus ascribed to Milton. The
leading facts are well known, and lie within a small
compass. It was found by Mr. Lemon in the State
Paper Office, together with a copy of Milton's
State Letters, in an envelope addressed to Mr.
Skinner, merchant, supposed to have been nephew
of Cyriack Skinner, Milton's intimate friend, to
whom two of his Sonnets were addressed. It bore
upon it the superscription, Joannis Miltoni Angli
de Doctrinâ Christianâ. These manuscripts appear
to have come into the possession of government at
the time that arrests and seizures of papers were
actively going on, during the public ferment attending the Popish and Rye-house plots. Many close
coincidences of phraseology and expression have
been traced, by critical industry, between the Latin
style of the Treatise, De Doctrinâ, and of Milton's
published Latin works.

The Bishop, though he did little, if any thing, to impugn the force of these evidences of the authenticity of the Treatise, marshalled a strong array of facts and arguments, in proof that a totally opposite conclusion was derivable from a scrutiny of the internal evidence.

We have evidence, he says, of Milton's Trinitarian belief in the 21st, 33d, 40th, 47th, 59th, 65th, and 66th years of his life, of which the two latter were the last. This evidence is supplied by his Ode on the Nativity, his Treatise on Reformation, his Sunday Instructions to his Pupils, his Paradise Lost, and his Treatise on True Religion. We have also evidence of his express declaration against Arianism in his 33d and 65th years, from his Treatises on Prelatical Episcopacy and on True Religion. His change of religious sects is no proof of any change in religious doctrine; because the Calvinists, Puritans, Presbyterians, and Independents, to whom he successively attached himself, were all Trinitarians.

These assertions he has elaborately illustrated by direct quotations from the works of Milton, irreconcilable with the opinions of the author of the work De Doctrinâ, except by supposing, what would altogether neutralise his authority, that at one and the selfsame period of his life he could be guilty of the most glaring and inexplicable contradictions.

The different spirit in which this work is written from that which generally pervades his controversial writings, furnishes another objection to its authenticity. In his principal prose works he has closely identified himself with them by the avowal of his dominant political opinions and prejudices; by references to the circumstances of the age in which he wrote, or to his own personal history; and by occasional passages of fierce invective or of surpassing grandeur of diction. In the work De Doctrinâ, on the contrary, all is calmness and moderation. It is a scholastic and metaphysical Treatise, unilluminated by any of those coruscations of fancy and eloquence which in his other works so forcibly recal the sublime author of Paradise Lost, or the Platonising and elevated Bard of Comus.

That the Bishop's arguments were not unsuccessful in exciting doubts of the authenticity of the Treatise in minds of a high order, will be apparent from the following letters from the present learned and venerable Archbishop of Canterbury, and the late Lord Grenville.

My dear Lord, ˙   London, March 23. 1826.
I have been too long without thanking you for your kindness in sending me your very interesting remarks on the late publication of what is called a posthumous work of Milton. Your arguments have great weight; and the long array of citations from works written at different periods of his life, which contain opinions altogether inconsistent with the heretical doctrines maintained by the author of the posthumous treatise, throw great doubts upon its authenticity. My copies, Latin and English, of this latter work are both in the country; so that I have not had opportunity of examining the passages which are adduced by the editor as proofs of the

correspondency of this work with the other works of Milton ; nor indeed would this busy season have allowed time for the comparison. Supposing the work to be Milton's, we can hardly acquit him of disingenuous conduct in using orthodox language in the works published during his lifetime, while he reserved his esoteric heterodoxy for publication after his death. I should like to see the arguments, if any there are, in disproof of your reasoning (for my private satisfaction I mean), but I have heard of no reply. I think the work in question so paradoxical that it can hardly do any harm, whoever may have been the real author.

Believe me, my dear Lord,
Most truly yours,
W. LONDON.

MY DEAR LORD, Charles Street, May 12. 1826.
I HAVE read with much attention, and with the strong interest which I feel in all that relates to his great name, your note on the work recently ascribed to Milton, and I really think your reasoning is as nearly conclusive as can be expected on such a subject.

The work De Doct. Xtianâ cannot have been the production of any short period in the life of any man, particularly of a blind man, though daily conversant, as we are told Milton was, and as every page of his great Poem proves him to have been, in Scripture reading.

No one who knows any thing of his character will suspect him of being capable at any time of

Y 4

publishing works countenancing one set of opinions, while he was secretly convinced of the truth of contrary doctrines, and was labouring in private for the ultimate promulgation of these last.

You have clearly shown that there is no considerable period between his fifty-ninth and sixty-sixth year, that of his death, during which he did not publicly express Trinitarian sentiments. The evidence resulting from the last of his theological works, that on True Religion, I think particularly striking. I was indeed surprised when I read in the Edinburgh Review the passage to which your Lordship adverts. Paradise Lost has long been as familiar to me, as frequent reading and the highest admiration of it could make it; and the impression which the Review describes had certainly never conveyed itself to my mind. The whole structure of that magnificent poem, to say nothing of particular expressions, seems to me to be undeniably in conformity with a belief in the Trinity; and no one acquainted with the character of the work, of its author, or of the times in which he wrote, can doubt that his poetry is as much to be received for a confession of his faith, as if it had been delivered with all the solemnity of a religious creed.

How far back then from the date of the publication of the Paradise Lost, will not the time employed in its composition carry the evidence of his opinions?

It can never be indifferent to us to ascertain that these opinions really are supported by the authority of so learned, so pious, and so sincere a man, — a man of such deep research, and endowed with one of the most powerful minds that was ever exercised on such subjects.

We may, I think, pronounce with much confidence, from the evidence which you have adduced, that Milton's tenets can at no period of his life have been those of an Arian. No presumption, therefore, nor any thing short of the most positive and indisputable evidence, should induce us to attribute to him an elaborate treatise in favour of doctrines which to the very close of his life he continued so openly to disavow.

Believe me ever,

My dear Lord,

With great respect and regard,

Your Lordship's most faithful

And obedient humble servant,

GRENVILLE.

P. S. I am not acquainted with the precise doctrines of the Churches of the Vaudois, " those who," in the language of Milton's exquisite Sonnet, " kept God's faith so pure of old." Can any inference as to his faith on the points now in question be drawn from this passage; or is the purity of which he there speaks to be understood only as contrasted with the errors of the Church of Rome, which in the following lines are more particularly referred to ?

MY DEAR LORD, Dropmore, May 25 1826.

I RETURN you many thanks for your interesting communication of your translations of two very striking pieces of poetry ; the latter of these was quite unknown to me, and I am much pleased with the turn of it, which is well preserved, and in some respects heightened in your translation. It is very flattering to me to see the idleness with which I sometimes give myself to this fascinating amusement, countenanced by the example and authority of one who knows so well how to employ his time to the best advantage, and to use it for the highest of all purposes.

Since I returned home among my books, for with them only I consider myself at home, I have turned to some accounts of the Vaudois churches; and I think it quite indisputable that no Arian or Socinian, nor any person whose religious opinions had any such tendency, could possibly express himself as Milton has, not in verse only, but as you observe in prose also, respecting the purity and orthodoxy of those churches.

This line of argument is, as I before took the liberty of observing to your Lordship, to be considered always in this case with a particular reference to the acknowledged piety and singular sincerity of Miltons' character. This last quality, as far as I know, has never been denied to him, except by one only of the numerous adversaries whom his opinions have at different times raised up against him. And this one, I am sorry to say, was the late Bishop Watson; who, in a 30th of January sermon, referred to by both Todd and Symmons, has charged him with the *grossest falsehood*. It would not be difficult to show that this coarse invective is wholly groundless, and that the passage in Milton's works to which it refers has been utterly misunderstood by every one of those

three critics upon it — by Watson, Todd, and
Symmons.
　　I have the honour to be,
　　　With high respect and regard,
　　　　My dear Lord,
　　　Most faithfully and truly yours,
　　　　　　　　　　GRENVILLE.

CHAP. XXIX.

LORDS LIVERPOOL AND ELDON AID THE COLLEGE. — THE
BISHOP'S VISIT TO THE AUTHOR. — HIS PERILOUS VOY-
AGE FROM BRISTOL TO SWANSEA. — HIS TRANSLATION
TO THE SEE OF SALISBURY.

1823.—1824.—1825.

IN the course of the session of Parliament of 1823,
the sanction and support of Government were given
to St. David's College by Lords Eldon and Liverpool, who concurred in annexing to it certain ecclesiastical sinecures, and some other pieces of preferment, in the gift of the Chancellor, by act of
parliament.

During the winter and spring of 1824, the Bishop's pursuits as an author, and the concerns of
the college, jointly occupied his time and attention.

In June, 1824, he paid a visit to the author at his
residence in Gloucestershire ; and by a happy but
fortuitous coincidence, the American Bishop of Ohio,
Dr. Chase, together with Sir Thomas and Lady Acland, and part of their family, were at the same time
assembled under his roof. Many neighbouring friends

joined the party on the day of their arrival; and few
of them will easily forget the lively interest which
all felt in witnessing the meeting, in a place so
remote from the metropolis, of two Bishops presiding over sections of the church of Christ in such
opposite hemispheres, both men of primitive and
devout feeling, — both also, at that very time, engaged in furthering the erection of a college for
clerical education, the one for a diocese, comprehending nearly the whole of South Wales, the other
for the vast and semi-cultivated province of Ohio,
in North America. They were themselves no less
gratified by this unexpected meeting. The Bishop
of St. David's, tempted by its being the height of
summer, fixed, when he quitted Blaise Castle, to go
by the steam-boat from Bristol Hotwells to Swansea.
The morning of his departure proved so stormy,
that his hosts would fain have induced him to re-
voke the plan ; but his arrangements were all made,
and he proceeded in spite of their earnest re-
monstrances. The following letter will show that
the anxiety they felt on his account, as the day advanced, was not without reason.

TO J. S. HARFORD, ESQ.

DEAR SIR,   Abergwilly Palace, July 8 1824.
I THANK you for your kind inquiries after the
issue of my perilous voyage, for indeed (as I was
informed after our arrival in port) we were once
so near the rocks, and in so much danger, that the
boats and anchors were got ready ; and the wreckers
were seen crowding down to the shore, expecting

plunder. But (thank God) we arrived safe at the Mackworth Arms, between one and two o'clock in the morning. I was much indebted to Mr. Grove for his kind attention in assisting me from the packet to the inn. I had heard so much of the difference between the steam packets and other vessels, that I was induced to make the experiment, but now think the passage from Bristol to Swansea a longer voyage than I would recommend to any friend who has time and money to spare. But being safe at home, I am not sorry for my experience, and for this additional proof of God's merciful protection in the time of danger.

I have the pleasure of informing you that Poll is quite well, and seems much pleased with his fine cage, which is greatly admired. He is fond of the warm atmosphere of the kitchen, but is occasionally brought into the breakfast-room to amuse us with his company.

I thank you for the passage of the Agamemnon, which struck me with its resemblance to Gray's language —

Αυτη ἐιπους λεαινα συγκοιμωμενη Λυκῳ,

might have suggested to Gray his

"She-wolf of France," &c.

I had allotted yesterday for an excursion to Lampeter, but was prevented by the rainy weather. To-day there is an amendment in the wind and the barometer, therefore I hope soon to get a sight of St. David's College.

The shield for my coat of arms to be placed in your castle travelled safe with me, and shall be put in hand as soon as I can see the painter.

Pray be so good as to add Mrs. Burgess's name
to Mrs. Harford's list of guinea donations towards
a printing press for Bishop Chase, which, if you
will pay for me, I will repay you when we meet.

Remember me kindly to Mrs. H., and believe
me to be,

Yours very truly,

T. St. David's.

In the spring of 1825, the See of Salisbury
became vacant by the death of Dr. Fisher, and
the Bishop of St. David's was appointed his successor. It has been very generally reported that
he was indebted to the influence of his old friend,
the Bishop of Durham, for this mark of royal
favour; but he himself assured me this report
was altogether unfounded. Much surprise 'and
regret were expressed at the time, in various
quarters, that he should have been willing to part
from his Welsh diocese, and perhaps it would
have been more entirely for his happiness had he
steadfastly adhered to his ancient station. His
quitting it was even regarded by many as the in-
fraction of an avowed determination to live and
die there; but it has already been stated on his
own authority, that the utmost he ever said in this
way was, that he should be perfectly content and
happy should it prove so. He had now, however,
reached his sixty-eighth year; his stall at Durham
involved a long annual journey thither; and this,
united to the fatigue of frequent travelling through
his own very extensive diocese, had become onerous
to him. But these considerations, he assured me,
would not have induced the step, had there not

been, in addition to them, a motive which pressed
upon his most intimate feelings. Mrs. Burgess,
who was much of an invalid from rheumatism,
ascribed it in a great degree to the dampness of
Abergwilly, and was therefore anxious for the
change. There were also other reasons which
influenced his decision. His various schemes for
the improvement of his diocese were now in a
great measure accomplished. Its slender income
had been doubled by his liberality. The College
was in the course of erection and endowment.
It is true, that he somewhat hazarded the final
success of the plan by quitting the diocese, since
it was impossible to foresee in what light it would
be regarded by another. He acknowledged that
he could not repress anxiety upon this point; but
was persuaded that the importance, and even the
necessity of the undertaking were so undeniable,
that he might venture to assure himself it would
find a cordial friend and supporter in his successor.
These anticipations were more than verified, and
he was quickly relieved from any solicitude on this
head, by the enlightened judgment and the active
energy with which the plan was appreciated and
prosecuted by Dr. Jenkinson, who succeeded him
in the See of St. David's.

Seldom has any Head of a diocese quitted it for
another accompanied by sentiments of veneration
and regret more sincere and general than those
which were expressed towards Bishop Burgess, both
by the clergy and gentry; and his own feelings
were not a little affected at the prospect of the approaching separation. They were softened, however, not only by the considerations already men-

tioned, but also by the local attachment which he
felt towards Salisbury. It was the place in which
he had commenced his public career as chaplain to
Dr. Shute Barrington, whose friendship had endeared it to him by innumerable pleasant associations. He was also, from the same cause, acquainted in a general way with the diocese, and he
delighted in the cathedral of Salisbury, and in the
bowery walks which skirt the precincts of that majestic and elegant fane.

What were the general sentiments and feelings of
the clergy throughout the diocese of St. David's
in the prospect of his departure are faithfully depicted in the following address presented to him,
among others, by the Archdeaconry of Carmarthen.

> To the Right Rev. THOMAS BURGESS, late
> Lord Bishop of St. David's, now Lord
> Bishop of Salisbury.

We whose names are underwritten, clergy and
laity of the Archdeaconry of Carmarthen, in the
diocese of St. David's, beg leave to approach your
Lordship, and to express our deepest regret at the
irreparable loss we have sustained by the removal
of your Lordship from the superintendence of this
See.

Your Lordship found the diocese of St. David's,
in the year 1803, in a most dilapidated state in
every view. The churches and ecclesiastical buildings were generally in a ruinous condition; many of
the clergy were incompetently educated, and dis-
graced their profession by ebriety and other de-

grading vices; but your Lordship, by requiring a
strict attention to duty from the Commissaries
General and rural Deans, succeeded in restoring
the churches in some districts to a state of exemplary neatness; and by submitting to become
your own examining chaplain, and requiring superior learning and theological knowledge from the
candidates for Holy Orders, by enforcing the law
against irregularities, and by withholding institution from all who were not competently skilled
in the language of their parishioners, your Lordship has gradually furnished the diocese with a body
of clergy much superior to that which we ever possessed before.

Your Lordship's enjoining that all candidates for
orders should have passed seven years at one of the
licensed grammar schools contributed materially
to this reform; and your having succeeded, against
many difficulties, in founding a college for the future
education of candidates for the Church, has crowned
your Lordship's public services.

But this is not all. While your Lordship was
occupied in these laborious undertakings, and in
attending to the detail of the various minor, yet
harassing duties of this too extensive diocese, you
were incessantly engaged in composing learned
works, in answer to the heretical cavils of the
enemies of our Church Establishment; and though
possessed of deep learning, which qualified you to
figure in the first ranks of literature, you wrote
numerous familiar religious tracts and catechisms
for the instruction of the youth of your diocese.

Nor must it be forgotten, that instead of confirming only in the county towns, your Lordship

z

confirmed in almost all the market-towns in the diocese, and thus brought confirmation, in a manner, to every man's door.

These are such important services as can never be forgotten, and if to them we add your Lordship's liberal and princely subscriptions towards building the College, churches, chapels, and every useful undertaking, and, in a most disinterested manner, running out the episcopal leases, with the view of improving the revenues of the See, the aggregate will form such an accumulated mass of public service, as can scarcely be paralleled in any period of the Church.

While we thus presume to trouble your Lordship with the expression of our deep and heartfelt regret for the severe and unexpected loss we have sustained, permit us, at the same time, my Lord, to offer our humble congratulations on your Lordship's elevation to the See of Salisbury, through his Majesty's spontaneous and most gracious favour; to which we add our cordial wishes that your Lordship may enjoy your new dignity in health, comfort, and happiness, to an extended period of life.

Then follow the names of the subscribing clergy, headed by that of the late Rev. Mr. Beynon, Archdeacon of Cardigan.

A subscription was at the same time zealously entered into for presenting the Bishop with a beautiful piece of plate, in testimony of these sentiments. It was entitled the Cambrian Vase, and emblematically alluded to his eminent services.

CHAP. XXX.

TESTIMONIES OF AFFECTIONATE VENERATION TO THE
BISHOP FROM VARIOUS CLERGYMEN IN HIS WELSH
DIOCESE.

THAT the sentiments conveyed in the address,
which closes the preceding chapter, were truly expressive of the feelings of the reverend body from
which they emanated, the writer of these pages has
had many occasions of knowing, and he may, with
equal truth add that the name of Bishop Burgess
still lives in the affectionate veneration of the clergy
of South Wales. Those, in particular, to whom he
was personally known delight to dwell upon his
various excellencies, and to bear their testimony
to the purity and elevation of his Christian character. In proof of this assertion, some extracts
shall here be introduced from written memorials
of the Bishop, kindly transmitted to the writer by
three highly respectable parochial incumbents of
the diocese of St. David's. Though drawn up
wholly without concert, their descriptions will be
found remarkably concurrent with each other, and
with the general tenour of the preceding pages.

" I feel the liveliest interest," says the Rev. Mr.
Byers, " in the task which you have undertaken ;
for I sincerely loved and revered that good and holy
man, and am persuaded that a biographical memoir
of him will prove most welcome, not only to that
branch of the Christian church of which the good
Bishop was an overseer and an ornament, but to the
church of God throughout the world, since the name

of Dr. Burgess has been honourably associated with
theology and literature for more than half a century. But his name will be more especially associated, in the memory of all who enjoyed the privilege
of his friendship, with what is greater than the reputation of learning, I mean with every thing that
is single and unaffected in personal piety, humble
and self-denying in life; simple and urbane in deportment: conscientious and independent in the
exercise of episcopal patronage, and rigidly faithful
and exact in all that he regarded as his duty, whether in reference to his public office or private and
social life. All this is well known to those who were
privileged to have free access to his study and his
table, and to whom he was wont to open the rich
stores of his mind, with a simplicity and a humility
seldom witnessed, and to develope the feelings and
workings of a heart in which most obviously dwelt
purity and kindness.

" I myself certainly had, as you observe, full opportunities of studying his character; the more
so from the occurrence of particular circumstances,
which brought me into close and frequent communication with him. Conscientiously exact in his
closet duties, and accustomed to find time daily for
meditation and the perusal of some of the more eminent devotional works, he enjoyed a most enviable
serenity of mind. His fine countenance was an index of his character; there sat on it a meekness
and placidity which were truly engaging, mingled
with a dignity and a depth of expression which inspired veneration.

" His characteristic virtue, his prominent grace,
which could not escape the observation of any who

ever communicated with him, was *humility*. He had, through grace, obeyed the apostolic injunction in putting on 'kindness, humbleness of mind, meekness.'

" He was ever anxious to avoid wounding the feelings of others; and when necessity was imposed upon him to reprove an offender, it was obvious how much pain the act cost himself. I can illustrate this by an instance, one of several which occurred within my own observation. A Welsh curate, of low origin, attainments, and habits, convicted of disreputable conduct, and imprisoned in the county gaol for debt, wrote to the Bishop imploring him to pity his case, and to send him some relief to support him during the period of his confinement. The Bishop replied by faithfully pointing out the disreputable line of conduct which had brought him into this condition, and by giving him a very serious but mild reproof, together with a hint of the consequences which might ensue from his present disgraceful position. By the same post he enclosed to me the supplicatory letter, with a private injunction to inquire strictly into the case, in search of any mitigating circumstances which might spare him the pain of noticing it publicly: he also enclosed a ten pound note, desiring me, if it appeared necessary, to convey it to the wretched man to meet his immediate emergency; and, added the Bishop, with his characteristic modesty and conscientiousness, ' let Mr. . . . know distinctly that he owes not this gift to me, but to a kind Providence which places it at my disposal in the very moment of his distress.'

" Of his conscientious and independent disposal of

z 3

preferment, I had many proofs during my acquaintance with him of sixteen years. Happening one
day to call at the palace, the Bishop mentioned a
living just become vacant, and said it was astonishing
what a number of applications had been made for it
in the course of eight-and-forty hours. He appeared
dissatisfied with the various candidates named to him,
and expressed his wish to fix on some truly good
man with a family, to whom the living might be of
real service. I ventured to name a curate to him,
whose ministerial fidelity and moral character had
been highly spoken of in my hearing a day or two
before. He had a large family, and had been labouring with much success in a laborious but very
poor curacy. He instantly desired me to inquire
further and very particularly about him. I did so,
and soon reported the result. He thanked me for
the trouble I had taken, without saying any thing
more ; but a few days after, he kindly called on me
to say, that he had offered the living to the gentleman I had named, who had joyfully accepted it.
On this occasion I know the Bishop passed by the
urgent recommendation of a person of great influence in favour of a respectable individual, in order
that he might prefer a deserving man with a large
family, who had worked hard for many years on a
curate's pittance. Happy those who serve in the
ministry of the Gospel under such a Bishop."

" Of the Bishop's literary labours and self-denying life," writes the same clergyman, " few can have
any conception. I was frequently admitted to see
him on business, even as early as six in the morning,
when, rather than detain me, he has seen me in his
dressing-room. Often he kindly remarked, your

time is not your own, and is as precious to you as mine is to me; scruple not to send to me when you really want to see me."

" On one of my early morning visits, about eight o'clock, in the winter, I found him seated, in his great coat and hat, writing at a table in a room without a carpet, the floor covered with old folios, and his candles only just extinguished. " I have been writing and reading," he said, " since five o'clock." At another time I breakfasted with him one morning by appointment, at his hotel in town ; and found him, at eight o'clock, about Christmas, writing by candle-light, the whole room being strewed with old books, collected from various places in the metropolis. The untiring perseverance with which he prosecuted his researches for evidence on any particular subject is inconceivable."

" I expected," says the same clergyman (who was privileged to spend some days in his society, at the outset of their acquaintance), " to find in him a profound scholar and a learned divine ; but his conversational powers were also truly engaging on subjects of general literature and science ; and whilst he appeared to listen with a suavity and humility to others, as though he was sitting at their feet obtaining knowledge, he himself opened the most various stores of information, and proved that he had diligently inquired into such branches of science as chemistry, medicine, anatomy, botany, &c.

" I must be permitted to advert to one other point in the Bishop's character which was truly admirable. With the caprice of this world's friendship, or with its reproachful adage, ' out of sight, out of mind,' he had no fellowship. There was nothing vacillating or worldly about him. All was simplicity, steadfastness, and high principle In bearing this high testimony to his worth, I am far from expressing my own sentiments only. I doubt if there be a clergyman in the diocese of St. David's who would not cheerfully echo and confirm it. The uniform, kind, and unostentatious hospitality at the Palace of Abergwilly will be long remembered.

" It affords me the most sincere gratification thus to dilate on the high excellence of that character which you are desirous of setting before the world in its just light. I loved and honoured the Bishop in life; his memory is dear and precious to me: and I cherish the consolatory hope, that the time is not distant when, through the infinite mercies of God in Christ Jesus, I may be permitted to join him in the realms of eternal bliss. Having often served under and ministered with him in the church below, blessed and joyful is the anticipation of resuming that glorious service in the church of the first-born in heaven."

The following testimony to the Bishop is from the pen of the Rev Mr. Vincent : —

" Never was there a Prelate who was more respected by his clergy than Dr. Burgess; indeed, it would be difficult to give an adequate idea of their feelings of veneration and affection for his character. In all their difficulties, they applied to him as to a common parent, in whose bosom they felt sure of finding sympathy, and who they knew was ever ready to afford them the most wholesome and salutary counsel.

" He was in the habit of keeping a book, in which he registered the name of every active and efficient

Clergyman who came under his notice, and to this he referred whenever a living or important curacy became vacant ; so anxious was he that every church in his Diocese should have a minister fearing God and doing good to the souls of men.

" He gave one of the best livings in the county of Pembroke to a very eminent and popular Clergyman, and the presentation was accompanied by a truly kind letter, reminding him of the high responsibility of the situation in which he was about to be placed, and, at the same time, encouraging him in the most affectionate manner to continue faithful and diligent in the discharge of his ministerial functions.

" The Clergyman in question has long since entered into his rest ; he always kept this letter with his sermons, and said that it furnished him with a stimulus to constant and unremitting exertion.

" No Clergyman, who was active and faithful in the performance of his duties, could be long without receiving some intimation that his Lordship knew and approved of his conduct.

" He eminently bore the character, as well as the name, of Pastor Pastorum.

" The constant attention which he paid to the affairs of his diocese, and the numerous works which he published, left him but little time at his command ; yet I never heard a Clergyman complain that he called on any occasion at the Palace and found the Bishop difficult of access.

" His manners were remarkably affable, but, at the same time, grave and dignified. His meek and venerable deportment seldom failed to make a favourable impression upon those whose prejudices led them to undervalue his sacred office; and I have known more than one Dissenter constrained to acknowledge that they never beheld a person who had more the appearance of 'a man of God.'

" The following anecdote is well known, and perfectly authenticated. A Baptist minister took upon him to make an oration over the remains of one of that sect in the church-yard of a parish near the town of Cardigan. Proceedings were, in consequence, instituted against him in the Bishop's Court by the minister of the parish, who was resolved to prosecute such an irregularity. In his distress, which was great, he went to the Bishop, and acknowledged how wrongly he had acted, but pleaded ignorance and entreated forgiveness. His Lordship pointed out to him the illegality as well as the impropriety of his conduct, and told him that he had made himself liable to severe ecclesiastical censure, but that, being convinced the sorrow he expressed was sincere, he would take care that further proceedings against him were stayed. The leniency of his Lordship, and the mildness with which he tempered his grave reproofs, made such an impression on the poor man, that he exclaimed on leaving the Palace, — 'I do believe, if there is a godly man upon the earth, it is the Bishop.' From that time he occasionally attended the parish church; and instead of any longer venting, as he had been accustomed, virulent invectives against the Church and her members, he conducted himself towards both with marked deference and respect.

" When the Bishop and his lady quitted Abergwilly, they were universally regretted in the neighbourhood, and particularly by the poor, who followed them with blessings, and bewailed their loss with indications of heart-felt sorrow. I particularly noticed one poor man, in whose coracle I crossed the river: as he paddled along he frequently ejaculated, ' Ay, he was the friend of the poor ! ' "

" The Bishop " (says the Rev. Mr. Thomas, Vicar of Cardigan) " was in the habit of conversing freely with his clergy, and advising with them as a father, in all things connected with their sacred duties.

" He ever manifested particular anxiety for the spiritual welfare of his diocese, and never lost sight of the youthful portion of its population. At confirmations, he gave three or four small tracts, specially adapted to the occasion, to every one whom he confirmed. These he always took with him in his carriage, packed up in small parcels ready for the purpose. He was a liberal subscriber to charity schools, and he frequently gave exhibitions on particular subjects to the different grammar-schools of the Diocese."

Mr. Thomas then enters into various interesting details illustrative of the Bishop's Christian character; but they are so similar to those already given, that it would be useless repetition to introduce them.

The following anecdote, communicated to the writer by the Rev. Mr. ——, will attest the firm and manly support he was ready to give to his Clergy, when unwarrantably opposed. A week-day evening lecture had been established by one of them in his parish church, to which some of the parishioners offered so much vexatious opposition, that the Clergyman was compelled to exercise his

just authority in resistance of a determined interference with his ministerial jurisdiction. It soon
became necessary to refer the question, by a common
appeal, to the higher authority, and the decision was
in favour of the Clergyman. His situation before
things were brought to this issue was very trying,
much unjust obloquy being industriously cast upon
him. The Bishop, aware of this, and being well
acquainted with all the circumstances that had occurred, left him not to contend, uncountenanced,
with his opponents, but manifested his private view
of the case by immediately attending the evening
lecture himself, and continuing to do so for some
time. His considerate countenance and support
at once abashed the opposing party, and cheered
the heart of a conscientious and excellent man.

CHAP. XXXI.

VARIOUS LETTERS — TESTIMONY OF DR. JENKINSON, BI-
SHOP OF ST DAVID'S, TO THE NECESSITY AND VALUE OF
THE COLLEGE — FURTHER SPECIMENS OF THE BISHOP'S
SACRA PRIVATA — DEATH OF THE BISHOP OF DURHAM.

1825 and 1826.

WE are now to think of the Bishop as fixed in his
new Diocese, and occupied in the discharge of its
professional duties. We shall hereafter contemplate
him in this character; but the general objects of
our narrative will be furthered by the insertion in
this place of the following letters; and, when we
add that those from Mrs. Hannah More were writ-

ten at the age of eighty, we think our readers will
doubly admire their vivacity and energy.

TO MRS. HANNAH MORE.

My dear Madam,   London, Feb 5 1825
I arrived here on Wednesday afternoon from
Durham, a journey of 260 miles, in very little more
than forty-eight hours, from which you will judge
that I am (thank God) in good health. I was not
here long without getting possession of your valuable
little volume, " The Spirit of Prayer," which I am
reading with great pleasure, and, I hope, profit. If
the profit of your readers should be in proportion to
the pleasure received from it (I conclude from myself that all must be pleased with it), you will have
employed your hours of sickness to very good purpose. The Bishop of Durham speaks of it with
delight. When I called on him on Thursday he
read to me several passages from it with great empressement. Our very venerable friend is looking
almost as well as I ever remember him. It is, this
year, forty years ago since I had the pleasure of
being introduced to you by him at the Palace of
Salisbury. He has been lately subject to a complaint of the erysipelas kind, incident to extreme old
age, but appears to have shaken it off for the present.
His spirits, his recollection, his love of books, and
interest in literary subjects, are as lively as ever.

I came to London to attend the opening of the
session, and was present at the debate on the King's
Speech. The address was moved by Lord Dudley
and Ward with great ability, but (as I feel on the

subject) with too favourable a view of what are called
the Roman Catholic claims. If the Roman Catholics
should petition Parliament this session, it is probable that the majorities in both Houses will be
different from what they have lately been, lessened
in the House of Commons and increased in the
Lords. The mover of the address (speaking of the
Popish agitators) said, " They have already lost all
those that wavered, and they may ere long shake
those that are still firm."

I hope that I shall have the pleasure of hearing
from one of your young friends a favourable account of your amended health. To them I beg to
be kindly remembered, and

     I am, my dear Madam,
        With affectionate regard,
          Your sincere Friend,
            T St. David's.

TO THE BISHOP OF ST. DAVID'S.

My dear Lord,   Barley Wood, Feb 27. 1825
Though my hand will probably never recover,
yet it is so far improved that I can write a little at
a time, but not without pain. I must, however,
compel it to thank you for your kind inquiries.
Your last letter recalled many long-past but pleasing scenes to my mind. Forty years since we first
met at the Palace at Salisbury !! I thank God
that excellent Bishop is not only living, but possesses
all his admirable powers, both of body and mind,
in their full force. As to myself, if I was a disciple
of Prince Hohenloe, I should say my recovery was

a miracle. It is a curious circumstance that I can
venture to assert, I have been raised up from
twenty apparently mortal diseases after having been
given over. But what is very remarkable, I have
been reckoning up no less than twelve physicians
(and almost as many apothecaries) who have attended me at different times and places, not one of
whom is alive! They taken, I left! Mr. Wilberforce, to whom I sent a list of their names, says,
that if I had lived three centuries ago, Dr. Carrick
(my present kind physician) would have had me
burnt for a witch, lest I should kill him also. God
has doubtless spared me for further repentance and
preparation. I ought to record, to the honour of
those honourable men, the M. D.'s, that in my whole
life I never paid but two fees!

Thanks to my Merciful Father I am better in
health than for the last two years, and able in the
mornings to see my friends. Apropos of friends,
I must tell you how they pamper me. I am almost
maintained at the public expense. Such continual
presents of game, venison, &c.

At my age this reprieve must be short; but
relief from exquisite pain is a great mercy. I have
not quitted my chamber for three years and a half,
but have had many blessings in it. I sometimes
hope that Blaise Castle may attract you on your
way to your Palace and your College, and that I
may see you once more. The Misses Roberts have
left me, and Miss Frowd is now lady of the bed-
chamber.

I fear this long letter has tried your eyes too
much: how are they?

If I thought Mrs. Burgess was with you, I would present my best respects to her.

Ever, my dear Lord,

Yours very sincerely,

H. MORE.

Written at several times : —

Miss Frowd is distributing for me at my schools above 600 books. The care and cost of these schools are heavy ; but the time is short.

I presume you have seen Davison on Prophecy. I have had a copy of this valuable work given me. I told the author, the last time I saw him, that I hoped Lord Liverpool would not long allow him to be confined to an obscure village.

TO THE SAME.

MY DEAR LORD,   Barley Wood, July 1. 1825.

I HOPE I may by this time congratulate you on your being set quietly down in your beautiful Palace, the naming of which brings back so many pleasing reminiscences. It is rather cruel to fall upon you so soon ; I therefore enclosed to your excellent dean a letter relating to a very meritorious individual, Mr ——, which was, in fact, intended for your Lordship. A more deserving man will not easily be found.

My contemporaries are dropping away fast before me. Your Predecessor ; the Dean of Canterbury ; the all-accomplished Sir William Pepys, &c. We have just lost a neighbouring Clergyman, for whom I had formerly the good fortune to obtain a small living in a parish where I have a school. I

used to say, other good men were going to Heaven,
but old Jones was there already. For sixty-one
years he never omitted his Sunday duty but four
times. He is dead at near ninety years of age,
being no longer able to mount a pulpit. That
dear Bishop of Durham gave me 50*l.* to provide him a curate. As he only lived out half
the year after I received this sum, enough was left
to pay his funeral expenses. His poor widow, who
has been his wife sixty years, has saved a little for
herself and daughters; and the ten Clergymen who
attended him to the grave will, I doubt not, help
us out in some way or other.

I hope Mrs. Burgess will feel the benefit of a
purer air.

I have taken a great interest in the fate of
Lieutenant ——, who is broke, and for ever disqualified to serve in the army, because he could
not wound his conscience by joining, as an officer,
in firing, bell-ringing, &c. in a Popish procession
at Malta. He has been to see me. He is a very
sensible correct young man, but, though connected very highly, and a relation of the Archbishop of Canterbury, he is left to starve for dis-
obeying orders. I will not say whether he was
right or wrong, but surely there are greater sins
left unpunished than following the dictates of a too
tender conscience. He is only twenty-eight years old.

I seldom write so long a scrawl, and, as Shakspeare's Dogberry says, I have, as a favour, bestowed all my tediousness on you.

Adieu, my dear Lord.

Your very faithful and obliged,

H. MORE.

A A

I am much obliged by your last valuable present, your letter to your late Clergy ; there is but one deficiency in the gift, which is, that you did not send me a portion of your learning to accompany your book ; though it is a little hard to expect that you should furnish sense for the reader as well as the writer.

The following from the Bishop of Durham will be read with interest, as having been written in his ninety-second year : —

My DEAR LORD,   Mongewell, July 14. 1825.

It is no inconsiderable addition to the pleasure which I feel in your translation to Salisbury, that you find the house and grounds in good order, and your comfort and Mrs. Burgess's increased by the state in which I put them both, at the expense of 8000*l.*, in 1785.

May every circumstance, as you become better acquainted with the Diocese, be productive of all that you can wish.

Worthing, thank God, has done great things for me. Miss Colberg's health is improved, but not to the extent I feel anxious it should be. Remember her and me to Mrs. Burgess, and believe me,

Your affectionate Friend,
S. DUNELM.

I congratulate you on having such a Dean and such a Chancellor.

TO THE BISHOP OF SALISBURY.

MY DEAR FRIEND, Wint Col, Feb 27 1826.
The principal topic of your last letter induces
me to utter what a thousand times I have thought,
viz. that your promotion to St. David's was a
blessing to that diocese. Not to mention innumerable other benefits conferred on it by you, that
you have erected a College for solid, sound, and
Christian education, will of itself be enough to call
forth the praises and thanks of grateful posterity.
My heart has always been with you in this work,
and I would now most willingly send you, as you
request, an abstract from the main body of our
statutes, if I had authority for so doing. The reverse, however, is the fact ; but I will most gladly
return answers to any questions which may not
concern the " Arcana Domûs.
Your affectionate Friend,
G. I. HEREFORD,

The College of St. David's found, as has been
intimated, in Dr. Jenkinson, the new Bishop of that
see, a firm and enlightened supporter
In the winter of 1826, the Bishop of Salisbury
was highly gratified by the following letter from his
Lordship on this subject. —

MY DEAR LORD,
Abergwilly Palace,
Jan 13 1826
I AM very much obliged to you for your two last
letters. You were most heartily welcome to the
A A 2

use of my house at Durham, and I hope you did not leave it sooner than was convenient to Mrs. Burgess and yourself.

On the 27th of December Mr. Harford, whom I had long been expecting, came here, and on the 28th I accompanied him to Lampeter for the purpose of seeing the College. We did not attempt to return the same day. Mr. Cockerell met us there. I was very much gratified with all I saw. I think the College is a very handsome building, exceedingly well contrived, and adapted for the purpose for which it is intended, and that it does very great credit to Mr. Cockerell's taste and judgment. I shall be heartily glad when it is fully established and fairly brought into operation, as I think there can be no doubt that it will be conducive in a very great degree to the welfare of the diocese. The judicious regulations established by your Lordship have, I am persuaded, contributed most materially to the present improved character of the clergy of this diocese. These regulations it is my intention to continue.

When the College shall have been opened long enough, then I apprehend it to have been your intention that the licensed grammar schools should become preparatory seminaries for the College, and that every candidate for orders, who has not been at one of the Universities and taken a degree, should be required to have been four years at the College.

[After various other remarks his Lordship adds,]

The more I reflect on the subject, and the more I become acquainted with this diocese, the more I

am convinced that the College is the only measure
which affords a prospect of any effectual remedy for
the evil inseparable from the system which unavoidably prevails in consequence of the necessity of
generally dispensing with an academical degree ;
which, of course, throws open the profession to many
who could not otherwise ever have aspired to it,
and a considerable proportion of whom are utterly
disqualified for it.   At my ordination in November
last, I refused to admit some of the candidates to
examination from their not having been at one of
the licensed grammar schools for the required period
of seven years, others for want of a title, and one
I rejected on account of insufficiency.   I have since
learned that the latter candidate, within three weeks
after his rejection, enlisted as a common soldier ! !
Another whom I refused to admit for want of a
title, has, I am told, subsequently married a woman
who keeps an alehouse at Llandilo.   All this shows
that it is impossible to be too cautious in admitting
young men to holy orders in this diocese.   The
candidates, while at the licensed grammar schools,
have too often been obliged to live at inns or public
houses, where they have necessarily witnessed scenes,
and associated with company exposing them to the
danger, and unless they are endowed with great
strength of character, to the certainty of acquiring
tastes and contracting habits utterly incompatible
with the profession for which they are destined.
For these evils and abuses the College will prove
the best and only effectual remedy, and the only
adequate security against the admission of improper
persons to the profession.

A A 3

With the sincerest sentiments of esteem and respect, I remain,

My dear Lord,
Faithfully yours,
J. B. St. David's.

Part of the winter of 1826 was spent by the
Bishop of Salisbury and his lady at Bath and
Clifton, for the health of the latter. We thus became neighbours for several weeks, and our meetings were frequent. In reverting to them, I re-
collect with particular interest a drive with him in
his carriage from Clifton to Bath, in the course of
which he made some striking remarks on the importance of habitually cultivating and maintaining
a devotional frame of mind.

After touching on the mental serenity and the
firmness of purpose which are its characteristic
accompaniments, he proceeded (casting aside the
reserve which he generally maintained in reference
to his own religious feelings) to repeat to me, with
equal simplicity and fervour, a fasciculus of prayers,
collects, and select passages from psalms and hymns,
with which, variously modified, he told me he was
in the habit of commencing the day. All that he
thus said proved how truly his religion was an in-
dwelling principle of holy living; a salient spring
of pure and heart-felt joy, and that the Bishop of
Salisbury, in the midst of continual engagements,
and the engrossing circumstances of station and
influence, retained the humble and devout feelings
of the retired Rector of Winston. The following
reflections written before he quitted the See of
St. David's will not unfitly come in here, and may

be regarded as a slight appendix to the chapter entitled his " Sacra Privata" : —

" In the midst of life we are in death."

" Watch and pray, for ye know not when the time is." — Mark, xiii. 33.

" Lord, so teach me to number my days, that I may apply my heart unto wisdom."

" Lord, increase our faith."

" Love is the fulfilling of the law."

" Oh, death! how bitter is the remembrance of thee to him who is at ease in his possessions ! "

" Oh! that they would consider their latter end."

" Immo vere ii vivunt qui ex corporum vinculis tanquam e carcere evolaverunt. Vestra vero quæ dicitur vita mors est." — *Scipionis Somn.*

" Quid aliud agimus, cum a voluptate (id est, a corpore), cum a re familiari (quæ est ministra, et formula corporis), cum a republicâ, cum a negotio omni sevocamus animum? Quid inquam, tum egimus, nisi animum ad seipsum advocamus, secum esse cogimus, maximè e corpore abducimus. Secernere autem a corpore animum nec quidquam aliud est, quam emori discere."— *Cicero.*

" Cicero in this passage explains what he means by abstracting one's self from the body. It is to turn the soul inwardly upon itself. It is to call it away from pleasure, from business, from politics, and to force it to self-inspection. Speaking in Christian language, it is to set our affections on things above, — not on things on the earth — to have our conversation in heaven — to lay up our treasure in heaven: not by a life of indolent contemplation, but by the active discharge of our duties in that station

A A 4

of life in which God has placed us. It is, by
' bringing forth much fruit,' John, xv. 5. , by
' letting our light so shine before men, that they
seeing our good works may glorify our Father who
is in heaven.' Matt. v. 16. ; ever looking unto
Jesus, the Author and Finisher of our faith."

On the 25th of March, 1826, an event occurred,
which, though quite in the course of nature, was
much felt by the Bishop. We allude to the death
of his old and beloved friend, Dr. Shute Barrington.
He had attained the advanced age of ninety-two,
and his fine faculties were unimpaired till within a
few days of his departure.

The funeral, in compliance with his own di-
rections, was so strictly private, that none of his
friends, excepting the executors, were invited to
attend, but when the day arrived on which the body
was to be conveyed to Mongewell for interment,
the Bishop of Salisbury gave a most touching proof
of his respect and affection Before seven in the
morning, the hour appointed for the procession
to leave Cavendish Square, he came thither on foot
from his own residence, and was recognised slowly
pacing up and down the pavement at a short
distance from his old friend's mansion, until the
hearse moved from the door, when he was seen
earnestly watching its progress, as if to catch the
last glimpse of that which contained all that was
mortal of one whom he had so sincerely loved and
revered.

Before finally bidding adieu to Bishop Barrington,
we will add a few particulars to those included in
our sketch of his earlier career.

To the end of his days he continued to administer

the rich and extensive patronage of his princely see upon the same high and disinterested principles which have already been particularised. Sound scholars, learned theologians, pious, active, and devoted parish priests, were men whom he delighted to honour and to advance, although, upon what may be termed open questions, they might not entertain precisely the same opinions with himself or with each other.

Gisborne and Paley; Bishops Burgess, Sumner, Gray, and Phillpotts; Faber and Davidson, Townsend and Gilly, Collinson of Gateshead, and Gray of Sunderland, were selected by the same discriminating patron to fill important situations in his diocese. The three last stalls, which became at his disposal, were bestowed upon persons whom he had never seen, until their useful writings recommended them to his notice.

Dr. Holmes found in him a generous friend, in the progress of his learned collation of the Greek Bible; and Dr. Bell, to whom the world is deeply indebted, as the founder of the Madras system, received from him the mastership of Sherborn Hospital — a valuable sinecure, which left him at full liberty to devote his time and thoughts to the extension of national education.

In each and all of these appointments, it was his wish and intention to select individuals whose talents, principles, and attainments best fitted them for the particular situations to which he appointed them. Nor were his regards confined to men eminent for learning or genius in the sacred profession. He loved and valued Christian piety for its own sake, and the humblest curate that came within his notice

in whose character and conduct he traced any thing
of the image of that Redeemer, in whom alone was
his trust, was sure to attract his esteem, and, if needful, his support. Party names with him weighed
nothing; principle and conduct were every thing.

His firmness of purpose, in adhering to these
principles of action, was sometimes put to a severe
test, but his presence of mind, united to a winning
courtesy, never failed him on any such occasion. It
was his constant maxim of conduct, and he often
gave it in counsel to patrons, never to make promises, nor even to encourage expectations. He
was one day accosted at court by Queen Charlotte,
for whom he entertained an affectionate and dutiful
respect, as follows : " My Lord, I have a favour to
ask of you. The living of ——, in your disposal,
is, I understand, vacant, and I shall be greatly
obliged if you will bestow it upon Mr. ——, for
whom I feel much interested." The Bishop, in the
most courteous manner, signified, in reply, his desire
to meet any wish expressed by her Majesty; but
added, that he felt bound to apprise her of the rule
which he had invariably laid down to himself with
respect to all such applications. He had no sooner
given utterance to it than the Queen stopped further
explanation, by exclaiming, " My Lord, I will not
say a word more · and I beg that no wish of mine
may lead you to violate so golden a rule."

But though he never made promises, he always
had a list, known only to God and to himself, of
the names of those who, he had reason to believe,
were most deserving of advancement and patronage.

The following incident illustrates at once his unbending principle and great kindness. A near relation of his, who had been gay and thoughtless, applied to him for advice about taking orders; adding, that he could venture to say, a great improvement had recently taken place in his principles and habits. The Bishop received him kindly; but before he would enter upon the subject, stipulated for the most frank and explicit replies to any questions he should put to him. In this way an acknowledgment was obtained, that he was influenced by the hope, that, as his relation, he would ordain and provide for him. And it further came out, that his wishes were fixed on a particular living then vacant, or on the point of becoming so, the value of which was about 500*l.* per annum. "And would this amount of income," inquired the Bishop, "entirely satisfy your wishes?" He eagerly replied in the affirmative. "You shall have it then," replied his Lordship, "but not in the way you propose. I cannot reconcile it to my sense of duty to ordain you, but I will immediately transfer as much stock into your name as will produce an annual sum equal to that which you have declared to be the acmè of your wishes, and may it prove to you all that you anticipate."

We have already stated that no hand was more open than that of Bishop Barrington to do generous acts, and to succour real merit in any station. There was nothing exclusive in his almsgiving. Though a determined opponent of political concessions to the Roman Catholics, he contributed most generously to the relief and assistance of the French emigrant clergy, many of whom enjoyed his hospitality and friendship.

Not few were the cases in which Dissenters of various denominations, encouraged by the fame of his diffusive beneficence, successfully applied to him for their own relief, or for objects of private charity. He was a generous supporter of the most approved public charities, and of institutions for the advancement of science and learning, particularly such as promoted the cultivation of the fine arts.

Among his other noble acts of munificence was the appropriation, in 1809, of the sum of 60,000l., which he received upon the renewal of the leases of some lead mines in the county of Durham, to the establishment of national schools in his diocese, and to the formation of a fund for the benefit of poor clergymen and their families.

So large, indeed, were his acts of public and of private charity, that even his ample fortune would not have sustained them had he not been careful to exercise, in other respects, a just and exact economy.

The existence of a branch of the Church of England in our remaining North American Colonies is very much to be ascribed to the influence and exertions of Bishop Barrington. In 1786, his Lordship drew up a very valuable and able paper, entitled " Thoughts on the Establishment of the Church of England in Nova Scotia." Its concluding paragraph, which was as follows, succinctly pointed out what he deemed the essential requisites, in order to give effect and permanence to the important object which he advocated. " Upon these measures, *the appointment of a bishop, a provision for an established clergy, and a seminary of learning to furnish a regular supply of ecclesiastics,* depends the very being of the Church of England in our remaining colonies of North America."

The government of Mr. Pitt, while it encouraged emigration to North America, was not insensible to the just claims of the settlers in those distant regions to share in the blessings ensured to their countrymen at home by a National Established Church, and therefore each of the above measures was approved and adopted

Dr. Inglis, father of the present highly respected Bishop of Nova Scotia, was appointed the first Bishop of that See in 1787. The Clerical Seminary was commenced in 1788, and chartered in 1802; and a provision for the clergy of the Established Church was finally arranged in 1813. To each of these important objects, the Bishop, in addition to his strenuous advocacy, added his liberal support.

In maintaining the dignity of his exalted station, there was a sober magnificence, an unostentatious splendour, which singularly befitted the solitary instance which our national establishment then presented of the Prince-Bishop. Those who ever saw him preside at the Assizes at Durham could never forget the happy union of the bishop and the nobleman in the whole of his amiable, courteous, and dignified deportment.

His state of mind, and the bent of his feelings, as he approached that hour which wrests from the great and the wealthy every earthly privilege and distinction, have been beautifully depictured by his friend and chaplain, the Rev. Mr. Townsend. We extract from his narrative the following particulars : —

" Literary curiosity, the comfort and refreshment of age, was an active principle in the Bishop to the last, and the love of literary novelty, next to devotion and benevolence, his ruling passion.

" Tea was brought in at half past seven, and at eight the Bishop ended the day as he had begun it, by the perusal of devotional books, or by private meditation and prayer. I well remember his telling me that he considered it to be a part of his duty to God to devote to Him the remaining strength of his intellect, by dedicating to His service those hours in which the faculties of his mind were most active and for that reason he never gave his restless and sleepless hours, which at his advanced age were unavoidably numerous, to prayer, and to devotional exercises. He preferred giving up the prime of his day, and the remnant of his intellect, to the Almighty; and he surrendered *the dross of his time*, such was his own forcible expression, to inferior subjects, to literary recollections, or to soothing remembrances of the friends he had lost, whose conversation he recollected with pleasure.

" At a quarter before ten, the family were summoned to evening prayer A slight supper was then served, and at eleven the Bishop retired for the night. The pleasantest hours which I passed with my lamented friend were those which elapsed between the removal of supper, and the entrance of the servant who attended him to his room. He was now ninety years of age, and he had long been accustomed to live in the constant anticipation of death Every night he composed himself to rest, not expecting to live till the morning. The conversations therefore which we were accustomed to hold at this hour were always grave and serious, though uniformly cheerful He regarded death, as a man of sound judgment and Christian principles will ever do — without fear, and without rapture; with well founded hope, though with undefinable awe — as a punishment decreed by the Almighty, yet as the introduction to a higher state of happiness than he could possibly experience (though he possessed every worldly enjoyment) in this state of his being. Though our conversation was sometimes directed to the literary or theological publications of the day, or to the actions, demeanour, or conduct of his more distinguished contemporaries, of whom he related numerous and most interesting anecdotes, yet the more frequent topics of our conversation were derived from the possible or probable approach of the period when the body should be committed to the ground, and the spirit return to its Maker. He delighted to dwell on these subjects. The nature of the future happiness, and future misery — the continuance of the

existence of the mental habits which are formed in this state,
and which constitute in some manner our future condition —
the extent of redemption — and the opposite opinions of Christians, respecting the invisible state , — these and similar considerations were alternately discussed in these calm and silent
hours , and he uniformly concluded these discussions by observing, " I know not, and I care not, what may be the real
solution of these questions, I am in the hands of a merciful
God, and I resign myself to His will, with hope and patience "
All our inquiries indeed upon these subjects, though they may
be very interesting, are merely speculative, and are always un-
satisfactory We cannot raise the veil which conceals the
future We must die before we can understand death ; yet
the sight of an old man, full of days, riches, and honours, at the
close of a religious and well-spent life, patiently expecting his
end, abounding in every virtue which can adorn mankind —
in humility, in patience, in kindness, in charity to all, in serene
submission to expected death, in implicit dependence upon
the mercy of a God, whom he believed to be his Friend, and
Father, by the Atonement, which had been accomplished by
the Mediator of the New Testament — the image of such a
man can never be obliterated from my memory , and the continued enjoyment of his conversation, till within a few weeks
of his death, while the strength of his body was gradually declining, and the intellectual, though not the spiritual powers
were decaying; that is, while he was beginning to be more
averse to worldly business, and more intent upon devotional
exercises, was a privilege which I cannot too much appreciate,
and which may be justly envied by all who can delight in the
society of the wise and good; or who would contemplate the
triumph of the spirit of man over the weakness of the mind,
and the infirmities of the body "

CHAP. XXXII.

PASSING OF THE ROMAN CATHOLIC EMANCIPATION BILL,
AND FEELINGS OF THE PROTESTANT PUBLIC RESPECT-
ING IT

1829.

In the autumn of 1828 the public mind was agitated
throughout Great Britain by reports that it was the

intention of the Duke of Wellington to make Roman
Catholic Emancipation a Cabinet measure, and to
support it in both Houses of Parliament by the
whole weight and influence of Government.

It was also stated that Mr. Peel, hitherto the firm
and unflinching opponent of emancipation, had
yielded to the same reasons which had swayed the
Duke's decision, and was prepared to bring a bill
to this effect into the House of Commons, and to
give it his unqualified support.

The first impression of the Protestant public
was incredulity; but when the fact became unquestionable, it naturally gave a violent shock (the
more violent in consequence of the quarter whence
the measure emanated) to their most deeply rooted
principles and feelings.

A sentiment of indignant hostility to the proposition was general among the great majority of the
members of the Church of England, and pervaded
also no inconsiderable portion of the Dissenters, so
that petitions against it poured into both Houses
of Parliament from every part of the country,
issuing from public meetings equally numerous
and influential, and attended not only by the Clergy
and the higher and leading members of their flocks,
but also by large bodies of respectable tradesmen
and yeomanry.

As long as the measure was in its progress through
the House of Commons, an active warfare continued
to be maintained against it out of doors ; and among
those who lifted a warning voice to the nation, the
Bishop of Salisbury was indefatigable. He addressed a series of letters on the subject to the Duke
of Wellington in one of the newspapers, in which

he strenuously denounced the intended measure as in a constitutional sense suicidal, and pregnant with future mischief and danger to the country. These letters, some of which were, in the first instance, transmitted in a written form to the Duke, led to a correspondence between himself and the illustrious Premier. The letters of the latter are written with his characteristic decision and energy; but the reasons which he urged in support of his intentions all resolved themselves into considerations of political expediency, arising out of the state of Ireland. The Bishop's opinions, on the contrary, were in the spirit of those of our Protestant ancestors, who were ready to incur any danger rather than to compromise those principles which identified opposition to the Roman Catholic religion, not only with the safety of the British Constitution, but with their zeal also for the Truth of God and the Glory of his Gospel.

On the 2d of April, 1829, in one of the debates on the question in the House of Lords, the Bishop, after saying that he could not reconcile it with his conscience to give a silent vote against the Bill, stated, in a brief but forcible manner, his principal objections.

He dwelt, in the first place, on the danger to be apprehended from the influence of that supreme spiritual authority by means of which the Pope extends his influence into foreign countries, and interferes with the temporal authority of sovereigns and states.

He then expressed his entire dissent from those who treated the question as one of mere political expediency, and maintained that it was impossible, upon any just principle, to view it separate from

B B

religious considerations. Did not the first canon
of our Church denounce the Roman Catholic religion as idolatrous and superstitious? Regarding
and treating it as such, had they not all in that
House repeatedly made a declaration, and bound
themselves by a solemn oath against Popery — an
oath, he added, from which — speaking individually
for himself — he felt he could not depart without
wilful and criminal prevarication?

He deemed, he said, any measure having for its
object the admission of Roman Catholics to seats
in Parliament to be utterly inconsistent with the
principles of the British Constitution, which was
exclusively and essentially Protestant; nor would
any argument ever convince him that Roman Catholics would fail to use legislative power, if committed to them, in a manner dangerous and injurious
to the interests of the Church of England. In the
very nature of things it must and would be so. How
could the Church of England otherwise than suffer
by giving such power to the members of another
Church, who are bound by principle to use their
utmost endeavours for the overthrow of the Protestant religion? — "My Lords," he added, "the
Bill for the admission of Papists into Parliament
appears to me contrary to the direct and literal
meaning of his Majesty's Coronation oath, in which
his Majesty, by the most solemn pledge, promises
to maintain, to the utmost of his power, the Protestant reformed religion established by law. The
Bill, as it appears to me, is not less contrary to a
much later pledge — the only pledge contained in
his Majesty's speech from the Throne — in which
his Majesty most graciously expressed his determin-

ation to preserve inviolate the established institutions of our country, of which a Protestant Parliament is one of the chief—the pillar and bulwark
of the rest, whereas the Parliament will cease to
deserve any such appellation when once the proposed concessions shall be made."

He concluded by intimating his apprehension
that the measure, if carried, would expose the
established Church to imminent peril, and the
country to the fatal mistake and bitter consequences
of sacrificing principle to expediency.

The passing of this act filled him with deep and
lasting concern, he did not cease to regard it as
the prognostic of further dangerous inroads upon
the Constitution ; and though no one more justly
appreciated the great and commanding qualities
which distinguish the Duke of Wellington, or the
debt of public gratitude so eminently his due, he
often lamented that the nation should have been
seduced by his influence into a measure fatal, as he
conceived, to its best interests and permanent security. " We owe all this," he often said, " to
the battle of Waterloo."

CHAP. XXXIII.

ANALYSIS OF THE CONTROVERSY RESPECTING THE DIS-
PUTED VERSE, 1 JOHN, V 7

THE Bishop from an early period of his theological
career was a zealous advocate of the doctrine of the
Trinity, as maintained by the Holy Catholic Church

from the apostolic age downwards. He regarded
it not as a mere speculative dogma, but as in the
highest sense a practical and vital Truth; closely
interwoven with the whole frame and texture of
the Christian Religion; intimately affecting in
its bearings the motives and springs of Christian
conduct, and regulating the approaches of the soul
to the Majesty of Heaven.

The force of this conviction may be traced
throughout his various theological writings. It is
vividly expressed in his first published sermon; it
breaks out in the midst of his critical remarks on
Mr. Granville Sharp's Tract on the Greek article,
it formed a leading subject in many of his Catechisms,
Charges, and Tracts, and in the latter part of his life
it led him to employ much of his time and thoughts
in defending the authenticity of the Disputed Passage, 1 John, v. 7., "For there are three that bear
record in Heaven, the Father, the Word, and the
Holy Ghost; and these three are one."

It was not that he deemed this Text * essential

---

* The following is a list of his publications on this subject —

A Vindication of 1 John, v. 7. from the objections of M.
Griesbach : in which a new view is given of the external evidence, with Greek authorities for the authenticity of the verse,
not hitherto adduced in its defence. 8vo 1821.

Adnotationes Millii, auctæ ex Prolegomenis suis, Wetstenii,
Bengelii, Sabaterii ad Joan 1. v 7. Unâ cum duabus epistolis
Richardi Bentleii, et observationibus Joannis Selden, C. M.
Psaffii, J F Buddei, et C. F. Schmidii de eodem loco. 1822.

A second edition of the Vindication, to which was added a
reply to the Quarterly Review, and a postscript in answer to a
publication entitled Palæoromaica 8vo 1823

A selection of Tracts on 1 John, v. 7. 1824.

A Letter to the Clergy of the Diocese of St. David's on a
passage of the second Symbolum Antiochenum of the fourth
century, as evidence of the authenticity of 1 John, v 1825.

to the proof of a doctrine which he traced as a golden thread pervading the whole texture of Divine Revelation * ; but as he had formed a strong opinion in favour of its authenticity after much patient study and laborious investigation, he felt impelled to place before the public the grounds on which he had come to this conclusion. To vindicate what he believed to be the integrity of the sacred writings, and to secure to the cause of orthodoxy the support of an important text, which he conceived had been surrendered on insufficient grounds, were his propelling motives.

The influence of Porson's critical authority, and the apparent consent of the learned world, had produced a general impression that the text in question

A Letter to the Rev Thomas Beynon, Archdeacon of Cardigan, in reply to a vindication of the literary character of Professor Porson, by Crito Cantabrigiensis, and in further proof of the authenticity of 1 John, v. 7. 8vo.

Remarks on the General Tenour of the New Testament regarding the Nature and Dignity of Jesus Christ Addressed to Mrs Joanna Baillie. 8vo. 1831

An Introduction to the Controversy on the Disputed Verse of St John, as revived by Mr. Gibbon; or, a Second Letter to Mrs. Joanna Baillie. 1835.

* It is an interesting fact, that the two greatest Greek authorities of modern times, Bentley and Porson, each avowed their conviction as critics and scholars that the doctrine of the New Testament is Trinitarian.

Bentley, writing to a friend with reference to the disputed verse, says, " You endeavour to prove that it *may* have been writ by the Apostle, being consonant to his other doctrine. This I concede to you ; and if the fourth century knew that text, let it come in, in God's name ; but if that age did not know it, then Arianism in its height was beat down without the help of that verse; and let the *fact* prove as it will, the *doctrine* is unshaken

The opinion of Porson has been already referred to, in the chapter on Unitarianism.

B B 3

was an interpolation either fraudulent or accidental. In his "Letters to Archdeacon Travis," Mr. Porson had two objects: one to prove the contested verse a forgery; the other to prove that Mr. Travis, who had undertaken its defence, was radically ignorant with respect to many of the points which the controversy involved.

Travis, it is said, was ambitious of the bench, and for a time acquired great credit by his publication — "I'll unbishop him *," was the exclamation of his redoubted antagonist, who already by anticipation beheld his victim laid low.

Infelix puer, atque impar congressus Achilli !

There is nothing of mediocrity in any part of these letters. It is difficult to say whether they are most distinguished by their extensive and pre-eminent learning, their singular ingenuity and acuteness, their keen irony and playful wit, or by their bitter sarcasm, their unrelenting severity, and the fierceness of their hostility and invective.

The triumph of Porson was as complete as a signal exposure of the ignorance and oversights of Travis could render it; but the main question, whether he had proved the disputed verse to be a forgery, was quite of another description. Undoubtedly he placed the arguments and the evidence opposed to its authenticity in a more striking light than any of his predecessors, and as far as the evidence of Greek MSS. is conclusive, he fully availed himself of the results of advanced and improved collation; yet it may justly be questioned

* These words were quoted to me by Bishop Burgess

whether, in other respects, he adduced any fresh
evidence, that would have been deemed materially
important by such crities as Mill and Bengelius.
To them the most formidable objections which he
has urged were familiar, and yet, in spite of them,
they had firmly advocated the authenticity of the
disputed passage.

This consideration furnishes a sufficient general
reply to a host of objectors, who, without giving
themselves the trouble to study the question, have
been accustomed to accuse Bishop Burgess of credulity, for having ranged himself on the side of
those eminent theologians. The manly integrity
of his character was far removed from the cow-
ardice, which would yield up an important text to
public opinion, however confidently expressed,
when his convictions were different. Neither let it
be imagined that, in these convictions, he stood
alone among his contemporaries. There were not
wanting some few in the foremost ranks of learning,
who, undazzled by Porson's authority, sided with
him, while others deemed the question still de-
batable. Among them were Bishops Horsley and
Middleton.

Having made these general observations, we shall
now proceed to offer a brief and popular statement
of the principal grounds on which Bishop Burgess
steadfastly maintained his own opinion of the authenticity of the verse in spite of the formidable array of
learning, argument, and evidence on the other side;
and in order to come at once to the point, we shall
state the objections to its genuineness, in a few
distinct propositions, and with the utmost force we

can impart to them, subjoining at the foot of each
the mode in which they were met by the Bishop.*

˙ Not a single Greek manuscript written before the
fifteenth century contains the controverted passage.

The apparently insurmountable difficulty created
by the absence of the verse from the Greek manuscripts is in some degree diminished by the fact,
that the great majority of them are comparatively
modern.

We have no Greek manuscript whatever of the
three first centuries.

Within the period extending from A. D. 301 to
900 we have only four — the Alexandrian, the Vatican, the Passionei MS., and one of Matthæi's.
— A. B. G. — 9.

The early Latin versions of the New Testament
were of the highest antiquity. What is called the
Vulgate is a revision by Jerome of these versions in
the fourth century. This revision he himself declares
that he executed by a reference to the authority of
the Greek original, or, to use his own words, " ad
Græcam veritatem."

Consequently the Vulgate furnishes important

---

* We are far from pretending in the following statement to
do more than bring forward the most forcible facts and arguments advanced by the Bishop in defence of the verse, and we
have entirely omitted any notice of the theories by which he
endeavoured to account for its absence from the Greek manuscripts, as none of them, we fear, can be deemed satisfactory.

evidence of the text of those originals at a period antecedent to the date of the earliest Greek manuscripts.

Now the majority of the MSS. of the Vulgate retain the disputed verse.* There are, it is true, some important exceptions; and Bishop Marsh has gone so far as to assert, that it is wanting in the most ancient manuscripts of the Latin version. Bishop Burgess replies, No. "It is NOT wanting in the most ancient MSS.; for we have none such older than the eighth century. Of these there are three in the library of Verona, and the seventh verse is found in each of them.

" There are cases," Michaelis observes, " in which the ancient versions are of more authority than the best Greek manuscripts, these being modern in comparison with the originals from which the Latin version was derived."

The same eminent critic says, in another place, " as it cannot be denied that the oldest Latin versions are of very high antiquity, notwithstanding some of their readings are false, their principal use in the criticism of the New Testament is, that they lead us to a discovery of the readings of the very ancient Greek manuscripts that existed prior to the date of any that are now extant." Mich. vol. ii. p. 121.

The Complutensian edition of the Greek Testament, published in Spain, A. D. 1522, and printed,

---

* It ought in candour to be added, that the argument from the manuscripts of the early Latin versions would carry much greater weight, but for the double fact that the verse is wanting in several of the more ancient, and that those which contain it present it in many different forms.

though not published, in 1514, that is to say, two
years before that of Erasmus in 1516, has the disputed verse. The editors declare, that the text
was derived from manuscripts of great antiquity.
Those who are opposed to the authenticity of the
verse, contend that it was probably introduced into
the Greek text of this edition from the Vulgate, or
on the authority of some modern MS. Mr. Porson
was of the former opinion, and maintains that the
style of the Greek is Latinised.

Wetstein undervalues the Complutensian edition;
but Michaelis, who appears to have examined it
with great accuracy, declares his conviction, " that
it was faithfully taken from MSS., and that those
Complutensian readings, which are in no MSS.
known to us at present, were actually taken from
MSS. used by the editors. So long, therefore," he
adds, " as we are without the MSS. from which this
edition was taken, it must itself be considered as a
valuable MS., or as a Codex Criticus, that contains
many scarce readings." Marsh's Michaelis, ii. 439.

What became of the MSS. of this celebrated
Polyglot edition of the Bible is involved in mystery.
The current story, that they were sold to a maker
of fireworks, and by him employed in the preparation of various devices of the pyrotechnic art, is
now pretty generally exploded.

Before the Complutensian Polyglot was delivered
to the public, Erasmus brought out his Greek Testament in 1516. It did not contain the disputed
verse. Being reproached with the omission in this
edition, and in a second, printed in 1519, he stated
his readiness to insert it in a future edition, provided
some one Greek MS. of authority containing it could

be adduced. It was found in the Codex Bri-
tannicus, or Montfortianus, a MS. Wetstein maintains of the 16th century, Griesbach of the 15th or
16th, and Dr. Adam Clarke of the 13th; accordingly
Erasmus introduced the text into his subsequent
edition of 1522.*

OBJECTION II

None of the ancient Greek fathers quote the
verse, although had it existed in their MSS. of the
Epistle of St. John, they would, as a matter of
course, have made much use of it in their contro-
versies with the Arians.

REPLY.

The defenders of the verse have not been able
to parry this objection by any direct evidence to
the contrary. It is true that Porson has somewhat overstated the degree in which its force is
admitted by Bengelius. The extent of the concession made by that eminent divine and critic is as
follows : " We as yet see no ancient Greek authorities for this verse, *except those which I have with
difficulty collected under head 23.*" He then introduces passages from Irenæus, Athenagoras,
Clemens Alexandrinus, Basil, Maximus, &c., none

---

* No great stress can, however, be laid upon this insertion
of the verse by Erasmus. His edition had been violently assailed, and his orthodoxy questioned ; he therefore, probably,
acted from prudential motives.

The Bishop never took up that part of the controversy which
relates to the readings of the Greek MSS employed by Robert
Stephens in his beautiful edition of the Greek Testament in
small folio. He lived to witness the discovery of the contested
verse in two additional Greek MSS ; a fact which will be noticed in its proper place.

of which, however, are adduced as quotations of the verse, but only as probable derivations from it.

The objection, therefore, is admitted by the advocates of the verse nearly to the full extent of Porson's assertion, and as the defence of its authenticity rests chiefly, as far as the evidence of MSS. is concerned, upon those of the ancient Latin versions of the New Testament, so the formidable difficulty arising from the silence of the Greek fathers is met by the authority of Latin fathers and Latin ecclesiastical writers.

There is a passage in Tertullian, a native of Africa, and a Latin Christian writer of the second century, which furnishes some probability that the disputed verse was in his copy of St. John's Epistle. The passage is as follows: "Ita connexus Patris in Filio, et Filii in Paracleto, tres efficit cohærentes, alterum ex altero, qui tres unum sint, non unus." Adversus Praxeam, 657. Editio Rigaltii.*

The words "qui tres unum sint," or, as some editions read, "sunt," are maintained by Grabe, Mill, Bengelius, and others, to be a quotation of the final clause of the disputed verse; Porson and

---

* Thus the connexion of the Father in the Son, and of the Son in the Paraclete, makes three coherent persons, one in the other: *which three are one* in substance, unum; not one in number, unus.

Bishop Kaye, in his learned and interesting work on Tertullian, p. 544., remarks on this passage to the following effect : — If Tertullian had been acquainted with 1 John, v. 7., a verse which clearly proved, according to his own mode of reasoning, the unity of substance and the distinction of persons in the Father, Son, and Holy Ghost, is it not contrary to all reason to suppose that he would have neglected to quote it, and chosen rather to refer his readers to the texts, John, x. 30 and xvi. 14. ?

Michaelis, on the contrary, maintain that Tertullian did not quote the verse.

That, although he cannot fairly be said to quote it, he had it in view in the preceding passage, is rendered the more probable by a remarkable passage in St. Cyprian, a venerable father of the African church, living in the third century, and a great admirer of Tertullian. He thus expresses himself in his treatise on the Unity of the Church : " Dicit Dominus — Ego et Pater, unum sumus: et iterum de Patre, et Filio, et Spiritu Sancto scriptum est. — Et hi tres unum sunt." * Now, the first part of this passage, viz. " I and the Father are one," is cited by Cyprian as having been " spoken by the Lord," and is a direct quotation of John, x. 30. He then goes on to say, And again of the Father, the Son, and the Holy Ghost, IT IS WRITTEN, " And these three are one." The words *it is written*, taken in connexion with the previous reference to the Gospel, imply also a quotation from Scripture. Where, then, *is it written* concerning the Father, the Son, and the Holy Ghost, " *these three are one*" — where but in 1 John, v. 7.? Hence arises a strong probability that Cyprian had the verse in his copy of St. John's First Epistle, and that he refers in the words, " *it is written*," to its concluding paragraph. Mr. Porson, on the authority of Facundus, a writer of the sixth century, urges the probability that Cyprian regarded " the Spirit, the Water, and the Blood," enumerated in the eighth verse, as mystically referring to the Father, the

* The Lord says. " I and the Father are one " And again, of the Father, the Son, and the Holy Ghost, it is written, " And these three are one "

Son, and the Holy Ghost; and therefore argues that the words, "these three are one," had reference to the eighth verse, not to the seventh.

This interpretation of the meaning of Cyprian is so forced and extravagant, that it deserves no credit upon the mere assertion of any individual, much less of a writer of no higher authority than Facundus. And where is the evidence of it? Cyprian himself drops not a hint to this effect. The first and the real author of this mystical gloss was St. Augustin, at the end of the fourth century; but he introduces it coupled with a qualification implying the interpretation to be far-fetched and questionable. After giving the natural and primary meaning of "the Spirit, the Water, and the Blood," in verse eight, he adds, hesitatingly, "If we wish to ascertain what these words signify, the Trinity itself not absurdly suggests itself." Si vero ea quæ his significata sunt, velimus inquirere, *non absurdè* occurrit ipsa Trinitas.

If Augustin could have appealed to the authority of Cyprian for this mystical gloss, he would not, it may be presumed, have introduced it thus doubtfully.

It was not till nearly two centuries after the æra of Augustin, that his mystical interpretation of the eighth verse was adopted by Facundus, who attempts, but without either reason or evidence, to fasten it also upon Cyprian. It deserves, by the way, to be noted that Facundus, in quoting the eighth verse several times, introduces in connexion with it the words in terrà, *on earth*[*] —which are not in general

---

[*] It may, however, be questioned whether the words " in terrà " were in the original MS. of Facundus. We know that they were interpolated in Bede.

found in MSS. omitting the seventh verse, and
which even Mr. Porson allowed, form, when they
occur, a possible antithesis to the words in the seventh
verse, in cœlo, *in heaven;* whence there is some
probability that the seventh verse was in the copy of
Facundus.

But the attempt to fasten this gloss upon Cyprian
through the medium of Facundus, is frustrated not
only by the facts glanced at above, but also by the authority of Fulgentius, a learned father who flourished
at the latter end of the fifth and the beginning of
the sixth century; prior by fifty years to Facundus.
He introduces the seventh verse as a quotation from
St. John with special reference to the authority of
St. Cyprian. His words are, " The blessed Apostle
John testifies, saying, There are three that bear record in heaven, the Father, the Word, and the
Spirit ; and the three are one." Which also the
most blessed martyr Cyprian confesses in his epistle
on the unity of the Church. And that he may
prove that there is one Church of the one God, he
adduces at the same time these testimonies from the
Scriptures. The Lord says, " I and the Father are
one — and again it is written concerning the Father,
the Son, and the Holy Ghost, *And the three are*
one."

Upon this passage Mr. Porson says, that Fulgentius fairly confesses he became acquainted with the
verse solely by the means of Cyprian , an assertion
which Bishop Burgess terms perverse, and which
even the learned advocate of Porson, Crito Cantabrigiensis, attempts not to vindicate.

It may be left to the plain sense of any intelligent
reader to determine, with the above quotations be-

fore him, whether Fulgentius does not quote the
disputed verse as St. John's, and subsequently refer
to its latter clause as having been quoted from the
Scriptures by Cyprian. The words of Fulgentius
are thus understood by Griesbach, who in consequence candidly states, that Fulgentius evidently
had the seventh verse in his own copy of St. John's
epistle, and also concluded that Cyprian had it in
his.

But if Cyprian quoted the verse, it must have
existed long prior to him, for even had he been dis-
honest he would scarcely have ventured to adduce
in so unhesitating a manner a novel interpolation ;
but his character was pre-eminently entitled to respect and reverence, and therefore Mill argues that
it existed in the MSS. of the African Church before Cyprian and Tertullian, and that it had thence
passed into the Latin copies of other nations.

Upon the whole, Bishop Burgess concludes, that
Cyprian did not interpret the eighth verse mystically or allegorically of the Trinity, because there
is not the slightest trace of such an intention in the
context of the passage in question in his writings ;
because Augustin, who first suggested this interpretation, makes no appeal to Cyprian in support of
it ; because nothing of the kind was ever imputed to
him by any ancient writer before Facundus, and because the authority of Fulgentius tends to establish
the very reverse of this supposition.

At the Council of Carthage, A.D. 484, an express
appeal was made to the seventh verse, by more than
400 Bishops of the Western Church, in their profession of faith, and no exception was made to
its authenticity by the Arian Bishops, who were

present at the Council. This fact, testified by Victor Vitensis, is of great importance. It not only tends to prove the existence of the verse at that time, but its recognition by all parties in the African Church. It strengthens the grounds of belief that Cyprian quoted the seventh verse, as also that Facundus has misrepresented and Fulgentius rightly stated Cyprian's meaning. It forms, in short, the crowning point of the testimony of the African Church in favour of the authenticity of the verse.

The author of the Prologue to the Canonical Epistles, ascribed by Erasmus, Le Clerc, &c. to Jerome (but without any sufficient evidence), had the verse in his copy, for he expressly refers to its existence in the Greek originals, and finds fault with the omission of it in many of the Latin MSS.

Mr. Porson and Bishop Marsh have availed themselves of the authority of the Prologue to prove that the verse was wanting as thus stated in many of the Latin MSS., but they ought to have added, that in whatever degree it is conclusive as to this fact, it is no less so as to its presence in various Greek MSS. when the Prologue was written. Its probable date is the sixth or seventh century.

OBJECTION III

Mr. Porson has asserted that, if the text of the heavenly witnesses had been known from the beginning of Christianity, the ancients would have inserted it in their Symbola or creeds.

REPLY III

Direct quotations are unsuited to the epitomising quality of creeds; but an ingenious argument in fa-

c c

vour of the probable existence of the text in Greek
originals of the fourth century, is derived by the
Bishop from a passage in the second Symbolum
Antiochenum, in the following clause, ὡς ειναι τη
μεν ὑποστασει Τρια, τη δε συμφωνια῾ Ἑν, *so that they
are three in personality, but One in agreement.*
Now the only place in the New Testament, in which
a unity of testimony is ascribed in direct terms to the
three persons of the Trinity, is 1 John, v. 7. This
passage made such an impression upon the late
Bishop Tomline, that he thus expresses himself in
a letter to Bishop Burgess : " The passage you
quote from the Symbolum Antiochenum is certainly
a very striking one, and adds materially to that
species of evidence in favour of 1 John, v. 7. Your
other quotations and observations have also considerable weight, and I willingly own that, upon the
whole, you have shaken my former opinion."

The inference in this case would, however, be
far more forcible if τρεις instead of τρια had been
the reading of the first clause.

The other quotations to which Bishop Tomline
alludes are various sentences, gleaned from the
Greek fathers by the industry of the Bishop, and
similar in their tenour to the above , of which the
following are specimens. Τα δε τρια κυριος ὁ Οεος
ἡμων. Και γαρ οἱ Τρεις Το ῾Ἑν εισι.* Of this sentence, ascribed to Origen, Fabricius says—Ad locum
1 Joh. v. 7. aliudi ab Origine non est dubitandum.

Maximus applies the same words to the Trinity,
and expressly quotes St John as his authority ; Πρ̣ος
δε τουτοις πασιν Ιωαννης φασκει, και οἱ τρεις Το ῾Ἑν

* But the Three are the Lord our God, for the Three are
One

ειτι. Gr. Nazianzen says, 'Εν, τα τρια Θεοτητι, και το εν, τρια ταις ιδιοτησι; and, again, και ταυτα τα τρια 'Εν.

The three are one in Godhead, and in their properties the three are unity, and these three are One. The last words are used also by Euthymius Zigabenus. *

In addition to the external evidence adduced by the Bishop in support of the authenticity of the text, he defended it also on various grounds of internal evidence.

That the omission of the seventh verse renders the context of the passage false in grammar and mutilated in sense he strongly maintained; a position in which he is, in some degree, supported by the opinion of Bishop Middleton, who, in his very learned and elaborate work on the Greek Definitive Article, thus expresses himself. —

" If the seventh verse had not been spurious, nothing could have been plainer than that TO εν of verse 8.. referred to εν of verse 7. As the case now stands, I do not perceive the force or meaning of the article; and the same difficulty is

---

* It would not be difficult to add to the number of similar quotations, but their bearing upon the point at issue, viz the authenticity of the text, it must in candour be allowed, is at best equivocal ; for, supposing the text to be genuine. though a Creed might not, for the reason already given, have quoted it, yet the Greek fathers, it may fairly be argued, certainly would. Their total silence respecting it is therefore inexplicable on the supposition of its authenticity. But the existence of sentences like these, instead of being a cause for wonder, on the supposition that the verse is spurious, was a natural consequence of the general belief in the doctrine of the Trinity, which prevailed in the Christian Church from the beginning. At this time controversy had given rise to rigorous and scholastic definitions.

briefly noticed by Wolfius." He then goes into an
elaborate exposition, on critical grounds, of the difficulty which he felt in reconciling the reading of
the eighth verse with the rejection of the seventh.
After fully allowing the great weight of the evidence against its authenticity, he closes thus:
" The objection, however, which has given rise to
this discussion, I could not, consistently with my
plan, suppress. On the whole, I am led to suspect,
that though so much labour and critical acuteness
have been bestowed on these celebrated verses, more
is yet to be done before the mystery in which they
are involved can be wholly developed "

Another point of internal evidence, which the
Bishop took great pains to establish and to illustrate,
was an almost necessary connexion, as he conceived,
of verse 7. with the context, and with the main
scope of the Epistle; as also an intimate correspondence between the general aim of the Epistle (the
verse being retained) and many important statements in the Gospel of St John relative to the
Divinity and Incarnation of Jesus Christ. This
unity of design and illustration between the Gospel
and Epistle depended, he conceived, in a great degree, upon the retention of the verse, and furnished
an almost conclusive proof of its authenticity.*

It was chiefly upon grounds similar to these, that
Bengelius, an able critic, and profound divine, while
he candidly admitted (with the single exception of

* The fullest development of this argument is contained in
the Bishop's " Second Letter to Mrs Joanna Baillie," enumerated in the list at the commencement of this chapter. Lord
Grenville, and Mr J. J. Gurney of Norwich, who is distinguished as a Biblical critic, expressed themselves, after reading
it, strongly disposed to regard the verse as genuine

the important testimony of the African Church)
the full force of the external evidence against the
verse, yet contended, unhesitatingly, for its authenticity. He concludes his vindication of it by declaring that, on studying the context of the passage,
the verse can be more certainly recognised than
the part of a leaf of a book long lost, every where
sought for, at length somewhere found, and proving
its claim to be restored to its former position by an
exact agreement in all its exterior points with the
part which was not lost. This alleged agreement
he denominates the " adamantine coherence of the
two verses."

Upon a general review of the Bishop's labours
and researches upon this interesting and much-
debated question, we think we shall not be deemed,
by the majority even of our learned readers, as going
too far in maintaining, that he has established the
existence of some strong points of external evidence
in its favour, and has added to their force by various
important considerations, coming under the head of
internal evidence, —

By placing in a strong light the argument in its
favour, furnished by many ancient MSS. of the
Latin version :

By arraying authority against authority; that,
for instance, of Selden, and Mill, and Bengelius,
and Horsley, against that of Newton, and Michaelis,
and Porson, and Marsh :

By showing how aptly, both in antithetical point
and grammatical accuracy, the disputed verse fits
into the place assigned to it; as also by arguing
ingeniously in its favour, from the similarity of the
train of thought which it developes, in connexion

with the context, to various important passages in
the Gospel of St. John ·

But, above all — for it must be allowed that the
above-mentioned particulars weigh but lightly
against the main difficulty, viz. the absence of the
verse from every Greek MS. of any authority, and
the total silence of the Greek fathers respecting
it — above all, we repeat, by the force and prominence which he has given to the remarkable and
continuous testimony of the African Church in its
favour.

This testimony, which had already been powerfully pressed home by Mr. Nolan, he has strengthened in a manner honourable to his researches
as a scholar, and his acuteness as a critic. His
able vindication of the passage in St. Cyprian,
upon which this testimony mainly depends, from
the comments and inferences of Mr. Porson, has,
been noticed in its proper place; and in the conclusion which he draws that it is a positive reference to
the disputed verse, if not a citation of it, he is supported, be it remembered, not only by very eminent
scholars of past days, but, in recent times, by the
authority of Griesbach.

The suffrage of the African Church in favour of
the verse ought not to be undervalued, when it is
considered how high a testimony Eusebius bears to
its integrity and purity, and how remarkably it was
protected (a short period only excepted) from the
influence of those great convulsions which for many
years agitated the Eastern and Western Churches,
and endangered the integrity of the sacred text.*

* To the Rev. Mr. Nolan's " Inquiry into the Integrity
of the Greek Vulgate," I am indebted for this remark.   His

Thus regarded, the first link of the chain of evidence in its favour, furnished by this church, is coeval with the second century; thence it descends through Cyprian, Fulgentius, Victor Vitensis, Marcus Celedensis, Phœbadius, Eucherius, Cassiodorus to the celebrated Council of Carthage, in the reign of Hunneric, the Vandal, at which 400 Bishops were present, when it was solemnly adduced by them in their Confession of Faith, and its authenticity unquestioned by the Arians present.

There is, however, it must candidly be avowed, an important link wanting in this chain of evidence; and that is, the high authority of St. Augustin. That he should have resorted to the eighth verse, for an argument in support of the doctrine of the Trinity, which he does in his mystical gloss upon it already cited, if the seventh verse had been in his copy of the Epistle, is highly improbable.

From what has been stated, our readers will, we trust, be able to form a correct opinion for themselves of the principal points of the evidence connected with a controversy which has employed the learning and industry of the greatest scholars and critics of modern times.

_____

work, which is equally learned and ingenious, developes, by many interesting facts and arguments the importance of the evidence furnished by the African Church in support of the verse

CHAP. XXXIV.

THE REV. L. CLARKE'S TESTIMONY TO THE EPISCOPAL
VIRTUES OF BISHOP BURGESS.

WE have now brought our memoir to a period at
which our readers will naturally expect us to give
some account of the mode in which the Bishop
discharged his various duties in the Diocese of
Salisbury. Our description of him, as Bishop of
St. David's, was in many particulars derived from
personal observation and local knowledge. We
cannot lay claim to the same advantage in respect
to his new sphere of labour, excepting in a very
inferior degree ; but we are happy to have it in our
power to introduce the following description of his
Episcopal virtues, from the pen of the Rev. Liscombe Clarke, a clergyman universally respected
and esteemed, and who, from having ably discharged
the important functions of Archdeacon of Sarum
and Bishop's Chaplain, from the year 1827 until
1836, when ill health led him to resign the first-
named office, had the closest opportunities of studying, to the life, the character and habits of his venerable Diocesan

TO J. S. HARFORD, ESQ.

MY DEAR SIR,
   You have desired me to furnish you with a short
account of the leading principles upon which our
late revered friend Bishop Burgess acted in the

Diocese of Salisbury, and of the practical results of his plans. I fear that the task which you have called upon me to perform will not be so executed as to prove worthy of your acceptance. Yet as I certainly had, during my intimacy and official connexion with that eminent Prelate for the larger portion of the time during which he held this See, many opportunities of forming a judgment of his character as a Christian Bishop, I am induced to comply with your request, from a desire to offer, however unworthily, my humble tribute of respect and veneration for the public principles and conduct of one for whom I entertained, also, an unfeigned personal attachment.

It is well known that Bishop Burgess was not translated to the See of Salisbury from that of St. David's till he had reached an advanced period of life, at which the responsibilities attaching to the discharge of the Episcopal functions in a new sphere of action must have been felt by him to be in no ordinary degree arduous. Much allowance must therefore be made, and, in fact, was made, by every considerate person, for some slight deficiencies; for a letter occasionally unanswered, or an official paper mislaid; for some well-devised plan for the good of the Diocese imperfectly carried out, some salutary regulation only casually enforced. It may, however, be fearlessly asserted, that the great leading principle which actuated him in all his views in his public capacity was a sincere desire to do his duty faithfully and conscientiously, for the promotion of true religion and the honour of God, to the encouragement of the active and zealous among the labourers in his Lord's vineyard, and to the increase of spirituality in that Church which he so much loved, and for the scriptural doctrines of which he contended so earnestly, but at the same time so meekly and charitably. The practical results of his high and holy aims, and the light emanating from his pure and bright example, were visible in the increased efficiency and more spiritualised affections and sentiments of many of the clergy over whom he presided.

Of the laity, too, all who conversed with or had occasion to consult him held him in the highest estimation for the guileless simplicity of his character, the stores of his learning, and the readiness with which he brought these to bear in social intercourse; for his unaffected humility, the peculiarly mild and benevolent tone of his sentiments in judging of the motives and conduct of others, the religious turn which he gave to many topics otherwise devoid of much interest, and the united ease and dignity of his demeanour. Many of them did not fail to express themselves gratified and honoured by his notice, and acknowledged that they seldom departed from his presence without having made some acquisition of human knowledge, some personal advance in Christian experience. For they had found in him that which realised their ideas of a Bishop whose "affections were set on things above, not on things on the earth;" who, at the same time that he was uninfluenced by mere worldly considerations, yet took a deep interest in promoting the welfare, both temporal and spiritual, of his fellow-creatures.

Such, my dear Sir, is (I firmly believe) a faithful sketch of the general character of that pious and good man. But you will probably expect that I

should enter a little more into detail as to the manner in which he performed the duties of his high
and responsible office. And I am myself the more
disposed to do so, because I think that his character
has not always been in this respect sufficiently understood or appreciated; in fact, there have been
some who did not scruple to charge him with a
neglect of the business of the Diocese. How this
originated I have never been able very satisfactorily
to discover. That it was the effect of prejudice in
some quarter or other I believe; for I can truly
say that, so long as I had the privilege and happiness of knowing the Bishop, he was intent upon discharging his duties with scrupulous attention and
diligence.

Considering the late period of life at which he
succeeded to the See of Salisbury, he obtained a
remarkably accurate knowledge of the topography of
the Diocese, and of the circumstances of the several
parishes comprised in the two counties of which it
then consisted. Indeed, his acquaintance with these
would have surprised me a good deal, if it were not
in my power to mention a minute, but not unin-
teresting, proof of the pains which he took to acquire them.

I found him one day engaged in tracing with his
own hand, notwithstanding the infirmity of his sight,
on a large map of Wiltshire, a number of circles, of
which the old-established stations for confirmation
were the centres, in order that, for the future, no
person might have to travel more than seven miles
from his home to be confirmed, and this (be it remembered) at a period when it had been customary
for Confirmations to be held at only the principal

market towns, and not unfrequently on the same days as the Visitation of the Clergy. I have also in my possession a Diocesan Atlas, if I may so call it, which he had caused to be prepared at a considerable expense by a surveyor, containing separate maps of all the Deaneries of the Diocese, with the names and relative position of the several parishes in each Deanery accurately delineated.

It was truly recorded of him, soon after his decease, that he had "devoted an exemplary attention to the affairs of the Diocese with the conscientious zeal of a man whose heart goes with him in the performance of the duties of his office; that his habits of business were active; and that he afforded facility of access at all times to those who had occasion to communicate with him." His fondness for professional study and literary retirement did, indeed, (as was also said,) induce a life of comparative seclusion; and hence, perhaps, many persons less acquainted with his general habits were inconsiderate, not to add uncharitable enough, to place to the account of indolence or negligence the gradually increasing infirmities of almost octogenarian age. Yet, as was truly testified in the record before alluded to, "he never lost sight, even for a moment, of the claims which the Church had upon him; and his loss was deplored, not more as a local bereavement, than as a great public deprivation of learning and talents devoted to its service."

Throughout the twelve years during which he presided over this Diocese he contributed liberally towards the improvement and increase of places of religious worship, and towards the erection and establishment of schools: he assisted in procuring, and in some instances provided out of his own pocket, for the augmentation of poorly-endowed benefices; he made himself acquainted with the names and characters of his clergy; and omitted no opportunity which was regularly brought before him, and in which he could safely and legally interfere, for correcting any neglect or irregularity in the ministration of the public offices of the Church, or enforcing a more adequate performance of parochial duties. Curates coming out of other dioceses were examined as to their general competency and the soundness of their religious opinions, besides being required to produce the ordinary testimonials of previous good conduct, before he would license them. And in order to obviate as far as he could, without undue rigor, the anomaly which certainly appears to exist in our Church, of intrusting a deacon who is not authorised to perform some essential functions, and to whom the Church assigns only a secondary and subordinate office, with the sole care of a parish, he would not accept titles for orders from deacons upon curacies of which the population exceeded four hundred, except in cases where the incumbent, or a curate in priest's orders, was resident: he required also that they should be deacons a full year before they applied to be ordained priests, and that they should remain in the same curacies to which they were ordained at first, for two years at the least.

Among the Queries which he addressed to the Clergy, and to which he requested to be furnished with answers, previously to his triennial visitations, were the following : —

How often is Divine Service performed in your

Church on Sundays, and at what hours? Do you
preach twice every Sunday? Is Divine Service
performed at your Church on Wednesdays and
Fridays, and is the Litany then read? Have you
always Divine Service on Ash Wednesday? Do you
usually preach on that day? Is the Church Service
daily and duly attended throughout Passion Week?
and do you always preach on Good Fridays?

Is there a Sunday School in your parish? Where
is it held, and do you personally superintend it? Is
there a Day School, or Free School, in the parish
for the poor? Is it in union with the National
Society? Is there any Grammar School? Is there
any Infant or Adult School? Are pains taken in
the Parochial School to prepare the children for
Confirmation, and are they taught to join at all
times in the Service of the Church? If you are
engaged in the conduct or superintendence, as
trustee, of a Grammar or Classical School, do you
take care that religious instruction in the evidences,
doctrines, and duties of Christianity is duly attended
to?

Is there any annual village feast or wake? Is
it attended with any disorderly consequences? Do
the churchwardens take care to prevent the pro-
fanation of the Sabbath? Do you observe any increase or decrease of crime among the younger part
of your parishioners? If an increase, to what do
you attribute it?

Surely the desire to obtain information from time
to time on such particulars speaks for itself, and argues no deficiency of interest in the religious state
of the diocese. And I must again notice, that at
the period in question several of those particulars

had not excited the general attention which they
have since attracted. Infant Schools were then but
few in number, and a Diocesan Board of Instruction
was not even contemplated.

It is unnecessary for me to do more than simply
to advert to the Church Union Society, for the
assistance of infirm and distressed clergymen, and
the numerous unseen channels through which he
ministered privately to the wants of many others of
his poorer brethren, whose cases were almost daily
coming to his knowledge, and were no sooner known
than relieved. But in connection with that Society,
which was mainly conducted through the instrumentality of the rural deans, I cannot deny myself
the gratification of quoting the high testimony
borne to the episcopal usefulness of my late revered
patron by one who also knew him well, the Rev.
Wm. Dansey, Rector of Donhead St. Andrew, and
Rural Dean of Chalke, in this county and diocese.
That very able and zealous clergyman, in the
Appendix to his valuable and interesting work on
the Name, Origin, &c., of Rural Deans, makes the
following honourable and impartial mention of the
late Bishop : —

" Such is the present constitution of the office
under the venerable Bishop Burgess, who has rendered it more effective during his occupation of the
See of Sarum, by enjoining on his rural deans
annual or more frequent inspection of churches and
chapels, with their ornaments and furniture, church-
yards, manses, &c. ; by circulating periodically
visitation articles of inquiry, to be formally filled up
by them, and deposited in the archives of the See;
by distributing mandates and prosecuting *inquisi-*

tions where necessary, by the instrumentality of deans rural; and, lastly, by holding a yearly conference of all the deans of the three archdeaconries of the diocese at the palace; reviving therein the image of those older conventions at which the deans rural, as the proper delegates and standing representatives of the parochial clergy, were heretofore wont to deliver their *acta Visitationis* to their diocesan, and to report and consult with him on the spiritual condition of their respective decanates."

Of the Church Union Society just now alluded to, which owes its origin entirely to him, and constitutes so striking an instance of his munificence, the diocese is at this time enjoying, and will continue, I trust, to enjoy, the permanent benefits. Upon the beneficial effects of his system in the discharge of the two most important branches of the episcopal functions — I mean the Confirmation of the young, and the Ordination of candidates for the pastoral office — I shall take leave to dwell a little more in detail.

As to the general importance of a decent and profitable administration of the scriptural and apostolic rite of Confirmation, there cannot be any diversity of opinion among those who duly consider its meaning, and the effects which may be expected to follow it. For baptism being a solemn covenant between God and man, into which it concerns all to enter through Jesus Christ, and infants being by our Church allowed to be baptized at an age too tender to admit of their performing at baptism what is required on their parts, which is therefore performed by proxies, it clearly becomes necessary that all should take some subsequent suitable opportunity of openly confessing Christ in the face of the Church, and of ratifying and expressing their own individual consent to their baptismal covenant. This is best done at the time of Confirmation, which is an ordinance admirably calculated to stamp a mark upon the minds of the rising generation at a very critical age. It will therefore, according to the manner in which it is administered and received, be the seal of piety or irreligion to thousands.

But it is sufficiently notorious that some years ago the mode of conducting Confirmations in many dioceses was unhappily such as to afford matter of grief to every sincere friend of religion and of the Church ; and it must be acknowledged that a better system did not prevail in the diocese of Salisbury than in others. It too often happened in every diocese that one of the most affecting offices of the Church was deprived, not only of the solemnity of an act of Divine worship, but also even of common decency and propriety. We cannot be thankful enough that the scenes of confusion which frequently prevailed on such occasions are now of comparatively rare occurrence, and that the administration of this holy rite is conducted with more method and on better principles.

Our late revered Diocesan effected a considerable improvement in this respect. He increased the number of places for holding Confirmations, and confirmed at some of them every year. He always appointed separate days for the visitation of the clergy and for confirming. The circular letters in which he desired every parochial minister to announce to their respective flocks his intention of

D D

confirming, and the form of address which he himself drew up and transmitted to them for that purpose, gave earnest expression to the great anxiety
which he felt that the solemn ordinance might be
properly conducted. He "entreated them to instruct their parishioners, both publicly and privately,
in the nature and benefits of Confirmation ; " and,
still more earnestly, to " appoint a day for the cele-
bration of the Holy Communion, soon after the
Confirmation, and to invite especially all who had
been recently confirmed to partake of that most
sacred ordinance." He directed " them also to remind parents of their natural duty, and sponsors
of their spiritual engagements to see, as far as in
them lay, that the young persons committed to their
charge were made duly sensible of their obligations
in these respects." These instructions were further
accompanied with a very useful series of questions
for elderly persons and others, who could not read
or retain in their memory the whole of the Church
Catechism, so framed that, while they comprised a
brief summary of the Catechism, they required only
the simple answers of " Yes," or " No."

At the time of Confirmation the arrangements in
which his system differed somewhat from the mode
more usually adopted were simple, and their effect
was impressive and edifying. Admission into the
church was allowed only to the catechumens, their
ministers, and their parents or guardians. All of
these were, if possible, admitted some half hour previously to the commencement of the service : thus
constituting one uniform congregation, they were
seated and silent, each in his proper place, (the
males on one side of the church, the females on the

other,) and had time to collect their thoughts, and offer up without distraction a prayer for the blessing of God on the ordinance in which they were about to participate, before the entrance of the Bishop, who, on proceeding to the chancel, found there a moderate number of young people, seldom exceeding seventy or eighty, in readiness for him. The ceremony, which consisted only of the Confirmation Service, commenced by the officiating minister reading the introductory preface. The Bishop then delivered to the division of catechumens about to be confirmed, who were kneeling before him, a few words of exhortation, in which he called their attention to the responses which they would have to make; but more especially he enjoined them to answer distinctly and individually, with an audible voice, that most important and heart-searching question, "Do ye here, in the presence of God and of this congregation, renew the solemn promise and vow that was made in your name at your baptism, ratifying and confirming the same in your own persons, and acknowledging yourselves bound to believe and to do all those things which your godfathers and godmothers then undertook for you?" He then confirmed them, repeating the Prayer of Confirmation after imposition of hands on four or six only, never more, at a time; pronounced over them the blessing; and dismissed them with a short charge, referring principally to the 17th chapter of St. John's Gospel, and very touching from its simplicity; in which he again pressed upon them a continual remembrance of that day's solemnity, the regulation of their future lives according to the tenor of their vows, and a Chris-

tian steadfastness in the doctrines in which they had
been instructed. This division was then allowed to
retire altogether from the church, and another
division was brought up from their seats, and confirmed and dismissed in like manner; and so
throughout the whole number of catechumens; the
Blessing and the Charge being repeated to each
division, till all were confirmed. The Bishop and
clergy then left the church.

The good effects of this simple arrangement were
obvious: there was but little noise and no unnecessary
detention in the church; and in very many cases
a manifest impression of the propriety and benefits
of Confirmation, and of respect for the venerable
Bishop himself, and, as I trust, for episcopal authority in general, was left upon the mind. And
within my own knowledge more than one instance
occurred of parents expressing, with tears of gratitude in their eyes, their sense of the improvement
which they had just witnessed in the mode of conducting this important rite.

You will, perhaps, wonder how the Bishop could
have borne, at his age, the fatigue of thus going
through the service, together with his charge, so
frequently in the course of one morning, when, perhaps 700 or 800 persons were confirmed. Indeed,
I often myself expressed to him my fears lest the
fatigue should be too much for him. But the
purport of his answer was always the same. "Be
assured," he would say, "that the lively interest
which I take in a rite every way so affecting, and of
such vast importance to the spiritual welfare of so
many of Christ's 'little ones,' precludes any feeling
of personal inconvenience. God grant that the

ceremony (however imperfectly I may have performed it) may be blessed to them, and that there
may have been vouchsafed to them, through me, a
portion of that heavenly grace which shall enable
them 'to continue his for ever.'" This was his
constant language on such occasions; and I have
since reflected, with a melancholy satisfaction, on
the gracious dispensation of Providence, which ordained that he should receive the first awful summons to prepare for his own departure out of this
world, and should have even entered upon the first
stage (if I may so speak) of his passage through the
gate of death to Christ's everlasting kingdom, while
engaged in administering the sacred rite in which
he always took so lively an interest, and which he
administered, as we have just seen, so effectually
for edification. You are well aware that, while in
the act of confirming in the parish church of Warminster, in the year 1835, he was seized with an
attack of paralysis, which, though slight and partial,
evidently affected his speech and bodily strength at
the time; and it may be doubted whether he ever
afterwards entirely recovered from its effects.

But if such was the unceasing anxiety of this excellent bishop to give a solemn and abiding effect to
the sacred rite of Confirmation, it will easily be believed that it was still more his earnest aim to admit
into the ministry, if possible, only such persons as
were duly qualified for it by their previous studies
and attainments, and, above all, by the purity of
their principles and the integrity of their moral
habits. It might be truly said of him that he acted
up to the apostolical direction of "laying hands suddenly on no man." His earnest prayer to God

was, that he might be enabled "faithfully and wisely to make choice of fit persons to serve in the sacred ministry of the Church." How often have I heard him declare that the Ordination Weeks were to him the most anxious and disquieting weeks of his life.* In fact, so great was his caution, and so firm was he in carrying out the principles which "guided and governed his mind," in this respect, that till his character was better understood, and the real kindness and benevolence of his heart more generally appreciated, he was thought by many to be unduly strict and particular.

One or two points in his system, with reference to the preparation which he required in those who applied to him for Ordination, deserve a more especial notice.

He instituted a preliminary examination for the candidates for Deacons' Orders to take place at Salisbury about three months previously to the Ordination Week. At this they were to appear personally, and to bring with them a written syllabus or abridgment of certain prescribed books, such as Pearson on the Creed, Butler's Analogy, Burnet's History of the Reformation and Pastoral Care, and they were required to give proof of their qualification for the performance of the public offices of the Church by reading aloud the Morning Service, in the Chapel, before the Bishop or his Chaplain, and a small congregation, consisting generally of the Dean and one or two of the Canons and Prebendaries of the Cathedral ; and a sufficient competency in this very important part of clerical duty was an

* Bishop Burnet's feeling, with respect to Ordinations, was precisely similar.

indispensable requisite for the candidate being permitted to proceed in his examination, which subsequently embraced a thorough acquaintance with the Bible, Ecclesiastical History, the Evidences of Christianity, and the Thirty-nine Articles of Religion with their Scripture Proofs ; some proficiency in Hebrew was also required.

But I would more particularly mention that the examinations were not confined to a literary and critical knowledge of the Bible and the other subjects referred to. The Bishop's anxiety extended to a still more important point ; and the following, which were among the questions usually required to be answered by the candidates, were calculated to test their moral and religious training and habits of previous self-examination : — " Have you, during the last seven years, been engaged in any secular profession? What books have you read on the qualifications necessary for Holy Orders ? What books have you read to enable you to judge of the fitness of your own talents and disposition for the Ministry of the Church, and to instruct you in the knowledge of yourself? What is the difference between the literary and spiritual preparation for Holy Orders ? What are the characteristics of personal religion ?

" What is the end and design of the Christian Ministry ? By what names are the ministers of Christ distinguished in the Scriptures ? Why are they styled Christ's Ambassadors ? Why are they styled Stewards of the Mysteries of God ? What are the duty and office of Christ's Ministers ? What especial motive have they to do this faithfully? When are men regularly called to the Ministry ?

What is the *outward* Call to the Ministry? What is the *inward* Call? Is the *inward* Call sufficient without the *outward*? Will the *outward* Call succeed without the *inward*?"

The Bishop himself compiled a small tract on the importance and difficulty of the Pastoral Office, and the danger of rashly undertaking it, which was put into the hands of the candidates, on their first appearance at Salisbury, and was afterwards read aloud and commented on. It contained, among other things, some of the most awakening and heart-stirring passages of Bishop Bull's well-known Sermon on the Pastoral Office, and a striking passage or two from Dr. Glasse's translation of Erasmus's Ecclesiastes on " the duty of parents and preceptors to prepare such as are destined for the ministry, even from their tender years, for the reception of Divine grace, and to instruct them chiefly in those things which may best fit them for their great work."

Among the subjects for the written exercises which were required of the candidates were the following : —

" No one can come unto me, except the Father, which hath sent me, draw him." John, vi. 44.

" Except ye be converted, and become as little children, ye shall not enter into the kingdom of heaven." Matt. xviii. 3.

" Holiness, without which no man can see the Lord." Hebrews, xii. 14.

" Know ye not that the friendship of the world is enmity with God?" James, iv. 4.

On the Ordination Service.

On the disposition of mind necessary for the due

observance of the Ordination Service, and on the personal responsibilities consequent on it.

A Summary of the Epistles to Timothy and Titus.

A written translation of the Latin pages of the tract (above referred to) " De Dignitate Sacerdotii Christiani."

" If ye then, being evil, know how to give good gifts unto your children, how much more shall your heavenly Father give the Holy Spirit to them that ask him." Luke, xi. 13.

I have it in my power to add some particulars of the mode of treating this last subject which he proposed for the adoption of the candidates; viz. scriptural proofs of the distinct Personality and Divinity of the Holy Spirit; an enumeration of the gifts of the Holy Spirit, and fruits of the Spirit; proofs from Scripture of the presence, communion, and fellowship of the Holy Spirit in the minds of believers in Christ; a statement of the duty and necessity of prayer for the presence and aid of the Holy Spirit incumbent on all men, but *especially on the ministers of religion*, and the assurance that such presence and aid will be granted, if prayed for in faith.

But I need not multiply evidences of the impressive character which he was anxious should be given to these examinations; those which I have already adduced are, I trust, sufficient for the purpose. And I think it will be granted that it was next to impossible, but that in the minds of the majority of persons ordained by him, after such strict and searching preparatory requirements, the seeds at least must have been implanted of such principles of duty and responsibility as tend to alienate the heart from mere worldly engagements, and from pursuits calculated to discredit our function and lessen our usefulness. That in all on whom he "laid his hands" these dispositions reached the height to be desired may not be true ; but I do not scruple to assert, of my own knowledge, that very many among the younger clergy did at the time of their ordination apparently form corresponding resolutions, and have since given satisfactory proofs of their striving to pursue and improve them. In the same proportion were the efficiency and influence of the parochial clergy increased, the spiritual interests of the diocese promoted, and the character of our apostolical Church exalted.

On the whole, we may, I think, safely conclude that, as among the Prelates of modern times none was more distinguished for personal piety and learning than Bishop Burgess, so the services also, which he practically rendered to the Diocese of Salisbury, were beneficial and permanent.

We who had so many opportunities of studying his character and appreciating his many virtues, may, I trust, be permitted, without the charge of presumption, to apply to him, in testimony of our admiration and gratitude for his unceasing exertions in the cause of true Religion, the language of St. Paul ; and as we know that like that great Apostle, towards the end of his labours, he waited patiently and "in the full assurance of hope" for his passage to eternity, we may venture to affirm that he "fought a good fight," that "his course" upon earth was "finished" with joy, that he "kept the faith ;" that the work given him by his divine

Master to do was effectually done; and that there
is "laid up for him a Crown of Righteousness,
which the Lord, the righteous Judge, shall give him
at that day."

Believe me, my dear Sir,

With every sentiment of respect and esteem,

Your faithful Servant,

LISCOMBE CLARKE.

CHAP. XXXV.

VARIOUS CORRESPONDENCE.

THE Bishop's correspondents to the close of his
life were numerous, including many eminent men in
the two Universities, and some of the most gifted
of his literary contemporaries. The topics chiefly
touched upon in their letters were connected with
the criticism of the Greek Testament, or with collations of MSS., or with one or other of the Bishop's
learned publications; so that, among the large mass
which have passed under the writer's examination,
there are not many suited to the taste of general
readers. The Bishop's own letters, of which but
few are in his possession, were in general brief, and
confined to the immediate point of business; they
were seldom discursive, and he rarely gave the rein
to fancy in them, or full expression to the noble sentiments of his kind and generous heart. No one was
ever more distant from professions of any kind.
Among his more intimate friends, and frequent correspondents, were the late Archdeacon Churton and

George Marriott, Esq. The letters of the former
bespeak the scholar, and breathe the cordial, affectionate regard of early and intimate friendship ;
those of the latter are fraught with pleasant literary
intelligence, with elevated Christian sentiment, and
with high respect for the Bishop's character and
office.

The late Rev. Lewis Way was another friend
with whom the Bishop corresponded for many years.
One of the links between them was a mutual interest in the objects and proceedings of the Jews'
Society, the existence and present flourishing condition of which may be traced back to the munificence
and zeal with which Mr. Way supported its funds,
and laboured in its cause, when pecuniary and other
embarrassments threatened its extinction. At this
critical period, Bishops Burgess and Ryder were
persuaded by him to become its joint patrons. The
respect felt by both of these excellent men for Mr.
Way's eminent Christian virtues ripened into cordial friendship and regard, under the influence of
his amiable and brilliant social qualities.

The present Chapter will be principally composed
of a select few of such of the letters referred to, as
will tend to illustrate the general object aimed at in
these pages.

TO THE REV. CHARLES DAUBENY.

Dear Sir, August 15 1825
The Thirty-ninth Canon of our Church directs
that " No Bishop shall institute any to a Benefice,
who hath been ordained by any other Bishop — except he shall appear, *upon due examination*, to be

worthy of his Ministry." I wish to fulfil the intention of this Canon; and for this purpose, though I cannot at once exact the various proofs of competency which I may require, yet there is one upon which I must be fully satisfied, before I take any decisive step towards disposing of the Vicarage of Warminster; I intend that the person who shall succeed to it shall first read prayers and preach in the Church, that I may know whether he has sufficient ability in reading prayers and in preaching for such a congregation as that of Warminster. The judges of his competency in these particulars might, perhaps, be the rural Deans of the district, and any two Clergymen selected for the occasion.

Incompetency of voice and of elocution is such an evil in our Church, wherever it exists, that I am anxious to provide against it in every way I can.

I wish, therefore, to profit by your advice and experience, and shall be glad to have your opinion on the subject of this letter. I have already appointed a commission for the examination of candidates for orders as to the competency before mentioned, previously to their coming to me for examination in Divinity.

I am, dear Sir,
Yours very sincerely,
T. SARUM.

TO THE LORD BISHOP OF SALISBURY.

My LORD, N. Bradley, August 22. 1825
I HAVE the honour to coincide perfectly in opinion with your Lordship on the subject of your last letter. The evil complained of, and which your

Lordship has in view to correct, has always appeared
to me a very serious one ; as nothing tends so much
to diminish the effect of our excellent service as the
careless or incorrect manner of delivering it : a circumstance which never fails to leave an unfavourable
impression on common minds. The fact is, every
person supposes he can read, and is therefore above
learning ; and the consequence is, that so few of our
Clergy read well. There has always appeared to
me to be some defect in our University system on
this head. In whatever degree your Lordship may
correct this evil so generally complained of, the
Church of England must be your debtor, whilst
the satisfaction arising from such a circumstance
cannot fail to be your Lordship's just reward.

I would only take leave to hint, that as Rural
Deans were not originally appointed with a view to
the office, with which your Lordship proposes to
invest them, it may be a subject for consideration,
how far, as individuals, they may be competent to
discharge it. In venturing to suggest this, I trust
the " Cobler will not be thought to have gone beyond his Last."

I have the honour to remain, with due respect,
Your Lordship's
Faithful and obedient Servant,
Charles Daubeny.

TO THE SAME.

My dear Lord,   Middleton, October 25. 1825
I am certainly no Solomon, nor you, I ween,
a native of Sheba, though you have now and then
puzzled me with hard questions, but never, I think,

more than to-day. I have neither the hymn of
Cleanthes, nor the golden verses of Pythagoras; —
the latter are to be found, I think, in the *Poetæ
minores*. In the absence therefore of printed authority, I was obliged to proceed as I could, to guess
now and then at the text, and so, right or wrong,
to correct the letter-press. I am truly sorry to
hear that your sight is worse than it used to be. It
is a comfort, however, that the eyes are less pained
by writing than by reading, and that there is one
near at hand who sees well for you and for herself.

I am ever, my dear Lord,
Your most obliged Friend and faithful Servant,
R. Churton.

TO THE SAME.

My dear Lord, Middleton, July 5. 1826
Much did I rejoice to see you in St. Mary's at
the Infirmary Sermon, — and the more, as I supposed you would be at the Commemoration in the
Theatre the next day. I inquired for you at the
King's Arms, and found you had been gone about
ten minutes. The day after I had the pleasure of
meeting your Lordship at Mr. Marriott's, I saw
Bishop Jebb at Mr. Norris's at Hackney. He
brought me back to town in his chariot, and I had
much interesting conversation with him and his excellent chaplain, Mr. Forster. They are extremely
anxious and pressing for the publication of more
Sermons of the ever dear Dr. Townson, having
almost by heart those already in print, particularly
that on the Rechabites. I have had a most kind
letter from my said good Lord of Limerick, and

am to hear from him again. He could not, as he once hoped, meet me at the Oxford Commemoration, but went to the Commencement at Cambridge.

We are to set off for Aberystwyth this day fortnight.

I am ever, my dear Lord, &c.,

R. CHURTON.

TO THE SAME.

MY DEAR LORD, Bronwydd, August 8 1826.

MY feelings have been gratified very frequently by the strong regret which your Lordship's departure from this Diocese has excited.

Mrs. Lloyd desires me to say how much gratified all here will be, if, on any occasion of visiting Lampeter, you can come to Bronwydd. At family prayers, she called for Luther's hymn, *because the Bishop had said he should wish to hear it on his death-bed.* T—— afterwards told us that the effect of it at the musical festival, in the Cathedral at York, last year, was tremendous.

Penpoint. Wednesday. — I resume my pen with unmixed pleasure. We have seen the College, and neither Tyler, George, nor myself, could wish any thing otherwise than we found it, or for any thing besides what we found. I remembered your Lordship's injunction to view it from the churchyard at Lampeter. On the road to Abergwilly, also, by Highmead, as well as on that to Llandovery, the view is immitably interesting. All the situations which I ever heard of for the College are far inferior to Lampeter. We united in wishing that the keep of the old castle may not be destroyed.

Lord Kenyon writes to me as follows : — I am very glad the Bishop is so well pleased with the appearance of his College, and trust that, by the goodness of God, he will be spared many years to witness and to contribute to its prosperity. It is one of the most blessed works of Christian piety and of devotion to its Diocese from a Bishop that centuries have furnished ; and as a Welshman, I am most anxious that my countrymen should duly estimate their obligations to its founder.

Adieu, my dear Lord.

I am ever devotedly yours,

G. W. MARRIOTT.

The Bishop was much pleased with the following passage in a letter addressed to myself by an invaluable friend, for whom he also entertained feelings of high esteem and affectionate regard, Sir Thomas Acland, describing his impression on a first view of the College.

" I have visited St. David's College, and I have come away exceedingly gratified with my visit, and not a little pleased that I have had a share, however small, in the production of so honourable a work. The design, the arrangement, the surprising economy of the execution, are extremely creditable to our friend Cockerell, and for his sake, as well as for the good Bishop of Salisbury's and yours, I sincerely rejoice in this success. It is now brought to a point that must ensure all that you can wish."

TO THE SAME.

MY LORD, King's College, Cambridge, June 16.

I BEG leave to return your Lordship my most grateful acknowledgments for your kind present. If the doctrine of a Holy Trinity of Persons in the Godhead be true, I should expect it to pervade the whole Scriptures, just as the fundamental doctrine of the fall and recovery pervades them. I should expect it to be taken for granted and incidentally expressed in a multitude of passages where there was no occasion for direct mention of it: "Let *us* make Man in *our* image;" "The Man is become as one of *us;* " " Go to, let *us* go down and confound their language." So again (in the Prophets), " The Spirit of the Lord shall rest upon him;" ".The Spirit of the Lord God is upon me;" &c. (Isaiah, xi. 2. and lxi. 1.), and a multitude of other passages of the same kind, are perfectly clear upon the presumption of the doctrine of the Trinity, but are altogether inexplicable without it; and the existence of such passages in the Volume of Inspiration is precisely what I should expect. They say to me, This is a doctrine which is to be received without gainsaying , since it is not only asserted where the occasion calls for it, but is assumed where you would not readily expect it to occur. The difference which I make between the direct and indirect passages is, that I would establish the doctrine on those passages alone which are sufficient to support it; but I would illustrate it without hesitation from those which, without expressly asserting the doctrine, appear to take it for granted.

I fear I convey my mind but clumsily; but I will make the matter clear by an easy illustration: —

The Divinity of Christ pervades the Scriptures in the way that I have mentioned. I find, accordingly, St. Paul saying, "He that spared not his own Son, but delivered him up for us all, how shall he not with him also freely give us all things?" On reading this I say, the Divinity of Christ is not mentioned here, but it is taken for granted; and on any other hypothesis the observation has neither force nor sense. Suppose the Lord Jesus to be only a creature, how can I, from the bestowment of him to suffer for me, infer, that God will bestow on me all the blessedness and glory of Heaven? If a man take pity on me when perishing with hunger, and give me a loaf or a lamb to supply my necessities, can I infer from thence that he will bestow on me a large inheritance? is the inference so clear that no one in his senses can doubt the truth of it? Yet this illustration falls infinitely short of the point to be illustrated. For if God will give me all things, I must number amongst them the everlasting enjoyment of Himself as my portion and inheritance; and then, upon any supposition but that of the Divinity of Christ, my argument must be, if God gave me a Creature, how shall he not give me the Creator? If he delivered up a Creature to suffer for me for a time, how shall he not deliver me from suffering to all Eternity?

Your Lordship will now see my meaning: I say that such passages as these, where the Divinity of Christ is not expressly mentioned, but only taken for granted, convey to my mind as strong a conviction of the truth of his Godhead as the more direct passages : and though I should not select such a passage to found the doctrine upon it, I should readily take it to elucidate and confirm what I had previously proved.

I am, my Lord,
Your Lordship's most indebted Servant,
C. SIMEON.

TO THE SAME.

MY DEAR LORD, Barley Wood.

I TAKE shame to myself for having delayed so long thanking you for your very kind and interesting letter.

I am delighted to see genius in the third generaation of my good Shepherd. The verses really are not bad.*

It will amuse you to hear that when one of our missionaries to Greece recently arrived in that once classical country, the only novelty he found was my little story of the Shepherd of Salisbury Plain in modern Greek. But I have not done yet — another grandson of this famous Shepherd, who has been digging out a chalk quarry, has sent me a present of the prettiest baby chair you ever saw, made by himself. I give this account, because *You* are the grand Spiritual Shepherd of Salisbury Plain, &c.

Ever yours, my dear Lord,
HANNAH MORE.

* Referring to some verses by a descendant of " The Shepherd of Salisbury Plain," sent her by the Bishop.

TO THE SAME.

My dear Lord,   Queen Square, Dec 6.
I presume that you must before this time have
reached Salisbury. I write chiefly to tell you the
substance of a most interesting recent communication from Bishop Chase ; of which you shall have
the full account, extracted from his letter, as soon
as I can forward it. He has been a visitation of
more than 800 miles, on one horse, this autumn,
and was solicited, in the course of it, to visit a tribe
of Oneida and Mohawk Indians, who were said to
be well disposed to the Church. He went, with
the aid of a guide, who introduced him to the Chiefs.
From them he learnt that they had long been in
possession of our Liturgy, published in London in
1787, in their language, and that the Elders of the
tribe used it in morning and evening service every
Sunday. They also administered Baptism, and lamented this as a great irregularity, from which
they much desired to be relieved by an authorised
Ministry. The Bishop preached to them through
an interpreter, and chose five of their most intelligent young men for gratuitous education at his
College, hoping finally to ordain them. What a
delightful instance of his persevering zeal, of the
value of his Diocesan Seminary in the extension of
the true Church and of our Liturgy ! With its
aid these poor Indians were able to form themselves
into something like a Christian body, and are quite
ripe for the benefit of a regular Church.

I saw the Bishop of Durham very well on Saturday.

> I am, my dear Lord,
> Most devotedly yours,
> G. W. MARRIOTT.

TO J. S. HARFORD, ESQ.

DEAR SIR,   Bath, March 12. 1827.
I THANK you for your very obliging letter; which
came to me the more acceptably from my not having
previously received any account of the opening of
the College. I wrote on the first of March to Mr.
Lewellyn, inclosing a letter from Mr. Sharon Turner,
with an offer of a copy of his historical works for
the College Library. I have recommended Mr.
Turner to send the books directly to Mr. Lewellyn.

The account which you give of the examination of
the students proves the necessity of an Institution
for Clerical Education very different from the existing Grammar Schools. I quite enter into the
feelings which you express respecting the first performance of Divine Service within the precincts of
St. David's College. And *Omen accipio*, a promising omen of the improvement which I trust that
the course of education pursued there will produce
in the future religious character of the Menevian
Clergy. I am sure you must have been highly
gratified, for your account of all that passed, strongly
reflects the impression which was made upon you.
I am to go to Salisbury to hold an Ordination on
the 25th. How soon after that I may have the
pleasure of visiting Blaise Castle, I am sorry I cannot

at present determine — so many have been my hindrances.

> Yours very truly,
>
> T. SARUM.

TO THE LORD BISHOP OF SALISBURY.

MY DEAR LORD, Rothley Temple, April 26. 1827.

HAD I not been extremely engrossed ever since my departure from Bath, I should sooner have taken the liberty of troubling you with a few lines, to express my regret at not having had it in my power to pay my respects to your Lordship before I came away. Had I not been called to a distance very suddenly and unexpectedly, I should certainly have done it, not from motives of ceremony but of real respect, and allow me to say regard. I should have been glad also to have had the honour of introducing two of my Oxonians to your Lordship, both destined to the Church by their own choice, one of them elected Fellow of Oriel, under circumstances much to his credit, about a year ago , the other, also of Oriel, having taken his B. A. degree a few months ago, with very honourable distinction.

I trust, from your Lordship's present See being nearer to Bath, I may have other opportunities of meeting you, from whose society it is no compliment to say, I hope to derive profit as well as pleasure. But I know the value of your time, and must only occupy it while I subscribe myself, with respect and attachment, my dear Lord,

> Your obliged and faithful servant,
>
> W. WILBERFORCE.

TO ARCHDEACON CHURTON.

DEAR CHURTON,   October 22. 1827.

SICKNESS realises and endears to us the consolations of Christianity. At that time especially, a
truly believing Christian feels sensibly the want of
a Saviour; and his faith is rewarded by the reflection
" I know in whom I have believed and trusted,"
and " He is faithful who has promised."

You have probably seen the verses which Dr.
Parr subjoined to his MS. Catalogue. They are
very good as far as they go ; but they do not go far
enough for a Christian :

Summe Deus ! grates a me tibi semper agendæ,
Quod bona librorum et . . .   frugis in aulâ est
Copia; mente fruor quod sanâ in corpore sano,
Natales læte numerans et carus amicis,
Discendi quod amor viget, atque instante senectâ,
Spes vitæ melioris inhæret pectore in imo

This I say is very good as far as it goes ; but a
Christian should have said more. He should have
said that the *melior vita* * which he, hoped for was
purchased for him by the death of Christ. I therefore propose the following conclusion :

Quam Christus mihi morte suâ meritisque redemit

With my best wishes for your perfect recovery,
I am, Dear Churton,
Yours most sincerely,
T. SARUM.

TO MR. J. BURGESS.

DEAR NEPHEW,   Southampton, Dec. 10. 1828.

I AM glad to find by your letter that you have
been so well employed in your College studies.

* The better life

There is one thing I strongly recommend you, which is always to have in view the profession for which you are intended, and to procure for your private reading Collyer's Sacred Interpreter, Burnet's Pastoral Care, and Gibson's Pastoral Letters. I wish you also to remember that Hebrew is as necessary for the Old Testament as Greek is for the New. You will have an opportunity, perhaps, before long of attending the Lectures of the Regius Professor of Hebrew, and I earnestly recommend you not to be content without making yourself a good Hebrew scholar before you take your Bachelor's degree; you will find a great advantage in having made this acquisition before you engage in the active duties of your future profession.

Before I dismiss this letter let me remind you of your Latin translation of the passage in Thompson.

Yours affectionately,

T. Sarum.

My dear Nephew,   Southampton,
                                    Dec. 22 1829.

You are probably before this time returned from College, having, as I suppose, passed your responsions during the last term. I shall be glad to hear from you some account of your examination, and what were the books and exercises in which you were examined. Your College exercises have, I conclude, given you frequent opportunities of cultivating the habit of Latin versification, and that you have occasionally found the translation of that passage of Thompson which I recommended to you not an unpleasant or unimproving occupation. I should have pleasure in perusing the whole of it completed, or any part of it that you may send to me. I should be much gratified by receiving from you an account of your public and private studies during the last term. If I have not already done it, I will take this opportunity of recommending to you the careful perusal of the present Bishop of Chester's (Dr. Sumner's) work on the evidences of Christianity, and at the same time of repeating my advice that you would make Grotius's invaluable treatise, " De Veritate Religionis Christianæ," the text-book of your studies on this subject. You have, if I mistake not, commenced and made some progress in the first of three of the most important years of your life, I mean the three which immediately precede the age at which young men usually become candidates for Deacon's orders ; and it will be of great consequence to you, that you keep that period frequently in view, and that you make a point of accommodating your private studies and pursuits very much to it. With our united kindest regards,

I am, my dear Nephew,

Your affectionate Uncle,

T. Sarum.

TO THE LORD BISHOP OF SALISBURY.

My dear Lord,   Clifton, 1829.

I lose not a moment in returning you my cordial thanks for your very kind bounty. I was just looking into my accounts to see what I could do in aid of the same case. My subscriptions are so numerous, that I have greatly exceeded my income this year. My schools alone cost me 240*l.* annually.

I thank you for your interesting letter. I wish you had mentioned the state of your health. May God long continue one of the ablest nursing fathers of our invaluable Church. My own health is far better than I could have expected at my great age (84). It has pleased my heavenly Father of his infinite mercy to grant me a long space for repentance of the past and preparation for the future

Mr. Huber of Geneva, who has been staying here, has had the goodness to translate many of my works into French May it please God to bless them. He sometimes works by feeble instruments, to show that the glory is all his own. I have lately received from Germany a copy of Cœlebs in that language, of which I cannot read one word.

I am bringing my affairs into a small compass. Among other things I have just sold the copyright of my too numerous volumes.

I should not have been guilty of all this egotism except to such a dear and honoured friend as yourself.

I have had a visit from dear Mr. Wilberforce, who is all life and spirit. He and you are, I think, my two oldest and best friends. Of my first set of contemporaries not one is left. I mean the Johnsons, the Burkes, the Beatties, the Reynolds's, the Porteus's, the Barringtons, &c. &c.

With my best respects to Mrs. Burgess,

I am, my dear Lord,

Your obliged and faithful

HANNAH MORE.

We could introduce various specimens of Mrs. H. More's correspondence with the Bishop, subsequent to the above; but from this time her letters became very brief, in consequence of the infirmities of great age. We cannot, however, withhold from our readers the following tribute which she pays to her old and revered friend, in connection with a description of the peculiar characteristics of Bishop Horsley's Sermons, sketched in the spirit of her best days, in a letter written many years before the date of the above, to the Rev. Lewis Way. "My taste is so—shall I say spoilt, or raised—by the old divinity, that a large proportion of the new does not gratify my palate. It has, however, been gratified, in a high degree, by Bishop Horsley's Sermons. They exhibit, in no ordinary degree, genius, profound thinking, originality, sagacity in penetrating and unfolding an obscure text, pellucid clearness in conveying it, general soundness of doctrine, deep learning displayed with better taste than in the old divines, not by loading the text, or crowding the margin, but by its results, in making his page more luminous and his exposition more scriptural. There are some faults arising from his naturally irascible temper and a want of spirituality—but I did not write for the purpose of eulogising Bishop Horsley. Our excellent living Bishop (St. David's) expressed as much pleasure as yourself at your rencontre, and was delighted at some curious book you lent him. He is indeed a Bishop of the old school, and is laboriously carrying on a work worthy of the best primitive prelates."

TO THE SAME.

My Lord,   Keswick, February 4. 1830.

I AM much obliged to you for your Charge, which I have read with profit as well as pleasure. The perusal has revived a wish which I felt (and I believe expressed) some years ago, that the Society for promoting Christian Knowledge would publish a select collection of such Charges, chronologically arranged. It would be historically, and also (we might hope) practically useful : and certainly such a selection might be made as would do honour to the Church of England. These are not times in which we should let the arms of our forefathers rust upon the wall.

I have materials for doing much, should it be God's will to grant me life, and leisure for employing them. My plans are to proceed, whenever I can, with the Vindiciæ, of which one volume is before the public ;—repelling the attacks both of Papist and Puritan, through the course of our Church history; and tracing the errors and practices of both to their causes and to their consequences. This I would follow up with Historical Sketches of the Monastic Orders; an arduous, but most important, as well as most interesting, undertaking, — for which I am well prepared.

Had all our Prelates deserved their elevation as well, and used it as worthily as the one whom I have now the honour of addressing, the Church would at this time have been in peace and safety, and the State would have been in no danger from within. I do not doubt of an eventual triumph; but there

may be much to suffer, and much to overcome before it be gained : the more cause, therefore, as your
Lordship well observes, is there for our best exertions.

I have the honour to remain,
My Lord Bishop,
With the greatest respect,
Your Lordship's obliged and obedient Servant,
ROBERT SOUTHEY.

TO THE REV. W. EVANSON.

DEAR SIR,   Salisbury, Feb. 11. 1830.
I AM here for a single day on business, and find
your very valuable volume of Goeze's Enlarged
Defence of the Complutensian Edition of the New
Testament, with which I am delighted and astonished:
delighted with the acquisition of such a work, which
I have long wished to see in English ; and astonished
at the persevering diligence which has accomplished
it ; pleased also with the manner in which it is made
accessible to the reader, by its Contents and Index.
I shall be most happy to undertake the expense of
printing it (Deo volente) before long.

I am printing here a letter addressed to the Bishop
of Norwich (occasioned by his Letter to the Popish
Bishops), in vindication of the opponents of the
Popery Bill from the charge of prejudice and bigotry,
intolerance and injustice. I have written it chiefly
for the purpose of re-asserting the principles on
which our opposition was founded, more fully and
argumentatively *ad hominem* than I could in any
other form. It is a friendly expostulation; for we

have been on friendly and intimate terms nearly
fifty years.

I am, dear Sir,
Yours very truly,
T. SARUM.

TO G. MARRIOTT, ESQ.

DEAR SIR,   Southampton, June 8 1830.
FOR the last ten days I have been confined to the
house by an obstinate sore throat, which did not
yield to medicinal remedies till the day before yesterday. In the mean time Bishop Ridley's " Fare-
well" and " Lamentation" have been read to me
more than once, to my great admiration of the truly
apostolical spirit of those little tracts. They have
reminded me much of St. Paul's Letters from Rome
during his imprisonment; and if it was not that St.
Paul was divinely inspired, and Bishop Ridley (must
I say?) not inspired, I should be almost inclined to
say, that the letters of Bishop Ridley (a prisoner in
London for Christ's sake) are not less edifying,
under present circumstances, and under any circumstances of privation or distress on account of
religion, than the letters of St. Paul, a prisoner at
Rome for the same Saviour's sake. I hesitated to
call Bishop Ridley *inspired*, in the usual sense of
the word, because I did not think that he wrote or
acted under any special revelation, as St. Paul did.
But I verily believe that he was supported by the
" grace of Christ," which is sufficient for all trials;
and enabled by it to dictate that which that grace
alone could have inspired, and bear what that alone
could have taught him to endure, not only with pa-

tience but with joy, not only with fortitude but with exultation; nay, with transport at the thoughts of the honour of suffering for Christ's sake, and for the true profession of the Gospel. I have been preparing a short Preface to these pieces, and a Table of Contents, which I have been hindered from completing by my engagements; at the same time I have been occupied in printing my anniversary discourse addressed to the Royal Society of Literature, and an Appendix to it on the Chronology of St. Paul's Second Epistle to Timothy, and his other Letters from Rome In page 75. of Ridley's "Lamentation" I perceive a defect in the Edition from which mine is printed, and which I did not anticipate; and that is an omission of some important references which have place in Fox's original copy.

I am, dear Sir,

Yours most sincerely,

T. Sarum.

TO THE LORD BISHOP OF SALISBURY.

My DEAR LORD,

Our dear invalid daughter has had a sad accident by a severe fall. It is hoped no permanent injury will be the consequence, but it must at least lead to a great protraction of her confinement and deprivations. I bless God that her spirit of cheerful patience is continued to her. He only knows how much of trial may be necessary to produce in us those dispositions without which we are not "partakers of the Divine nature," and therefore cannot be fitted for the divine presence, in earth or in heaven.

*   *   *   *   *   *

The following passage from Lucas's Sermons, vol.
ii. p. 134., will, I think, be much approved by your
Lordship. Vain are the highest attainments in
knowledge unless we " add to knowledge virtue,"
and to the illumination of the mind the *conversion*
of the heart, which completes the new creature. This
St. Peter truly calls " a participation of the divine
nature." 2 Pet. i. 2. The degree of prejudice
existing against the term *conversion* is, I fear, only
to be accounted for by some aversion from the duty
of seeking a change of heart. The old Adam in
us likes himself too well.

Horneck supplies many such passages as the above
from Lucas, and neither of them has ever been
thought Calvinistic.

I fear that my brother has not the book about
which your Lordship inquired, nor knows who has
it. He has not answered my inquiry. I told him
he need not, if his return would be (as the lawyers
say to a writ of execution when no goods are found)
Nihil. Adieu, my dear Lord.

I am, ever,
devotedly yours,
GEORGE MARRIOTT.

Sep 3. 1830

TO THE SAME.

MY DEAR LORD, London, March 22. 1831.
I THANK you for the judicious and seasonable remarks inserted in the Salisbury Journal. If every
·one would act in the spirit of those suggestions, our
supplications would rise up like incense, and might

F F

obtain that relief from our distresses which we look
for in vain from political changes : but we have
grossly misused the blessings bestowed on us by a
bountiful Providence, and must henceforth expect
to learn wisdom from experience of the bitter effects
of our ingratitude and folly.

Believe me, my dear Lord,

Most truly yours,

W. Cantuar.

TO THE SAME.

My Lord,   Keswick, April 12 1830.

If there be any work on Historical Evidence as
depending upon moral probability, and not upon
those ascertainable points on which deeds and dates
may be brought to bear, I am not acquainted with
it. We have, as in a court of law, to consider the
competence of the witness and his credibility, what
opportunities of knowledge he may have possessed,
if he be an original writer, or what authorities he
has followed when he treats of remote subjects, or of
times anterior to his own. Possibilities and proba-
bilities are then to be weighed ; how far the writer,
even with a fair intent, may have regarded the
things of which he wrote from an unfavourable
point of view ; and whether he had any specific purpose to serve, or cause to plead, which might induce
him, either deliberately or unconsciously, to give an
unfair statement. Thus the credit which we allow
to historical evidence must depend at last upon the
opinion which we form of the sincerity and discern-
ment of the witness. There can be no certain test ;
and this, where men are disputatious, must leave

many things infinitely disputable. Yet, on the whole, in most important points, methinks sufficient certainty may be attained by a judicious and equitable mind.

I ought to apologise for having thus needlessly stated considerations which must long have been familiar to your Lordship. But with regard to conflicting testimony, I may say something from experience. Frequently in my historical pursuits, and more especially when composing my History of Brazil, I have had the statements of opposite parties before me, and found them so contradictory, that there was evidently wilful falsehood on the one side. My rule was to give most credit to that where there was most right in the ground of the difference; and where I found both alike disregardful of truth, to frame the most probable statement that I could from both, referring the reader always to my authorities, and taking care never to present my own view of the matter as worth more than it was.

I have the honour to remain,

My Lord,

With sincere respect,

Your Lordship's obliged and obedient Servant,

ROBERT SOUTHEY.

TO THE SAME.

My Lord,   Liverpool, February 22. 1831.

I ANXIOUSLY desire to maintain my connexion with the Established Church; but after many inquiries and efforts, I find the obstacles in the way of my ordination *so numerous*, that I fear I shall be obliged to give it up, as not within my reach.

" My heart's desire and prayer to God is, that
Israel may be saved," and that I may be permitted
to prolcaim the glad tidings of a crucified Saviour to
the long-neglected and scattered sheep of the house
of Israel; but in order to this I find ordination *absolutely necessary*, for by conversing with them upon
the word of God I do but very little.

I should feel greatly obliged if your Lordship
would direct me by your counsel how I may be
enabled to do this great work as a minister of Christ,
and of the Church of my choice.

An opportunity presented itself of my receiving
ordination among the Moravians, but I shall not feel
satisfied in taking any such step till I hear from your
Lordship.

I am, &c. &c.

HENRY S. JOSEPH.

TO MR. H. S. JOSEPH.

SIR,   London, March 7. 1831.

On the important subject of your letter, I cannot
venture to *direct* you, or indeed to give you any
advice, but in conformity with the direction of St.
James, " If any of you lack wisdom, let him ask of
God, and it shall be given him. But let him ask in
faith, nothing wavering," and with St. John, " If we
ask any thing *according to his will*, he heareth us."
But before you ask the divine counsel, be sure that
your motives are purely spiritual. And then, if Providence clearly opens a way for you among any
sincere members of the Church of Christ, follow it
in a spirit of faith, devotedness, and self-denial.[*]

[*] Mr. Joseph was subsequently ordained in the Church of
England.

The Moravian Church is, I believe, a branch of the true Church of Christ.

I am Sir,

Your obedient Servant,

T. Sarum.

TO THE LORD BISHOP OF SALISBURY.

My Lord,   Keswick, May 16. 1830.

I am much obliged to your Lordship for your Anniversary Discourse, and have perused it with great satisfaction. The reasoning is, in my judgment, conclusive; and no reasonable person would require more evidence in a case where so much was hardly to be expected or hoped for.

Your Royal Society may do more for Literature than its elder Sister has ever done for Science. For invention has well been called "a solitary thing;" but there are great objects in literature which can only be accomplished by co-operative labour, and by the funds of a collected body.

I have the honour to remain,

My Lord,

Your Lordship's obliged and obedient Servant,

Robert Southey.

Extract of a Letter from the Bishop of Salisbury to a Friend in 1830.

" I have read the passage in question, and I think the author mistaken in his views of our existence after this life. I believe that when we die our future condition is fixed, and that we shall at once be in a state of happiness or misery.

F F 3

" The Redemption of man by Christ may very naturally be a subject of grateful contemplation in another life, for the very thought of Atonement must suggest the recollection of Sin propitiated and forgiven. But in this recollection there will not, I imagine, be any abatement of happiness, but rather a participation of the joys which Angels feel over the sinner that repenteth," &c. &c.

TO ALFRED CASWALL, ESQ.

My dear Nephew,   London, June 30. 1831.

I thank you for taking so early an opportunity of writing to me from Bonn. I am glad that you have seen M. Scholz, and that you are pleased with his reception of you. I possess (I believe) every thing that he has published, his Historia Textus, his Biblio-critical Travels, his German Translation of the New Testament, and the first volume of his *Greek* Testament. I wish you would ask him when we may expect the second volume; I wish you would also ask him if he can give me any information respecting the Greek MS. of the New Testament, which M. Harenburgius says was shown to Paulus Antonius at Venice, by a Greek of high authority. This is mentioned by M. Harenburgius in his Melitema de Pericopis Biblicis. The passage is as follows :*

" Ostendit Paulo Antonio Græcus auctoritatis non modicæ codicem Græcum Venetiis, in quo pericopa illa (1 John, v. 7.) legebatur."

---

* A Greek showed Paulus Antonius (at Venice) a Greek manuscript of no inconsiderable authority, which contained the passage, 1 John, v. 7.

We leave London this day for Salisbury. Your aunt unites in kind regards to you, with

Yours affectionately,

T. SARUM.

TO G. MARRIOTT, ESQ.

DEAR SIR, Palace, Salisbury, Feb. 23. 1832

IT is so long since I heard from you, that I cannot help being apprehensive lest the illness of yourself, or of some part of your family, has occasioned your silence. I am at present free from all my late winter maladies, and am endeavouring to keep so by the help of almost daily airings when the weather will let me. My seventy-sixth year seems rather too late to begin the system of cold water, which has been so beneficial to you and to Lord Teignmouth.

I have very lately become acquainted with a writer of the 17th century, who has a great deal of excellent theology and morality, John Smith of Queen's College, Cambridge. The volume which the Dean of Salisbury has lent me is entitled Discourses by John Smith, late of Queen's College, Cambridge, 1673. I am printing one of Arrian's Discourses of Epictetus in Greek, Latin, and English, which I think will interest you. I shall be glad to hear that you are all well.

Yours most sincerely,

T. SARUM.

TO J. S. HARFORD, ESQ.

DEAR SIR,   Palace, March 20. 1832.
I RETURN you many thanks for your very interesting and most seasonable little tract.* It is calculated to do most extensive good, and from the
account which you have given me of its great sale
it cannot fail to do so. I have lent to one of our
Canons the copy which you were so good as to send
me, and he has given an order to the bookseller
here to procure copies for sale and distribution.

I am impatient for the perusal of your translation
of the Agamemnon, and should be glad to receive
it by any early conveyance. With our united kind
regards to you and Mrs. Harford, believe me,
                    Your's most sincerely,
                              T. SARUM.

TO THE LORD BISHOP OF SALISBURY.

MY LORD,   Llangela, January 8. 1834.
BY a letter received from Mr. Harford, I am
informed of your Lordship's kindness in having
paid the amount of one year's income of the three
Scholarships, which you were so good as to express
your intention of founding at St. David's College,
and also of your Lordship's wishes respecting the
names they are respectively to bear, and the conditions on which they are to be bestowed. Having
been honoured on a former occasion by a commu-

* The tract referred to was a narrative of conversations
held with C. Davies and W. Clarke, two of the Bristol rioters,
some days before their execution in January 1832.

nication from your Lordship on this subject, I am
requested by Dr. Lewellin to express on behalf of
St. David's College the grateful sense with which
we receive this fresh mark of your kind favour
towards it, and also to assure your Lordship that it
shall be our earnest endeavour to appropriate these
benefactions in conformity with your commands.
Mr. Harford also informs us that it is your Lordship's intention to confer upon us an additional
obligation, by devoting a bequest of Mrs. H. More's
to a fourth prize, for the best examination in certain
subjects, which he has specified. It would be highly
gratifying to us, if your Lordship would allow us to
call at least one of the four Exhibitions by the name
of Burgess, as a memorial of your Lordship's unceasing regard and liberality. The College itself
will, we trust, long continue to record your exertions, to which it is, under Divine Providence, mainly
indebted for its existence. And we should be happy
if we might be permitted thus to testify our sense
of your continued kindness, when the termination
of your Lordship's official connexion with it had
destroyed the claim it might otherwise have retained
upon your patronage and support.

I have the honour to be,

My Lord,

Your Lordship's most obliged

and faithful Servant,

ALFRED OLLIVANT.

The above letter calls for a few particulars
explanatory of the facts adverted to in it, and of
the practical results of St. David's College. It
had been finally completed and opened for the

reception of students on the 1st of March, 1827,
and the experience of six years had realised, in
all leading particulars, the anticipations of its
founder. It had secured to the Diocese of St.
David's precisely what its peculiar circumstances,
as already detailed, required — a system of sound
education, and strict academical discipline, with a
limited scale of annual expense, the rate of which,
it may not be out of place to add, is now reduced
so as completely to meet the exigencies of the
southern part of the Principality. Already the
beneficial effects of the Institution were felt and appreciated in the superior character and attainments
of the Clergy who had been educated within its
walls ; still, however, some such means of rewarding merit were wanted as would tend to excite
among the students a generous emulation, and
prove a stimulus to superior proficiency. With this
view the able and respected Vice Principal of the
College, in the course of a letter which he published
in the Carmarthen Journal in the year 1833, in reply to the censures of an anonymous assailant of the
Collegiate system, expressed his conviction that great
benefits would result to the Institution, if a sum of
money were raised by subscription adequate to the
foundation of several Scholarships, to be given away,
like those at the Universities, to such as might pass
the best examination in certain specified subjects.
This letter caught the eye of the Bishop of Salisbury, and he lost no time in requesting Dr. Ollivant
to explain his views on the subject more in detail.
The consequence was, his entire approbation of the
plan, and his generous resolution to found four
Scholarships of the annual value of 10*l.* each on the

principle proposed. A small proportion of the funds
in support of them were derived from two bequests
left to the Bishop's disposal ; but the principal part
of the endowment was supplied by his own munificence. Two of these Scholarships are, by his own
direction, called " The Eldon Scholarships," in
honour of Lord Eldon. They are to be adjudged,
as also the third, severally, to three of the students,
natives of the Principality, who shall pass the best
examinations in Hebrew, the Classics, and the Welsh
language, and in the evidences of Christianity.
The fourth is open to all the members of the College, and is to be given for the best examination in
the history and contents of the Bible, and in the
evidences of Christianity,

The appeal of Dr. Ollivant was also generously
responded to in various other quarters, and the result
has been the establishment of no less than fourteen
Scholarships, five of 20*l.* per annum each, the others
of different values, but none under 10*l.* per annum.

The late Bishop Van Mildert was a generous contributor of 500*l.* to this fund.

The Principal and Professors have thus been supplied with the means of conferring appropriate distinctions and rewards on the more meritorious
students, who have been enabled in consequence to
obtain the advantage of such an education as the
College affords at a considerable reduction of expenditure.

The Bishop's correspondence furnishes manifold
proofs of the delight which he felt in liberally contributing to objects of charity and beneficence, both
public and private. In the course of the year 1828,
he made a donation of 500*l.* to the Clergy Orphan

School; and both at this and at other times he transmitted discreet and effectual aid, through his friend
the Archbishop of Dublin, to several converted
Roman Catholic Priests, placed by their change of
religion in a state of great destitution.

Among the latest of his many benevolent acts was
the building and endowment of a National School
at Laverstock, near Salisbury, and the erection of a
gallery in the Parish Church for the accommodation
of the children. The Incumbent had called upon
him in order to implore a small contribution in aid
of this good work, when the Bishop, after minutely
ascertaining the facts of the case, and the poverty
of the parish, delighted and surprised him by mu-
nificently taking upon himself the whole expense.

CHAP. XXXVI.

THE BISHOP'S LATTER DAYS.

THE old age of Bishop Burgess was the serene and
gentle sunset of a life directed to the noblest objects,
and influenced by high and holy motives. The
vigour of his intellect, and the energy of his application, were very little abated after he had reached
that period of life, the usual characteristics of which,
to use the forcible words of the Psalmist, are
" labour and sorrow." His temperate habits, the
placidity of his disposition, and his habitual admixture of active with sedentary pursuits, contributed
in no small degree to this immunity from the usual
infirmities of advanced age. On his library table,
to the close of his life, were sure to be found the
newest and most accredited works on Theology and

Biblical Criticism, both English and Latin, with the contents of which, in spite of his defect of vision, he made himself master to the full extent required by his own special objects of pursuit and research. Occasionally he was aided in this respect by his Chaplain, Dr. Radcliffe. Treatises of practical piety and devotion were no less sure to be within his reach; and in some of these his written notes attested the care and interest with which they had been perused. He amused himself with writing Latin verse to the last, and composed a few lines in this language, expressive of the devout tendency of his affections, within a month of his death. English poetry, which had been one of the delights of his youth, lost none of its charms for him after he grew old. To store his memory with its choicest beauties was a practice that never forsook him. Even as late as 1830, when he was in his seventy-second year, he made himself master in this way of the finest sonnets of Milton, and would challenge his niece, Miss Pinkerton, whom he had induced to do the same, to a frequent repetition of them. He also committed to memory at the same age whole chapters of the Bible.* Among the characteristics

* The following note pleasingly exemplifies the above interesting fact : —

To Miss Pinkerton.

My dear Niece, May, 1830
" I am glad to hear that your cold is better, and that you are going on so well with our scripture lessons. I have been obliged to content myself with learning the first chapter you refer to, perfectly by heart, and refreshing my memory occasionally with those that follow, so that I expect to be junior in the class when we meet again.
Yours affectionately,
T. Sarum.

of his mind, cheerfulness and hope continued predominant, for they were nourished by principles
which maintained their vigour and freshness to the
last. What was it to him that the shadows of
evening were gathering round him, and the day
of his mortal pilgrimage hastening to its close?
"He knew in whom he had believed," and "his hope
was full of immortality." He was fully aware of
his advancing infirmities, and of the gradual decay of
his physical powers; but the principal regret these
changes caused him was the consequent abridgment
of his powers of active usefulness, and his increasing
disqualification for discharging his Episcopal functions in the spirit of his more vigorous days. The
"Comforts of Old Age," written by his friend
(the friend, too, of every benevolent object) Sir
Thomas Bernard, was a book in which he took much
pleasure; and it will be seen by the following
tabular memoranda which he drew up of its leading
topics, with how much of self-application he had
perused it: —

Discomforts of Old Age	Comforts of Old Age.
1 It unfits for public life.	1 Literature and useful employment of time.
2 It is attended by infirmity of body	2 Reflection on the past.
3. It diminishes the power of animal enjoyment	3 Cheerful habits.
4 It is a state of anxiety on account of the approach of death	4. Cultivation of agreeable thoughts
	5 Restraint of vain desires. Ditto of vain anxieties.
	6 Prospects of Eternity Hope of Heaven.

At the end of this statement he adds, —"But none

of these things move me: neither count I my life dear unto myself, so that I might finish my course with joy." Acts, xx. 24. Such was the spirit in which the Bishop met the advances of age ; such the radiance which illumined his approach to the valley of the shadow of Death. Yet he had had to encounter not a few prejudices when he first settled in his new diocese. He was already in the decline of life when he was translated to Salisbury, a stranger to almost every one in the place, active and energetic in the discharge of his professional duties, and fond of exercising an unpretending hospitality, but having no taste for large parties, and often silent in them. While, therefore, he was loved and revered by all who had the privilege of his intimate acquaintance, and while the Clergy, in particular, bore witness to his uniform kindness and facility of access, those who only saw him casually, or in a formal manner, were apt to misconstrue the mixture of gravity and shyness in his address to strangers into coldness, and even into distance. Upon being questioned on literary or theological topics, he was easily drawn out, and his conversation became instructive, amusing, and animated ; but he had very little of the pleasant small-talk which makes up so much of the current coin of general society. He was quite aware of this deficiency, and would often, when listening to the conversation of ladies, tell them, with a smile, how much he would give for their power of running on so long upon agreeable nothings. But if causes like these did produce in some quarters misconceptions to his disadvantage, they were partial and temporary ; and long before he had reached the end of his career, esteem and veneration for his character pervaded the whole diocese. How much of courage and firmness of purpose was blended in his character with benignity and meekness, was proved in 1831, at the time of the Bristol riots, when so general an expectation prevailed at Salisbury of dangerous insurrectionary movements there also, and of the popular fury being blindly directed against the Church and the hierarchy, that the Bishop was advised, nay, strongly urged by many of the neighbouring gentry, who waited on him for the purpose, to quit the palace, for a time, for some securer residence. " No," he replied, energetically raising his hands; " this is my post of duty, and nothing shall induce me to abandon it."

It has been urged to his prejudice, that, owing to the absorption of his time in learned pursuits, he was an unpunctual correspondent. It would be too much to say that the charge is wholly without foundation ; but I am convinced, after much inquiry, that it has been most grossly exaggerated. The controversy about the disputed verse, and books in general, were his amusement, and were dismissed when business required his attention. Yet, it is very possible that frequent long absences from home upon visitation and confirmation tours, and sometimes defects of memory, may have often retarded his answers to important letters, and thus have given apparent ground for such a censure, but those who best knew the Bishop will attest, that neglect of this description was the exception, and not the habit of his life. The writer of these pages was among his frequent correspondents, and ever found him most punctual. The first thing done after breakfast at Salisbury was the reading and an-

swering of letters, both of which were duly entered
with his own hand in a book, specially kept for this
purpose.   Nothing else was attended to till this
occupation was finished.

Whenever the health of Mrs. Burgess induced
him to leave home for any length of time, he was in
the habit of fixing at a place sufficiently near to
Salisbury (it was generally Southampton) to allow
of his spending a day there in each week for the
transaction of business.

The Bishop's two nieces, the Miss Pinkertons,
were much his companions, and were treated by
him with an affection almost paternal.   The eldest,
whose Christian character had particularly endeared
her to him, was cut off, to his great grief, pre-
maturely, by consumption.   The younger, whose
sedulous attentions added greatly to his comfort,
was married in the year 1833 to the Rev. C. B.
Pearson, eldest son of Dr. Pearson, Dean of
Salisbury.   He eventually gave this gentleman the
valuable prebend of Fordington, on the understanding that, in the event of a renewal of the lease of the
estate of that name, he should augment the vicarage
of Fordington to 300*l*. per annum; an arrangement
which he had the happiness of effecting in the
Bishop's lifetime.   His infant son, born in 1834,
attracted much of the Bishop's notice and affection.
He delighted in having it brought to see him, and in
making his musical boxes play for its gratification.

The frequent intercourse which this family alliance
produced between himself and the Dean of Salisbury contributed in many ways to his advantage.

The Dean, whose influence, from office, and not
less from acknowledged ability and high character,

G G

was naturally great, often proved a kind and useful medium of communication between the Bishop and the members of the Chapter, and was anxious to manifest, by every attention in his power, the affectionate regard and esteem which he felt for his Diocesan.

Mr. Pearson rendered the Bishop much valuable assistance, by often acting as his amanuensis, and by reading to him works in the learned languages.

The impressions produced upon him by the intimate opportunities which he thus enjoyed of contemplating his character, are justly and feelingly depicted in the following extract from one of his letters.

" He was truly an object of my most unfeigned respect and veneration. His deeds of charity and active benevolence were known of all men, but his character in private, the '*vita interior hominis*' was neither generally known nor appreciated. He was a man of whom the race is just disappearing from the earth — one who resembled the ancient fathers of the Church in simplicity and holiness, in extensive learning and scholarship, as well as in the calm and meditative turn of his mind. The present day has called forth a different character among the heads of the Church. The busy, bustling, innovating spirit of the times seems to require men less firmly attached to ancient usages, less imbued with the learning and spirit of a recluse, more sharp-sighted and skilled in politics. I have a great respect and esteem for the present governors of the Church; but I must confess I turn from them to contemplate with the highest veneration the simple, straightforward, self-denying and holy course of the good Bishop of Salisbury.

After the intercourse with and knowledge of him which it has been my privilege to enjoy for the last four years, united to the impressions produced on my mind by his private books and papers, as to the course of his secret studies and devotions, and his high principles of public conduct, my conviction is, that if ever there was an upright and holy man, whose single aim and object was to 'exercise himself to have always a conscience void of offence both towards God and towards man,' it was he. I should not say all this to most people, lest it should seem the partial praise of a relative, but you will believe it to be the inward conviction of my heart; and I can truly comprehend the feeling which prompted Bishop Burnet to say with respect to his intercourse with Archbishop Leighton, 'For what I have seen and heard of him, I know that I shall have to give account to God in a most particular manner.'"

The Archdeacon of Sarum, the Rev. Francis Lear, who paid a feeling tribute to the Bishop's memory in an obituary sermon, depicts in the following expressive terms the temper and frame of his spirit:—

" The peace of which we have been speaking was largely vouchsafed to our late venerable Diocesan : he was one whose mind was stayed on God, and who was, according to the gracious promise in the text, kept by that God in perfect peace. He was emphatically a man of peace. I appeal to all who were in the habit of conversing with him, and who really knew his character, if I am not fully justified in using that term. There was something in his manner and appearance, nay, even in the very sound of his voice, which spoke of peace, all was calm and quiet around him and within him, the world, with

G G 2

its noise and restlessness, was ever shut out; he
heard of it only as we hear the roar of the stormy
ocean, borne to us by the wind from afar ; he had
no heart for its turmoils, no hand in its schemes,
and seldom turned so much as a look towards its
commotions. The same stillness prevailed in his
dwelling which reigned in the mind of its owner :
his was a calm which seemed to spread itself from
his own heart to the hearts of those with whom he
held converse. I do not think that the most ruffled
spirit could have remained in his presence without
being tranquillised; there was a serenity in his manner which would have acted as oil on the troubled
waters : all that was disturbed and violent would,
if brought in contact with one so placid, have died
away. There is a peace which the world giveth,
and which they that are of the world enjoy ; there
is a peace which a naturally placid temper gives ;
and there is a peace which arises from mere outward prosperity. Sadly indeed do they mistake,
and awfully will they be deceived, who suppose that
a state of mind so low, so earthly, and so unspiritual
will bring a man peace at the last ! But how different was that peace which he of whom I speak
enjoyed ! It sprang from far other sources, it rested
on quite another foundation, it had respect to a far
other recompense; it had, as I firmly believe, the
Holy Spirit for its author, Christ for its rock, and
Heaven for its end."

During the winter of 1835, the Bishop solaced
some of his leisure hours by adding a few additional
stanzas to Bishop Ken's well-known evening hymn—

" Glory to Thee, my God, this night," &c.

and printed some copies of them for distribution
among friends. These octogenarian verses, though
not of a nature to endure the severity of morose
criticism, forcibly illustrate the simplicity and fervour of his devout affections. For instance, after
expressing the most entire resignation to the Divine
Will, whether for life or for death, and paraphrasing
these words of St. Paul — " To depart and to be
with Christ is far better " — he pursues the train of
thought as follows : —

TO DIE, AND WITH THE LORD TO BE,

" With John, and James, and holy Paul,
    And dearest friends long gone, and all
    The spirits of just men perfect made,
    Midst purest joys that never fade

" Come then the maladies that may
    Close, at thy bidding, life's short day,
    And find me so prepared t' obey
    The call, so prompt to watch and pray ;

" That, thankful for my sins forgiven,
    The Saviour's love, the hope of Heaven,
    I may my final rest attain,
    From sorrow free, and sin and pain,
    The Christian's everlasting gain "

" Oh, may my soul on thee repose," &c. &c.*

The following letter will be read with interest in
connexion with the above devout effusions.

* The succeeding extract will show how much the Bishop's
heavenly anticipations were in unison with those of the sainted
George Herbert, as expressed to a friend not long before his
death. " I now look back upon the pleasures of my life past,
and see the content I have taken in beauty, in wit, in music,
and pleasant conversation, is now all passed by me like a dream,
or as a shadow that returns not, and is all become dead to me,
or I to it, and I see that as my father and generation have
done before me, so I also shall now suddenly (with Job) make

G G 3

TO THE LORD BISHOP OF SALISBURY.

MY DEAR LORD,   · Lambeth, February 13 1835

I RECEIVED your kind letter, and your two little
inclosures in prose and verse, not indeed on New
Year's Day (as you intended), but on the day preceding my entrance on my seventieth year, a time
of life, when those who have lived to any useful
purpose have learned fully to appreciate the sentiments so feelingly expressed in Bishop Ken's original hymn, and the additions which you have made
in the same spirit of pious devotion.

The prose extract is a valuable portion of a very
excellent book, great part of which I read in the
intervals of leisure which I could command in the
autumn.

With many thanks for your interesting present,
and kind recollection of me, and hoping for the

---

my bed also in the dark; and I praise God I am prepared for
it; and I praise Him that I am not to learn patience now I
stand in such need of it; and that I have practised mortification, and endeavoured to die daily, that I might not die eternally; and my hope is that I shall shortly leave this valley of
tears, and be free from all fevers and pain; and, which will be
a more happy condition, I shall be free from sin, and all the
temptations and anxieties that attend it; and this being past,
I shall dwell in the New Jerusalem; dwell there with men
made perfect; dwell where these eyes shall see my Master and
Saviour Jesus; and with him see my dear mother, and all my
relations and friends. But I must die, or not come to that
happy state. And this is my content that I am going daily
towards it, and that every day which I have lived hath taken
a part of my appointed time from me; and that I shall live the
less time, for having lived this and the day past."— WALTON's
Life of Herbert

benefit of your prayers at this critical juncture of the affairs of our Church,

I remain, my dear Lord,
Very faithfully yours,
W. CANTUAR.

TO THE SAME.

MY DEAR LORD, Pall-Mall, March 5.

I RETURN you my grateful thanks for your Lordship's letter and promise of a copy of the Appendix to Sir A. Carlisle's essay. It will be doubly valuable to me as one fast approaching to the appointed age of man, and more particularly as recommended by your Lordship, who, while you advance to that better country to which you allude in your motto, still continue to point out to your followers the way that leads to peace and happiness. If I might be allowed to re-translate your Lordship's lines sent to me on a former occasion, I would say —

> Sit Veritatis fas mihi lumine
> Lenire curas, corpore et in gravi
> Mulcere me fessum senemque,
> Spe placidâ melioris ævi.

I am, my dear Lord,
Yours very faithfully,
W. HEBERDEN.

TO THE REV. W. DANSEY.

DEAR SIR, Palace, 1835

YOUR precious volume of the poems of Flaminius came safe to hand. The fourteen accompanying pages of the fifth part of your Rural

Deanery Lucubrations are also very acceptable.
I am preparing to send to the Rural Deans who
have been appointed since my incumbency in this
See, an officially sealed appointment. I may, perhaps, send you one by to-morrow's post, to which
the attention which you have lately paid to this
subject, may probably suggest some additions as to
the Decanal duties.

Yours very faithfully,
T. SARUM.

TO THE SAME.

DEAR SIR,   Christ Church, January, 20. 1835

YOUR approbation of my portion of an Evening
Hymn induces me to think that you will not tire of
the subject if I send you an addition to it. Instead
therefore of the line,

" The Christian's everlasting gain,"

I add the following —

> That thus, enlarged from earth's gross clay,
> My soul in pure existence may
> Join with the Church of God above
> In hymns of gratitude and love,
> To God, the Author of all good,
> And Him, who bought us with his blood,
> And the Holy Spirit of both in one,
> In homage round th' Eternal Throne.

I believe that death to a Christian, who dies in
penitence and faith, is an everlasting gain, by its
freeing him from pain, sorrow, and sin; but it is
much more. And what more, I have *alluded* to on
the authority of Scripture rather than expressed.

If you have a copy of Bishop Butler's Sermons,
I wish you to read his second sermon on Human

Nature, because to that sermon, what I have to say on the use of verbal criticism in the investigation of moral truth has a reference.

I am, dear Sir,
Yours very faithfully,
T. SARUM.

TO THE SAME.

DEAR SIR, Palace, Salisbury, July 27. 1835.

IN looking over the list of letters sent last week to the rural deans to invite them to our Church Union Meeting on the 11th of August, I am apprehensive that you may not have received such a letter from me. If this should be a duplicate, it affords me an opportunity of sending you a copy of a hymn much used in the Scotch Church, not unworthy of Flaminius, or your friend Barnard * ; and

* The hymn was as follows. —

The hour of my departure's come,
I hear the voice that calls me home ;
At last, O Lord ! let trouble cease,
And let thy servant die in peace.

The race appointed I have run,
The combat's o'er, the prize is won ;
And now my witness is on high,
And now my record's in the sky.

Not in my innocence I trust,
I bow before Thee in the dust ;
And through my Saviour's blood alone
I look for mercy at thy throne.

† It was for sinners such as me
Thou diedst upon th' accursed tree,
And every groan thou utter'dst there
Embalms a contrite sinner's prayer.

† This stanza was added by Miss Catherine Fanshawe in her last illness.

at the same time of adding that I am as comfortably convalescent as could be expected after my late
illness at Warminster and at my time of life.

I think I have before informed you that the
Dean will preach on the day of our Church Union
Meeting.

                    I am, dear Sir,
                         Yours very faithfully,
                                   T. SARUM.

TO THE LORD BISHOP OF SALISBURY.

                         King's College, Cambridge,
MY LORD,   March 19. 1835.

I FEEL extremely indebted to your Lordship for
your little poetical present, to every word of which
my heart responds.   I am myself *dying* daily ; and
I find that to be the best and happiest mode of
living.   Why should we not be taking Pisgah views
of the promised land, and tuning our harps that we
may be ready at any moment to join the heavenly
choir in their songs of praise to " Him, who hath
loved us, and washed us from our sins in his own

— — —

> I leave the world without a tear,
> Save for the friends I hold so dear ;
> To heal their sorrows, Lord, descend,
> And to the friendless prove a friend.
>
> I come, I come, at thy command,
> I give my spirit to thy hand ;
> Stretch forth thine everlasting arms,
> And shield me in the last alarms
>
> The hour of my departure's come ;
> I hear the voice that calls me home ,
> Now, O my God ! let trouble cease,
> Now let thy servant die in peace

blood ? " or, rather, I would say, to Him who loveth and washeth us from our sins. The Psalmist has strongly suggested this distinction, in calling upon all that is within him to adore and magnify his God for *present* and *existing* blessings; "*forgiveth, healeth, redeemeth, crowneth, satisfieth,*" and if we be in a right frame of mind, we shall receive *all* God's dispensations in the same way, tasting nothing but love even in his chastisements. The words your Lordship quotes from Mrs. Hannah More's Memoirs, as having been used by her sister Martha in her last illness, — '' I love whatever comes from God, I love my sufferings," — struck me also. Is not this, indeed, the proper disposition to be exercised in the hour of trial. St. Paul (What ? was *resigned ?* No :) *took pleasure* (εὐδοκῶ) in trials of every description : he had scarcely the word *resignation* in his vocabulary ; and we also according to the grace given to us, should almost banish that word, except in very grievous trials indeed, and substitute for it the Apostle's εὐδοκῶ. It is a joy to me, my Lord, to see that this is the happy frame of mind which you enjoy under the infirmities of age, when the grasshopper may be a burthen to *the body ;* but tribulation itself is an occasion of nothing but joy to *the soul.* If only we believe that our very hairs are all numbered, and the minutest occurrences are ordered by Infinite Wisdom for our good, we neither have, nor can have, any thing but what should be to us a source of joy.

At this time last year, this was my blessed experience on what was thought by all to be the bed of death : and I am anxious so to improve my few re-

maining hours, that, when the closing scene shall
actually arrive, I may be thus highly favoured again,
and have an abundant entrance ministered unto me
into the kingdom of our Lord and Saviour Jesus
Christ.

Since my restoration to health, circumstances of
more than ordinary importance have engaged my
attention. I have been called to dispose of no less
than six livings, in all of which I have placed
Ministers, without reference to any thing but their
peculiar fitness for the place they are sent to occupy.
This is the great reform wanted in our Church;
and if generally carried into effect by all who have
patronage in the Church, it would supersede all
occasion for any further reform. If it did not stop
the mouths of Dissenters, it would diminish their
numbers, and effectually prevent their increase.

At our last Jews' Auxiliary Society, of which
your Lordship is the president, I dropped a few
hints which produced a great effect amongst Ministers, as well as the Undergraduates; and as my
views are both peculiar and important, I take the
liberty of transmitting a paper to you containing
them. Religion is understood by many in its rise
and progress in the soul, but by very few in its more
perfect state. Even the Apostles themselves, for
six years after the day of Pentecost, did not see
their duty towards the Gentiles; and so it is even
with good and pious Ministers at this day in reference to the Jews: and if the contents of my paper
be duly considered, I cannot but hope that many of
our brethren, and even fathers in the ministry, will
exclaim, " Then hath God appointed ME to seek the
salvation of the Jews, and I am shamefully remiss

if I do not exert my talents and my energies for the promotion of it.".

I am, my Lord,

Your Lordship's most obliged and

obedient Servant,

C. SIMEON.

TO THE SAME.

King's College, Cambridge,
April 4. 1835.

MY LORD, MY DEAR LORD,

I AM this moment returned from the table of the Lord, and think I am performing an acceptable service to my Divine Master in returning a few lines to your Lordship, in answer to the letter which I received from you this morning. You notice my observation relative to the word "resignation." I love the high tone of Christian morals. " Rejoice evermore: in *every* thing *give thanks :* for THIS is the will of God in Christ Jesus concerning you." I see no exception here : nor would I make any in my own experience. I read that "*all* the ways of the Lord are mercy and truth unto such as keep his covenant and his testimonies." But what is *truth ?* Is it not an accomplishment of a promise ? Shall I be RESIGNED then to a *mercy* coming *in this way ?* I pray daily, " Thy will be done on earth as it is done in heaven." And if *actively,* why not *passively* also ? I do not read of the 'Apostles being RESIGNED to their imprisonment and beating ; or of Paul and Silas being RESIGNED to their stripes, and feet in the stocks. The former " rejoiced that they were counted worthy to suffer ; " and the latter " sang praises to

God at midnight." I grant that the *occasion* of their sufferings gave an elevation to their minds; but sufferings of whatever kind are, in fact, sent and apportioned by God himself, without whom not a sparrow falls to the ground: and our privilege under them is to say, "The cup which *my Father* hath given me, shall I not drink it?" Shall I not then be thankful for it, under a full assurance, that it is amongst the "*all* things that are to work together for my good?" The great secret is, to have it well settled in our minds what our *desert* is; nothing will appear heavy then. On the contrary, every thing which is sent to keep us from our *desert*, will be welcomed as a blessing in disguise.

But even this is *low ground*. It is our privilege to soar above all this. I have been preaching on those words (Isaiah, xliii. 4.) "Since thou wast precious in my sight, thou art honourable, and I have loved thee;" and I ask, Were the Jews "precious, and honourable, and loved" above all the people upon earth, and are Christians less so? If they were so blessed as having been redeemed from temporal bondage, am not I as redeemed by the blood of God's only dear Son? Am I then precious in his sight, and shall not he be so in mine? Am I "honourable and beloved" in his estimation? what then shall I quarrel with, or complain of, that comes from him? If you want to see my *desert*, see the two last verses of the 42d chapter; and if you want to see the extent of God's mercy, see the first three verses of the 43d chapter; and then if you want to see what kind of *resignation* befits us, see my text; and then be as querulous under any trials, or if you please, as re-

signed, as the remembrance of such mercies will
admit of.

Now, my Lord, you will forgive the fulness of my
heart, and pardon the expression of it. It is your
own kindness and condescension that embolden me
thus to divulge the secrets of my heart; and the
rather, because I feel assured that there is a responsive chord in your heart, that will vibrate to the
touch. Your own expression, that " we are bought
with a price," shows that we should be equally ready
to glorify our God either by life or death, both the
one and the other of which are to be numbered
amongst our treasures. " All things are yours,
whether life or death, if ye be Christ's." This, my
Lord, it is our privilege to feel; and I hope that
every day which shall be added to your Lordship's
life will bring you to a richer enjoyment of it.

And now let me thank your Lordship for the kind
present which you did me the honour to send me
about a week ago, and to which you have added
the last page by this day's post. I am quite of your
Lordship's opinion, that " the Gentiles being a law
unto themselves," is only as distinguishing them
from those who had a law revealed to them: and
whilst I do not enter much into the *vexata* question
of innate ideas, I feel assured that every one has a
sense of right and wrong operating in accordance
with the light that has been vouchsafed to him; and
that every one is bound to get his mind enlightened
in order that that consciousness may aid him in
fleeing from evil and in doing good. To us who
enjoy the full light of the Gospel, this divine principle is a source of the deepest humiliation and of
the sublimest joy. I have a consciousness that I

ought to lie at the foot of the Cross, and I have a consciousness that I do so. I have a consciousness that I perform no duty aright; but I have a consciousness that God hears my sighs, and treasures up my tears : and taking this consciousness in connection with God's promises, I rejoice in hope of the glory of God.

With many thanks to your Lordship for your condescending kindness towards me,

I remain, my dear Lord,

Most truly yours,

C. SIMEON.

TO THE REV. C. B. PEARSON.

DEAR NEPHEW,   April 12. 1835.

I WAS glad to receive from you, a good account of my niece's health, and to hear that your present situation has proved beneficial to her.

I yesterday finished the labour of examination of candidates, who are to be ordained to-morrow. If I should live to this time next year, I shall probably devolve the greater part of the examination on the archdeacon, after having been personally engaged in it just half a century. I became Bishop Barrington's chaplain early in 1785.

With my best wishes for your and your wife's health,

I am, yours affectionately,

T. SARUM.

TO THE LORD BISHOP OF SALISBURY.

MY LORD,

AT your Lordship's advanced period of life, the wonder is, that you should still retain such powers of mind and body. But to you who are looking simply, as the wounded Israelites to the brazen serpent, no change can come amiss. When it is said of our blessed Lord, that he came to seek and to save that which was lost, we want nothing more. Out of the word "lost," we can both of us spell our names with more satisfaction, than if our respective names had been there. We might in this latter case have doubted, whether we were the individuals intended; but in the word as it now stands, we can have no more doubt than of our own existence. Blessed prospect for those who feel their lost state by nature!

Through mercy I am singularly strong at this time, and am preaching to very large audiences three times every week. I wish to work while it is day. The night is very shortly coming, when I shall cease to work; but when I shall hope to enter on a bright and everlasting day.

I am, my dear Lord,
Your devoted Servant,
C. SIMEON.

King's Coll, August 20. 1835.

CHAP. XXXVII.

THE BISHOP'S SEIZURE AT WARMINSTER. — THE AUTHOR'S
LAST INTERVIEW WITH HIM.

On the 16th of June, 1835, the Bishop held a confirmation in the parish church of Warminster. He slept the preceding night at the house of the Rev. Mr. Dalby, a clergyman high in his regard and esteem, whom he had himself appointed to the vicarage. In the course of the service, while discharging the functions of his sacred office, the Bishop suddenly sunk down, from a slight attack of apoplexy, in a state of insensibility, at the communion table. Through the prompt assistance of a medical gentleman present, who bled him in the arm, he was quickly restored to consciousness, and conveyed back in a sedan chair to the vicarage, where he received the most considerate attentions from his kind host and hostess. He was well enough to return to Salisbury the next day; and amended so rapidly, that on the 28th of the month his thanks were publicly offered in the usual form in the Cathedral, and he was soon after able to enjoy society, and partially to resume his former avocations.

Before the close of the month I spent some days with him, and found him composed, serene, and cheerful. His recent seizure, however, had fixed a strong conviction on his mind, that the term of his mortal pilgrimage could not be distant, and that he had received a merciful warning to make ready for the final summons. The bent of his thoughts and meditations corresponded with these impressions. He talked in his usual pleasant way upon literary topics, but seemed desirous of directing the current of thought to objects of higher interest. The beatific vision of Christ in a future state was a subject he had in past days delighted to converse upon with any intimate friend, and he was now humbly rejoicing in its anticipation. " I receive," he said, " my recent illness as an intimation from the great Head of the Church that my day of active service is almost closed. It is a pleasing reflection to me that it was in the act of prayer I sunk down at Warminster. " He then added, that his thoughts at the time were much in unison with a passage that he admired in one of the hymns of Marcus Flaminius, translated by the Rev. W. Barnard. He pointed it out to me as follows : —

Blessed Jesus — rescue me :
Thou alone canst set me free,
Loose the prison-house of clay,
Bear me to the realms of day,
Teach my ransom'd soul to sing
Glory to th' Eternal King,
Glory to the Blessed Son,
And the Spirit — Three in One.

He then requested me to read him the same passage, together with a few additional lines, in the Latin original.

Jesu benigne subveni,
Tuamque dextram porrige.
Tu morte, mortuum, Tuâ
Olim evocasti ex inferis ;
Nunc vitâ me vivum tuâ
Perire ne rursum sinas.
Humana fae spernam omnia,
Nudumque te nudus sequar ;

Et ponderosi corporis
Me solvi tandem nexibus:
Ut pura mens et integra
Ævo potita Cœlitûm,
Te sanctum et optimum Patrem
Et Sempiternum Spiritum
Laudare nunquam desinat.

The poems of Flaminius have been alluded to in a preceding chapter. The Bishop greatly admired them, and, as their author's history is little known, and the facts are interesting, we subjoin the following particulars His family name was Zarrabini; that of Flaminius was assumed. He was born at Imola A. D. 1498, was educated with the utmost care by a pious and learned father, and displayed even in early youth indications of genius, which fixed on him the admiring attention of some of the greatest men of that golden age of modern literature.

He pursued his studies at the University of Bologna, and after some years spent in Rome, attached himself to Mattheo Giberti, Bishop of Verona ; at which place, and at Padua, he spent several happy years, dividing his time between his patron's palace and a delightful villa which he gave him on the lake of Garda. Here he devoted himself to the study of the Greek philosophy, and to the composition of those beautiful Latin poems which were the admiration of his contemporaries, and which still continue to be read with much interest. Tiraboschi speaks of him thus : — "I am now treating of the sweetest, the most amiable, the most modest of all the Latin poets of that age, that is, of Marc Antonio Flaminio, a name not less dear to virtue than to the muses. He inspired all who knew him with equal sentiments of admiration and tenderness."*

The villa on the lake of Garda was his beloved home; but though his tastes were of the simplest kind, and his habits temperate, he suffered severely from a weak and debilitated stomach, and was forced to travel in 1538 to the South of Italy in pursuit of health. Wherever he went, his literary acquirements and amiable manners procured him friends. At Naples he became acquainted with the Spanish reformer, Valdez, and with others who were inclined to the Protestant communion.

His own mind was soon deeply interested in the questions at issue between the two churches, and emancipated itself, in a great degree, from the shackles of popery. The Reformers indeed claim him as their own, but as he lived and died in the communion of the Church of Rome, he can only, with propriety, be classed with such men as Erasmus, who, whatever might be their restraining motives, were almost but not altogether Protestants. Possibly he had not been able to make up his mind on all the various points which enter into the controversy. He was a beautiful example of genius clothed with humility, and walking in the paths of purity and peace. Of his Latin poetry Roscoe has observed, that it has the simplicity and tenderness of Catullus, without his licentiousness. Often, indeed, he strikes the lyre to sacred themes, and celebrates

---

* Io parlo del più dolce, del più amabile, del più modesto fra tutti i poeti Latini di questo secolo, cioè di Marcantonio Flaminio, nome caro alla virtù non meno che alle muse, e che in tutti color che il conobbero destò sentimenti di ammirazione al pari che di tenerezza. — *Tiraboschi*, lib. iii. c. 31.

in lofty numbers the praises of the Saviour of men, and the wonders of redeeming love.

It was natural that such an author should be a favourite with Bishop Burgess, and he felt pecularly obliged to the Rev. W. Dansey, the learned Vicar of Donhead St. Andrews, near Shaftesbury, for procuring, at no small pains, a copy of the Latin poems of Flaminius for him, and also an elegant paraphrase of many of them, executed by the late Rev. E. W. Barnard, and edited by Archdeacon Wrangham.

As the Bishop appeared to me unequal to the fatigues of business, I strongly urged him, in the course of our conversation, to employ a secretary for his correspondence, telling him that I felt persuaded it would tend to prolong his life. " I am not at all anxious," he replied, " for prolonged life ; I trust I am willing to resign it whenever God may please. I have long been making this my aim. The best state of existence here below is dashed with much sorrow." The text, Heb. iv. 15., " We have not an high priest who cannot be touched with the feeling of our infirmities," being repeated to him, as one pregnant with consolation, " Yes," he replied ; " but the most sustaining words to me are these : ' Being justified by faith, we have peace with God.'" Rom. v. 1. "It is obvious," he added, " that 'peace with God' is the result of a true faith, and hence it follows that justifying faith is something far beyond the mere assent of the understanding to Divine testimony. The peace spoken of is the result of faith in the atonement of Christ. When Bishop Bull," he went on to say, " was in his last moments, his son-in-law, with a view of administering to his comfort,

reminded him of the good he had done by his life
and writings, and of his various exertions in the
cause of religion; 'My only hope,' replied the Bishop,
'is in the mercies of God through the merits of
Christ.'" Then addressing me, he added, " In this
sentiment I entirely accord."* We next conversed a little upon public affairs, and in particular
upon the attempts which had recently been made
by some of the Dissenting Sects to excite bitter feelings of hostility against the Established Church. The
very different spirit, or rather the cordial respect and
attachment manifested towards it, at this critical
juncture, by the Wesleyan Methodists, called forth
his marked commendation, and he spoke with much
esteem of that community of Christians — "What a
different front should we present as a Church to our
opponents," he observed, "were it not for internal
divisions among ourselves — minor differences of
opinion among good men, upon what may be termed
open questions, ought not to separate them from
each other, or to provoke party-feeling. Division
in the Church makes us a rope of sand."

* Not only this declaration, but the whole tenor of the
Bishop's sentiments, as expressed in these pages, proves how
entirely he rested on the merits of Christ as the sole ground of
our justification We are the more particular in drawing attention to this point, because we are aware, that though from
first to last he never built on any other foundation, there are
statements in some of his printed works which have been censured as defective with respect to this vitally important doctrine.
The fact is, he felt jealous lest the term justified by faith *only*,
should be so construed as in any degree to impair the obligation
to a life of Christian holiness. It was, therefore, his object, on
the one hand, to give prominence to the great doctrines of
Grace, and, on the other, to the awful certainty of human responsibility , but in attempting to define their respective bearings, and mutual dependencies, he was not always free from
ambiguity or contradiction.

After further remarks upon this and upon some other topics of public interest, he again adverted to his own precarious condition, and spoke of the wisdom and the happiness of making preparation for death the object of our years of health and strength. "What a reproach," said he, "to the inconsideration of Christians as to the consequences of death, is that fine saying of a Pagan, 'Tota philosophorum vita commentatio mortis est.'" * Religion, he feared, was too generally supposed to consist in little more than a decent compliance with established forms, instead of being *that* which is the end and aim of all devotional forms, — the grateful homage of a renewed heart, the worshipping of God in spirit and in truth.

He then referred to a sermon of Scougal's, published by Bishop Jebb, upon that text, "Many shall seek to enter in, and shall not be able;" adding, "It is one of the most awful that I know."

This led him to touch upon the difficulties which any one, who is bent upon pursuing a steadfast course of consistent piety, must be prepared to encounter in the world, not only from a multitude of contrary attractions and temptations, but also from the shafts of calumny and ridicule. Not only religious laymen, but even clergymen, he observed, were often exposed to this trial. He had known many most laborious and useful clergymen stigmatised by reproachful appellations, chiefly, he believed, because they were more zealous and earnest in their preaching, and in

* The whole life of philosophers is a contemplation of death, a sentiment in Cicero's Tusculan Disputations, lib. 1. c. 30, but borrowed, like many other of his noblest thoughts, from Plato.

discharging their pastoral duties, than some of their neighbours.

"Then," added he, "there are excellent observances which have been cast off because they are thought to savour of popery; fasting is one of them, and another is a greater attention to discipline in our Colleges and Halls."

He afterwards turned the conversation on the best devotional writers, and expressed great delight in a little work of Fenelon's, entitled "Reflections for every Day in the Week."

"It was happy," he observed, "for Fenelon, as a Christian, that adverse circumstances banished him from the gay circles of Paris to the duties and seclusion of his diocese. He writes like one who well knew how and where true peace is to be found."

In allusion to his growing infirmities, he said, that, fearing the time had arrived when he was become incapable of efficiently discharging the important duties of his office, he had not long since requested permission to resign his bishopric, but had been informed, in reply, that a resignation of this description was deemed, for many reasons, inadmissible.

It gave me much pleasure to hear from him that it was his intention to leave his valuable library, consisting of 10,000 volumes, to St. David's College, Lampeter; and also a sum of money to enable the College to enlarge their present library for the reception of so great an addition. This bequest was made by a codicil to his will, which he showed me. After his death it could no where be found, but Mrs. Burgess, with prompt affection, completed his liberal intentions, by making an immediate payment of the sum that had been specified. The proposed enlargement has since been accomplished in a manner very creditable to the good taste of the members of that learned body, who are now in possession of a library which does honour to the munificent spirit of their founder.

Such in substance, and in some parts in his very words, was one of the last conversations I had the privilege of holding with my revered friend. We never again met, though I frequently had the pleasure of hearing from him. In the course of my visit he communicated to me many of the particulars of his early life recorded in this volume. Like the thread of Ariadne, they have guided me through what would otherwise have proved an inextricable labyrinth.

CHAP. XXXVIII.

THE BISHOP'S LETTER TO LORD MELBOURNE. — LETTERS TO DR. SCHOLTZ. — HIS LAST ILLNESS AND DEATH. — EULOGISTIC TRIBUTES TO HIS MEMORY FROM THE BISHOP AND DEAN OF SALISBURY, AND FROM ARCHDEACON BERENS.

1836 to 1837.

In the autumn of 1835 the Bishop and his family spent some months at Lyme, in Dorsetshire, where I received from' him the following letter in reply to some queries of mine respecting his college life: —

DEAR SIR,   Lyme, August, 29. 1835

YOUR very kind letter deserved an earlier answer. The state of my health is ($\chi\alpha\rho\iota\varsigma$ $\tau\omega$ $\Theta\epsilon\omega$) considerably better than when I had last the pleasure of seeing you at Salisbury. I am not however so firm on foot, as I was the day before my illness at Warminster. But I am thankful for my freedom from pain, and from any apparent symptoms of relapse. My health indeed is, perhaps, quite as good is usual at my time of life, or that is wanted for my present duties, for these duties I consider as very much circumscribed by the *providential discharge* (as I am accustomed to call it), from the more active engagements of my station which I received by the merciful visitation, which occurred at Warminster.

I was ordained in the year 1782 by the Bishop of Winchester. My title was a scholarship at Corpus C. C. Oxford. My excellent friend Mr. Tyrwhitt persuaded me to continue my classical studies at the University after I took my bachelor's degree, and his generous friendship enabled me to do so by an annual donation, equivalent to what I might have obtained from a curacy, till I was engaged in the office of college tutor, which more than supplied all my wants.

Mrs. Burgess's health was a good deal affected by the late hot weather, but I am happy to say she is now much better. I have hardly room to say that,

I am, dear Sir,

Your's most sincerely,

T. SARUM.

Towards the beginning of winter he returned to Salisbury, in order to hold an ordination, and accomplished the journey without much fatigue; but the trembling hand-writing of his letters indicated the decay of his physical powers, and various expressions in them proved how fully he was himself conscious of the fact. Under these circumstances, great was my surprise at receiving from him, in the early part of the spring of 1836, a printed letter, addressed to Lord Melbourne, deprecating in vigorous and glowing language, and with great argumentative force, an assertion made by that noble Lord in his speech on moving the second reading of the Irish Church Bill, to this effect, " that the doctrines of the Roman Catholic Church are fundamentally the same with those of the Church of England."

This letter is comprised in so brief a compass, and is so remarkable a production, as the able and spirited remonstrance of an octogenarian Bishop, writing from the verge of the tomb to the Prime Minister of the day, that our readers will not, we think, deem it out of place in the Appendix to this volume.*

It is due to Lord Melbourne to add, that he returned a very courteous and respectful answer to this letter, but waved any attempt to grapple with its arguments.

In the course of 1836, the Bishop addressed three printed letters successively to Dr. Scholtz, the learned editor of an elaborate and critical edition of the Greek Testament, in which he pointed out some remarkable contradictions between certain passages in the Prolegomena to that work, and the statements of his note on 1 John, v. 7., respecting the age and date of the Greek MSS. containing the disputed verse.

* See Article III in the Appendix

Copies of these letters the Bishop circulated among most of his learned correspondents; and the replies of some of them (among which was that of his old and much valued friend Dr. Routh) proved that they concurred with him in the justice of his criticisms. The Rev. Mr Faber thus notices the Bishop's unabated mental vigour and energy : —

" Though I do not feel myself by any means at home in the general merits of the question, it excites my admiration, mingled with much satisfaction, that in despite of the severe affliction of your sight, you should still be able to follow these studies with all the vigour and freshness of youth."

It has been already stated, that up to a very recent period, the only MS. known to contain the disputed verse was that entitled the Montfort. By the researches of Dr. Scholtz, it has been discovered in two more, the Neapolitan and Ottobonian, the former, as he conjectures, of the eleventh century, the latter of the fifteenth. The Bishop regarded these discoveries as a triumph, and anticipated similar results from further researches. Dr. Scholtz acknowledged, in very respectful terms, the receipt of the letters ; he allowed that the MS. in question added something to the evidence in favour of the authenticity of the verse, but maintained that they were of very little weight when compared in authority and antiquity with the multitude omitting it. To this letter the Bishop replied only a few weeks before his death. repeating the charges of contradiction already noticed, which the Doctor had not attempted to rebut, and reiterating his own opinions.

He passed through the spring and summer of 1836 in tolerable health, but during the autumn became severely indisposed, and suffered much from difficulty of respiration, which was regarded by his medical attendants as a symptom of incipient dropsy. It was treated as such so successfully, that he was greatly relieved before the approach of winter, when being advised to change the air of Salisbury for the milder climate of Southampton, a place to which he and Mrs. Burgess had long been partial, they removed thither early in November. The tone of his conversation with various friends shortly before he set out, bespoke a settled conviction that the time of his departure was at hand, and there was a beautiful admixture of humility and faith in all that he said on the subject.

To one of those friends, whose Christian fidelity and judgment naturally inspired confidence, he addressed himself in the following terms of touching simplicity just before he received from his hands the holy sacrament: —

"I feel that, in all probability, I shall not long survive this attack; I wish, therefore, to be tried as to the foundation on which I am resting. Will you give me your view of the frame of mind, and the particular objects of faith and dependence, which a person thus situated ought to contemplate and to cherish? What should be my views and feelings in the near prospect of an eternal world? When you have given me your sentiments, I will tell you my own." His friend, in reply, repeated to him, in the language of Scripture, some of those sublime promises to which, in a dying hour, the most learned and eminent of the sons of men must have recourse for consolation, equally with the illiterate and the humble. To the whole tenor of what was thus said the Bishop cordially assented, and expressed the strong consolation he had derived from various passages of Scripture which he quoted ; all bearing upon the mercy of God to the penitent believer in Christ Jesus.

During this conversation, his calm but expressive emotion attested the depth of his feelings. His voice faltered, and tears of mingled penitence and immortal hope coursed down his venerable cheeks. To another valued friend he said, in adverting about the same time to similar topics, — "I think, on looking back to my past life, I have acted for the most part conscientiously ; but how unworthily, how shortly ! Oh, what a comfort there is in looking to Christ ! I scarcely like to use that expression, common as it is, of looking to the cross; it is a *figurative* term, whereas I want something substantial. I had rather make mention of Him who died, than of the instrument by which he suffered."

Soon after reaching Southamptom, he addressed the Dean of Salisbury, and his sister, in the following letters : —

MY DEAR DEAN,   Southampton, Nov. 11.
I HAVE lately thought much of Mr. Simeon's very interesting words, which you were so kind as to send me at Salisbury. A Christian can have no doubt of the truth of Christianity, and of its doctrines, as declared by men who died for their profession of it. He who is a real believer in the Gospel can have no spiritual wish unfulfilled.

Mrs. H. More's " Consolations of Prayer " have

been lately read to me, and I was much pleased
with a short sentence, similar to those of Mr.
Simeon, — " The Christian feels that he is entering
on a state where every care will cease, every fear
vanish, every desire be fulfilled, every sin be done
away, every grace perfected."

Have you seen any thing of Mr. Clarke ?   Our
last accounts of him were rather more favourable,
and I shall be glad to hear them confirmed.   With
our united kind regards to you all, I am,

My dear Dean,
Yours very faithfully,
T. SARUM.

TO MRS. RHODA BURGESS.

MY DEAR SISTER,   Southampton, Dec. 20. 1836.

YOUR letter of this morning finds me in a considerable degree of pain, which I am almost ashamed
to mention to you, who have experienced so much
suffering in the course of a not very short life;
shorter, however, than mine by many years.   I am
glad, but not surprised to hear so good an account
as you send me of your adopted daughter, whom I
have always thought an invaluable companion to
you.   Accept my best wishes that the approaching
season may always return to you in health and good
spirits, and with a grateful remembrance of the mercy
which we have to commemorate.   Love God your
Creator, love God your Saviour, love the Holy
Spirit your teacher, instructor, comforter, and sanctifier.   With every good wish from my wife to you
and Miss R——. I am. my dear sister,

Yours very affectionately,
T. SARUM.

The following reply to an application from Lord
Sidmouth for his consent to accept the resignation
of the Vicar of Potterne, a gentleman far advanced
in years, in favour of his curate, a highly respectable clergyman, is very honourable to the Bishop's
memory. And not less so to Lord Sidmouth were
the terms in which, in a second letter, his Lordship
expressed his entire acquiescence in the wisdom and
propriety of the Bishop's decision.

TO VISCOUNT SIDMOUTH.

MY DEAR LORD,   Southampton, Dec. 1836.

I HAVE had a variety of applications for the
exchange, which is the subject of your letter, but I
have always objected to it. My first objection is
on very general grounds, namely, to the principle
of exchange, which in my opinion is very seldom
admissible, except in cases of extreme ill-health.
My next objection is to the irregularity of this case,
it being intended, that the present incumbent should
continue to occupy the parsonage house after the
exchange, so that the new incumbent would not
occupy his legal place of residence. My third objection is to the injury which, by consenting to this
application, I might be doing to a successor, to whom
this, one of the largest livings in the Bishop's gift,
might prove, if vacated in the ordinary course, a
valuable acquisition. There are few persons whom
I would so willingly oblige as your Lordship, but I
should be sorry to think that one of the last acts,
perhaps the very last, of my episcopal life, should
be an act of favour against law, rule, and precedent.
My health, which you kindly enquire after, is some-

what improved by my residence here, though I am
still an invalid,

Believe me, my dear Lord,

Yours most sincerely,

T. SARUM.

During the first two months of his residence at
Southampton, the Bishop, though in a state of increasing debility, was not seriously ill ; but early in
January, 1837, the difficulty of respiration from
which he had suffered in the preceding autumn
recurred, with aggravated symptoms. Mr. Maule,
his usual medical attendant at Southampton, was
first called in, and subsequently Dr. Oke. In the
course of their visits he often diverted the conversation from himself and the symptoms of his complaint to books and to topics of literary interest,
and charmed them by the easy and agreeable flow
of his observations, and the mild serenity of his demeanour.

Though much of the business of the diocese, in
consequence of his declining health, was now done
by commission, he still attended to it as far as his
strength permitted, and daily dictated official letters ;
but the fatigue which this employment caused him,
proved that he was making efforts beyond his
strength.

His chaplain and relative, the Rev. Henry Deane,
who was with him in the closing scenes of his life,
attests the anxiety which he manifested to make himself acquainted (notwithstanding his great debility),
with the particulars of the new duties which had devolved upon him by the recent annexation of the
archdeaconry of Dorset to the diocese of Salisbury.

Mr. Deane placed several papers conveying information upon the subject on the chair by his bedside, only two days before his death.

Among his latest notes was one to the Rev. Mr. Dansey, conveying a charitable donation for a fellow-creature in distress.

It was not till the 2d or 3d of February, that the attached friends who watched over him were painfully impressed with the conviction of his immediate danger. The embarrassment of breathing became daily more oppressive; and in spite of his efforts to spare the feelings of relatives by suppressing any outward demonstrations of suffering, the fact was often evident from his clasped hands and declining head. Though his patience was truly exemplary, he sometimes expressed anxiety lest his very slight acquaintance with pain, the consequence of habitual good health, should interfere with that perfect submission to the Divine will to which he aspired.

Owing to the inclemency of the winter, he was deprived at this time of his usual airings in the carriage; and on attempting to take walking exercise in the house, the exertion so affected his breathing that he often returned to his chair quite exhausted. On one of these occasions, he said, "There *must* be something to bring every one to his journey's end The days of our years, as the Psalmist says, are threescore years and ten; after which it is labour and sorrow. Why should I be taking so much care and pains, just as if I wished to live for ever, when, as you know (addressing a friend), I do not wish to live any longer than it pleases God." The affectionate attentions of Mrs.

Burgess were unceasing, and he often repaid them by grateful acknowledgments, and by the assurance that they ministered essentially to his comfort. In the same spirit he responded to the assiduous care of his attached man-servant Michael, and of his other attendants.

About this time an account appeared in the " Christian Observer," of the last illness and death of the Rev. Mr. Simeon, of King's College, Cambridge. It was read to the Bishop, who listened to it with marked interest, and desired to hear some parts of it a second time. Soon afterwards, while slowly pacing the room, he was heard repeating in a low but emphatic voice, and as if applying the words to himself, some of the most striking expressions of humility, faith, and hope, uttered on the occasion referred to by that eminent Christian.

There was something inexpressibly interesting, and which will find a response in every Christian bosom, in the feelings with which he himself continued to regard the approaches of death. Deeply sensible how much of imperfection mingles with and mars the best actions and obedience of our fallen race, the idea of passing into the presence of the Great Supreme, infinite in purity and holiness, impressed him with solemn awe, and led him again and again to try by the test of Scripture the foundation of his immortal hopes. His self-communings, and the particular texts which sustained and animated his faith, he himself recorded, with his almost dying hand, on some loose sheets of paper, and the following is a copy of this interesting document : —

" May I die the death of the righteous, and may

my last end be like his," was the expressed wish of
one who by his duplicity seems to have forfeited
the blessing of which he expresses himself desirous.
What his precise view of the blessing was, is not evident. Another and a better judge on the subject
says, "Mark the perfect man, and observe the upright; for the end of that man is peace."

But, as all have sinned and fallen short of the
glory of God, and as it is true, that "no man liveth
and sinneth not," vain will be any man's depend-
ance on his own performances and uprightness for
acceptance with God. A sense of pardon will alone
bring a man peace at the last. "Being justified
(that is, acquitted of our sins, and forgiven) through
faith in the atonement of Christ, we have peace
with God ;" Romans, v. 1. For by Christ we are justified and acquitted of all things from which we
could not be acquitted and justified by the law of
Moses. A sense of pardon was the ground of
David's peace : "I said, I will confess my sins unto
the Lord, and so thou forgavest the iniquity of my
sin. Blessed is the man whose iniquity is forgiven,
and whose sin is covered. Blessed is the man, to
whom the Lord imputeth not sin."

David's expression is remarkable —"to whom the
Lord imputeth not sin, and in whose spirit there
is no guile," *i. e.* no subterfuge, no concealment.
Sin to be forgiven must be forsaken, especially the
sins that most easily beset us.

> Teach me to live that I may dread
> The grave as little as my bed:
> Teach me to die that so I may
> Triumphant rise at the last day.

GROUNDS OF CHRISTIAN CONSOLATION

Learn of me, for I am meek and lowly of heart, and ye shall find rest unto your souls. Matt. xi. 29.

Him that cometh unto me, I will in no wise cast out. John, vi. 37.

No one will truly go to Christ who does not feel the want of a Saviour.

This feeling can arise only from the sense of sin. I said, I will confess my sin unto the Lord, and so Thou forgavest the iniquity of my sin. Ps. xxxii. 5.

Blessed is he whose transgression is forgiven, and whose sin is covered. Ps. xxxii. 1.

The blood of Christ cleanseth from all sin. 1 John, i. 7.

By Him we are justified.

Being justified by faith, we have peace with God. Romans, v. 1.

My peace I give unto you, not as the world giveth, give I unto you. John, xiv. 27.

Lord, increase our faith. Luke, xvii. 5.

Lord, I believe, help Thou mine unbelief. Mark, ix. 24.

O Lord, we beseech Thee, mercifully hear our prayers, and spare all those who confess their sins unto Thee, that they whose consciences by sin are accused, by Thy merciful pardon may be absolved through Christ our Lord. Amen.

Now the God of hope fill you with all joy and peace in believing, that you may abound in hope through the power of the Holy Ghost. Romans, xv. 13.

CHRISTIAN RECOLLECTIONS.

Come unto me all ye that travail, and are heavy laden, and I will give you rest. Matt. xi. 28.

To Thee, oh Lord! I come, weary and heavy laden with the burden of my sins. To Thee I confess them in heart-felt and sincere humility.

To Thee alone, oh Lord! my Creator, my Saviour, my Comforter, and Sanctifier, I look for mercy and forgiveness.

I have confessed to God the sins of my past life, I think of them daily with grief and contrition. I think of them as most deserving of God's anger and punishment. But I console myself with the remembrance of God's promise of forgiveness to confessed and forsaken sin. If we say that we have no sin, we deceive ourselves, and the truth is not in us. But if we confess our sins, God is faithful and just to forgive us our sins, and to cleanse us from all unrighteousness. 1 John, i. 8, 9.

God so loved the world that He gave his only begotten Son, that all who believe on Him should not perish but have everlasting life. John, iii. 16.

There is no peace with God without pardon, and no pardon without belief. Being justified by faith, being pardoned through faith, we have peace with God.

There can be no doubt that the doctrines of the New Testament, delivered by Apostles and Martyrs, who died in verification of them, must be true. There can be no doubt that God is, and that He is a rewarder of them that diligently seek Him. I believe that God sent His Son into the world to be the Saviour of the world. I believe that the Son of God came into the world to save sinners by His

death on the cross, and that without that atonement
there is no salvation.

I believe that the Holy Spirit of God is the
Teacher, Instructor, Comforter, and Sanctifier, and
that through Him only we believe in Christ.

I believe that Christ was made Sin — that is, a
sin-offering for us, that we might be made the righteousness of God in Him. 2 Cor. v. 21. The blood
of Christ cleanseth from all sin. 1 John, i. 7.

On the 11th of February the Bishop dictated his
last letter to a literary friend, but in so low a voice
as to be scarcely audible, and he had great difficulty
in franking it.

On Sunday the 12th of February he appeared a
little better, and was able to listen with interest to
the church service and a sermon. His mind was
peaceful, calm, and happy, and he conversed pleasantly in a low voice with those around him. After
tea he repeated Mrs. Heman's beautiful sonnet,
written on her death-bed, on hearing the Sabbath
bells *, until he came to the concluding lines, —

---

* The Bishop greatly admired this sonnet. It is as follows : —

" How many blessed groups this hour are bending,
Through England's primrose meadow-paths their way
Towards spire and tow'r, 'midst shadowy elms ascending,
Whence the sweet chimes proclaim the hallow'd day !
The halls, from old heroic ages grey,
Pour their fair children forth ; and hamlets low,
With whose thick orchard-blooms the soft winds play,
Send out their inmates in a happy flow,
Like a free'd vernal stream : I may not tread
With them those pathways, to the feverish bed
Of sickness bound : yet, oh, my God ! I bless
Thy mercy, that with Sabbath peace hath fill'd
My chasten'd heart, and all its throbbings still'd
To one deep calm of lowliest thankfulness."

" I may not tread
With them those pathways, to the feverish bed
Of sickness bound yet, oh, my God ! I bless
Thy mercy, that with Sabbath peace hath fill'd
My chasten'd heart, and all its throbbings still'd
To one deep calm of lowliest thankfulness."

In attempting to repeat this passage his voice
faltered, and he was mastered for a few moments
by strong emotion; but recovering himself, he exclaimed, " Let me finish them, I *wish* to finish them ;"
and then calmly proceeded to the end of the sonnet,
while all around him were much affected. He had
continued to this time to read family prayers in the
evening. On this day he did so for the last time.
His voice was very weak, but deeply earnest. It
had long been customary with him to have a chapter
of the Bible read after prayers, together with Fenelon's " Reflections " for the day. On this occasion
he selected for himself a Confession of Sins, and
part of the Office for the Sick, from a Book of
Devotions.

On the evening of the 13th of February the
Bishop was so unwell, that he retired early to his
room, never again to leave it. During the three
ensuing days he lay in a state of great debility, but
was not materially worse. In this state of prostra-
tion he gave a manifest proof how strong the ruling
passion was even in death. He had sent to the
press at the close of the preceding week a final letter
to Dr. Scholtz, defending his own views respecting
the controverted verse. He asked for the proof
sheet on the very day on which he thus took to his
bed, but it was not ready. On the next day, the 14th,
his servant procured and brought several copies

of it to him. The Bishop rallied for a moment *
on being told it was come, and desired that he
might be supported in bed while he franked two
covers enclosing proof sheets to his friends, Dr.
Babington and the late Rev. Francis Huyshe. With
the aid of his man-servant and of Mrs. Burgess he
at length accomplished his object, though with great
difficulty.

With this effort the Bishop resigned every earthly
anxiety, and his thoughts became wholly absorbed
by religious meditation and prayer.

On the evening of Thursday, Mr. Maule, his
assiduous medical attendant, on taking leave of him,
expressed the hope that he would be able to lie still,
and obtain some rest; to which the Bishop replied,
" The only rest I desire, or have ever sought for,

---

* This instance of the rally of mental energy, at the signal of
a cherished and favourite object — even under the approaches
of death — is not unlike an interesting fact connected with the
closing scenes of the life of venerable Bede His last days had
been employed on his translation of the Gospel of St. John
into the Saxon language The day before his death the person
that wrote for him, observing his weakness, said, " There now
only remains one chapter, but it seems difficult to you to speak."
" It is easy," he replied, " take another pen and write as fast
as you can." About nine o'clock he sent for some of his brethren, to divide among them a few articles that were in his
chest. While he was speaking to them, Wilberch, the amanuensis above referred to, said, " There is now, master, but one
sentence wanting," upon which he bid him write quick, and
soon after the young man said, " It is now done, " to which
Bede replied, " Well, thou hast said the truth — it is now
done. Take up my head between your hands, and lift me, for
it will please me much to sit over against the place where I
have been wont to pray, and where I may yet invoke my heavenly Father " Being thus seated, he said, " Glory be to the
Father, Son, and Holy Ghost ," and as he pronounced the last
words, expired. *Vide* CHALMERS' *Biographical Dictionary.*

is pointed out in those comforting words,—'Come unto me all ye that are weary and heavy laden, and I will give you *rest;*'" uttering the last words with all the emphasis in his power: "And as for peace, through faith we have peace with God; and if we have peace with God, we have peace with all the world. Is it not so?" He then added a cordial "Good night."

He continued to grow weaker until the ensuing evening, when so decisive a change took place, that his medical attendants declared the struggle was well nigh over. His sight seemed to be gone — he appeared to be scarcely conscious of any thing that was passing around him — his utterance became very indistinct—and the oppression on his breathing was extreme. His old servant, who for months had scarcely lost sight of him, was unwearied in his attentions to his dying master, and studious of every thing that could alleviate his sufferings. He was sensible, which he proved by his rejection or acceptance of any thing that was offered, and as long as he was able he never omitted to add his thanks for every attention. Throughout the night of Saturday his breathing grew shorter and shorter, till about two on the morning of Sunday, the 19th of February, when he gently breathed his last.

The funeral took place in Salisbury Cathedral on the 27th of February. The shops of the city were closed by general consent, and the cathedral was crowded. The body left Southampton early in the morning, and reached its last home about one. It was met at the great western door by the Clergy of the Chapter, headed by the Dean, and followed by those of the city, and of the immediate neighbour-

hood. The moment it entered the precincts of that
venerable fane, the organ poured forth its rich
volume of majestic sound, while the voices of the
choir responded in those sublime words, "I know
that my Redeemer liveth." The place selected for
the grave was the south transept, near those of the
relatives of Bishop Ken. The service was read very
impressively by the Dean, and as we committed the
remains of this eminent servant of God to the silent
tomb, I could not but reflect, What would now avail
the purple and the mitre which adorn that coffin —
what the dignified title of Bishop of Salisbury, and
all the reputation of the critic and the scholar, had
he not also been, in heart and life, a true disciple
and follower of Jesus Christ?

> " Tell them it is an awful thing to die ;
>   'Twas ev'n to *him* , but, the dread path once trod,
> Heaven lifts its everlasting portals high,
>   And bids the 'pure in heart' behold their God."

"What I was as an artist" (the sculptor Bacon
desired might be graven on his tomb) "appeared to
me of some importance while I lived, but what I
really was as a believer in Christ Jesus is the only
thing of importance to me now."

The following tribute paid to his memory by
Dr. Denison, his successor in the see of Salisbury,
at the first meeting of the Church Union Society
after the Bishop's death, is not less impressive
than just. After touching on the utility and excellence of the Society, and mentioning that the
system of charity which it embraced had first been
organised by Bishop Burgess, in the diocese of St.
David's, he thus proceeds : —

"And as circumstances have thus led me to ad-ı ert to his name, may I be allowed to pay a passing tribute to his departed worth.

" It is not necessary for me, and would be presumptuous, to speak of that with which the world at large is well acquainted, viz. his deep erudition and extensive and exact studies in both sacred and profane learning. It would ill become me, a stranger, to speak to you, who knew and loved him, of that which I can know only by report, the gentle and unobtrusive virtues of his private life ; how with meekness, humility, and Christian charity, he lived in good repute with men, and adorned the doctrine of God his Saviour in all things But I may be allowed to speak of that which the occasion suggests, viz. the deep feeling he entertained of the importance of the work of the ministry, and his careful anxiety for its due discharge. It was this high sense of the nature of the ministerial office, which made him scrupulous and exact beyond almost all other bishops in ascertaining the qualifications of those whom he admitted to administer in holy things. It was this same sense which made him feel deeply the importance of supplying the place of those whose ministrations failed through age or infirmity, and led him, in two successive dioceses, to establish institutions whose operations should especially be directed to the supply of this want. Nor did it seem to him enough to watch during his life with anxious care over this his favourite object, but even in his death, while he delegated the charge of this society to those who, he well knew, would earnestly endeavour to supply his place, he so endowed it by his own munificence * as not to allow the execution of

* The Bishop bequeathed the sum of 3000*l.* to the Salisbury Church Union Society.

his object to be altogether dependent upon the zeal of others.

" We may believe that he did in this a work well pleasing to the Lord ; and we should not fail to add our endeavours that his efforts be not in vain."

Conceived in the same spirit was the following impressive tribute paid to his memory by Dr. Pearson, Dean of Salisbury, in a sermon preached in the cathedral, upon the Easter Sunday following his death : —

" And here I cannot but remind you of one who will, I doubt not, have his share in the glory and the happiness of that celestial day. I refer to the late venerable Bishop of this diocese. How sincerely he was beloved and revered I need scarcely say. The feeling of attachment and respect to his memory is universal; and I am happy in having this opportunity, which I cannot but deem peculiarly appropriate, of adding my grateful testimony to that of so many others, to the various graces and virtues of his character. To the talents and the learning of our late excellent diocesan ; to his inflexible integrity and consistency, both of principle and conduct ; to his public spirit, and his patriotic love of all our ancient, and especially our ecclesiastical, institutions ; to his disinterestedness and liberality ; to his active benevolence and diffusive charity ; to the kindliness of his affections, and the sweetness of his manners, — a just and general tribute has been and will continue to be paid.

" The subject which we have been considering rather leads me to speak of the *Christian* character of our late venerable Bishop, and of that faith and hope which have been completed and realised in the happiness of a future world. His reliance on his Saviour's merits for pardon and acceptance in the sight of God was simple and sincere. Blameless and abundant as he was in every good work, he depended for salvation only on the atonement of Jesus Christ. This gave peace to his conscience, and enabled him to rejoice 'in hope of the glory of God.' He truly loved his Redeemer, and earnestly desired the extension of his kingdom. He was 'a lover of good men,' and delighted in their society. He was a father and friend to the poor. He was spiritually minded, which is 'life and peace.' How fervently he desired, and how diligently he pursued the perfection and the happiness of a higher world, those who conversed with him most confidentially and unreservedly best know. He aspired to the communion of prophets and apostles, of saints and angels, and, more than all, to a nearer and more intimate approach to 'God the Judge of all,' and to 'Jesus the Mediator of the new covenant.' The anticipation of this blessed and glorious termination of his earthly course cheered him amidst the infirmities of age, and the prospect of the grave. His faith triumphed over the last great enemy; and he is, doubtless, now safe in 'the resting-place of the spirits of the just,' awaiting, in joyful hope, the adoption, that is, 'the redemption of the body,' in that day when, with the assembled Church of the redeemed, he shall rise radiant and immortal from the tomb."

The following extract from a charge of Archdeacon Berens (a justly respected name) is added, on account of its characteristic fidelity of description :—

" To those who knew the Bishop intimately, and

saw him in the retirement of his own family, there was, in his demeanour, something singularly engaging. There was an unruffled calmness, a quiet cheerfulness, a gentle and unaffected courtesy and kindness of manner, which well befitted a Christian bishop. Familiarly acquainted, as he was, with the classical and theological literature of all ages ; possessed of a memory, even in advanced years, remarkably retentive and well-informed in the current literature of the day, his conversation was most instructive and interesting , and he was particularly pleased when he could give to the intercourse of friendship any thing of a religious character. The prayers which he used in his family were the prayers of the Liturgy, but those Collects were especially selected which were the most strong and explicit in expressing reliance upon the Atonement of Christ, and upon the sanctifying influences of the Holy Spirit. I never knew any one who appeared to live in more constant anticipation of the time when he should be summoned to his last account, or who was habitually sustained by a more lively faith in the merits and mediation of the Redeemer."

The facts detailed in this volume, and the impressive testimonies which have been quoted, may well absolve the Author from placing before his readers a particular summary of the intellectual and moral qualities which shed so bright a lustre on the character of Bishop Burgess. But he may be allowed to add a very few remarks on his merits as an Author.

As a Controversialist, he was a rare instance of tenacious earnestness and zeal in maintaining and defending his own opinions, or challenging those of others, without the slightest admixture of polemical bitterness. Controversy was always carried on by him in a courteous and Christian spirit, and he gave no advantage to an opponent by want of temper, or by any ebullitions of spleen or impatience.

He possessed, as a critic, much skill in detecting the weak points or fallacies of an argument, and placing his own sentiments in an advantageous light. Whatever was the subject of which he treated he never failed to bring the stores of deep study and extensive learning to bear upon it, though it is to be regretted that his conclusions were sometimes drawn in stronger terms than the premises warranted, and that his judgment did not always keep pace with the march of his erudition.

The elegant flow and the lucid expression of his Latin style have been often and justly admired ; and he composed in his native language with vigour, correctness, and elegance.

The publications of the Bishop were very numerous, and tended to attract particular attention to many interesting subjects connected with classical learning and research, with the doctrines and evidences of Christianity, or with the criticism of the Sacred Writings. Of the principal of these a list is printed in the Appendix, and a summary of some of the most important has been given in the preceding pages. The republication, either in whole or in part, of his ablest treatises, would be highly honourable to his researches as a scholar, his acuteness as a critic, and his piety as a Divine. Had he, however, directed his powers of application and his learned attainments to fewer topics, or concentrated them on some select subject of general interest, he might have enriched the literature of his country with more permanent monuments of his fame.

As it is, he has left behind him numerous materials for thought, and great stores of learning to aid the researches of the student and the critic; but in whatever light posterity may regard his writings, the name and memory of Burgess will not cease to be revered in the Church of Christ as a model of Episcopal virtue and Primitive Piety.

A handsome monument, erected to his memory in the Cathedral of Salisbury, bears the following inscription from the pen of Dr. Pearson, Dean of Salisbury.

Sacred to the Memory of
The Right Reverend THOMAS BURGESS, D D F R S
Late Lord Bishop of this Diocese,
And Chancellor of the most noble Order of the Garter ,
Who departed this life, regretted and revered, February 19th, 1837,
aged 80 years

This venerable Prelate received his early Education
on the foundation at Winchester College ;
From whence he was elected Scholar, and afterwards became
Fellow and Tutor, of Corpus Christi College, Oxford
At that seat of learning, he was distinguished by his talents and attainments ,
and after a residence of some years was appointed
Examining Chaplain to Dr Shute Barrington, then Lord Bishop of Salisbury ;
Who, on his translation to the See of Durham, preferred him to a
Prebendal Stall in that Cathedral
In the year 1803, he was promoted to the Bishopric of St David's
His praise in the administration of that extensive Diocese, and, still more,
in the foundation of St David's College, for Clerical Education
in the Principality of Wales, is in all the Churches
After twenty-two years of faithful and unremitting labour, he was
translated to the See of Salisbury ,
Where, among other Ecclesiastical and Charitable Institutions, he founded
and endowed the Church Union Society for this Diocese
The learning of this eminent Prelate was extensive and profound, and
his critical talents were of a high order
Of this his numerous publications bear ample testimony
His literary studies embraced a wide and varied circle , in the zealous
pursuit of which he was chiefly instrumental
in forming the Royal Society of Literature, of which he was elected
the first President
But the principal employment of his life, from its earliest to its latest
period, was devoted to the elucidation and defence
of Scriptural and Catholic Verity, as professed and inculcated by
the Church of England
His love of primitive Christianity was deep and unalterable
He had imbibed the great principles of the English Reformation , and was
firmly persuaded that their maintenance,
in all their original purity and integrity, was inseparably connected with
that of constitutional freedom, and of true religion
His manners were simple, yet dignified , his temper singularly sweet,
placid, and equable ;
His spirit generous candid, and disinterested ;
His charity liberal and diffusive
His faith was sound and unwavering ; his life pure, and unspotted
from the world
His end was peace, and his hope, through Christ,
full of immortality.

K K 2

APPENDIX.

No. I.

MR. GRANVILLE SHARP'S RULE.

In adverting to the publication of the second number of the Museum Oxoniense, we stated that the Appendix would give some account of a remarkable treatise which it included, entitled " Remarks on the Uses of the Definitive Article in the Greek of the New Testament, containing many new proofs of the Divinity of Christ, from passages which are wrongly translated in the common English Version," by Granville Sharp, Esq. This tract, which we are assured by its author would never have seen the light but for the intervention of Mr. Burgess, who selected it from various others placed at his disposal, has given rise to much animated discussion on critical questions of great interest connected with the scriptural evidences of the Divinity of Christ. In these discussions Mr. Burgess took for a series of years so prominent a part, that it becomes the duty of his biographer to place before his readers, in as popular a form as the subject will authorise, a general sketch of the nature of the controversy.

Mr. Sharp, who was an able linguist, and devoted to the study of Sacred Literature, maintains, in this tract, that the force of various texts bearing strong testimony to the Divinity of Christ, had been in a great degree sacrificed by the translators of our English Bible, from their not having adhered to the following critical canon, which he maintained was established by the genius of the Greek language, and by the practice of its best writers, both sacred and profane.

When two personal nouns of the same case are connected by the copulative (καὶ — and), if the former has the Greek definite article and the latter has not, they both relate to the same person. Example: 2 Peter, c. i. v. 1. ἐν δικαιοσυνῃ τοῦ Θεου ἡμων καὶ Σωτηρος ἡμων Ιησου Χριστου, which, according to the rule, should be rendered thus Through the righteousness of Jesus Christ, our God and Saviour.

Titus, ii 13 Προσδεχομενοι την μακαριαν ελπιδα, και επιφα-νειαν της δοξης του μεγαλου Θεου και σωτηρος ημων Ιησου Χριστου

Waiting for that blessed hope, and the glorious appearing of Jesus Christ, the Great God and our Saviour

A comparison of these texts with the translation of our English Bible, will at once show an unlearned reader how much the fulness of their evidence in support of the doctrine in question is augmented by the above change in the particles. In fact, the words " the great God and our Saviour Jesus Christ," in the last text, may be understood, as translated in our Authorised Version, to refer to two distinct persons, whereas the Greek idiom, as developed by Mr Sharp's rule, strictly confines their application to one and the same person, viz Jesus Christ

Among other texts, the following are instances of similar mistranslation — 2 Thess. i 12 ; 1 Tim v. 21. , Ephes. v 5.

Various modifications of the above rule were given by Mr Sharp, and certain exceptions, the nature of which he carefully defined These were subjoined to a new edition of the original tract, which was soon after published by Mr. Burgess, who added from his own pen, " A plain historical proof of the Divinity of Christ, founded on Christ's own testimony of himself, attested and interpreted by his living witnesses and enemies, the Jews " This part of the volume was a popular abridgment of the able sermon which he preached in 1790 It was annexed to Mr Sharp's treatise, for the convenience of unlearned readers, and was also printed separately for the use of his own parishioners He published a second edition of the above Treatise, in 1801, after his elevation to the Episcopal bench, with the following letter addressed to Mr. Sharp —

" DEAR SIR,

‘ I HAVE great pleasure in presenting you with a new edition of your valuable tract That you have very happily and decisively applied your rule of construction to the correction of the common English Version of the New Testament, and to the perfect establishment of the great doctrine in question, the Divinity of Christ, no impartial reader, I think, can doubt, who is at all acquainted with the original language of the New Testament I say decisively applied, because I suppose in all remote and written testimony, the weight of evidence must ultimately depend on the grammatical analogy of the language in which it is recorded I call the rule yours , for though it was acknowledged and applied by Beza and others to some of the texts alluded to by you, yet never so prominently, because

singly, or so effectually, as in your remarks In the addition
to the former edition I wished to excite the attention of a learned
and declared enemy to the doctrine of our Saviour's Divinity;
but he is no more ; and I do not know that he even expressed,
or has left behind him any opinion on the subject, or that any
other Socinian has undertaken to canvass the principles of your
remarks. The public has, however, lately seen an ample and
learned confirmation of your rule, drawn from a very minute,
laborious, and candid examination of the Greek and Latin
fathers, in ' Six Letters addressed to Granville Sharp, Esq ,
respecting his Remarks on the Uses of the Definitive Article
in the Greek Text of the New Testament. London, 1802 ' I
have taken some pains to improve the ' Plain Argument for
Christ's Divinity,' which I before subjoined to your ' Remarks.'
In this edition I have prefixed to it a table of evidences by Dr
Whitby, which I hope the younger part of your readers will
find useful to them in pursuing the different branches of this
most important subject ; and you, I think, will not disapprove,
because it is conducive to the principal purpose of your tract "

The important conclusions deducible from Mr Sharp's rule
and the authority of such a scholar as Mr. Burgess, naturally
attracted the attention of the learned world to the subject. It
was attacked and ridiculed by writers of the Unitarian school
with great asperity, though with little of critical acumen. But
the able treatise in support of its validity, alluded to in the
preceding letter, soon afterwards appeared from the pen of Mr
(now Dr.) Wordsworth, and Master of Trinity College, Cambridge. Mr. Wordsworth's defence of the rule was conceived
in the true spirit of induction. He reasoned thus : — If Mr.
Sharp's rule be valid, then will the interpretation of the texts
affected by it, quoted in the writings of the Greek fathers, be
in correspondence with its tenor , for whatever opinions may
be entertained of those venerable writers in other respects, it
will not be denied that such men as St Chrysostom and .St
Basil are competent authorities upon questions connected with
the structure and idiom of their native tongue Accordingly he
examined with this view works of seventy Greek and nearly
sixty Latin fathers, extending from the second to the twelfth
century, a period of one thousand years, besides other theological writings; and the general result was, a complete confirmation on the part of the Greek fathers of Mr Sharp's rule.

The result as respects the Latin fathers was of less importance, because they were only translators (unlearned often) from
the Greek. Their observance of the rule is less uniform and
consistent, but Jerom (from his superior learning, himself a

host,) is among those who do support it; and as respects one of the most important of the texts referred to, viz Titus, ii 13., fifty-four Greek authorities, and no less than sixty of the Latin fathers and divines interpret it according to Mr Sharp's canon. The candour and impartiality displayed by Dr Wordsworth in this investigation were not less signal than his indefatigable industry and research, and it may justly be asserted that its conclusions have never been refuted

One of the objections urged with most confidence against the critical authority of Mr. Sharp's rule was the illiterate character of the sacred writers, and the improbability that those whose Greek style was so far removed from classical purity, would be correct or uniform in practice with respect to such delicacies of expression as are involved in the use of the Greek Article A very learned and competent authority, the late Bishop Middleton, has ably refuted this objection. He has shown (in his work on the Greek Article) that though the Apostles and Evangelists write not with the elegance of learned Athenians, their use of the Article is purely and correctly Greek ; and that whatever apparent deviation from it takes place, which is rare, is chiefly in quotations from the Septuagint, or in a few passages, literally translated from the Hebrew. The LXX were servile translators, and every where kept as close to the original as the Greek idiom would admit

Bishop Middleton's conclusion is, that, with certain limitations, which do not interfere with the preceding interpretation of the texts affected by this controversy, Mr Sharp's rule, and his application of it to the New Testament, is in perfect conformity with the usage of the best Greek classics, and with the syntax of the Greek tongue ; and he adds his conviction, that the passages in question were understood by the fathers as Mr. Sharp would translate them ; and as without doubt they will be translated at some future period. — *Vide* " Middleton on the Greek Article," 8vo., second edition, pages 79, 90, 91. 152.

Professor Stuart, of America, in an elaborate Treatise published in the Biblical Repository of that country, endeavours to prove, by a reference to Greek authorities, that the critical canons of Middleton, with respect to the Article, admit not of the universality which he claims for them, but are subject to exceptions which much weaken the force and certainty of his conclusions Yet even Stuart admits that where definiteness is a main object, the article which might otherwise be omitted is inserted This being conceded, the light reflected on the question at issue, by Mr Wordsworth's tract, becomes increasingly important, for he clearly proves, by a reference to undeniable

fact, that the most learned and illustrious writers of the Greek
Church recognise, by their unanimous consent, by their authority, and by their inferences, the validity of the contested rule
in the case of the principal texts affected by it, texts in which
definiteness was peculiarly essential.

No. II.

A LETTER to the Right Honourable LORD VISCOUNT MELBOURNE,
on the Idolatry and Apostasy of the Church of Rome, in Proof
that the Doctrines of the Church of Rome are not fundamentally
the same with those of the Church of England. By the BISHOP
of SALISBURY.

MY LORD,
THE bill which gave occasion to the letter, which I have now
the honour of addressing to your Lordship, has been abandoned. But the opinion which your Lordship, in moving the
second reading of the bill, maintained, respecting the supposed identity of the fundamental doctrines of the Churches
of England and of Rome, is still before the public, and may be
the ground of other projects of ecclesiastical innovation, similar
to the momentous measure of the discarded bill, if, on re-consi-
deration of the opinion then maintained, you should not see
its incorrectness My Lord, if the public prints have faithfully reported your speech, in moving the second reading of
the *Irish Church Bill*, your Lordship is represented to have
said, that the doctrines of the Roman Catholic Church are
fundamentally the same with those of the Church of England.
A Roman Catholic writer, in his project for the re-establish-
ment of popery in Ireland, has lately asserted, that " if we
except extreme unction, the Protestants admit *all the other
leading rites* of " the Catholic Church," leaving his uninformed readers to suppose that, excepting the article of extreme unction, there is very little difference between the
Protestant and Roman Churches in their religious tenets
This is an old stratagem of the Roman Church for the removal
of Protestant prepossessions against her communion, and apprehensions of danger from any association with it. This favourable aspect towards the Church of Rome is a great and
fatal delusion, as we unhappily know too well, from its influence on the legislature in 1829, when it was contended that
the admission of Papists into Parliament would tranquillise
Ireland, strengthen the Church of England, and give satisfaction to all parties. The same favourable feeling towards the

Church of Rome seems to have possessed your Lordship's mind, when you confidently asserted that fundamentally her doctrines were the same with those of the Church of England But, my Lord, the doctrines of the Roman Church are so far from being fundamentally the same with those of our Church, that they are fundamentally and essentially opposed to them, and subversive of them. The Church of Rome has not left us at a loss to know what are the *fundamental* articles of her creed. Your Lordship will, I doubt not, readily admit, that all doctrines are to be so denominated in both Churches, which are held in each to be necessary to salvation. Such are the doctrines which are contained in the creed, commonly called Pope Pius's Creed, which at once presents this broad difference between the Church of Rome and all other churches — that all who deny her doctrines are pronounced by her to be accursed In that creed are contained the following articles of her faith, without the belief of which she declares that no one can be saved — The supremacy of the Pope and of his church, transubstantiation, the sacrifice of the mass, the worship of saints, the veneration of images and relics, purgatory, penance for the remission of sins, seven sacraments, &c

These articles of Pope Pius's Creed are fundamental doctrines of the Church of Rome, and *not* of the Church of England, but were rejected by her three centuries ago, as idolatrous, impious, and heretical And so utterly at variance are they with the doctrines of our church, that they are subversive of our whole Protestant establishment Yet on the supposed approximation of the two churches was founded much of that fatal delusion which led to the extinction of the purely Protestant character of the British legislature, by the admission of Papists into the great council of the nation. In consequence of this recent anomaly in our constitution, and the utter forgetfulness of the anti-British as well as anti-Protestant spirit of Popery, much encouragement has been given to it in Ireland, to the great detriment of the Established Church, and of the true profession of the Gospel

The peculiar doctrines of the Church of Rome in Pope Pius's Creed are preceded by the Nicene Creed, which creed being common to both churches, has probably contributed to the supposition that the doctrines of both churches are fundamentally the same But, my Lord, the doctrines of Christianity contained in the Nicene Creed are so perverted by the Church of Rome, from the true sense of Scripture, by the additions of the Papal creed, as to constitute a very different profession of faith from that of the Gospel and of the Church of England In the Scriptures we are taught that there is

only *one* God, and in the Nicene Creed we profess it But
the Church of Rome, by her adoration of angels and saints,
and prayers to them for spiritual and temporal blessings, becomes a worshipper of *many* gods The Scriptures teach us
that there is *one* Mediator between God and man, and only
one name under heaven by which men must be saved , but in
the Church of Rome every saint is a mediator, and every
mediator a saviour By the Scriptures we are taught that
Christ offered himself *once* on the cross for the sins of mankind The Church of Rome professes in the mass to offer up
Christ *every day* as a propitiatory sacrifice to God. In the
Gospel we are taught to honour the Son even as we honour
the Father But in the Church of Rome greater honour is
paid to the Virgin Mary than to the Son, or to the Father.
The Church of England believes that Christ in his *divine*
nature is omnipresent, and that he is nowhere *bodily* present,
but in heaven at the right hand of God. The Church of Rome
teaches that Christ is bodily present in the consecrated bread
of the Eucharist, and in every particle of bread that is eaten
at the Lord's Supper Nothing more strongly shows the fundamental difference of the Church of Rome from the Church
of England than the *doctrine*, that the bread and wine are
changed by consecration into the body and blood of Christ ;
and the *worship* of Christ under the *visible forms* of bread and
wine ; the belief of which the Church of Rome declares to be
necessary to every man's salvation , but which the Church of
England pronounces to be idolatry, — to be abhorred of all
faithful Christians *

You object, my Lord, to the imputation of idolatry, as applied by the Protestant prelates of the Irish Church to the
Church of Rome The charge of idolatry was so applied by
our Reformers of the sixteenth century, who were born and
bred Papists, and knew by their own experience and knowledge what Popery was. It is so applied in our Liturgy and
Homilies; and has been so applied by the best informed and
most learned † Protestants from their time to the present It
may be sufficient to quote the testimony of Bishop Jeremy
Taylor · — " We know idolatry is a damnable sin, and we
know that the Roman Church, with all the artifices she could
use, never can justify herself, or acquit the common practice
[image-worship] of idolatry "‡ It is the legitimate language

* Declaration subjoined to the Communion Service
† Bishop Jewell, Archbishop Whitgift, Bishop Bilson, Bishop Andrews,
Bishop White, Archbishop Usher, Bishop Davenant, Bishop Jeremy
Taylor, Bishop Downman
‡ Dissuasive from Popery, p 10 Preface

of parliament, and has been the language of your Lordship's own solemn declaration, as often as you have taken your seat in either house of parliament,—in terms expressive of the most unequivocal *belief* that " the invocation or adoration of the Virgin Mary, or any other saint, and the sacrifice of the mass, as now used in the Church of Rome, are superstitious and idolatrous " *

When your Lordship, in your speech on the Irish Church Bill, condemned the charge of idolatry against the Church of Rome, as an insult on the Irish population, it must have been on the supposition that the worshippers of one supreme God are incapable of idolatry. But, my Lord, the profession of belief in one God, and the worship of one supreme God, are no proof that the members of the Church of Rome are not idolatrous by the worship of the Virgin Mary and other saints. The Jews, who were under the immediate and peculiar government of God, were addicted to idolatry from the time they left Egypt, uniting the worship of Baal with that of Jehovah, in spite of God's awful judgments against it, and in defiance of the national calamities which it frequently brought upon them, till they were finally punished for it by the total overthrow of their nation, and their captivity in Babylon. The most enlightened people of pagan antiquity were worshippers of one supreme God, at the time that they had many subordinate deities, national, domestic, and local, like the deified angels and saints of modern Rome.

For an exact parallel between Pagan and Papal idolatry, I may refer your Lordship not only to Dr Middleton's celebrated Letter from Rome, but to the author of a tract, entitled " A true and lively Representation of Popery, showing that Popery is new-modelled Paganism, and perfectly destructive of the great Ends and Purposes of God in the Gospel," published in London in 1679; a period, when the *increase* of *Popery* extorted from the legislature a remedy†, which we have lived to see *repealed*, to the *great increase* and encouragement of Popery —a remedy, the wisdom and expediency of which nothing was wanting to prove, but *its loss* (what if it may be but a temporary loss?) and the renewed and dear-bought experience which has followed this repeal

Your Lordship objects to that part of the petition of the Protestant Prelates of Ireland, which appeared to you to be couched in injurious, uncharitable, and unchristian language towards the Roman Catholic Church of Ireland   " The words

---

* Declaration (30 Car 2), " I , A B , do solemnly and sincerely, in the presence of God, profess, testify, and declare, that I believe," &c.
† 30 Car 2 , A D 1678, repealed 1829

usurpation, idolatry, and blind superstition," you observe, " are not terms of conciliation, nor were they fit language for a bench of right reverend prelates." The language is justified by the example of the many great authorities before mentioned, from Bishop Jewell down to Archbishop Usher, who have proved the Church of Rome to be usurping, idolatrous, and superstitious. The words are not terms of conciliation; but they are the language of truth, of history, and (as before mentioned) of parliamentary authority. What other term, indeed, than *usurpation* can be given to the assumption of universal dominion over the Church of Christ, which the Pope and the Church of Rome have employed to the degradation of sovereigns, the interdict of kingdoms, and the massacre of provinces? What other terms can with truth be applied to the bowing down in prayer before the images of saints, and to the adoration of Christ under the visible forms of bread and wine, than those which are employed by our church and parliament, and constitutionally adopted by your Lordship?

Your Lordship laments the great errors of the Church of Rome; and you scruple not to deprecate the spirit of some of her doctrines. But experience has abundantly shown, that those errors are not to be reformed, nor her doctrines mitigated, by conciliation and concession To call idolatry, superstition, and apostasy by any other terms than by their own appropriate appellations, is not to conciliate the church that is guilty of such corruptions, but to confirm her members in their errors, and to mislead uninformed Protestants. The Prophet's denunciation is true in respect of religion above all other subjects . " Woe unto them that call evil good, and good evil; that put darkness for light, and light for darkness."

The disuse of the old parliamentary terms, Popery, Papistry, and Papists, and the common use of the term Catholic instead of Popish, — of Catholicism instead of Popery, — of *real presence* instead of transubstantiation, — cannot fail to confound the understandings of uninformed and unthinking Protestants, and to propagate pernicious errors The Church of Rome is falsely called *Catholic,* and most inconsistently denominated *Roman Catholic.* It never was the Catholic or universal Church of Christ, either in authority or doctrine: — not in authority; for it never had dominion over the Eastern Church, nor over the whole Western Church, for the first ten centuries, nor after the beginning of the sixteenth.

Nor can a church be Catholic in doctrine, which has added to the generally received faith of Christians sundry articles of belief, as necessary to salvation, which are mere "novelties and heterodoxies," as they are called by Barrow at the close of his never-answered and unanswerable Treatise on the Pope's supremacy. The boasted term *Catholic*, as applied to the Church, is a novelty unknown to the Scriptures, and to the primitive Church of Rome, and though used by the Greek Church in the fourth century, was not admitted into the Roman Creed till after the fifth or sixth century. The Papal Church, therefore, has not the claim of antiquity for the term *Catholic*, nor even the authority of the Trent Creed for the *mode* in which it is applied. For in that Creed the Church of Rome is called *Catholic Roman*, and not *Roman Catholic*. But whether entitled Catholic Roman, or Roman Catholic, nothing can excuse the incongruity of combining in one appellation two contradictory terms, *universal* and *particular*, so as to call it either an universal particular, or particular universal Church. *

Your Lordship condemns in harsh terms the employment of Protestant missionaries in Ireland, as if it were placing the Irish population on a level with the worshippers of Juggernaut. Your Lordship is evidently not aware of the state of Popery in Ireland, or of the extent of that blind superstition and idolatry which is stated in the petition of the Protestant Prelates of Ireland, or of the details which have been given of it in various publications from the time of the Reformation to the present. Of its present state, I can refer your Lordship to a very recent account in a tract entitled *Popery in Alliance with Paganism*, by John Poynder, Esq. especially in Letters XII. and XIII. concerning the *Water Idolatry* in Ireland. Of a former period the following is by the Bishop of Down in 1686, — the learned, the pious, the excellent Jeremy Taylor, in the preface to his *Dissuasive from Popery.* —" We have observed amongst the generality of the Irish such a declension of Christianity, so great credulity to believe every superstitious story, — so little sense of true religion and the fear of God, so much care to obey the Priests, and so little to obey God, — thinking themselves more bound to swear on the Mass-book than on the four Gospels, and St. Patrick's Mass-book more than any new one, — these and so many other things of like nature we see daily, that we being conscious of the infinite distance which these things have from the spirit of Christianity, know that *no charity can be greater than to persuade the people to come to our Churches, where they shall be taught all the ways of godly wisdom, of peace and safety to their souls.*"— I shall give one particular instance of their miserable superstition and blindness, for which

* " And whereas the Papist boasts himself to be a Roman Catholic, it is a mere contradiction, as if he should say, universal, particular, or Catholic schismatic." — *Milton's Tracts on True Religion.*

I refer your Lordship to the whole very instructive passage from
p. xii to p. xviii

Deeply as we are interested in the responsibility imposed
upon us by our connection with India to diffuse the light of
religious and moral truth among its inhabitants, this responsibility, as it respects Ireland, is increased in a tenfold degree in
proportion to our religious and political affinities with it, as
well as its vicinity, — in proportion, too, to *that* declension
from the light of the Gospel, which your Lordship laments and
deprecates in the errors of the Church of Rome, — in proportion also to the duty entailed upon us of maintaining, in its
primitive truth, that Gospel which we have the highest historical authority* for affirming was preached in these islands by
some of the apostles; and consequently the duty of *opposing
the establishment of any religion contrary to the Gospel*; — and
lastly, in proportion to the long neglect of these Protestant
duties towards Ireland in past times

The three historical characteristics of the Christian Church
in these islands, — Apostolical, Episcopal, and Protestant, —
as it subsisted *before the end of the sixth century*, should never
be forgotten, as motives of attachment to its authority, and of
zeal in its defence, as evidences of its antiquity and independence on the Church of Rome, and means of disabusing the
minds both of Romanists and Dissenters, — of Romanists, ignorant of the *compact between Pope Adrian and Henry the Second,*
so late as the twelfth century, by which Popery was first introduced into Ireland, and of Dissenters forgetful of the *origin of
Dissent* in the *sixteenth century*

Your Lordship is of opinion that " Protestant missionaries in
Ireland have not the quality essential to missionaries, — of
disinterested parties, and that it is to be doubted whether
missionaries have been productive of that good which has been
generally ascribed to them." What purer interest, or more
righteous motive, can any man have than the conversion of his
fellow-creatures from idolatry and blind superstition, by the
diffusion of the Gospel, and a pure profession of Christianity
among them? And if we may judge of the beneficial effects of
missionary labours in the cause of religion from the success of
one individual, we might resolve all doubts on the subject by
an appeal to the life of Swartz, which has lately been read by
the public with so much interest, from the pen of the Dean of
Salisbury. But, great and influential as were his talents and
example in our *eastern* empire, the success of our *home* missions
in the reign of Edward VI, by the zeal and piety of Bernard

* Clemens Romanus, Eusebius, Theodoret, Gildas, &c.

Gilpin, for the instruction and conversion of a benighted population, bred up in the errors of Popery, is more to the purpose of meeting your Lordship's objection to the employment of Protestant missionaries in Ireland. Bernard Gilpin, who was Rector of Houghton-le-Spring, in the county of Durham, was also a licensed preacher, and in that capacity itinerated through Northumberland, Yorkshire, Westmoreland, Cumberland, and Cheshire, which were the chief scenes of those missionary labours which have transmitted his name to posterity, as *the Apostle of the North*. " If a missionary be one who carries forth the torch of Revelation in order that he may diffuse its light over dark places of the earth, Bernard Gilpin was justly entitled to that appellation. He laboured for the conversion of souls who had no other means of coming to the knowledge of the Gospel. In the reign of Edward VI. he had received a general licence for preaching, which he possessed in the reign of Elizabeth, and of which he made a most important use. "*

An ample field appears to present itself in the south of Ireland for similar exertion in the dissemination of the Gospel, in co-operation with the resident clergy, by licensed preachers, by school catechists, and Bible readers. The success of the circulating schools of Wales, instituted in the last century †, for the instruction of the Welsh poor in their own language, affords great encouragement to such missionary labours for the instruction of the Irish poor, by the mutual aid of the two languages, Irish and English, in the Protestant principles of the Established Church. Under such institutions, especially if aided by parliamentary grants for the building of glebe houses, chapels of ease, and school houses, and protected by the due administration of the laws, Protestant congregations might be created in the 860 devoted parishes with as much facility as we see new associations grow up in England under the shadow of Dissenting Meeting Houses and Roman Chapels. In their view of enlarging the means of general instruction, it does not seem to have occurred to the framers of the Irish Church Bill that, as lay impropriations are held on no other original right of tenure than are the proscribed benefices, a large portion of the benefits intended, through sequestration and confiscation by the abandoned bill, might be obtained by a property tax of ten per cent. on the average annual value of lay impropriations,

---

* Lives of eminent Christians, vol ii p 43
† Instituted by the Rev Griffith Jones, in 1730, and continued under his superintendence for more than twenty years, — conducted by the liberality of Mrs Bevan for nearly twenty years, till the time of her death, — and, after a long Chancery suit, confirmed by the Decretal Order of Lord Chancellor Eldon, in 1807.

to be applied exclusively to their respective parishes, without
depriving any parish of its Protestant character, or any ecclesiastical incumbent of his vested rights

I have the honour to be,
My Lord,
Your Lordship's
Very obedient servant,
T. SARUM.

Palace, Salisbury, Nov 18 1835

No. III.

PRINCIPLES UPON WHICH BISHOP BURGESS LISTENED TO
APPLICATIONS FOR ORDERS IN THE CHURCH OF ENGLAND
FROM VARIOUS INDIVIDUALS WHO HAD BEEN DISSENTING
MINISTERS.

IT is well known that Bishop Burgess admitted several individuals, who had been dissenting ministers, to holy orders in
the church of England, and the wisdom of his conduct in this
particular has been occasionally questioned. The following
extract of a letter to the author, from the Rev. Mr. Meek,
who was one of those thus ordained, explains in so satisfactory
a manner the principles upon which the Bishop acted in all
such cases, that it is made public with the permission of its
respected writer

After paying a very high tribute of affectionate and respectful regard to the Bishop's memory, he thus proceeds : —
" I shall ever regard it as one of the greatest mercies and privileges of my life, that I was admitted by him to ' holy orders,'
was nominated to my first curacy, was preferred to my first
benefice, encouraged in all my literary labours, and honoured
by his friendship and correspondence for several years

" You are aware that, before I was admitted to holy orders
in our beloved and apostolic church, for many years I exercised my ministry among Dissenters This at once brings me
to a part of the Bishop's history, concerning which you desire
information. The conduct of Bishop Burgess in admitting to
ordination several who had been dissenting ministers has been
incorrectly represented by some, and, in my opinion, unjustly
condemned by others. By Dissenters, it was said, the Bishop
held out *temptations,* to some of their ministers to conform to
the Established Church. Such was not the fact in a single

instance. My knowledge of the circumstances of nearly every case of this nature fully justifies me in saying, that Bishop Burgess required the fullest satisfaction as to sincerity, character, and fitness, before he gave encouragement to any such applicant to hope for ordination I know several dissenting ministers, who are now clergymen, who so far from being allured and encouraged by the Bishop to conform, felt that his Lordship discouraged their advances to the church, by requiring of them delay and sacrifices, which, though most painful, were exacted by the Bishop, as evidences to himself and to the church of their sincerity.   As the Bishop did me the honour of consulting me on several cases of the kind, — this, connected as it is with my own experience, enables me to speak with accuracy on the point.   At first, in the case of dissenting ministers seeking admission to the church, the conditions were, a printed declaration of reasons for conformity, testimonials as to character and fitness from their dissenting connections, twelve months' cessation from their dissenting ministry, a certificate of their actual communion with the church of England during that time, a nomination to a curacy in his diocese, and the usual examination required of candidates previous to ordination. From these regulations the Bishop departed, so far as I know, only in one instance, and in that he had special reasons, which in his own mind fully justified it.   One instance in particular, as showing the Bishop's conscientious caution and strictness, I notice.   A respectable dissenting minister, strongly recommended by the Dean of ——, sought ordination of the Bishop ; his testimonials were in all respects satisfactory.   At an interview which the applicant had subsequently with the Bishop, his Lordship discovered that he laboured under certain physical infirmities, and therefore decided at once on refusing him ordination.   On me devolved the painful task of communicating that decision.   From the Bishop's letter, authorizing that communication, now before me, I make the following extract . —

  " ' You are at liberty to state to Mr ——, that my objections to receiving · him as a candidate for orders, are to his voice and his lameness.   In admitting as candidates persons who have been dissenting ministers, by an indulgence at variance with the general usages of the Established Church, I should think myself inexcusable if I did not endeavour to limit that indulgence, as far as possible, to *perfection* of talents and character , but in all cases to the absence of every thing, which in *my own* apprehension is exceptionable.'

  " The gentleman thus rejected, I ought to state, subsequently obtained ordination from the late venerable Bishop of

Norwich, and is a respectable and useful clergyman. In another instance, reports to the prejudice of a candidate for orders, under like circumstances, reached the Bishop, who, on that ground, expressed to me doubts about receiving him as a candidate. The Bishop would not admit the gentleman, who is now a beneficed clergyman, to ordination, till he obtained from the best sources the satisfaction he required, and not till the expiration of full three years from the cessation of his dissenting ministry. The examination of such candidates for ordination was not less strict than was required of the more *regular* candidates. Previously to my own ordination, having before entered, and resided some time at Cambridge, I had, with the other and regular candidates, to go through all the exercises required of deacons and priests, which continued daily at the palace, from Tuesday morning to Saturday. The Bishop himself examined me two days in Latin and Greek. I have been thus particular in my notice of these facts, as showing, in opposition to the opinions of some, especially of Dissenters, that the Bishop did not invite, or tempt by laxity, dissenting ministers to conform to the church. I shall be excused if I add, that the Bishop, in this indulgence, never allowed himself to be influenced unduly by the recommendation of others. When it was known that I desired to enter the church, a noble lord, who had honoured me with his notice when I was a disssenting minister, voluntarily sent me a kind letter to be handed to the Bishop, recommending me to his Lordship's favour. This letter, however, the Bishop desired might only be seen by him at the time of my ordination; and was not read till he had received all the satisfaction he usually required in such cases.

" I am aware, as you doubtless also are, that by some the indulgence of Bishop Burgess, in ordaining dissenting ministers, has been condemned as an irregularity in the church, and as approximating to injustice to those who seek admission to holy orders by the regular and expensive way of university education. On this subject I think I can pretty accurately state the Bishop's reasons. Those dissenting ministers to whom the Bishop extended this indulgence, though few in number, were generally such as had enjoyed the advantages of dissenting institutions for education for the ministry; they were men who, having exercised their ministry among Dissenters for years, had not only gained experience in ministerial duties, but in quitting dissent, had to make a sacrifice of all their professional income, and to endure the reproaches of abandoned connections. Some, I know, had to sacrifice a larger amount of income than they could reasonably expect from any curacy they might obtain in the church. Such sacrifices the Bishop justly regarded as vindicating the purity of their motives. He kindly felt that the advances of such candidates to the church ought not to be repelled or prejudiced by the fact of their previous nonconformity, the error of which they discovered and renounced, and who from conscientious preference desired to transfer their ministry to the church. A *sudden* transfer the Bishop did not sanction; he required at first an interval of twelve months, and latterly of *three* years. The Bishop considered that, as conformity subjected such to the loss of previous income, and to the expenses of an interval of one, two, or three years, before ordination in the church, it would be hard to require of them the usual university course; though in two or three instances, which came under my own knowledge, he recommended this where practicable, and his recommendation was acted on. I may add to this, the Bishop felt that the labours of such ministers (who thus conscientiously renounced dissent), *in* the church and in *defence* of the church, would tend to the advancement of her true interests. How far his Lordship felt and judged correctly on this last point it becomes not me to pronounce, but must be left to the judgment of others to decide. My own conviction is, — of course I exclude my own humble labours, — that *conformists*, from their *experimental* acquaintance with dissent, have been found in our days among the most able and efficient defenders of the church against dissenting bitterness and misrepresentation. And I cannot but regret that more such conformists in heart (and I know many) do not find a door of admission into the ministry of the Church of England."

A LIST OF THE PUBLICATIONS OF BISHOP BURGESS, TO THE YEAR 1823.

(THE PRINCIPAL OF THOSE WHICH FOLLOWED HAVE BEEN ENUME-
RATED IN THE CHAPTER ON 1 JOHN, V. 7., OR IN OTHERS)

1. Observationes in Tragœdias Burtoni Pentalogia com-
plexas. 1778

2. Burtoni Pentalogia, seu Tragœdiarum Græcarum Delectus, ed. 2da. cui accedunt Observationes et Index Græcitatis
2 vols 8vo. 1779.

3. Ricardi Dawes Miscellanea Critica, iterum edita. 8vo.
1781.

4. Essay on the Study of Antiquities, 2d edition. 8vo.
1782.

5. The Salisbury Spelling Book, for the Use of Sunday
Schools 1786.

6. Conspectus Criticarum Observationum in Scriptores
Græcos et Latinos 8vo. 1788.

7. Initia Homerica, seu excerpta ex Iliade Homeri, cum omnium locorum Græca Metaphrasti. 8vo. 1788. ed. 2da 1820

8. Remarks on Josephus's Account of Herod's rebuilding of
the Temple of Jerusalem. 8vo 1788.

9. Sententiæ Philosophorum e Codice Leidensi Vossiano
12mo. 1788.

10 Tractatus Latini, Crevier, &c 1788. 8vo.

11. Considerations on the Abolition of Slavery and the Slave
Trade, upon grounds of natural, religious, and political duty
8vo. 1789.

12. The Divinity of Christ proved from his own Declarations,
attested and interpreted by his living Witnesses, the Jews. A
Sermon, Oxford 1790

13. Child's First Lessons in Religion 1790 12mo

14. Remarks on the Scriptural Account of the Dimensions
of Solomon's Temple 8vo. 1790.

15 Reflections on the Controversial Writings of Dr Priestley relative to Religious Opinions, Establishments, and Tests.
8vo. 1791.

16 Emendationes in Suidam. 1791. 4 vols. 8vo.

17. Gravinæ Opuscula. 12mo 1792.

18. Musei Oxoniensis Fasciculus I. 8vo. 1792.

19. First Book of Hooker's Ecclesiastical Polity. 8vo. 1793.

20. Aristotelis Liber de Poetica cum Animadversionibus Thomæ Tyrwhitti variisque Lectionibus Venetis, &c. 1794.

21. Musei Oxoniensis Fasciculus II. 1797.

22. Moral Annals of the Poor. 1797.

23. Aristotelis Πεπλος, sive Epitaphia Heroum Homericorum Opusculum ab H. Stephano primum editum, hac editione pluribus epitaphiis auctum. 12mo 1798.

24. Thomæ Tyrwhitti Conjecturæ in Æschylum, Euripidem, et Aristophanem ex autographo editæ, adjectis ejusdem ad Dawesium Observatis. 8vo. 1798. Reprinted by Mr. Elmsley, with Notes, and Epistolæ Diversorum ad Tyrwhittum. 1822.

25. The Spirit of Prophecy the Testimony of Jesus. A Sermon. 8vo. 1802.

26. Johannis Tzetzis Carmen περι διαφορας ποιητων e Codice Bodleiano.

27. Sharpe on the Greek Article, Durham. 1803. 12mo.

28. Charity the Bond of Peace and of all Virtues A Sermon. 1803.

29. De Pocseos ortu et versificatioue. Gr. and Lat. 12mo

30. Initia Paulina, sive Introductio ad Lectionem Pauli Epistolarum 12mo 1804

31 A Sermon preached at the Anniversary of the Royal Humane Society. 8vo. 1804.

32. Christmas Gift. 1805 12mo.

33. First Principles of Christian Knowledge. 12mo. 1804.

34. The peculiar Privileges of the Christian Ministry considered in a Charge delivered to the Clergy of the Diocese of St. David's, in the Yeai 1804. 2d ed. 1810.

35. A Sermon preached before the Lords Spiritual and Temporal in Westminster Abbey, on Jan. 30. 1807.

36. Copper-plate Copies of Hebrew Letters and Words 1807.

37. Practical Christianity 12mo. 1806

38. A Hebrew Primer 12mo. 1807.

39. Hebrew Reader. 2 Prts. 12mo.

40. Hebrew Elements, or an Introduction to the Reading of the Hebrew Scriptures 8vo. 1807. 4th edit. 12mo. 1823.

41. A Charge delivered to the Clergy of the Diocese of St David's, in the Year 1807.

42. A Sermon preached before the Society for the Propagation of the Gospel 1808

43 Prayers in Time of War, and Public Danger. 1808.

44. A Companion for Ash Wednesday. 1809.

45 The Arabic Alphabet, or an Introduction to the Reading of Arabic. 1809.

46 Maxims of Health for the Use of the Poor. 1810

47. Motives to the Study of Hebrew, two Parts 12mo. 1810.

48 Selecta Loca Prophetarum ad Messiam pertinentia Hebraice et Græce, 12mo 1810.

49 Extracts from Bishop Bull's Sermon on the Difficulties and Dangers of the Pastoral Office. For the use of Candidates for Holy Orders To which is prefixed an Introduction De Dignitate Sacerdotii Christiani 1811.

50. Reflections on the Judgment delivered by Sir John Nicholl, against the Rev. T. W. Wickes : — printed and distributed 1811, but not published

51. Elementary Evidences of Christianity 3d ed. 1812.

52 Bishops and Benefactors of the Church of St David's vindicated from the Misrepresentations of a recent Publication · a Charge delivered to the Chapter of St. David's in 1811. 4to. 1812.

53. Johannis Sulgeni Versus Hexametri in laudem Patris Sulgeni, Archiepiscopi Menevensis. E Codice MS Cottoniano. 1812.

54 Faith founded on Reason, or a Rational Christian's Profession of Faith ; being a Summary of Christian Doctrine, extracted from the Exposition of the Apostle's Creed, by the Right Rev John Pearson, D D. Lord Bishop of Chester, with a Creed of Evidences by the Editor. 12mo 1812.

55 Jones's Catechism on the Thirty-nine Articles. 12mo. 1812.

56. The First Seven Epochs of the ancient British Church. A Sermon. 8vo 1813.

57 A Charge in 1813. 8vo.

58. Bishop Bull's Letter to Mr. Nelson on the Corruptions of the Church of Rome, in relation to Ecclesiastical Government, the Rule of Faith, and Form of Divine Worship, in answer to the Bishop of Meaux's Queries. 18mo. 1813.

59 Brevis Conspectus Historiæ Ecclesiasticæ. 1813 .

60 Hebrew Etymology 12mo 1813.

61. The Protestant's Retrospect 12mo. 1813.

62. Two Letters to the Clergy of the Diocese of St David's on the Independence of the ancient British Church on any foreign Jurisdiction. 8vo 1813

63. Friendly Advice to Servants, Apprentices, and Workmen, consisting of useful Maxims, Scripture Extracts, and moral Proverbs, together with some Christian Thoughts on Stage Entertainments. 1813.

64 An Introduction to the Doctrine of the Holy Trinity 1814

65. Tracts of various Writers on the Doctrine of the Holy Trinity, and on the Nicene and Athanasian Creeds, to which is added, an Introduction to the Doctrine of the Trinity, by the Editor 12mo. 1814.

66 Rudiments of Hebrew Grammar. 1814.

67 Samaritan and Syriac Alphabets. 12mo. 1814

68. A Charge addressed to the Clergy of the Diocese of St David's. 1814

69 The Gospel Way of Salvation. A Tablet on Pasteboard. 1814.

70. A brief Memorial on the Repeal of the Statute relative to the Doctrine of the Trinity 8vo 1814

71. A Protestant's and Papist's Manual, containing a Papist's Reasons for not conforming to the Church of England, and a Protestant's Answer to them. 1814

72. Ecclesiæ Christianæ Primordia. 8vo 1814.

73. A Letter to the Lord Bishop of Durham on the Origin of the Pelasgi, and on the original Name and Pronunciation of the Æolic Digamma 1814

74 The Bible, and nothing but the Bible, the Religion of the Church of England. 8vo 1815.

75. The Truth to which Christ came into the World to bear witness, and the Testimony of Christ's Contemporaries to his Declaration of his Divinity, confirmed by his Discourses, Actions and Death, a Sermon, 8vo 1815, being a Sequel to a Sermon preached at Oxford, 1790.

76 A Good-Friday Address to our Countrymen, the Roman Catholics, on the Character and Authority of St Peter. 1815.

77. Miss Smith's comparative Vocabulary of Hebrew and Arabic, to which is prefixed as a Praxis, the Carmen Toghrai. 12mo 1815.

78. Evidence of the Divinity of Christ, from the literal Testimony of Scripture, containing a Vindication of Mr. Sharp's Rule from the Objections of the Rev. Calvin Winstanley; with Observations on Right Principles of Interpretation 2d Edition 1815.

79. Three Addresses to Persons calling themselves Unitarians. 1815

80 Appendix to Hoare's Life of Sharp. 4to

81. A Volume of Tracts on the Independence of the Ancient British Church, on the Supremacy of the Pope, and the Inconsistency of all foreign Jurisdictions with the British Constitution, and on the Differences between the Churches of England and of Rome; to which is prefixed a Map, showing

the Limits of the Pope's Jurisdiction at the End of the Fifteenth Century. 8vo. 1815.

82 The Scripture Evidence of the Divinity of Christ, extracted from Bishop Pearson's Exposition of the Apostles' Creed. 1815.

83. Chrysostomi Selecta 12mo. 1815.

84. Queries addressed to Persons calling themselves Unitarians 1815.

85 A Collection of such Scriptures as ought to be seriously and frequently considered by all those who either are preparing for Holy Orders, or are already ordained. In Hebrew, Greek, and English. 12mo 1816

86. The Unitarian Catechised. A folio page 1816.

87. The Protestant Catechism. 8vo. 1818.

88. Reasons why a New Translation of the Bible should not be published without a previous Statement and Examination of all the material Passages, which may be supposed to be misinterpreted Second edition 8vo 1819.

89. English Reformation and Papal Schism 8vo. 1819.

90. Three Words on General Thornton's Speech. 8vo. 1819.

91. An easy Way by one Duty to serve Religion, to double your Income, and to prolong Life; or Devotion, Frugality, and Health promoted by the Observance of Lent; to which are added, Extracts from the Works of the Rev W. Jones, Lessius, Cornaro, and Cheyne. 1819

92. Three Letters to Dr. Phillimore (by Philopatris). 1819.

93. A Volume of Tracts on the Divinity of Christ, containing the Bible, and nothing but the Bible; Evidence of the Divinity of Christ; a brief Memorial, and Three Addresses to Unitarians; to which is prefixed a Preface, containing Strictures on the recent Publication of Mr. Belsham and Dr. Carpenter. 8vo. 1820.

94 Remarks on the Western Travels of St. Paul, as an Evidence of the Truth of Christianity, and an Argument of Prescription against the Supremacy of the Pope, and of the Church of Rome. 1820.

95. Popery incapable of Union with a Protestant Church. 8vo 1820

96. Scripture and Antiquity united in a Christian's Testimony against the recent Publications of Mr. Belsham and Dr. Carpenter. 8vo. 1820.

97 The Challenge answered in Defence of the Authenticity of Matthew, xxviii. 19. 12mo 1820

98 A Vindication of 1 John, v. 7., from the Objections of M. Griesbach. 8vo. 1821.

99. Dr Owen's Tract on the Nature of the Protestant Reli-

gion, and its present State in the World, to which is prefixed a Letter to William Wilberforce, Esq 12mo. 1821

100 A Vindication of Bishop Cleaver's Edition of the Decretum Lacedæmoniorum contra Timotheum, from the Strictures of R. P. Knight, Esq 8vo 1821

101 Adnotationes Millii, Bengelii, Wetstenii, &c in 1 Joann v. 7.

(*The two preceding were printed and distributed, but not published*)

102. Marci Celedensis Explanatio Fidei. 1821.

103 A Speech delivered in the House of Lords on the Roman Catholic Question 1821

104. The Church of England Man's Elementary Catechism; or First Lessons in the Doctrine of Christ and his Church. Eleventh Edition 1822.

105 Arrian's Epictetus. 12mo.

106. A Speech intended to have been delivered in the House of Lords on the Roman Catholic Question. 1822

107 The Greek Original of the New Testament asserted, in Answer to a recent Publication, entitled Palæoromaica 1823.

108 A Vindication of 1 John, v. 7, from the Objections of M Griesbach Second Edition. To which are added, a Preface in Reply to the Quarterly Review for March, 1822, and a Postscript in Answer to a recent Publication, entitled Palæoromaica. 1823.

109. Christianity of Stoicism, or Selections from Arrian's Discourses, &c 12mo. 1822.

110 Tertulliani Liber de Præscriptione adversus Hereticos, Latine et Anglice. 12mo.

111 Milton contrasted with Milton and the Scriptures. 8vo.

THE END.

LONDON:
Printed by A SPOTTISWOODE,
New-Street-Square.